GALE BUSINESS INSIGHTS

*Gale Business
Insights Handbook
of Social Media
Marketing*

GALE BUSINESS INSIGHTS

Gale Business Insights Handbook of Social Media Marketing

Miranda Herbert Ferrara, Project Editor

GALE
CENGAGE Learning®

Detroit • New York • San Francisco • New Haven, Conn • Waterville, Maine • London

GALE
CENGAGE Learning·

Gale Business Insights Handbook of Social Media Marketing

Project Editor: Miranda Herbert Ferrara

Production Technology Support: Luann Brennan

Production Service: Graphic World Inc.

Composition: Graphic World Inc.

Manufacturing: Rita Wimberley

Product Manager: Michele P. LaMeau

Publisher: David Forman

Cover: Apps Download or Sync to Mobile © iStockPhoto.com/pictafolio.

LIBRARY OF CONGRESS CATALOGING-IN-PUBLICATION DATA

Gale business insights handbook of social media marketing.
    pages cm. -- (Gale business insights)
  Includes bibliographical references and index.
  ISBN-13: 978-1-4144-9931-4 (softcover)
  ISBN-10: 1-4144-9931-0 (softcover)
  1. Internet marketing--Social aspects. 2. Marketing--Social aspects. 3. Social media--Economic aspects.
  HF5415.1265G34 2013
  658.8'72--dc23   2012048076

Gale
27500 Drake Rd.
Farmington Hills, MI, 48331-3535

ISBN-13: 978-1-4144-9931-4

ISBN-10: 1-4144-9931-0

This title is also available as an e-book.
ISBN-13: 978-1-4144-9938-3; ISBN-10: 1-4144-9938-8
Contact your Gale, Cengage Learning, sales representative for ordering information.

Printed in the United States of America
1 2 3 4 5   17 16 15 14 13

Table of Contents

Preface

The *Gale Business Insights Handbooks* series is a collection of thematically focused volumes centered on the specific projects, tasks, and activities in which businesspeople currently engage. The series will be helpful for both the student taking business classes in undergraduate and/or advanced degree programs, such as a Masters of Business Administration (MBA), or the working professional who needs a quick refresher on a particular business topic. The entries in each *Handbook* contain both theoretical information on a topic and practical applications for everyday situations in businesses of any size.

Topic Selection

Each volume of the *Gale Business Insights Handbooks* series contains a hand-selected collection of the most relevant, current, and useful topics. Entry topics have been selected for the *Gale Business Insights Handbooks* series through a variety of methods to assure that the most timely and most studied topics are covered.

- Business textbooks, both domestic and international, were surveyed to identify key topics being covered and how those topics are taught in the classroom.

- Business journals and trade publications were monitored to identify key trends and current event business topics happening around the world.

- Discussions were held with business school professors and business professionals to determine what specific tasks, activities, and projects most commonly occur in today's business world.

Handbook Features

Each volume includes entries on topics appropriate to that volume's particular theme. Unlike a traditional encyclopedia, however, each entry is oriented toward practical applications as well as theory.

Each entry in a *Gale Business Insights Handbook* volume begins with an *In This Essay* section that clearly outlines the topics and key concepts covered.

Throughout the text of the entry there are also five *icons* used as visual cues to indicate paragraphs or sections of text where key terms or particularly important or helpful information can be found. The icons are more fully explained in the *User's Guide* following this preface.

The *Handbooks* feature both in-text *key terms* and a cumulative list of *glossary terms*, which the authors and editor feel will aid overall reader comprehension of the topic.

Authoritative Sources

Entries have been compiled by combining authoritative data from government sources, professional associations, original research, and publicly accessible sources both in print and on the Internet. These sources include general academic periodicals and books as well as websites and blogs. Every entry in a *Gale Business Insights Handbook* contains a *bibliography* of print and electronic sources for further information and research.

Fully Indexed

Each *Handbook* has been fully indexed to allow researchers to locate relevant information quickly.

About *Gale Business Insights Handbook of Social Media Marketing*

The *Gale Business Insights Handbook of Social Media Marketing* examines the questions, "What is social media marketing?" and "How can it be used in my business?" This volume focuses on building an internal business case for using social media, highlighting its importance, the benefits it can provide, and how to implement a successful strategy and measure its effectiveness. Entries examine such topics as the types of social media and their followers, how to increase discoverability, how to define and protect your brand, legal challenges with social media, and more.

Suggestions Welcome

Comments on this *Handbook* and suggestions on topics for future *Handbooks* are cordially invited. Please write:

The Editor
Gale Business Insights Handbooks
Gale, Cengage Learning
27500 Drake Rd.
Farmington Hills, Michigan 48331-3535

Gale, Cengage Learning, does not endorse any of the organizations, products, or methods mentioned in this title.

User's Guide

Throughout the text of each entry in the *Gale Business Insights Handbook* series, there are five icons used as visual cues to indicate paragraphs or sections of text where key terms or particularly important or helpful information can be found.

Icons

 For More Information — Indicates a paragraph or section of text where a resource or list of resources is located. These resources will be helpful to discover further information on the concepts outlined in each entry (such as addresses, websites, or other sources).

 Helpful Hint — Indicates a paragraph where a helpful tip or idea, suggestion for consideration, or best practice is located. These suggestions may be helpful when putting concepts presented in the entry into practice.

 Know This — Indicates a paragraph where a key concept or larger theme that must be known to understand the main idea of the entry is located.

 Tools to Use — Indicates a paragraph where the reader will find a mechanical or technical measuring device or software application that could be leveraged for calculating or applying concepts outlined in the entry. This icon is also used to indicate where there are descriptions of how standards are acquired.

 Key Term — Indicates the paragraph and provides the definition of an essential term in an entry necessary to understand the overall topic and core concepts presented. The individual key terms are also aggregated into a full glossary at the end of the *Handbook* volume.

List of Contributors

Erin Brereton
Journalist, editor, and legal, finance and business marketing consultant
BENEFITS OF SOCIAL MEDIA
CHOOSING THE RIGHT MEDIA FOR YOUR
    SOCIAL MEDIA CAMPAIGN

Heidi Cardenas
Freelance writer specializing in human resources, business and personal finance and small business advice
REPRESENTATION OF THE BRAND
PREPARING FOR A LONG-TERM SOCIAL
    MEDIA CAMPAIGN
MANAGING YOUR SOCIAL MEDIA CAMPAIGN
BENEFITS OF SOCIAL MEDIA TEAMS

Thomas Hill
Central Connecticut State University
UNDERSTANDING SOCIAL MEDIA AND ITS
    EFFECTS
DIVERSIFICATION OF SOCIAL MEDIA
    CONTENT STRATEGY
TRANSPARENCY OF SOCIAL MEDIA MARKETING
MEASURING SOCIAL MEDIA EFFORTS
CONVERGENCE OF MARKETING, DATA,
    AND TECHNOLOGY
PROTECTING THE BRAND

Alexandra Horblitt
Freelance writer
UPDATING SOCIAL MEDIA EFFORTS

Page Huyette
Montana State University
TAKING ADVANTAGE OF INTERACTIVITY
BUILDING A RELATIONSHIP

Shannon Johnson
Mercer University School of Law
Author of A-Z Guide to Federal Employment
Law for the Small Business Owner
MARKETING TO A GLOBAL SEGMENT

Karla Lant
Northern Arizona University, Extended
Campus: Masters of Administration Program
Feature Writer, Education.com
Gadgets and Tech Writer, San Francisco Examiner
Life Insurance Writer, The Simple Dollar
SENTIMENT ANALYSIS

Sherrie Negrea
Freelance Writer, Versatile Writing
BUILDING A CASE FOR SOCIAL MEDIA
CREATING A CONGRUENT SOCIAL MEDIA
    MARKETING PHILOSOPHY
CREATING SOCIAL MEDIA MARKETING STRATEGY

Jeff Somers
Author of the *Avery Cates* series and *Trickster*
INTERNAL SOCIAL MEDIA INTERFACES
PREPARING FOR PARADIGM SHIFTS
DIMINISHING RETURNS OF SOCIAL MEDIA
CONSISTENCY AMONG ALL SOCIAL MEDIA OUTLETS

Eric Stirgus
Freelance writer
DEVELOPING BRAND LOYALTY THROUGH
   SOCIAL MEDIA COMMUNICATION

Victoria Treder
Attorney and Commentator
MARKET SEGMENTATION
SOCIAL MEDIA MARKETING STRATEGIES
KEEPING UP WITH THE COMPETITION
LEGAL CHALLENGES WITH SOCIAL MEDIA

Ahlam Yassin
Freelance writer
INCREASING ONLINE DISCOVERABILITY

Building a Case for Social Media

In This Essay

- There has been a paradigm shift on how companies promote their products to their consumers because of the Internet
- Social media has four main classifications: social commerce, social community, social entertainment, and social publishing
- The popularity of online shopping has increased the amount and helpfulness of social media marketing
- Social media marketing requires little start-up cost but does require time to maintain, which does cost money

Introduction

In the twentieth century, businesses and companies promoted their products and services with the buying public the traditional way: they paid for advertisements that appeared in newspapers and magazines and on radio and television. In the first decade of the twenty-first century, that began to change. With the emergence of a new online phenomenon called social media, the rules changed. Prospective customers were no longer reading newspapers or magazines or watching television as much as they once did. The percentage of consumers around the world who watched television in a typical week declined from 71% in 2009 to 48% in 2011 (Accenture, 2012). If they did read newspapers, it was likely to be online, where ads were not as prevalent as in the print edition. At the end of 2010, for the first time more people read news online than in a newspaper (O'Dell, 2011). If consumers sat down in front of their television, they often had a laptop, smart phone, or an iPad in their hands. When they saw an ad for a new product, they searched for it online and then asked friends on

Facebook whether any of them had bought it. Then they tweeted the news to their followers on Twitter.

One of the basic principles of marketing, according to social media expert Jan Zimmerman, is to "fish where your fish are," or to reach your customers where they shop or congregate. Since social media began captivating attention in the first decade of the twenty-first century, more and more customers are not only shopping online but also spending their time on a social media platform. Facebook, which became available to anyone age 13 or over in 2006, reached 1 billion monthly active users in 2012 (Facebook.com, 2012). Twitter, a social networking site also launched in 2006, had 500 million active users as of 2012 (Statistic brain, 2012b). In addition, YouTube, the video-sharing website, logged 490 million unique users each month in 2012 (Statistic brain, 2012a).

In addition to these major pillars of the social media world, new social networks are constantly entering the marketplace, providing innovative ways for businesses to engage with prospective customers. Pinterest, for example, a pinboard-style photo sharing website, was developed in 2010 on an invitation-only basis and was opened to the public two years later. By 2012, the website had more than 4 million unique visitors a day, and studies showed that customers who found a product on Pinterest were more likely to buy it than those who found it on other social platforms (Cabalona, 2012).

Consumers have shifted their time and allegiance from printed media to online media, and increasingly to social networks. For certain demographic groups, social media is where these consumers spend most of their time online. In 2012, it was estimated that 98% of 18- to 24-year-olds use social media (Statistic brain, 2012a). Of all adults online, more than 91% use social media regularly (Bodnar, 2012b). If businesses and companies want to market their products where their consumers are, social media is a good place to find them. How businesses can use social media to drive up sales, however, is a more complicated challenge that depends on many variables, including the type of business and its marketing objectives.

Defining Social Media and Social Media Marketing

Social media is an array of online services that combine two-way communication and content sharing. What differentiates social media from

Facebook whether any of them had bought it. Then they tweeted the news to their followers on Twitter.

One of the basic principles of marketing, according to social media expert Jan Zimmerman, is to "fish where your fish are," or to reach your customers where they shop or congregate. Since social media began captivating attention in the first decade of the twenty-first century, more and more customers are not only shopping online but also spending their time on a social media platform. Facebook, which became available to anyone age 13 or over in 2006, reached 1 billion monthly active users in 2012 (Facebook.com, 2012). Twitter, a social networking site also launched in 2006, had 500 million active users as of 2012 (Statistic brain, 2012b). In addition, YouTube, the video-sharing website, logged 490 million unique users each month in 2012 (Statistic brain, 2012a).

In addition to these major pillars of the social media world, new social networks are constantly entering the marketplace, providing innovative ways for businesses to engage with prospective customers. Pinterest, for example, a pinboard-style photo sharing website, was developed in 2010 on an invitation-only basis and was opened to the public two years later. By 2012, the website had more than 4 million unique visitors a day, and studies showed that customers who found a product on Pinterest were more likely to buy it than those who found it on other social platforms (Cabalona, 2012).

Consumers have shifted their time and allegiance from printed media to online media, and increasingly to social networks. For certain demographic groups, social media is where these consumers spend most of their time online. In 2012, it was estimated that 98% of 18- to 24-year-olds use social media (Statistic brain, 2012a). Of all adults online, more than 91% use social media regularly (Bodnar, 2012b). If businesses and companies want to market their products where their consumers are, social media is a good place to find them. How businesses can use social media to drive up sales, however, is a more complicated challenge that depends on many variables, including the type of business and its marketing objectives.

Defining Social Media and Social Media Marketing

Social media is an array of online services that combine two-way communication and content sharing. What differentiates social media from

List of Contributors

Erin Brereton
Journalist, editor, and legal, finance and business marketing consultant
BENEFITS OF SOCIAL MEDIA
CHOOSING THE RIGHT MEDIA FOR YOUR
   SOCIAL MEDIA CAMPAIGN

Heidi Cardenas
Freelance writer specializing in human resources, business and personal finance and small business advice
REPRESENTATION OF THE BRAND
PREPARING FOR A LONG-TERM SOCIAL
   MEDIA CAMPAIGN
MANAGING YOUR SOCIAL MEDIA CAMPAIGN
BENEFITS OF SOCIAL MEDIA TEAMS

Thomas Hill
Central Connecticut State University
UNDERSTANDING SOCIAL MEDIA AND ITS
   EFFECTS
DIVERSIFICATION OF SOCIAL MEDIA
   CONTENT STRATEGY
TRANSPARENCY OF SOCIAL MEDIA MARKETING
MEASURING SOCIAL MEDIA EFFORTS
CONVERGENCE OF MARKETING, DATA,
   AND TECHNOLOGY
PROTECTING THE BRAND

Alexandra Horblitt
Freelance writer
UPDATING SOCIAL MEDIA EFFORTS

Page Huyette
Montana State University
TAKING ADVANTAGE OF INTERACTIVITY
BUILDING A RELATIONSHIP

Shannon Johnson
Mercer University School of Law
Author of A-Z *Guide to Federal Employment Law for the Small Business Owner*
MARKETING TO A GLOBAL SEGMENT

Karla Lant
Northern Arizona University, Extended Campus: Masters of Administration Program
Feature Writer, Education.com
Gadgets and Tech Writer, San Francisco Examiner
Life Insurance Writer, The Simple Dollar
SENTIMENT ANALYSIS

Sherrie Negrea
Freelance Writer, Versatile Writing
BUILDING A CASE FOR SOCIAL MEDIA
CREATING A CONGRUENT SOCIAL MEDIA
   MARKETING PHILOSOPHY
CREATING SOCIAL MEDIA MARKETING STRATEGY

Jeff Somers
Author of the *Avery Cates* series and *Trickster*
INTERNAL SOCIAL MEDIA INTERFACES
PREPARING FOR PARADIGM SHIFTS
DIMINISHING RETURNS OF SOCIAL MEDIA
CONSISTENCY AMONG ALL SOCIAL MEDIA OUTLETS

Eric Stirgus
Freelance writer
DEVELOPING BRAND LOYALTY THROUGH
  SOCIAL MEDIA COMMUNICATION

Victoria Treder
Attorney and Commentator
MARKET SEGMENTATION
SOCIAL MEDIA MARKETING STRATEGIES
KEEPING UP WITH THE COMPETITION
LEGAL CHALLENGES WITH SOCIAL MEDIA

Ahlam Yassin
Freelance writer
INCREASING ONLINE DISCOVERABILITY

Building a Case for Social Media

In This Essay

■ There has been a paradigm shift on how companies promote their products to their consumers because of the Internet

■ Social media has four main classifications: social commerce, social community, social entertainment, and social publishing

■ The popularity of online shopping has increased the amount and helpfulness of social media marketing

■ Social media marketing requires little start-up cost but does require time to maintain, which does cost money

Introduction

In the twentieth century, businesses and companies promoted their products and services with the buying public the traditional way: they paid for advertisements that appeared in newspapers and magazines and on radio and television. In the first decade of the twenty-first century, that began to change. With the emergence of a new online phenomenon called social media, the rules changed. Prospective customers were no longer reading newspapers or magazines or watching television as much as they once did. The percentage of consumers around the world who watched television in a typical week declined from 71% in 2009 to 48% in 2011 (Accenture, 2012). If they did read newspapers, it was likely to be online, where ads were not as prevalent as in the print edition. At the end of 2010, for the first time more people read news online than in a newspaper (O'Dell, 2011). If consumers sat down in front of their television, they often had a laptop, smart phone, or an iPad in their hands. When they saw an ad for a new product, they searched for it online and then asked friends on other types of websites is that it has the ability to allow users to talk back and forth and share messages, video, audio, or multimedia with others.

With the requirements of two-way communication and content sharing, a website would not be defined as a social media platform unless it allows visitors to provide feedback on the site. Similarly, although there are many rating sites for restaurants, hotels, and tourist sites, these were not considered part of the social media landscape until they allowed visitors to post comments on these sites. TripAdvisor.com, a travel website, is a social media platform because it allows users to post reviews and recommendations of restaurants and hotels they visit. An e-newsletter or a blog that does not invite responses would not be defined as social media.

When businesses write content that is used to market products by popularizing them online through the use of text, video, or audio messages, they are engaging in social media marketing. The ultimate goal of using these social media services or channels is *relationship orientation* with potential customers (Zimmerman and Sahlin, 2010). "Everything that applies to a new business applies to social media," Zimmerman said. "This is a new tool, but the people and business principles haven't changed."

Relationship orientation: *A focus to establish, maintain, and enhance relationships with customers.*

Whether a business is updating its Facebook page, putting a product image on Pinterest, or sending a tweet about a new product line, it is engaged in building relationships with prospective customers. With social media, customers have the ability to respond to that message or share the content of the message with other users. In this process, the brand becomes more familiar to the customer and creates top-of-mind visibility.

"When it comes to social media, it isn't about selling," said Robbin Block, a Seattle-based marketing strategist and author of *Social Persuasion: Making Sense of Social Media for Small Business.* "The uber goal is to get your product sold; otherwise why would you be doing it? The way that you communicate is the critical thing in social media. It's a way of engaging people so that they feel you're having a conversation with them."

Over time, that engagement can ultimately improve a company's profits as visitors to social media sites are converted into customers. That process requires a substantial time commitment to promote a product across the social medium spectrum. Yet the time invested may create a following of loyal customers who will spread the word about a brand or product on social media networks.

History of Social Media

Packet switching:
A method of data transmission in which a message is broken into a number of parts that are sent independently and reassembled at the destination.

Social media traces its history to the origins of the Internet. The precursor to the Internet was ARPANET (Advanced Research Projects Agency Network), a network based on *packet switching* that connected computers at different universities and research laboratories in the United States. The network was launched in 1969, when a student programmer at the University of California, Los Angeles, sent the message "login" from his computer to a computer at the Stanford Research Institute (located in Menlo Park, California). Over the next decade, the network grew to include more than 200 host computers throughout the world. By 1982, the protocols on the network became standardized and ARPANET became one component of the worldwide network of interconnected computers that came be known as the Internet.

The creation of what former U.S. vice president Al Gore called the "information superhighway," which was sanctioned through U.S. federal legislation in 1991, laid the groundwork for one of the two key components of what would become social media—the ability to host two-way communication. The creation of message boards and online forums allowed asynchronous communication, which was followed by instant messaging in the 1990s, and Yahoo groups and Google groups, which were both launched in 2001.

Another development that moved the Internet one step closer to the creation of social media networking was the blog, which evolved from the term *weblog*. The blog became popular in the late 1990s as a way to publish commentary on a particular subject, often with interactive features allowing visitors to leave comments on the posted content.

"Blogging took the elitism out of publishing and it gave experts a public forum to share their expertise," said Lorrie Thomas Ross, author of *The 36-Hour Course to Online Marketing* (Thomas, 2010). "You could be the CEO of a company or you could be someone in a small town in the middle of nowhere sharing your expertise." Blogging was also the precursor to Twitter, a microblogging service that allows users to send posts with a maximum of 140 characters.

The launching of Facebook attracted millions of people to social media networking, and the growing popularity of this type of service spurred other newcomers to enter the market: Tumblr, a microblogging platform; Foursquare, a location-based social networking website for mobile devices; Google+, a multilingual social networking service; Delicious, a social bookmarking web service; Digg, a social news website; Reddit, a social news and entertainment site; Instagram, an online photo-sharing site; Kickstarter, a website that provides tools to raise funds for creative projects through crowd funding; and Yelp, a local directory service with user reviews. As of 2012, social networking accounted for 22% of all time spent on the Internet, or one in every four and half minutes, in the United States (Social networks, 2010).

Classifying Social Media

Businesses that want to take part in social media networking can easily be overwhelmed by the number of channels and platforms available. As of 2012, there were more than 200 social media networking sites, a number that is rapidly growing according to Jure Klepic, a marketing professional with Lucule Consulting in New York City. One way to sort out the array of social media channels is to group them in categories. Although many social media experts have come up with classification systems, the framework created by Tracy Tuten and Michael Solomon, co-authors of *Social Media Marketing* (Prentice Hall 2012) navigates through the social media array with a simple and straightforward approach. Tuten and Solomon divide up social media networks into four zones: Social Community, Social Publishing, Social Entertainment, and Social Commerce.

Social media is used for both personal and commercial purposes, so some functions will overlap in two or more zones. "That's the nature of social media," Tuten and Solomon write. "All social media are networked around relationships, technologically enabled, and based on the principles of shared participation."

The following summarizes each zone and the social media networks that it includes:

Zone 1: Social Community

Social media channels in this zone focus on relationships and common activities of people who share similar interests. Social communities offer two-way and multi-way communication, collaboration, conversation, and sharing information. Other social media networks may involve relationship-building, but interacting, collaborating, and creating relationships are the primary purposes for social communities. Social communities include social networking sites, message boards, and forums and wikis.

The social media networks that fall into this zone are Facebook, Twitter, LinkedIn, and Google+.

Zone 2: Social Publishing

Sites offering social publishing assist users in sharing content with an audience. Social publishing channels include blogs, microsharing, and media sharing sites, social bookmarking, and news sites.

The social publishing sites included in this zone are Blogger, Blogspot, Technorati, YouTube, Flickr, Pinterest, Picasa, SmugMug, SlideShare, and Scribd.

Zone 3: Social Entertainment

Social networks that offer sites providing opportunities for play and enjoyment are the focus of the social entertainment zone. These sites include social games, socially enabled console games, alternate reality games, virtual worlds, and entertainment communities.

Social entertainment sites included in this zone are: Come2Play, Second Life, MySpace, Zynga, and uGame.

Zone 4: Social Commerce

Social commerce sites allow people to buy or sell products and services online. Another feature these sites offer is the opportunity to interact and collaborate with other online shoppers during the shopping experience. These sites include reviews and ratings, deal sites and deal aggregators, social shopping markets or online malls, and social storefronts.

Here are some social media sites that specialize in social commerce such as Facebook, LivingSocial, Groupon, Snipi, VideoGenie, TripAdvisor, and Payvment.

Should Businesses Use Social Media Marketing?

Understanding the social media networks that constitute these four zones is a good first step for a business thinking about delving into social media marketing. Although social media marketing can link businesses with millions of consumers, experts caution that it may not be the right solution for all businesses. "Every organization is different," said Ross, the chief executive officer of The Marketing Therapist, based in Santa Barbara, California. "That's why there are marketing consultants out there."

For a new business trying to build *brand awareness*, social media marketing should not be the only strategy that is used. "If nobody's ever heard of you before, they're probably not going to like your Facebook page," Block said. "They're not going to see what you're posting." To build brand awareness for a new business, Block recommends a traditional public relations strategy, consisting of promoting a business in the newspaper or a specialized publication in the field. Once the brand or product is better known in the buying public, consumers can be directed to the company's website, and then the focus can switch to building social connections.

Brand awareness:
The degree to which consumers precisely associate a brand with the specific product.

What is most important for a business is determining where its audience is and targeting it there. "If you want to find people online, and if your current prospective customers are using social media, that's the best way to reach them," said Zimmerman, author of three books on marketing and owner of Watermelon Mountain Web Marketing, based in Albuquerque, New Mexico. "If you're trying to reach people who ride the buses, then that's where you want to put your advertising—on the buses or on the subway."

Larger companies with extensive marketing departments are more likely to have extensive social media marketing campaigns because they have the staff to work on building and maintaining pages on Facebook and other networks. "Big corporations are some of the biggest users of social media," Zimmerman said. "They have the most money and the most time. They'll have 24 people working on social media. For a small business, in most cases, the owner is the one doing the marketing."

Regardless of the size of the company, social media marketing should not be seen as a panacea to a business's marketing needs. Many marketing experts advise small and large companies to use social media in addition to, rather than instead of, traditional forms of marketing such as print advertising and media relations. "Social media marketing is essential, but it's not a replacement for other kinds of marketing," said Solomon, a marketing professor at Saint Joseph's University in Philadelphia. "It's not a panacea." Social media marketing, however, can enhance a traditional advertising and sales promotion strategy by reaching new customers and maintaining relationships with those customers. "It's a much more powerful and effective way to achieve some of these objectives," Solomon said.

Advantages of Using Social Media Marketing

One of the chief advantages of using social media marketing is its cost. Joining a social network such as Facebook or Twitter is free, and any business can develop a presence on a social media network. This makes social media marketing a highly attractive strategy for many small businesses.

"For a very new business with a very small budget, it's a very cost-effective way to achieve some early objectives—creating awareness for a product and creating some buzz around a brand," advised Solomon. "As they go on, they will do some traditional marketing."

What also makes social media marketing a cost-effective approach is that once consumers discover a new brand or product online, they can spread the message to their friends and followers on social networking sites without the company's involvement. A popular product can go viral in the social media world, with postings and images of it posted on a number of sites.

A shopper strolling through downtown Manhattan in search of a cashmere sweater, for example, might use her smartphone to log onto Facebook and ask her friends which stores they recommend in her location. The shopper could also log on to Pinterest and look for pictures of a cashmere sweater that other people have posted. She could do a simple Google search for cashmere sweaters near her specific location. Another possibility would be to rely on her mobile device, which can detect her location and present results for nearby stores to visit.

Although social media marketing may seem like an inexpensive strategy, many companies do not realize the extensive investment of time that is required to maintain a Facebook page or a Twitter account. The rule of thumb is to spend two hours a week per channel, according to Zimmerman, "if they're going to do it well and master it." Those two hours might be spent uploading new images of products on a Facebook page, sending out a Twitter message about a new business development, and responding to customer comments on a ratings site. "It's free in the sense that it doesn't cost them advertising," Zimmerman explains. "But time is money."

Trends Affecting Social Media Marketing

If businesses want to reach their customers online, an increasing number are turning to social media marketing to achieve this goal. One reason is because customers are choosing to shop there. In 2011, 70% of all Internet users aged fourteen and older purchased something online (Data points, 2012). Although e-commerce only accounted for 6.6% of all retail sales in 2011, marketing experts expect that number to rise dramatically, possibly reaching 20% of total retail sales by 2022.

The popularity of online shopping has affected all age groups, from teenagers to the elderly (Data points, 2012). The demographic shopping online more than any other is consumers between the ages of 35 and 64. In 2011, between 73 and 75% of consumers in this age bracket made at least one purchase online, the survey showed. The most popular online purchases are apparel and accessories; books, music, and videos; and toys and hobbies.

Another trend driving the growth of social media is the popularity of smartphones. The mobile revolution presents a powerful outlet through which customers can access the Internet from any location. In 2012, more American mobile customers owned a smartphone than a regular talk-and-text device (Lunden, 2012). As of March 2012, smartphones were in use by 50.4% of American consumers, the first time that smartphone penetration exceeded 50%.

What does the prevalence of smartphones mean for social media marketing? With more smartphones in use by the buying public, more consumers have the ability to shop online 24 hours a day. In 2012, 64% of smartphone owners shopped online using their mobile devices, a number that had quadrupled since 2010 (mCommerce, 2012).

Besides shopping online, smartphones allow people to spend more time on social media. In 2012, 73% of smartphone owners were accessing social media networks daily through social apps, and another 19% were connecting to social media channels weekly (Apps, 2012). More Facebook users now access the social networking site from a mobile device than from a desktop computer. In 2012, 57% of Facebook's users logged onto the website from a mobile device (Protalinski, 2012). Similarly, 60% of Twitter users accessed the microblogging service from a mobile device in 2012 (McGee, 2012).

"Mobile devices have expedited the use of social media through the applications," Ross said. "The Facebook app, the Twitter app, the Instagram app—it makes it quick and easy. Mobile phones are with us 98% of the time, which means we probably sleep with our cellphone, so if we have our mobile phone with us, we are more likely to upload a picture on our Facebook page or on Pinterest."

The constant access to the Internet through mobile devices, tablets, and computers has changed the way consumers buy products. Before a consumer even walks into a store and talks to a salesperson, 60% of the buying cycle is already over according to Kipp Bodnar, co-author of *The B2B Social Media Book: Become a Marketing Superstar by Generating Leads with Blogging, LinkedIn, Twitter, Facebook, Email, and More* (2012).

"We live in a customer-centric marketing world now," Bodnar said. "Customers can do their own research now. They are completely in control of the buying process. Social media marketing is a way to incorporate that 60% of the cycle so that your company will be top-of-mind when your customer actually gets to a sale."

Promoting your business on social media networks allows customers who are browsing Facebook, Twitter, or Pinterest to learn about your products and services either from your own postings or from reviews from other consumers. In short, social media marketing will put your company's brand in front of the increasingly large audience of people accessing social media networks from their mobile devices, tablets, and home computers.

How Businesses Use Social Media

As the buying public has migrated to social media and ecommerce, businesses that invest in social media marketing are finding their efforts to be beneficial. In 2012, 87% of small- and medium-sized businesses said social media has been somewhat helpful or helped a great deal, according to a survey by Vocus and Duct Tape Marketing (Path to Influence).

The survey of 400 small- and medium-sized businesses shed light on the particular benefits of social media:

- It increased annual sales because businesses had more capability to reach out to prospective customers
- It provided insight on customers' demands and requirements
- It allowed businesses to promote products to customers they might not have been able to reach normally
- It allowed businesses to alert customers to last-minute deals and special events that might not have been worth the time without social media outlets

TABLE 1 Helpfulness of Social Media to Small- and Medium-Sized Businesses

0%	Hurt
10%	No effect
58%	Helped somewhat
29%	Helped a great deal

The small- and medium-sized businesses that found social media to be only somewhat helpful or to have had no effect gave the following reasons:

- They had no dedicated staff member to keep up with postings on Facebook and other social media sites

- Their use of social media was limited

The report concluded: "Those that say social media is not helpful also say they've invested little effort. Social media is hard work and you get out of it what you put into it" (Vocus, 2012).

Facebook was the clear favorite among social media platforms that the businesses were using, according to the Vocus survey. Facebook was being used by 73% of the businesses, followed by LinkedIn (61%), Twitter (55%), YouTube (47%), and Google+ (44%) (Path to Influence). Those social platforms also had the top ratings as the most helpful platforms in the survey.

These rankings, however, were completely upended when the businesses that were surveyed were asked which social medium platform they would likely use in the future. The businesses ranked Google+ (14%) and the photosharing sites Instagram (14%) and Pinterest (13%) as the platforms they plan to use in the next year. Those sites were followed by Reddit, a social news website (12%); and Tumblr, a microblogging platform and social networking site (12%). With the exception of MySpace, Facebook had the lowest projection for growth, with only 7% of businesses planning to use it (Vocus, 2012).

Future of Social Media Marketing

In the future, social media marketing will increasingly become targeted toward the location of customers based on their smartphone. Niche targeting will allow someone to walk by a restaurant and then

Marketing: *The process to create, develop, and define markets that satisfy the needs and wants of individual and business customers.*

Marketing mix: *The balance of marketing techniques required for selling the product: 1) Price; 2) Product; 3) Promotion; 4) Place. Also known as the Four (4) Ps.*

receive a text message from the restaurant alerting the consumer to a special deal offering US$1 off on a meal. Using Twitter, the business could also Tweet its special discount to the customer walking by the storefront. Although this technology already exists, customers now have to opt in to whether they want to receive such location-based messages.

To create a more effective presence in the world of social media, businesses will have to make a significant upfront investment in time and staff allocation to establish a presence on various social platforms. "There's a lot of time that goes in upfront," Solomon said. "And there's also an ongoing commitment that the company has to make." If a company creates a page on a social media platform but does not maintain it, the page may become obsolete or attract negative comments that go unmonitored. Despite the challenges associated with social media marketing, most of the businesses surveyed by Vocus said they planned to increase their use of social media.

As the chart shows, businesses have different outlooks and approaches on using social media marketing. The type of social media marketing campaign a business undertakes will depend on whether it is selling products and service to other businesses or to consumers, whether it has a dedicated staff to maintain pages on social websites, and whom its target audience is. "You have to find the proper allocation of time and money to put toward any medium," Block said. "It's all economics—how do we allocate scarce resources?"

Although there are many variables in determining which path to take, marketing experts agree that social media should not be ignored. When considering a *marketing* plan, it is just one part, albeit an important one, of a company's *marketing mix*.

TABLE 2 Future Plans for Social Media

2%	Not sure
14%	Keep social media use around the same
39%	Increase use of social media a lot
45%	Increase use of social media a little

SOURCES OF ADDITIONAL INFORMATION

American Marketing Association. http://www.marketingpower.com
Mobile Marketing Association. http://www.mmaglobal.com
Social Media Marketing Association. http://socialmedia-marketingassociation.com

BIBLIOGRAPHY

Accenture. (2012, January). Consumers intend to buy fewer televisions as they migrate to other consumer electronics devices, Accenture survey finds. *Enhanced Online News*. Retrieved January 29, 2013, from http://eon.businesswire.com/news/eon/20120109005244/en

Barone, L. (2012, September). Are 87 percent of small businesses using social media wrong? *Small Business Trends*. Retrieved October 25, 2012, from http://smallbiztrends.com/2012/09/vocus-social-media-survey.html

Block, R. (2010). *Social persuasion: Making sense of social media for small business [kindle edition]*. Seattle, WA: Block Media.

Bodnar, K. (2012a). *The B2B social media book: Become a marketing superstar by generating leads with blogging, Linkedin, Twitter, Facebook, email, and more*. Hoboken, NJ: Wiley Publishing.

Bodnar, K. (2012b, June). 21 Internet marketing stats that will blow your mind. *Hubspot Blog*. Retrieved October 25, 2012, from http://blog.hubspot.com/blog/tabid/6307/bid/33328/21-Internet-Marketing-Stats-That-Will-Blow-Your-Mind.aspx

Facebook.com. (2012). Timeline. *Facebook.com*. Retrieved October 30, 2012, from http://newsroom.fb.com/content/default.aspx?NewsAreald=20

Fitchard, K. (2012, August). Carrier data confirms it: Half of U.S. now owns a smartphone. *Gigaom*. Retrieved October 31, 2012, from http://gigaom.com/mobile/carrier-data-confirms-it-half-of-us-now-owns-a-smartphone/

Foong, Louis. (2012, June). Interesting infographics: B2B social media. *The Alea Group*. Retrieved October 25, 2012, from http://www.louisfoong.com/interesting-infographics-b2b-social-media/

Klepic, J. (2012, August). Social media is much more than just social and media. *The Huffington Post*. Retrieved October 25, 2012, from www.huffingtonpost.com/jure-klepic/social-media_b_1776403.html

Lightspeed Research. (2012, May). Apps: Fun or functional? *Lightspeed Research*. Retrieved October 31, 2012, from http://www.lightspeedresearch.com/press-releases/apps-fun-or-functional/

Lunden, Ingrid. (2012, May). Nielson: Smartphones used by 50.4 percent of U.S. *TechCrunch*. Retrieved October 31, 2012, from http://techcrunch.com/2012/05/07/nielsen-smartphones-used-by-50-4-of-u-s-consumers-android-48-5-of-them/

McGee, Matt. (2012, June). Twitter: 60 percent of users access via mobile. *Marketing Land*. Retrieved October 30, 2012, from http://marketingland.com/twitter-60-percent-of-users-access-via-mobile-13626

Moses, Lucia. (2012, April). Data points: Spending it. *Adweek*. Retrieved October 31, 2012, from http://www.adweek.com/news/advertising-branding/data-points-spending-it-139582

Nielsenwire. (2010, June). Social networks/blogs now account for one in every four and a half minutes online. *Nielsenwire*. Retrieved November 2, 2012, from http://blog.nielsen.com/nielsenwire/global/social-media-accounts-for-22-percent-of-time-online/

O'Dell, Jolie. (2011, March). For the first time, more people get news online than from newspapers. *Mashable.com.* Retrieved January 28, 2013 from www.mashable.com/2011/03/14/online-versus-newspaper-news/

Protalinski, E. (2012, June). Facebook: Over 955 million users, 543 million mobile users. *CNET News.* Retrieved October 31, 2012, from http://news.cnet.com/8301-1023_3-57480950-93/facebook-oer-955-million-users

PRWeb UK. (2012, May). mCommerce quadruples in just two years. *PRWeb.* Retrieved October 30, 2012, from http://www.prweb.com/releases/2012/5/prweb9536719.htm

Statistic Brain (2012a, July). Social Networking Statistics. Retrieved October 29, 2012, from http://www.statisticbrain.com/social-networking-statistics/

Statistic Brain. (2012b, September). Twitter statistics. Retrieved October 30, 2012, from http://www.statisticbrain.com/twitter-statistics/

Thomas, L. (2010). *The McGraw-Hill 36-hour course: Online marketing.* New York: McGraw-Hill.

Tuten, T., & Solomon, M. (2012). *Social media marketing.* Upper Saddle River, NJ: Pearson Education.

Vocus.com. (2012, September). Path to influence: An industry study of SMBs and social media. *Vocus.com.* Retrieved October 29, 2012, from http://www.vocus.com/blog/smb-social-media-influence/

Zimmerman, J., & Sahlin, D. (2010). *Social media marketing all-in-one for dummies.* Hoboken, NJ: Wiley Publishing.

Understanding Social Media and Its Effects

In This Essay

- To harness the power of social media for marketing, companies should take care to learn about and understand the various social media venues and how they are used

- Risk management is an important aspect of a company's involvement in social media, where negative reports can spread quickly

- Social media can be used to assess and gauge consumer buying behavior and therefore influence those behaviors by establishing relationships

Social media allows individuals to communicate instantly. Social media, with its numerous ways of connecting around relationships and interests, has dramatically changed the marketing landscape. Information dissemination is no longer under the sole control of its owners or marketing managers. Traditional media, including television, newspapers, magazines, and radio, is no longer the primary information. Major Internet search engines see their niches diminishing as well.

What does this mean for marketing communications? It means that companies need to understand how social media affects reaching their audiences. It also means that businesses may need to develop marketing strategies using social media channels. This means learning and using the channels particular to their target audience. It means expanding their reach to all relevant audiences, employees, vendors, and industry trade groups—the groups that mean success or failure as a business. Moreover, influence is largely built on the strength of relationships.

Social media is not limited to the major platforms such as Facebook, Google+, or Twitter. It extends to all of the venues used by consumers to solicit information, which includes texting, e-mails, and traditional media. Nonetheless, traditional media does not have the primacy it once enjoyed, so businesses need to adapt their marketing strategies to use social media in a proactive way that enhances their brand and messages. Businesses cannot ignore social media. The customer-driven nature of social media gives it primacy over traditional media. According to *Demystifying Social Media*, "…it no longer makes sense to treat it as an experiment" (Divol, Edelman, & Sarrazin, 2012).

If businesses cannot ignore social media, how should they view this form of communication? As mentioned previously, companies should view it as a part of its communications array for information dissemination. A successful company will target their information to the mainstream audience in the venue in which they are comfortable. Having access to product information or service messaging builds a company's relationship with its target and secondary audiences. Additionally, integrating social media into the overall marketing plan means a comprehensive strategy in combination with traditional marketing tools (Hanna, Rohn, & Crittenden, 2011).

In this virtual world, a business does not have sole control over who creates its marketing messages. "It's no secret that consumers increasingly go online to discuss products and brands, seek advice and offer guidance" (Divol et al., 2012). The loss of control has caused reservations for marketing managers and the managers who oversee them. With consumers using a growing variety of venues, some managers find it difficult to determine which venue is best for their brand. In addition, some decision makers find it difficult to determine the return on investment (ROI) to substantiate the investment of finances and staffing to make use of this resource (Divol et al., 2012).

Marketing managers see social media as a means of connecting to their target audiences. Looking at social media as a strategy or system for a company's product or message branding is still taking hold with many companies. To understand social media's effects, especially for these decision makers, the best place to start is with a basic grasp of social media. Then, once a framework for social media is established, the next step is to see how social media can affect a business. During this step, social media is viewed for branding, for communicating company messages, and for managing risk for a company. Finally, the company should examine relationships and how to harness them in light of social media marketing (Divol et al., 2012).

Understanding the Social Media Climate

What is social media? Social media are the venues consumers use to collect information about products, brands, companies, interests, etc. Social media are the means by which consumers develop relationships around the companies they purchase from, the products they use, the issues they support or the recreational activities they love. These venues flourish and generate dynamic interaction, with and without business input (Currie, 2009).

Social media takes many forms. Currie (2009) notes the following forms of social media tools:

- Social networks (Facebook and MySpace are friends-based)
- Blogs (interest-based)
- Mobile text messaging
- RSS feeds (interest-based)
- Microblogs (Twitter is interest-based)
- Video sharing (YouTube and interest-based)
- Podcasts
- Wikis (Wikipedia)
- Image sharing (Flickr, Pinterest)
- Widgets
- Social bookmarking (Digg, Delicious)
- Mobile websites
- Virtual worlds (Whyville)

These forms of social media are ranked by type, kind, and level of interaction. With the variety of forms and the development of more venues day by day, it presents a challenge to determine which channels best serve marketing needs. In addition, social media types overlap each other, making the determination even more challenging (Currie, 2009).

Marketing managers meet the challenge by using a combination of social media tools. Social networks offer the highest level of interaction. They help their members socialize, exchange information, and form communities. Blogs offer interaction between author and reader. Mobile texting offers instant messaging among friends and by extension to followers in the microblog universe. RSS feeds are important ways to access news services. It is important to note that each of the venues have a different level of interaction (Currie, 2009).

A company's product or message determines which tool is best for reaching customers. It also depends on the venue used by that company's target audience. As a result, companies need to go where members of their audience are getting their information and interact with them when they are available. Additionally, each tool comes with an array of metrics. Referring to those metrics allows a company to gauge the effectiveness of that tool in their marketing efforts. Marketing managers find the two-way nature of social media requires greater efforts (Divol et al., 2012).

Risk Analysis and Social Media

Before using social media, there is a need to discuss the role of risk assessment. Risk assessment involves social media in two ways. First, risk assessment analyzes the degree to which an event adversely affects a company. Then, risk assessment analyzes the potential for escalation of an adverse event (Kasperson et al., 1988).

For the purposes of this article, an adverse or risk event is any situation or circumstance with the potential of negatively impacting a company's brand, product, or message. In a strictly technical definition, managers view risk as the probability that an adverse event will occur. Risk management is the execution of policies in response to a risk event and managing the groups the event affects (Kasperson et al., 1988).

The potential for negative perceptions generated by company spokespersons, news reports, advocacy messages, or products is an intangible yet real threat given one's business climate. It is not unusual to see an adverse event go viral in social media with startling frequency (Divol et al., 2012). Needless to say, avoiding or minimizing those occurrences is a growing area for risk assessment application.

Kasperson et al. (1988) indicate that consumers view risk in a much broader context. Consumers view a risk event in terms of the following:

- Who delivers the messages about the risk event.

- The amount of, or lack of, usable information in risk event messages.

- The perceived threat generated by the event.

- The degree to which a person can control the risk event.
- The familiarity with or personal knowledge of the risk event.

Along with these factors, consumers also judge the perceived veracity of the messenger. A good example is the amount of negative coverage in the aftermath of Hurricane Katrina, due to the lack of commitment by FEMA "to transmit critically important information immediately to as many people as possible. Literature suggests that companies who are slow to disseminate information can cause the unintended effect of being viewed as not forthcoming (Currie, 2009)." This makes them seem less truthful.

There are some situations where an audience is related to an adverse event but not directly affected by it. These groups would be considered a secondary audience for a company. A narrow application of risk assessment on this group can escalate a negative perception. The negative effect relates to a perception of inequity (i.e., the perception that the company favors some groups over others). Social media can be a key tool in managing perceptions (Currie, 2009; Kasperson et al., 1988).

An unintended effect is escalating negative commentary in social media. Currie (2009) and Kasperson et al. (1988) attest that limiting information dissemination can result in escalating risk on the part of a company's secondary audiences.

A broad framework for assessing risk needs to be applied when managing social responses and the public experience of a risk event. The escalation or social amplification of an adverse event increases in stages. Kasperson et al. say that social amplification begins with the risk event and then moves to characteristics of the event. Once the characteristics become known, then the next stage is disseminating information about the event. Next, interpreting and responding to the risk event's information takes place. After the event is interpreted and response generates, the next stage is the spread of the event's impact.

Finally, Kasperson et al. say the negative effect a company experiences can be lost sales, increased regulation, stock downturns, and litigation. Using those same stages, a positive effect a company experiences is increased sales, community support, favorable media treatment, and improved interaction with secondary audiences (Currie, 2009).

Successful risk management takes into account public perceptions in addition to the cause/effect nature of pure risk assessment. Social amplification can affect a risk event in two ways: it can increase an event's effects or attenuate them. Social media helps a business manage both aspects of social amplification.

Understand the Role of Marketing Today

Understanding the types of social media available and their functions helps determine the most effective tools for a company to use (Currie, 2009). Understanding how the public perceives risk is key in developing a company's marketing strategies (Kasperson et al., 1988). Traditional marketing is a one-way communications method of propagating a company's messages, branding, and advertising (Kasperson et al., 1988).

As mentioned earlier, the information distribution once was the sole province of a marketing or public relations manager. These managers chose the information channels such as mass media, spokesmen, industry trade groups, etc. These sources rated as expert level. On the flip side, consumers had few choices for getting their information.

The marketing climate has drastically changed. This result is largely because of the Internet and the resulting ease of accessing social media. Divol et al. describe it: "marketing's primary goal is to reach consumers at the moments, or touch points, that influence their purchasing behavior." This means that consumer behavior has changed. It is no longer linear and marketing strategies need to adjust accordingly.

Suffice it to say, non-marketing managers are aware of social media's effect, especially in terms of reaching customers. Divol et al. (2012) state that, "the vast majority of [non-marketing] executives have no idea how to harness social media's power." They go on to explain, "This is due to the seemingly nebulous nature of social media [. . .] there's no single measure of social media's financial impact and many companies find that it's difficult to justify devoting significant resources, financial or human, to an activity whose precise effect remains unclear."

With the current marketing climate, social media can play an effective role in a business' overall marketing strategy. That role is two-fold: recognizing the purchasing process and applying social media at those junctures that best influence buying behavior (Divol et al., 2012). That interaction is not just between company and customer, but extends to a company's fans, advocates, and also detractors. As a result, social media has become a highly influential factor in marketing planning.

Understand Consumers' Purchasing Today

Consumer buying behavior follows a journey. That journey begins with considering a product, followed by its evaluation. Then there is buying and experiencing the product. The last stages of the process are advocating for the product and bonding with it or becoming a zealot. Managers can influence the purchase process through *touch points*. These touch points are monitoring, responding, amplifying, and leading (Divol et al., 2012).

Touch points: *A point of contact or interaction, especially between a business and its customers.*

Consumer Buying Process

Monitoring social media lets organizations become aware of the conversations, trends, and information shared about them. Building on the information gained from monitoring helps to respond to trending issues in the form of crisis management or customer service. Both crisis management and customer service allow engagement where consumers use the product (Divol et al., 2012). It provides the opportunity to remedy a negative experience or improve delivery of a product's benefits.

Furthermore, through amplification, a company can call attention to trends that promote positives about its products. It can clarify or influence the sources of comments that potentially damage its product's effectiveness. At the final stage, leading, companies can introduce new uses for its products, launch new products, or encourage the development of product zealots (Divol et al., 2012).

Consumer Evaluation and Social Media

Consumers make decisions upon their purchases dependent on the likes of their social networks. "We have a natural inclination to emulate those we like, admire, find attractive as these attributes also contribute to the 'guilt by association' impression of self-identity" (Solis, 2012). Consumers also rely on their online communities for research and advice. Again, this dynamic interaction drives social media's influence. Managers' ability to guide or interject effectively into that dynamic contributes to a marketing program's success.

Anderson, Huttenlocher, Kleinberg, and Leskovec (2012) indicate that similarities between communities' members influence how members evaluate each other. It also influences recommendations between members based on status. Expanding on Anderson et al., communities form around interests (networks, forums, and microblogs), friends and family (networks), or experts (blogs and microblogs). As a result, it is possible to predict how an aggregate will respond to or evaluate products and messages (Anderson et al., 2012).

Gilbert and Karahalios (2009) discuss tie strength. A tie is a relationship between two community members. It can be strong or weak: "Strong ties are the people you really trust whose social circles tightly overlap your own. [...] Weak ties, conversely, are merely acquaintances." (Gilbert & Karahalios, 2009). The strength of the ties determines whether and how much information flows between the ties. Therefore, relationships affect the type of information shared. They also affect the quality and quantity of information shared. Further, Gilbert and Karahalios state that tie strength has seven dimensions: intensity, intimacy, duration, reciprocal services, structural, emotional support, and social distance. While duration, emotional support, and reciprocal services are self-explanatory, the remaining dimensions need a brief explanation.

Intensity is the quantity of messages a user receives. Intimacy is the quantity of cherished words, shared photos, or information exchanged between two members. The structural dimension refers to communities that two members share. Lastly, social distance denotes the differences in education levels, political affiliations, demographics, and social media usage. The dimensions both complement and influence each other into strong or weak ties. They suggest that using tie strength and its dimensions predict the quality and quantity of information shared in a community. It also predicts response to that information (Gilbert & Karahalios, 2009).

Strong ties receive emotional, intimate, and frequent information. Weak ties trend toward less qualitative, less intimate information. Gilbert and Karahalios are quick to add that variables within each dimension may affect the flow of information across ties. As a result, tie strength bears further study. However, it is clear this work indicates relationships are essential in social media.

Understanding Social Media Engagement

Different products engender different responses. According to Understanding Social Media (n.d.), social media allows people to post anything—photos of new sneakers, tweets about a new restaurant—and as a result create marketing content. Managing or influencing that content creation, especially when the content is not company-generated, is challenging for businesses. However, developing a grasp of what motivates a consumer to engage in social media can boost marketing strategy effectiveness (Understanding Social Media, n.d.). Part of that knowledge relies on familiarity with functional products and hedonic products.

Functional products, according to Understanding Social Media (n.d.), are "primarily utilitarian products (e.g., hair dryers, washing machines and lawn mowers), with tangible, objective features that offer functional benefits, fulfill utilitarian needs, and are meant to solve problems. 'Hedonic products are items' (such as jewelry, perfumes, massages) with subjective, non-tangible features that fulfill experiential needs and whose consumption produces enjoyment and pleasure."

The authors suggest that functional products have "search attributes information in [their] advertising [and] results in a positive product experience." However, when the authors turn to hedonic products that are both subjective in nature and experiential for the customer, like perfumes or massages, the included "experience attribute information facilitates imagination which is so important in judging a hedonic product... This in turn results in more positive product evaluations." The information as well as product type motivates a consumer to use social media.

Understand Engagement's Importance

Information and experience initiate engagement. Revisiting Divol et al. (2012), engagement is the point at which a user connects with the brand, product, or message via social media. It is important because of the nature of the marketing climate. The companies that can navigate social media as well as initiate engagement are one step closer to executing effective marketing strategies.

Marketing is increasingly consumer-driven. Consumers want two-way communication with companies. Furthermore, they want to share their interests, opinions, and experiences about the products they use and the interests they support. As a result of this dynamic sharing and content creation, consumers rely more on their networks for information over company-generated information. Thus, engagement is important for reaching customers and for making purchasing decisions. Successful engagement relies on relationships, both user to user and user to company.

Social Commerce and Engagement

Social commerce: *The use of social network(s) to assist in e-commerce transactions.*

What underlies engagement? According to Solis (2012), "the social sciences of psychology, anthropology, communications, economics and human geography, et al., are essential in building meaningful relationships in influencing mutually beneficial behavior." Solis continues, "the A.R.T of Engagement, actions, reactions, and transactions become the fabric of holistic and connected experiences" Along with A.R.T., Solis sees *social commerce* as a function of social psychology. This science studies social influence and how people relate to each other. Consequently, social media demonstrates how people leverage that influence for social capital. That is, people earn their relationships, with individuals or with organizations, and the accompanying stature (Solis, 2012).

Solis divides social commerce into six areas of decision making:

- Social proof   Uncertainty causes people to do what others do.
- Authority   Experts guide decision making.
- Scarcity   Items that are less available have more value.
- Liking   People do business with people like themselves.
- Consistency   Uncertainty causes people to take few risks.
- Reciprocity   People want to repay favors with similar acts of assistance.

With social commerce, using some or all of the above aspects help consumers build social influence. With the exception of scarcity, Solis notes that each area relies on relationships. It complements the recurring theme of this discussion to understand social media. Involvement in customers' online experiences and making that experience memorable, will in turn cause customers to become more emotionally invested with that company.

Engage Customers Where They Use Social Media

Divol et al. (2012) remind us that there are four areas where companies can engage their customers in the buying process: monitoring, responding, amplifying, and leading.

Monitoring social media tools appropriate to a company's business makes it more aware of customer sentiment, product trends, and claims made about the company. Active monitoring informs company responses. As a result, marketing communications follow monitoring by letting company responses take on a dual nature. Crisis management can respond to customer-generated claims and potentially damaging issues resulting from the buying decision–making phases of considering, evaluating, or buying. The same monitoring also allows companies to respond to service complaints and product defects in regards to the buying decision–making phases of experience, advocacy, or bonding (Divol et al., 2012).

Companies make their online presence known through proactive messages. The messages can take the form of recommendations, advice, and activities. These are actions that promote positive tones in the consideration, evaluation, and buying phases of the purchasing process. It can also mean growing or providing forums around product experience. Companies can have exclusive activities for advocates and super advocates. These actions take the form of special deals and events that encourage this group to influence their networks on behalf of the company.

For touch points involving leading in social media venues, marketing strategies can focus on promoting brand awareness at the consideration phase. Next, organizing new product kickoff or special offers at the evaluation and buying phases, respectively, allow businesses to actively draw in customers to all aspects of their products. Finally, the last touch point, leading, affects the decision-making phases of experience, advocacy, and bonding. This last aspect of leadership fosters partnership with consumers to innovate products, to educate consumers, and to develop the crucial element of engagement.

Conclusion

This discussion has focused on social media's key aspects: relationships and engagement. Both aspects influence marketing strategies and planning.

The process starts with risk analysis and the need to see that successful social media management involved both knowing a product's or an event's risk position as well as the degree of a risk event's potential impact. Having such knowledge allows a company to manage and address public response. Risk assessment depends on a broad application of risk analysis methods (Kasperson et al., 1988). As a result, a company can influence and reach its target and secondary audiences through the appropriate social media channels. How a company manages a risk assessment contributes to positive or negative escalation (Divol et al., 2012).

Relationships affect social media and have a role in consumer buying behavior. Touch points in the buying process and elements of tie strength illustrate that relationships dynamically affect social media in a variety of ways rather than a straightforward approach (Gilbert & Karahalios, 2009). Furthermore, the touch points of monitoring, responding, amplifying, and leading serve as guidelines for companies in choosing social media tools as well as in when to contact their audiences. Knowing how product types, functional and hedonic, motivate consumers toward engagement is also relevant (Understanding Social Media, n.d.).

Subsequently, relationships are essential to effective engagement. Customers use social commerce in six areas in the decision making process. These areas are social proof, authority, scarcity, liking, consistency, and reciprocity. Consumers actively using these "pillars of social commerce" (Solis, 2012) employ various levels of relationships and degrees of influence to make their buying decisions. They leverage the relationships to earn stature in social media (Solis, 2012).

Whether individuals use their influence to affect marketing planning or companies affect customer buying decisions through engagement, the end result is increased communication and greater interaction through social media.

SOURCES OF ADDITIONAL INFORMATION

Demystifying Social Media. http://www.mckinseyquarterly.com/Demystifying_social_media_2958

Mashable. http://mashable.com/category/social-media/

McKinsey Quarterly's website. http://www.mckinseyquarterly.com/home.aspx

Michael Stelzner. http://www.socialmediaexaminer.com

BIBLIOGRAPHY

Anderson, A., Huttenlocher, D., Kleinberg, J., & Leskovec, J. (2012, February). Effects of user similarity in social media. *WSDM '12*. Retrieved January 2, 2013, from http://www-cs.stanford.edu/people/ashton/pubs/wsdm-sim.pdf.

Currie, D. (2009). Expert round table on social media and risk communication during times of crisis: Strategic challenges and opportunities. Retrieved December 4, 2012, from http://www.apha.org/NR/rdonlyres/47910BED-3371-46B3-85C2-67EFB80D88F8/0/socialmedreport.pdf.

Divol, R., Edelman, D., & Sarrazin, H. (2012, April). Demystifying social media. *McKinsey Quarterly*. Retrieved January 2, 2013, from http://www.mckinseyquarterly.com/Demystifying_social_media_2958.

Gilbert, E., & Karahalios, K. (2009, April). Predicting tie strength with social media. *CHI 2009*. Retrieved January 2, 2013, from http://sing.stanford.edu/cs303-sp11/papers/gilbert_tie_strength.pdf

Hanna, R., Rohn, A., & Crittenden, V. (2011). We're all connected: The power of the social media ecosystem. Kelley School of Business, Indiana University. Retrieved January 2, 2013, from http://topgan.cce.unsyiah.ac.id/Were%20all%20connected%20The%20power%20of%20the%20social%20media%20ecosystem.pdf.

Kasperson, R., Renn, O., Slovic, P., Brown, H. S., Emel, J., Goble, R., Kasperson, J. X., & Ratick, S. (1988). The social amplification of risk: a conceptual framework. *Risk Analysis*, 8(2), 177. Retrieved January 2, 2013, from http://elib.uni-stuttgart.de/opus/volltexte/2010/5307/pdf/ren27.pdf.

Solis, B. (2012, April) 6 pillars of social commerce: Understanding the psychology of engagement. *Socialmedia Today*. Retrieved January 2, 2013, from http://socialmediatoday.com/briansolis/484521/6-pillars-social-commerce-understanding-psychology-engagement.

Understanding social media: The effect of product type and brand information on consumers' social media use. (n.d.). Retrieved January 2, 2013, from http://www.aabri.com/OC2013Manuscripts/OC13004.pdf.

Benefits of Social Media

In This Essay

- Social media allows businesses to relate in a more personal, intimate way with their customers

- Many considerations should be looked at when planning a social media approach

- More people are using the Internet, so social media marketing can use that to its advantage

- Search engine optimization (SEO) and partnerships can increase the effectiveness of social media marketing strategies

- Social media marketing has a lower cost to use than traditional marketing strategies

Overview

A comprehensive social media presence can provide a business with various unique professional and promotional advantages.

If a website can be considered a company's virtual calling card, social media may be viewed as its follow-up call. Companies have a multitude of outlets through which to enter the social media realm: They can establish pages on Facebook, YouTube, Pinterest, and Twitter. They can create a blog. They can advertise, promote open positions, and recruit employees through LinkedIn.

Social media options continue to expand. Companies looking to market their products and services online can provide a *podcast*, release a promotional app, or build excitement or "buzz" by offering a discounted

Podcast: *A program, most often music or talk, made available in digital format for download over the Internet.*

promotion through Groupon, Living Social, or another similar service. Types of creative promotional options are limited only by the imagination of the promoter.

Information on Demand

Social media outlets usually have a set format, which means that visual customization may be as simple as adding a company logo. Also, the ease of posting to sites such as Facebook and Twitter allows organizations to send frequent, timely updates to their customer base to promote products and services.

Frequent social media posts can help companies remain relevant to consumers. A strong presence online helps businesses build their *brand* by establishing a defined identity.

Brand: *Name, term, symbol, sign, or design used by a firm to differentiate its offerings from those of its competitors.*

A Closer Customer Relationship

Social media allows companies to connect with their customers in a personal, intimate way. Although other marketing efforts, such as email blasts or direct mailing pieces, can be somewhat customized with, for example, a first name or personal introduction, social media contacts can be more closely tailored according to a customer's characteristics.

If a company has the personnel resources to monitor social media such as individual Facebook pages, the company can reach out to customers periodically to comment on their Facebook posts. Businesses can also suggest that purchasers indicate approval on sites such as Yelp, which features a heavy emphasis on user reviews, or that they "like" various items or articles on Facebook. Personalized contact can help companies directly communicate with and build a stronger connection to their client base.

Considerations

Companies may benefit from factoring several considerations into their social media approach. Answering the following questions may help web marketers plan how best to use social media:

- How can social media sites be used to connect with current and potential clients?
- What social media sites would best reach the client base?

- How could current web policy integrate or involve social media?

- How can rankings on search engine websites such as Google be improved so that the company website appears high up on the list of search results? How can social media help achieve that goal?

- What frequent updates would best promote the brand and products to consumers?

- How can social media be used to form personal connections with customers, and how should dissatisfied customers who contact the company through social media outlets be handled?

- How can social media outlets help foster new relationships with business partners?

- Can social media help reduce current marketing expenses?

Background

The Ever-Expanding Internet

Since its start in the 1960s as a small U.S.-based network, the Internet has grown rapidly in popularity and reach. It is now a truly world wide web.

In 1996, 23% of U.S. adults were online, according to the Pew Research Center. By August 2012, a similar Pew survey found that the number of U.S. adults regularly using the Internet had grown to 85%, with emailing and searching for information ranking highest on the list of typical online activities.

As Internet use has grown, the ways consumers and businesses use the technology also has evolved. The practice of going online has morphed into a more direct and targeted communication channel. One possible explanation for this change is the increased use of social media.

The University of California at Berkeley, which released research in June 2011 from an analysis of more than 41,000 adults in the United States who had participated in the Pew Internet and American Life Project between 2000 and 2008, cited the 2004 launch of Facebook and the 2008 creation of Twitter as two main drivers of the growth in social media's popularity.

The university's Berkeley Center for New Media reported that as of 2011, there were 2 billion social media users across the globe. Social media use is clearly a popular pastime. According to the Berkeley Center's study, social media users create enough data every day to equal the print collection of the U.S. Library of Congress, one of the largest libraries in the world.

New Online Avenues

Research indicates that social media use is not limited to instant messaging and posting photos. People are increasingly turning to online news sources for recent information relevant to their community and lifestyle. News outlets have played a hand in this change by establishing websites with interactive "social" features.

Television and print media remain a primary source of local and national news for many Internet users, as well as for people who do not spend time online. However, certain demographic attributes predict who will turn to the Internet for their news. Residents of large cities, who tend to be younger and more mobile, are more likely to find out about local news through Twitter, blogs, Internet searches, and media websites, according to a 2011 Pew Research Center report.

In some communities, word-of-mouth communication seems to have moved online. Also, more than one-third—41%—of adults are likely to proactively share news information on social networking sites, the 2011 study found. Suburban residents were the most likely to serve as what the Pew report called a "news participator" role.

An Inaugural Audience

Internet use reached a new milestone in spring 2012, when the Pew Research Center's Internet & American Life Project survey found that half of U.S. citizens age 65 or older (classified as "senior citizens") were using email and the Internet.

The senior age group is still the least likely overall to use the Internet. However, with 53% of the generation now online regularly, the increase is notable—as is the growth in senior cell phone ownership.

The Pew Research Center's 2012 report noted that 69% of seniors (people over age 65) owned a cell phone; in May 2010, the percentage of seniors owning a phone had been only 57%. Even the older seniors are using cell phones. In 2010, 47% of seniors age 76 and older owned a cell phone; by early 2012, that number had risen to 56%.

Social Media Grows More Popular

An increasing number of seniors also are embracing social media outlets such as Facebook and Twitter.

Although email remains seniors' most popular form of online communication, approximately one-third—34%—reported using social networking sites such as Facebook as of February 2012. Eighteen percent of U.S. citizens age 65 and older used social media on a daily basis, according to the Pew Research Center.

The rest of the United States is echoing the 65-and-over generation's trend. Overall, approximately 60% of U.S. adults use social networking sites such as Twitter and Facebook, according to Pew's 2012 Internet & American Life Project survey.

Small Businesses Embrace Social Media

Recent studies have shown that as more companies begin to use social media to promote their services and products, corporations with sizeable marketing budgets are not the only ones that are making social networking a priority.

In 2011 the International Data Corporation (IDC; www.idc.com), which provides market intelligence, advisory services, and events for technology and telecommunications companies, predicted that social networking technologies—especially those linked to mobile technologies—would soon be recognized as a mandatory component in every information technology company's business strategy.

IDC's forecast appears to have been correct. In a 2012 survey by the marketing company VerticalResponse, two-thirds of businesses with fewer than 100 employees reported that they were spending more time on social media in 2012 than they did in the previous year. Popular social media activities included locating and sharing content and blogging.

Nearly half—43%—of small businesses reported spending close to an entire day (six or more hours), on business-related social media activities. Eighteen percent said they spent eleven or more hours each week managing social media.

However, although use of social media among small businesses has risen, many survey respondents expressed concern about the time it took to post updates and create content. One-third of those answering VerticalResponse's survey said they would like to spend less time on sites such as Facebook and Twitter and more time focused on new business growth.

Small business CEOs, owners, and other high-ranking officials told VerticalResponse that they found searching for and posting content to the Internet to be the biggest drain on time. Learning about social media developments and use, analyzing data to see how the effort was working, and tracking competitors' social media use also ranked high.

Generating Business Exposure
Group Social Media Mentality

Both organizations that are made up of members or volunteers, and businesses seeking to promote their products and services can benefit from using social media outlets as a promotional tool.

A study that the Pew Research Center conducted in 2010 found that social networking sites had a particularly strong lure for Americans who were voluntarily active in groups and organizations: 82% of social network users are group participants. On Twitter alone, 85% of users were group participants, according to Pew.

Group-related research shows that social media sites can have a strong impact on engagement. Sixty-two percent of Pew's survey respondents said the Internet had a major effect on groups' ability to raise awareness of an issue, and roughly 55% said the Internet has played a major role in groups' ability to attract new members.

Social media presence may pay off particularly well for targeting *Generation Y* consumers. Internet users age 18 to 29 are the demographic that is most active in fan groups for products and brands, according to Pew.

Generation Y: *A person born between 1977 and 1992. Also known as Gen Y; Millennial.*

Increasing Traffic/Subscribers

For a company looking to expand its client base, informing new people about its offerings is an important step. A website offers companies the chance to market themselves 24 hours a day. For a site to be a successful marketing tool, it has to be clear, informative, and primed to be as visible and easy to find as possible. Companies also need to keep potential customers coming back to their site.

Consumers ages 25 to 44 who use Facebook expressed a willingness to let social media influence their buying decisions, according to a survey conducted in 2012 by email marketing software provider ExactTarget. The survey found that 42% of Brazilian consumers made a purchase after being exposed to a marketing message through Facebook.

In some countries, such as Brazil, social media sites have proven to be extremely successful marketing tools for companies. The recent Exact-Target survey found that 77% of consumers in Brazil who are online interact with brands on Facebook. Also, 26% of Brazilian consumers who are online interact with brands on Twitter, and 58% said they consistently read posts from their favorite companies.

Keeping Customers Happy

Social media use varies among countries. In Australia, only 55% of active Facebook users have opted to click "like" to indicate their feelings about a company's page on the site. In contrast, 89% of Brazilian Facebook users have clicked on the thumbs-up icon to indicate they support a company, according to ExactTarget.

Despite how their country of origin's citizens opt to interact on Facebook product pages, businesses may not want to rely solely on their social media presence to interact with their client base, particularly when dealing with unhappy customers.

Some customers will like products. Others will post a note of praise, and some will post something negative. Most dissatisfied customers who use social media to share their complaints do so after they have tried to contact the organization in another way. They turn to social media if they feel the problem was not resolved, according to *MIT Sloan Management Review* magazine. A 2011 article in that magazine, "When Unhappy Customers Strike Back on the Internet," notes that an upset commenter may feel more deceived than displeased, and suggests quickly addressing the issue with a heartfelt "we're sorry"-type reaction.

Improving Search Rankings
Search Engine Optimization (SEO)

Companies employ various methods to attract new customers and clients to their websites. Search engines such as Google and Firefox often play an important role.

There are several ways a company can increase its chances of appearing when someone uses Google or a similar site to search for a specific term or item. To offer users the best quality sites with the most content, according to Google, its search algorithms look for more than 200 signals when pulling up search results. Factors that affect search results include how often, and where, relevant terms appear on a web page.

Companies can incorporate *keywords* to help increase their website's chances of appearing high on a search engine's results list. For example, a manufacturer that sells hair gel might repeatedly mention the word *gel* in its home page text.

Businesses can also host a *blog* on their website to help improve search engine rankings. Blogs often include frequently updated content that other websites reference and link to, and Google's search algorithms, for example, favor web pages with fresh content and a large number of high-quality links. Some search engines consider multiple links to a page to be a sign that the page contains significant content.

Keyword: *On the Internet, a search term that a search engine uses to select websites to display in the search results.*

Blog: *A website on which an individual or group records opinions, information, etc., on a regular basis. Short for weblog.*

B2B (business-to-business) marketers: *Short for business-to-business or a commercial transaction between two businesses.*

Using a blog to build connections to other sites and help improve search engine ranking is a common practice. According to the report "Search Marketing: The State of B2B SEO and PPC Practices" from the marketing strategy magazine *BtoB*, in 2012 three-fourths of marketers described themselves as at least "moderately involved" in using search engine optimization to help improve their home pages' rankings.

The use of search engine optimization techniques to improve rankings has become more popular than paying directly for advertising designed to improve search results. According to *BtoB*, 44% of companies have used paid search options, such as pay-per-click advertising. These highlighted ads appear alongside search results and link directly to a company's website.

Social Media and SEO

Social media sites can also provide companies with an SEO boost.

Some *B2B (business-to-business) marketers* claim that maintaining a dynamic social networking presence can help businesses significantly increase traffic on their website. Social media outlets such as Facebook and Twitter give companies the opportunity to post frequent updates about products, promotions, and other news, which can in turn push viewers to the company's website to learn more.

Direct marketing publication *DM News* noted in a June 2012 article that because SEO is constantly evolving due to user trends, companies need to stay up to date on new terms, techniques, and ways of improving their ranking. It is crucial that companies create content that is tailored not only for their websites, but that will work on social networks and third-party sites as well. *DM News* advised studying how other sites, including social media outlets, share links and package content.

Creating New Business Partnerships

Although many companies are just starting to fully realize the potential marketing benefits social media can offer, research indicates its popularity as a promotional tool for businesses and professional organizations will continue to increase.

A 2011 study by IBM found that although only 42% of chief marketing officers (CMOs) are currently tracking third-party online reviews to gauge product acceptance, 82% of CMOs say they plan to use social media more frequently in the next three to five years to connect with both current and future customers.

In addition, 56% of CMOs said they viewed social media as "a key engagement channel," according to the study.

Connecting With Customers

Social media offers organizations a chance to build a more personal relationship with current and potential customers.

An e-book titled *The Definitive Guide to Social Selling: How to Sell to People, Not Contacts*, published in 2012 by two market research firms, InsideView and Focus, advises using social media outlets to learn more about customer needs and how to best meet those needs.

Some industries seem particularly well suited to using social media for customization. For example, in a May 2012 article covering highlights from the 2012 Advantage Conference on trends, *Travel Business Review* cited a senior buyer who spoke at the conference as saying that social media would allow travel planning companies that were planning to use discounts and other incentives to attract travelers to their services "to assess the travel preferences of the employees, and to formulate policies accordingly."

To obtain the best results, *The Definitive Guide to Social Selling* suggests combining marketing-based social networking with other posts that are friendly. Sharing articles or posts is also helpful. InsideView notes that social networking can help sales professionals tailor the company's message to effectively reach and influence customers and potential business partners.

Making Contact

Sales representatives can use social media to determine who might be the best prospective client or business partner contact at a company or organization, and when the best time is to contact them, according to InsideView.

A September 2012 *CRM* magazine article said that email has, for years, been the most widely overused marketing tool employed to reach customers. *CRM* Editorial Director David Myron explained that the popularity of email campaigns can be attributed to their "internally focused metrics (such as lead generation, return on investment and revenue)."

Myron noted that the best marketing plans use a social media strategy that involves posting items users will either like or link to.

Myron questions what element would make a reader opt to report or like a post the company makes on the reader's page. He then says value plays a key role, and suggests that companies include a helpful tip, reward, or other item to entice users to react. Engaged readers are more likely to either indicate approval or help spread the word.

Is a Facebook post more likely than an email to get forwarded from one marketing target to another? Myron says yes. He explains that a marketing-based email is focused on a company's interests (notably, its sales interests), whereas a personalized Facebook post that presents value to the reader indicates that the company takes customers' interests to heart.

Building Community

In an August 2012 *Marketing Week* article, author Bruno Teuber suggests that when establishing an online social networking presence, businesses should focus on customer interests.

Building a social network, such as a message board or listserv, into web and email communications can be a significant undertaking. However, increasing the level of engagement a company has with its community of customers creates "deeper engagement and advocacy that, in turn, will lead to higher sales and a greater degree of customer satisfaction," Teuber says in his article, "Social Communities Should Be Used to Encourage Sales." He offers Sephora as an example of a company that followed this strategy. The cosmetics retailer hosts a widely used online community designed for customers who want to discuss their enthusiasm for make-up. Rather than simply establishing a page on an existing social media site, the company has built a new social network around its brand.

Minimizing Marketing Expenses

One major advantage of social media is its minimal cost compared to traditional marketing tools. Like other types of online marketing, social media can also help companies reduce printing and postage costs associated with mailing promotional items to customers.

In the post-recession economy of the second decade of the 2000s, many companies have cut back on expenses—including producing and sending direct-mail marketing pieces to customers and potential clients.

To encourage use of its services, the U.S. Postal Service began its "Second Ounce Free" program in early 2012. The program offers organizations that use direct first-class commercial mail the chance to send 2 ounces of promotional materials for the same cost of sending a 1-ounce promotional mailing. However, even with the introduction of the program, the use of first-class mail continues to decline, with a 25% drop measured in the five years leading up to 2012, according to *DM News*.

Print promotional mailings may be down, but spending for social networking–related services continues to grow. International Data Corporation reported a 47% jump in social media spending, the biggest growth in spending for any technology category. IDC's "2012 U.S. Social Media Trends by Vertical" study found that retailers were making particularly strong investments in social media, and that "successful retailers are integrating their mobile, analytic and social media strategies into one cohesive business approach."

Getting Personal

Social media allows retailers and other organizations to assess customer behavior and accordingly send personalized offers direct to customers via mobile devices or other channels, according to IDC.

Companies can use social channels to build personal connections with clients, gauge customer needs, and obtain information to drive the organization's research, development, and growth goals. Using social media can also help businesses streamline internal operations, saving them both time and expense.

"Emerging uses in the construction industry for instance demonstrate how B2B organizations can leverage social media as a powerful collaboration tool to share project and material data, submit bids and review designs," said Eileen Smith, program manager for global technology and industry research organization at IDC.

Improving Sales

One potential barrier companies may face in promoting their products and services to new and existing customers involves ensuring that customers are able to access external websites on a frequent basis.

Many companies' current and potential customers spend the majority of their waking hours, eight or more hours a day, at work. However, in recent years, some workplaces have begun to limit or block access to certain sites—or the entire Internet—so that workers cannot view external websites while in the office.

Social media websites have been hit particularly hard. According to a 2012 study from Easynet and Ipanema Technologies, 67% of European chief information officers (CIOs) said their organization blocks Facebook. Sixty percent block YouTube, and 56% ban Twitter, according to *Total Telecom* magazine.

Blocking social media site access in the office can have a detrimental effect on a company's overall promotional strategy and presence in the marketplace. According to the Easynet and Ipanema study, European CIOs who failed to embrace social media risked demotivating staff, eliminating their company's competitive edge, creating ineffective marketing strategies, and alienating customers.

SOURCES OF ADDITIONAL INFORMATION

Groupon. http://www.groupon.com
Living Social. http://www.livingsocial.com
Yelp. http://www.yelp.com

BIBLIOGRAPHY

Advantage 2012 conference highlights changes in corporate travel policy. (2012). *Travel Business Review*, May 3, 2012.

Anwar, Y. (2011, June 7). So much for digital democracy: New study finds elite viewpoints dominate online content. University of California at Berkeley News Center. Retrieved December 3, 2012, from http://newscenter.berkeley.edu/2011/06/07/digital-democracy/

Austin, M., & Giamanco, B. (2012). *The definitive guide to social selling: How to sell to people, not contacts* [e-book]. InsideView and Focus, pages 3–8, 11–13.

Easynet. (2012). Social media shunned by CIOs [press release] *Total Telecom*. Retrieved Feb. 3, 2013, from http://www.ipanematech.com/wbNewsFront/newsDetail/id/125/wb_culture/en

Facts About Google and competition. (2012). Retrieved December 3, 2012, from http://www.google.com/competition/howgooglesearchworks.html#section1

Green, A. (2012, March). Marketers split on the impact of mixed postal promotions. *DM News*, 10. Retrieved December 3, 2012, from http://www.dmnews.com/marketers-split-on-the-impact-of-mixed-postal-promotions/article/228985/

Gullasken, Michael. Content marketing: The new SEO? (2012). *DM News, 42*. Retrieved December 3, 2012, from http://www.dmnews.com/plug-ins-search-marketing/article/242831/#

IBM STUDY: Digital era transforming CMO's agenda, revealing gap in readiness [press release]. (2011). Retrieved December 3, 2012, from http://www-03.ibm.com/press/us/en/pressrelease/35633.wss

IDC predictions 2012: Competing for 2012 [press release]. (2011). International Data Corporation. Retrieved December 3, 2012, from http://www.idc.com/getdoc.jsp?containerId=prUS23177411

IDC study reveals emerging social media trends across vertical markets [press release]. (2012, July 11). International Data Corporation. Retrieved December 3, 2012, from http://www.idc.com/getdoc.jsp?containerId=prUS23688012

Launch announcement: BtoB issues "State of B2B SEO and PPC Practices" report [press release]. (2012, February 22). *Yahoo! Finance*. Retrieved December 3, 2012, from http://finance.yahoo.com/news/launch-announcement-btob-issues-state-171000409.html

Madden, Mary, and Zickuhr, Kathryn. (2012, June 6). Older adults and Internet use [press release]. The Pew Research Center's Internet & American Life Project. Retrieved Feb. 2 2013, from http://www.pewinternet.org/Reports/2012/Older-adults-and-internet-use.aspx

Miller, C., Rainie, L., Purcell, K., Mitchell, A., & Rosenstiel, T. (2012, September 26). How people get local news and information in different communities [press release]. The Pew Research Center's Internet & American Life Project. Retrieved December 3, 2012, from http://www.pewinternet.org/Reports/2012/Communities-and-Local-News/Summary-of-Findings.aspx?view=all

Myron, D. (2012, September). What email marketers can learn from social media. *CRM*. Retrieved December 3, 2012, from http://www.destinationcrm.com/Articles/Columns-Departments/Front-Office/What-Email-Marketers-Can-Learn-from-Social-Media-84271.aspx

New research finds email has driven more than two thirds of online Brazilians to purchase [press release]. (2012, July 13). ExactTarget. Retrieved December 3, 2012, from http://www.businesswire.com/news/home/20120713005052/en/Research-Finds-Email-Driven-Thirds-Online-Brazilians

Purcell, K., Stewart, A., & Rainie, L. (2010). The social side of the Internet. Pew Research Center's Internet & American Life Project. Retrieved December 3, 2012, from http://www.pewinternet.org/Reports/2011/The-Social-Side-of-the-Internet.aspx

Rainie, L., Smith, A, Lehman Schlozman, K., Brady, H., & Verba, S. (2012). Social media and political engagement. Pew Research Center's Internet & American Life Project. Retrieved December 3, 2012, from http://pewinternet.org/Reports/2012/Political-engagement.aspx

Survey shows small businesses investing more in social media, but juggling resources [press release]. (2012). Vertical Response. Retrieved December 3, 2012, http://www.verticalresponse.com/about/press/small-business-social-media-survey-results-infographic

Teuber, B. (2012). Human touch needed if web ads are to have right impact. *Marketing Week*. Retrieved December 3, 2012, from http://www.marketingweek.co.uk/opinion/human-touch-needed-if-web-ads-are-to-have-right-impact/4003397.article

Tripp, T. M. and Grégoire, Y. (2011) When unhappy customers strike back on the Internet. Retrieved Dec. 3, 2011, from http://sloanreview.mit.edu/the-magazine/2011-spring/52303/when-unhappy-customers-strike-back-on-the-internet/

Creating a Congruent Social Media Marketing Philosophy

In This Essay

■ A business entering into social media marketing should create a business plan before getting started

■ There are three stages in the development of most social media marketing strategies

■ Metrics should be developed that work with the requested social media marketing strategy and should be measured often

Overview

Once a business has committed itself to social media marketing, it will need to create a strategy to implement it. This phase of the marketing campaign will require establishing goals for the business to implement on the selected social media platforms. After creating specific objectives, such as increasing website traffic or improving brand awareness, the business will need to develop metrics to measure its return on investment (ROI) generated from its social media marketing efforts.

Like any marketing campaign a business undertakes, a social media marketing program must be tailored to the specific business and the goals it considers important in promoting its products and services. Businesses that sell to other businesses (B2B) will likely have different social media marketing objectives than businesses that sell directly to customers (B2C). The goals and implementation of social media marketing for small businesses will be different from the strategy a large company will undertake.

After implementing the social media marketing strategy, businesses should define a set of goals for measuring the effectiveness of the campaign.

Benchmark: *A standard, or a set of standards, used as a point of reference for evaluating performance or level of quality.*

For some, the metric to use may be website traffic; for others it may be "Likes" on a Facebook page. Regardless of the measurement used, marketing experts agree that the single most important objective is whether the social media marketing campaign increases sales for the business, which many marketers consider the only *benchmark* that matters in any type of marketing strategy.

Creating a Social Media Marketing Goals Statement

A business entering the world of social media should begin by creating a Social Media Marketing Strategic Goals Statement (Zimmerman, 2010). Similar to a business plan, the statement should include a business profile, including its products and online presence, its social media marketing goals, its budget for this campaign, and what metrics to benchmark. The form should conclude with a marketing profile that lists the business's target markets, a value proposition (why should a customer buy from this company?) and a list of competitors, including their websites, blogs, and social media pages.

Once the statement is completed, it can be shared with the company's top executives as well as with its board of advisors or directors. The statement will help the business explain the rationale for involvement in social media, the strategy it will implement, and how it will be measured. By setting specific objectives within specific time limits, the statement will allow the business to determine whether the social media marketing campaign is generating ROI, according to Jan Zimmerman, the author of three books on social media and web marketing and owner of Watermelon Mountain Web Marketing in Albuquerque, New Mexico.

Defining Goals

When establishing social media marketing goals, a business should first decide what it wants to accomplish by creating a presence on social media platforms. The social media marketing goals should then be driven from those objectives according to Tracy Tuten, coauthor of *Social Media Marketing* (2012). For a large company like Dell, for example, social media is used systematically as an integrated part of its marketing program; social media is part of everything that Dell does to provide information to consumer groups and services to customers.

For other companies, a social media marketing campaign might be more event- or campaign-oriented. A beer company might sponsor a festival or create a game on Facebook that increases awareness of its product. A clothing store might run a traditional sale promotion that has a two-week limit on it. The business owner could then Tweet its followers and let them know they have two weeks to buy the product at a special discount. Although this type of campaign may be temporary, if it matches the marketing objectives, it can help the organization reach its goals, Tuten said.

Other types of companies might use social media to provide customer service for their products. Before the advent of social media, most customers who needed help with a product such as a computer would call the company's help desk to get the information they needed. Now they can find the same information on a social media platform. Best Buy, for example, launched an initiative called Twelpforce, a forum for employees to offer technical advice on Twitter. Its Twitter handle is @Twelpforce, and as of 2012, it had more than 47,000 followers (Twelpforce, 2012).

Goals and Benefits

Although the goals of a social media marketing campaign depend on the business and the specific goals it has identified, there are common priorities for businesses that are about to start, or have already started, this marketing strategy. In a 2011 survey, MarketingSherpa, a research firm, interviewed more than 3,300 marketers to determine what their most important social media objectives were. The survey found that the top three objectives were: 1) increasing website traffic through social media integration (56%), 2) developing an effective and methodical social marketing strategy (51%), and 3) achieving increasing measurable ROI from social media marketing programs (50%) (Balegno, 2011b).

For the most part, the ranking of these objectives mirrors the top benefits identified with social media marketing in other surveys of marketing managers. In a 2012 survey of 3,800 marketers conducted by Social Media Examiner, the top three benefits of social media marketing were increased exposure, increased traffic, and provided marketplace insight (Stelzner, 2012).

Increasing Website Traffic Through Social Media Integration

The top objective in the MarketingSherpa survey—increasing website traffic—can be a direct result of an effective social media campaign. Businesses that are active on social media sites can draw customers to their websites. To succeed, businesses need to target their customers on social media platforms by posting information, commenting on other posts, and sharing links with others. Research conducted in 2011 showed that 31% of website referral traffic came from sharing online (Petersen, 2011). The study reported that of those new website visitors, 82% came from social networking sites—38% from Facebook, 34% from blogs and bookmarking, and 17% from Twitter. Sharing via e-mail accounted for the remaining 17%.

This type of marketing is known as inbound marketing, in which businesses are found by people who are learning about and shopping for products on the Internet. Inbound marketing relies on attracting customers to a business's website through search engines, blogs, and social media. This strategy contrasts with traditional outbound marketing, in which businesses or marketers push a message out through trade shows, seminars, e-mail blasts, cold calling, and advertising.

Improving Brand Awareness or Reputation

Customers must know something about a company's brand before they will purchase one of its products. Building brand awareness, therefore, is key to increasing sales. Social media provides a platform for companies to increase brand awareness by extending their reach to larger audiences. This strategy can also increase the visibility and frequency with which customers are exposed to a particular brand. A company's marketing team can engage potential customers on social media sites and monitor what consumers are saying about its brand. Furthermore, when social media users share information about a brand, that can have a powerful impact on increasing sales. A 2009 Nielsen survey found that 92% of individuals globally trust the messages or recommendations they receive from friends. The messages they least trust are text ads on mobile phones, trusted by 29% of those surveyed (Nielsen).

Developing an Effective and Methodical Social Marketing Strategy

When launching a social media marketing campaign, businesses should first identify who their target customers are and then determine on which social platforms they can be found. A business selling infant apparel, for example, may want to engage potential customers on a parenting website or a blog for new mothers. The business should then craft a message and post it on that social media channel. A business that provides computer services may want to converse with clients about its services on Twitter, whereas a bridal company may find potential customers on Pinterest.

The messages businesses post on a social media site should be a soft rather than a hard sell. "Social media is better for branding, customer retention, customer loyalty, and even for text support than it is for pushing sales," Zimmerman said. "People aren't going to read a string of messages that are one advertisement after another."

The ideal message on a social media channel should be something that can be consumed in a five-second read according to Lawrence Lerner, owner of LL Business Consulting. The message must also be placed in context: An airport is not the ideal place to advertise pool supplies. With social media, however, businesses can find the right outlet for whatever product or service they are selling so that they can appeal to their target markets.

A business starting out with social media should begin with one platform and create an effective message that engages with users. Once that proves successful, the business can expand to another platform. For social media to be effective, businesses must spend two hours per week per channel, according to Zimmerman. Her recommendation: "Start with one thing, do it well and master it. Don't try to do everything at once."

Measurable ROI from Social Media Marketing Programs

Once a business reaches the break-even point—the number of sales required for revenues to equal total costs—it can calculate its ROI (return on investment) from any incoming profits. Determining the ROI from a social media marketing campaign, however, may be difficult to calculate if the business sells products both online and from a bricks-and-mortar store or if it sells products on different Internet channels. The business must be able to identify both the costs and revenue from its social media marketing, which may be tricky to separate if sales are also generated offline. To help businesses sift through this data, a number of companies have developed tracking software that allows companies to monitor sales from social media.

Converting Social Media Followers to Paying Customers

Another factor that should go into determining ROI is tracking leads from social media sites. Because exposure on social media should be aimed at a "soft" sell, one of the objectives of social media marketing is to generate leads.

The audience on social media presents an enormous pool of potential customers. As of 2012, Facebook reached 1 billion monthly active users and Twitter had 500,000 million users. Businesses may seek to capture as many social media users as they can to their website. However, to convert these social media users into paying customers can be a lengthy process. The classic conversion funnel shows that visitors from social media are first considered as prospects and then leads. Of those original visitors, only 2 to 4% are expected to become buyers (Zimmerman, 2010).

Measurable Lead Generation from Social Marketing

If a business is attracting more traffic to its website from social media, it is generating leads that can be converted into paying customers. As mentioned earlier, using social media marketing to generate leads is a multistep process. To start attracting traffic, an organization should sign up for social media accounts and then interact with users and contribute content that people want to learn about.

When social media users land on a webpage, they will make up their mind about that site within the first eight seconds according to Vinny La Barbera, a business marketing blogger. He suggests that social media users be directed to targeted landing pages that have limited navigation options and a contact form at the top of the webpage. These landing pages should include "strong, clear calls to action" such as signing up for a free trial of the business's service.

Improving Search Engine Ranking Positions

Using social media can improve a business's search engine ranking in a number of ways.

One method of improving a search engine ranking is to create backlinks, in which a website is listed as a link on other websites. The best way to build backlinks is to post high-quality content that people will want to share on social media networks. A.J. Kumar, co-founder of Single Grain, a digital marketing agency in San Francisco, suggests that businesses find ideas for future content marketing posts on social networking websites. For example, if the business owner simply Tweets, "How Do I SEO (search engine optimization)" a number of topics will appear that can be turned into content marketing pieces (Kumar, 2012).

Another way to increase search engine rankings through social media is to display social sharing buttons on the top and bottom of a website or blog. Businesses can also use social media to brand themselves as experts within their industry by adding content to websites and blogs relating to their products and services.

Integrating Social Media Marketing Data with CRM and Other Marketing Systems

Customer relationship managment (CRM) is a system for managing a business's interactions with customers, clients, and sales prospects. Although CRM systems are traditionally internal databases of customers and clients, companies can now use software that tracks social media campaigns for CRM. For example, comments generated by social media users about a particular company or product can be tied into a CRM system so that the company can generate sales leads, ideas for new products, and strategies for improving a company's image and brand (Diana, 2011). The new software tools allow companies to locate and use the millions of messages that are being generated on a daily basis about the company's products, advertising campaigns, and reputation.

Customer relationship managment (CRM): *A model for managing a company's interactions with customers, clients, and sales prospects using technology. Also known as CRM.*

Integrating Social Media Monitoring and Analytics into a Single Dashboard

At one time, businesses managed the flood of social media conversations one post at a time. That process has changed, however, with the development of social media tools that allow businesses to monitor, update, manage, and maintain several communication channels at the same time. These tools compress all the social media outlets a company is tracking within a single *dashboard*. One of the more popular social media tools is Hootsuite, which allows users to create a dashboard that tracks preferred social media channels. Although Hootsuite charges a monthly fee, other social media dashboard tools such as Threadsy and Myweboo are free (Bale, 2010).

Dashboard: *A web page which collates information about a business.*

Recruiting Interdepartmental Staff to Perform Social Marketing Activities

Developing a social media marketing campaign is a time-consuming process for small businesses as well as larger companies. The sole proprietor of a small business may have to manage the social media marketing in addition to running the company, unless he or she outsources the work to a marketing firm. For a large company, employees from various departments will need to be involved in social marketing, and as more people participate, a formal process with guidelines will need to be developed.

In a 2011 report, MarketingSherpa identified three phases of social marketing maturity through which organizations must evolve to create an effective social media marketing strategy. The process a company follows in planning, executing, and measuring the effectiveness of its social media marketing activities determines its phase of social marketing maturity (Balegno, 2011a).

As organizations advance from one phase to the next, it will achieve a more effective social marketing campaign and process to execute the program. MarketingSherpa's report found that of 3,300 marketers surveyed, 35% said their organization was in the trial phase, 46% were in the transition phase, and 19% were in the strategic phase.

The size of an organization has a direct effect on the advancement of its social media marketing. Large organizations with more than 1,000 employees were more than twice as likely to have reached the strategic phase than smaller organizations with fewer than 100 employees (Balegno, 2011a).

Improving the Quality and Cost Efficiency of Customer Support Programs

With the power of social media in the hands of customers, businesses need to pay attention to what their customers are saying about their products and services. Rather than treating this interaction with apprehension, however, businesses can use social media platforms to partner with their customers and improve the delivery of their services. One way to do this is to engage with customers on Twitter about service issues, similar to Best Buy's Twelpforce program. Customers who are already on Twitter find it faster and easier to contact a company about a service problem than going through its help desk. The power to influence millions of potential customers by engaging them in the conversation is the incentive for engaging with customers.

Developing Metrics for Social Media Marketing

If small and large companies are investing time and money in social media, they want to know how effective their efforts are. Because social media marketing relies on computers, this strategy is easy to quantify in terms of the benchmarks the business develops. The amount of data available from online marketing far surpasses what is available from traditional marketing (Zimmerman, 2010). The ability to measure the effectiveness of social media activities is what makes it a valuable tool for public relations and advertising.

With the avalanche of messages on numerous social media sites, businesses may want to know which channels drive more traffic to their websites. Do Likes on Facebook mean anything for a business's bottom line? Do people buy a product after reading Tweets posted by a business? How many social media users who visit a website become paying customers?

There are a number of *metrics*, or tools of measurement, that can be measured from social media marketing. In general there are two types of data that can be measured:

Metrics: *A standard of measurement used to gauge a company's performance.*

- **Internal performance measurements:** This involves monitoring how effective a social media marketing strategy is in achieving goals such as increasing website traffic and the percentage of website visitors who convert into paying customers.
- **Business measurements:** These are costs associated with the business operations, including cost of customer acquisition, the cost of staff or outsourced marketing, average dollar value per sale, break-even point, and ROI.

Choosing What to Measure

Organizations using social media marketing can measure many key performance indicators (KPI) associated with social media marketing programs. Whether all these indicators are useful, however, depends on the particular business and its key objectives. If the business's goal is increasing website traffic, it should measure the number of visitors to its hub site. If it wants to measure traffic on a new blog, then that is what it should measure.

Although some organizations may find Likes on a Facebook page less useful, some companies track Likes so they can push information out to those users according to David Steinberg, a social media expert and founder of XL Marketing. Other experts argue that a business's sales are the only true measurement of the success of a social media marketing campaign.

Key metrics used to evaluate a social media marketing program include:

Website traffic: Websites must have a baseline level of traffic to provide the people who will purchase its products and services. In addition to sales, more visitors to a website means there is a higher likelihood that they will engage with the site's blog, click on its social media buttons, share the site with friends, and interact with the brand.

Brand awareness: It is crucial for businesses to increase brand awareness. If consumers do not know about a company's brand, they will not buy its products or services. In addition, if customers are familiar with a brand and learn about it through social media platforms, they will be in a better position to recommend it to their friends on Facebook, Twitter, or other social media channels. Businesses can measure their brand awareness on social media using various tools. Klout, for example, evaluates a business's activity across social networks and gives it a score ranging from 10 to 100. The company can also determine how many people the business influences, how much it influences them, and how influential is the audience. These scores should be recorded monthly to give a business a snapshot of its effectiveness in improving brand awareness.

Leads: Businesses that become active on social media sites can interact with consumers who may become potential leads for their products or services. If consumers become aware of a brand, they may connect with the company's website, where they may move through the conversion funnel to become paying customers.

Financials: Businesses need to measure their costs, sales, and revenue to determine when they reach the break-even point and start making a profit. Using analytical tools, businesses can determine which sales arrive from social media sites and the amount of revenue they generate.

Search marketing: Content on social media should be optimized the way it is on a website so that a company's posts can rank high in search results. Social media posts can be optimized by using appropriate search terms or keywords and then optimizing the content, navigation, and structure to create a profile or message that will attract the most visitors.

Most Useful Metrics for Small- and Medium-Sized Business

In a 2012 report, Vocus, a company that provides software for public relations, marketing and communications professionals, surveyed 400 small- and medium-sized businesses and organizations to assess their view on social media. When asked which metrics they were using, the top three answers were website traffic, number of new customers/clients, and number of likes. Larger companies were more likely to conduct more complicated data analysis that included demographics and conversations (Path to Influence, 2012).

The report further analyzed the usefulness of the metrics and the degree to which they are currently being used by small- and medium-sized businesses. The most useful metrics were increase in revenue/sales, increase in foot traffic, and number of new customers mentioning social media. None of those three metrics, however, was the measure most used by the businesses surveyed. The metric most used by the businesses in the survey was increased traffic to a website. As the report noted, "Metrics such as sales and increased foot traffic score high among SMBs (small- and medium-sized businesses) in terms of usefulness but are not as widely adopted because of the challenge of tying sales directly to social media efforts."

Although metrics are extremely important to determine effectiveness of social media marketing, they must be simple and easily accessible for businesses to use. Determining the origination point for customers who arrive at an organization's website seems to be a key stumbling block in analyzing the computer-generated data. Once established, the metrics should be measured on a monthly basis and recorded in a spreadsheet to monitor the increases or decreases over time. This is a necessary time investment for any social media marketing effort since by measuring the impact of a social media campaign, the organization can better focus its marketing time and resources.

SOURCES OF ADDITIONAL INFORMATION

American Marketing Association. http://www.marketingpower.com
MarketingSherpa. http://www.marketingsherpa.com
Mobile Marketing Association. http://www.mmaglobal.com
Social Media Marketing Association. http://socialmedia-marketingassociation.com

BIBLIOGRAPHY

Bale, K. (2010, November 9). Top 10 social media dashboard tools. *Socialbrite*. Retrieved December 7, 2012, from http://www.socialbrite.org/2010/11/09/top-10-social-media-dashboard-tools/

Balegno, S. (2011a). 2011 social marketing benchmark report. *MarketingSherpa*. Retrieved November 12, 2012, from http://www.marketingsherpa.com/resources/MS-2011-Social-Marketing-Benchmark-Report-EXCERPT.pdf

Balegno, S. (2011b, May 3). Marketing research chart: top social media objectives for 2011. *MarketingSherpa*. Retrieved November 19, 2012, from http://www.marketingsherpa.com/article/chart/top-social-media-objectives-2011

Diana, A. (2011). Social media advances crm to increase revenue, market share and brand. *CRMSearch*. Retrieved December 7, 2012, from http://www.crmsearch.com/index.php

Kirk, A. (2012, September 17). 4 social media goals every business should measure. *Social Media Examiner*. Retrieved December 7, 2012, from http://www.socialmediaexaminer.com/4-social-media-goals/

Kumar, A.J. (2012, August 1). 3 ways to use social media to improve your rankings. *Social Media Examiner*. Retrieved December 7, 2012, from http://www.socialmediaexaminer.com/3-ways-to-use-social-media-to-improve-your-search-rankings/

LaBarbera, Vinny. How to generate leads with social media. *Business Marketing Blog*. Retrieved December 7, 2012, from http://www.businessmarketingblog.org/how-to-generate-leads-with-social-media/

Nielsen global online consumer survey: trust, value and engagement in advertising. (2009, July). Retrieved December 4, 2012, from http://blog.nielsen.com/nielsenwire/wp-content/uploads/2009/07/trustinadvertising0709.pdf

Path to influence: an industry study of SMBs and social media. (2012, September). *Vocus*. Retrieved October 29, 2012, from http://www.vocus.com/blog/smb-social-media-influence/

Petersen, Rob. (2011, June 10). Social media sharing increases website traffic +30%. Here's why. *BarnRaisers*. Retrieved December 4, 2012, from http://barnraisersllc.com/2011/06/social-media-sharing-increases-traffic-30/

Stelzner, M. (2012, April). 2012 social media marketing industry report. *Social Media Examiner.* Retrieved November 20, 2012 from http://www.socialmedia examiner.com/SocialMediaMarketingIndustryReport2012.pdf

Tuten, T., Solomon, M. (2012). *Social media marketing.* Upper Saddle River: Pearson Education.

Twelpforce Best Buy (2012). *Best Buy.* https://twitter.com/twelpforce

Zimmerman, J., Sahlin, D. (2010). *Social media marketing all-in-one for dummies.* Hoboken, Wiley Publishing.

Creating a Social Media Marketing Strategy

In This Essay

- A step-by-step approach to social media marketing
- Ways to engage customers
- Using crowdsourcing to create social media buzz
- International social media campaigns
- Social media marketing failures

Overview

As social media has emerged as a dominant force in the online world, companies have been forced to rethink their marketing strategies. Marketing has evolved from paid advertisements in magazines and newspapers and on the radio to messages posted on social media platforms. Companies such as adidas, which once redesigned its websites every year to reflect new sports celebrities and products, are now posting to social media the same marketing content.

Simply posting messages on a Facebook page or on a Twitter account, however, will not attract the volume of customers necessary to have an impact on sales. To create a successful digital marketing strategy, a business must learn to craft its messages for social media and make them heard over the millions of posts added to those platforms every day. What works on one social media platform will not necessarily work on another. The type of message used will depend on the nature of the business and whether it is selling directly to customers or to other businesses.

Another variable to consider when creating a social marketing strategy is whether the business wants to target customers on the growing smart phone market. The rules for social media are different on mobile devices, and businesses must tailor advertising to the smaller screens of smartphones. This adds another dimension to the already complex landscape businesses must navigate to market their products using social media.

A Step-by-Step Approach to Social Media Marketing

Businesses should approach the creation of a social media marketing strategy by considering three main points:

1. Listening and monitoring. In this step, businesses should determine what is occurring on the social media site: who the users are, which messages engage them, and who is posting the messages.

2. Customer service. In this step, businesses should respond to customer's comments, positive or negative, about their products on social media sites.

3. Marketing. This step can focus on brand marketing and increasing user awareness of particular products and services. It can also be about performance marketing and whether the business' investment in social media marketing is resulting in more sales.

Brands that follow these steps are more likely to be successful in attracting visitors through social media sites and converting them into paying customers. The goal is not only to reach a company's target customer, but to engage them, getting them to explore a product and ultimately purchase it.

Ways to Engage Customers

To create a marketing plan for social media, businesses should use a variety of tactics to engage potential customers. Attracting social media users to a company's Facebook page, for example, where they can "Like" the page and receive posts from the company in their message stream, is one way to build brand awareness. How companies can draw customers to their Facebook pages, however, must be explored in the marketing plan.

Offering discounts or coupons for products and services, running competitions, or launching fundraising campaigns can all be used to lure potential customers onto a company's Facebook page. This will increase awareness of the brand and ultimately draw users to its website. Some Facebook pages already have the ability to function as an e-commerce site and can offer a "cart" for customers to purchase products. The cart can be connected directly to the company's website, providing a seamless transition from the social media platform.

The Fundraising Approach

One way to draw customers to a company's Facebook page is to develop a fundraising campaign that enlists the help of social media users in choosing where to donate the money. Target used this approach in 2012 when it launched a Facebook campaign to enable fans to vote for schools they felt should receive a portion of the company's US$5 million "Give with Target" initiative. The campaign earmarked US$2.5 million in grants to schools in need, as well as US$2.5 million in Target GiftCards to schools selected by its fans.

Target invited people to visit its Facebook page and vote for their local school so that it could qualify for a maximum of US$10,000 in gift cards. For every 25 votes a school received on the company's Facebook page, Target donated a US$25 gift card to the school. In addition, Target pledged to donate US$25,000 grants to 100 in-need schools selected by the company. Four of those schools would get an extra perk: a visit by Disney Channel actress and recording artist Bridgit Mendler, who would ride on a "Bullseye Bus" with Target volunteers to celebrate with staff and students at each of the four schools.

Although the fundraising program may not have directly led to increased sales of Target products, it had a significant impact on building the company's brand identity, said Marko Muellner, vice president of marketing for ShopIgniter, a Portland, Oregon, social media and e-commerce company that worked with Target to design its Facebook campaign so that visitors could select schools. "There were no products involved but it was a fantastic place to do a one-time promotional campaign," Muellner said. "It created a ton of momentum. There was a lot of competition for people voting for their schools on the Facebook page. That did a lot for Target and growing its brand community."

The Facebook Advantage

On October 4, 2012, Facebook announced that it had reached a milestone of one billion people actively using the social networking site each month. This record made Facebook the most popular social media platform for users around the world. The top five countries where people connected from at the time it reached this milestone were Brazil, India, Indonesia, Mexico, and the United States (listed in alphabetical order) (Facebook, 2012).

The explosive popularity of Facebook also made the platform the top choice for companies looking to market their products on social media. Marketers are attracted to Facebook because of its versatility. Companies can sell products directly to consumers, but they can also buy ads on Facebook and target them to users who match an identified demographic market. For example, a company specializing in wedding photography in Philadelphia can pay for ads next to the message stream of users who have indicated on their pages that they are getting married and who live in the Philadelphia area.

A survey of 3,800 marketing professions conducted in 2012 by the Social Media Examiner, a social media marketing website, found that Facebook was used by 92% of marketers, followed by Twitter, LinkedIn, blogs, and YouTube (Stelzner, 2012). The survey also showed that Facebook remained the most popular platform among marketers who were either just getting in the profession or among those with more experience in the field.

Best Practices with Facebook

Dunkin Donuts "Keep It Coolatta" When Dunkin Donuts released its slushy coffee drink, Coolatta, in the summer of 2009, it decided to create some excitement around this new product by launching a giveaway campaign on Facebook. The program, however, was not strictly a Facebook strategy; it also involved Twitter, resulting in an increase in fans to both platforms. The goal of the campaign was to gain access to "friends of friends" and to reward loyal customers with daily prizes.

In an advertisement outlining the four steps of the giveaway, Dunkin Donuts urged fans to head to a Dunkin Donuts and buy their favorite Coolatta. Customers were then asked to take a picture of themselves drinking or holding their plastic cup of Coolatta and post the photo as their profile pictures on the Dunkin Donuts Facebook page. When they posted the photo on their Fan Page wall, they were instructed to add the caption #CoolattaGiveaway, creating the link to Twitter. The customers were then entered into a daily sweepstakes of prizes with a summer theme—air conditioners, a summer wardrobe, JetBlue flights, and more.

Although these types of giveaway campaigns are now common, Dunkin Donuts' was one of the first of its kind. After the campaign began, pictures of Coolattas were splattered across the web, and Dunkin Donuts' Twitter following increased from about 23,000 to 43,000 fans. As Mashable, a website that reports on digital innovation, commented, "The campaign's focus on tying social media with offline experiences is a great way to immediately make their Facebook presence relevant to the bottom line" (Van Grove, 2009). Since the campaign launched, the number of Dunkin Donuts' followers on Facebook skyrocketed from 800,000 to more than 8.3 million in 2013.

Ford's Virtual Digital Car Launch A first in the world of automobile marketing took place in 2011 when Ford Motor Company created the first digital car launch on Facebook. Rather than the traditional release of a new model at an auto show followed by mass media marketing, Ford chose to introduce its 2011 Ford Explorer to the world solely on Facebook. Under the headline "What would you go do in the 2011 Explorer?" Ford asked its fans to post the story of their dream adventure anywhere in the United States on its Facebook page. The winner, selected by the automaker, would be able to take their trip at the expense of Ford.

One of the key elements of the virtual auto show campaign was that it ran as an all-day event. Its goal was to attract 30,000 Facebook fans to its page. (By 2013, the Ford Explorer page had more than 228,000 fans.) The all-day event began just after midnight on July 26, 2010, when a "Reveal" tab appeared on the Facebook page. The next morning, a video featuring the Explorer appeared on the page, along with photo displays, live chats, and question-and-answers on its Facebook wall. In addition to the activity on the page, Ford bought digital ads on hundreds of websites in an attempt to drive people to the Facebook page.

By the numbers, the virtual launch was a spectacular success. During the day of the virtual auto show, 75,000 Facebook fans logged on, more than 1 million views of the video were recorded on YouTube, and the event was the number one Twitter trend of the day. The online *buzz* took place six months before the actual product was available for sale. As

Buzz: *When discussing the Internet, excited attention relating to a new or forthcoming product or event.*

Jeff Bullas, a digital marketer, noted on his blog: "There is one thing for sure that a car company that spends twice as much as its competitors on digital media, has led the way on use of social media since 2009 and has just announced its best profit results in more than a decade ($6.6 billion profit for 2010) is doing something right" (2011).

Success with Twitter

With its 140-character limit, Twitter can be a difficult platform on which to generate a social media marketing campaign. This restriction requires marketers to use more creativity in launching a campaign on the site. Nevertheless, Twitter is attractive to marketers because of its real time connection, which can be advantageous in getting out timely messages.

Microsite: *A separately promoted part of a larger website with a separate URL designed to meet discrete objectives.*

In 2011, American Airlines marked the 30th anniversary of its AAdvantage loyalty program by running a Twitter contest called "Tweet to Win 30K Miles." The contest was part of a larger campaign called "Deal 30," featuring 30 partner deals and promotions spread out over 30 weekdays. A *microsite* was created to promote the daily promotions, which included the Twitter contest on the fourth day. To participate, members had to record their AAdvantage number on the microsite, tweet the #Deal30 hashtag, and follow AAdvantage on Twitter for a chance to win. The airline then picked 30 followers to win the 30,000 miles.

The goal of the campaign was to drive followers to the Deal 30 microsite, where they could qualify for a variety of giveaways, and to generate followers to the newly created @AAdvantage Twitter account. Even though the contest involved a number of steps, the microsite attracted more than 27,000 entries, and the @AAdvantage Twitter account showed a 70% increase in followers.

A simpler Twitter campaign was launched by Kraft Macaroni and Cheese in 2011 to build its following on the social media channel. Taking a cue from the childhood game "Jinx," Kraft set up the contest so that it would qualify any two Twitter users who individually used the phrase "mac & cheese" in a tweet posted at the same time. Kraft would then send both a link noting the "Mac & Jinx," and the first one to respond would receive five free boxes of Kraft Mac & Cheese and a t-shirt. The campaign allowed Kraft to gather fans on Twitter while generating positive feedback for the brand from its followers.

Successful Pinterest Campaigns

Many marketers have successfully branched out into other social media channels, beyond Facebook and Twitter, to promote their products. Pinterest, a pinboard-style photo sharing website that allows users to set up theme-based image collections, has been a site used for promotional campaigns by a variety of brands.

British Midland International ran a contest called "Pinterest Lottery" that awarded fans with free flights to any of the airline's destinations. The airline pinned numbered photos from five destinations around the world on its Pinterest board, and users selected images from the airline's board and repinned them on their own boards. At the end of each week, the company would randomly choose a number, and users who had repinned an image with that number was eligible to win a pair of free tickets to one of the airline's destinations.

Kotex created a campaign in Israel using Pinterest which it called "Kotex's Women's Inspiration Day." After finding 50 inspiring women and discovering what they were pinning on Pinterest, the company sent the women a virtual gift. The women who pinned the gift received a real gift in the mail, based on something they had pinned. The campaign resulted in nearly 100% of the women posting something about their gift on Pinterest and other channels, including Facebook, Twitter, and Instagram. The 50 gifts generated a total of 2,200 interactions on social media platforms.

Another Pinterest contest was launched by Peugeot's Panama unit, which rewarded fans who completed a Pinterest puzzle. The automaker's profile on Pinterest showed images of cars over two or more boards on the social media site. For each car, one of the boards was missing. Fans were asked to find the missing pieces by going to Peugeot Panama's Facebook Page or their website.

Checking into FourSquare

FourSquare, a location-based social networking site in which users "check-in" at venues with a mobile device, is another platform businesses are using to promote their products. In 2010, The History Channel created a FourSquare page to supplement its social media efforts on Facebook and Twitter and to find a new way to connect with its viewers. Although The History Channel cannot claim a physical location where viewers could check in, it does have a brand page that users can follow. When fans check in to various locations around world, such as the Tower of London or the Lincoln Memorial, a tip from The History Channel appears, offering an interesting tidbit about the background of the site. The campaign drew 202,000 followers to The History Channel's FourSquare page, and although it may not have had a direct impact on the channel's ratings, it helped generate excitement about the historical sites fans have visited.

In 2011, Starwood Hotels began offering an extra bonus of 250 "Starpoints" when a guest checked in with a confirmed reservation and logged onto FourSquare. The points could be redeemed for a night at a Starwood hotel, which can cost 3,000 or more Starpoints. The program is used around the world at all 1,051 Starwood hotels, which includes Sheraton, W. Hotels, Westin, and the St. Regis. Since the campaign began, the chain has given away nearly 10 million points and at the same time strengthened brand loyalty with its customers.

Using Crowdsourcing to Create Social Media Buzz

Crowdsourcing:
Obtaining services, ideas, or content by soliciting contributions from a large group of people, especially the online community.

If a company wants to create something new, why not get fans involved in suggesting ideas through social media? That is what Mountain Dew did when it launched a *crowdsourcing* project called Dewmocracy in 2007. During the three-year campaign, fans of the soft drink suggested new flavor combinations, and a select number worked with Mountain Dew to name the flavors, design the labels, and choose the marketing and advertising agencies that would be in charge of the launch. When the crowdsourcing campaign ended in 2010, the brand had gained three new flavors—Distortion, Typhoon, and White Out—that made it to store shelves. White Out is now a permanent part of the brand's soft drink line.

Crowdsourcing can energize a company's fans and generate buzz about its brand. It can also generate ideas or identify customer priorities that the company may not have considered. The strategy can work on a number of social media channels to engage with customers or it can be set up through the company's website.

One of most popular crowdsourcing campaigns is My Starbucks Idea. The brand created the campaign in 2008 to generate ideas for developing better products, improving its services, and creating new community involvement projects. Customers can submit and view ideas on a special website set up for the campaign or through the My Starbucks Idea's Twitter account, which by 2013 had more than 36,000 followers.

Since the campaign began, customers have suggested more than 130,000 ideas for new products, experiences, and community involvement. To keep customers engaged in the process, Starbucks regularly announces the new products or services that were suggested by customers on its website and Twitter feed. Examples of customer ideas that made to the stores are steel-cut oatmeal topped with fresh blueberries, a vanilla spice latte, and the peppermint mocha instant brew flavor.

In addition to serving as an idea generator for new products, crowdsourcing can also be used to engage customers on corporate social responsibility (CSR) projects. Companies can use crowdsourcing to generate new ideas and build engagement with targeted audiences. In 2010, Social Impact, a company focused on driving engagement on social issues, commissioned a survey of 216 top executives at companies who are responsible for philanthropic or social outreach projects. The survey showed that 44% of the executives had used crowdsourcing by asking customers to provide ideas and help in decision-making (Massey). Moreover, among the executives surveyed, 95% reported that crowdsourcing was valuable to their corporate social responsibility program.

International Social Media Campaigns

Although the major social media networks were created in the United States, their platforms are used worldwide. Social media campaigns can connect people around the globe on a personal level that was not possible even at the beginning of the twenty-first century.

One of the most widely praised international social media marketing campaigns is Iceland Wants to Be Your Friend, a project developed for the Icelandic Tourist Board in 2009. Created by the firm TakkTakk (which means "thank you thank you" in Icelandic), the campaign developed Iceland as a colloquial voice on several social media platforms to engage potential visitors who might visit the island. Here is how TakkTakk introduced Iceland on a website created for the campaign:

Halló humans on the Inter-net.

My name is Iceland. I am an island, full of mountains and glaciers and hot water and sheep and many nice Icelandic people, who like to make music, and who are sometimes cold.

(Maybe you have seen me on your tele-visions, or your Inter-net.)

I have heard that many humans use the Inter-net to make friends, and to talk about themselves. I decided to do this, too.

I stay put in the middle of the ocean, but here are my Inter-nets for you to klikk on with your mouse or your finger:

From here, readers could click on a button for one of five social media channels—Facebook, Twitter, Tumblr, Vimeo, or Flickr—to learn more about Iceland's waterfalls, volcanoes, and lagoons. Each message readers posted on each of these platforms was answered by "Iceland" in the same stylistic voice, which created a consistency across the social media channels.

The campaign was lauded by marketing and tourism professionals around the world. The project was praised as a "lesson in the aesthetic value of consistency, simplicity and friendliness" and offered as a model of social media marketing for businesses large and small (Mortimer, 2010). When the campaign ended in 2012, it had attracted 88,000 fans on Facebook and 16,000 followers on Twitter. (The Icelandic Tourist Board later chose to develop a more traditional website called Promote Iceland, aimed at attracting tourists and investment to the country.)

Social Media Marketing Failures

Fans have the ability to post comments on social media sites, so there is a possibility that some campaigns may not go as planned and generate negative publicity for the company. Among the reasons for the campaign's failure are lack of planning before execution or lack of management by employees with enough social media experience to make well-informed decisions.

One social media marketing project that backfired was a Twitter campaign launched by the Australian airline Qantas. In 2011, the airline created a backlash on Twitter when it held a #@GoWallabies contest and selected as the winner a Twitter follower who promised to dress like Radike Samo, an Australian rugby player, by wearing blackface with an afro wig. Two sports fans selected as winners had their photo taken with the Fiji-born player, appearing with their faces painted and their hair styled in afros.

Weeks later, the airline launched another Twitter campaign that also became a public relations disaster. A month earlier, the airline had grounded its fleet due to labor disputes, affecting thousands of passengers. The bad timing did not stop it from launching a Twitter contest that invited users to answer the question, "What is your dream luxury inflight experience? (Be Creative!) Answer must include #QantasLuxury." Coming off the negative publicity of the cancelled flights, the airline received a barrage of Tweets that were far from flattering. "BREAKING NEWS: Qantas introduce #QantasLuxury class. Same as standard class, but the plane leaves the ground" was one example of the responses.

Qantas responded by Tweeting: "Wow! Some very creative tweeps out there. Keep the entries coming #QantasWeHearYou." This response, however, did not acknowledge the difficulties the passengers encountered with the grounded flights, nor did the airline discuss how it would prevent such problems in the future.

Businesses should be prepared to counter negative comments on social media in a timely fashion. The company should assign someone to track all complaints, respond to them quickly in a public forum while remaining positive, and deal with the details privately. If this strategy is followed, businesses will be able to stop minor complaints from exploding into public relations fiascos.

In responding to the complaints, businesses should be respectful and may even use a humorous tone to keep the mood friendly (Horner, 2012). They should admit the mistake, following the customer service policy that the customer is always right, and publicly send an apology on the social media site. Then the customer should be contacted privately and offered a discount or benefit to compensate for their negative experience. Finally, the business should discuss on the social media site how it will fix the problem so that it will not happen again, a gesture that will hopefully earn back the trust of its customers.

SOURCES OF ADDITIONAL INFORMATION

American Marketing Association: http://www.marketingpower.com
Mobile Marketing Association: http://www.mmaglobal.com
Social Media Marketing Association: http://socialmedia-marketingassociation.com

BIBLIOGRAPHY

Bullas, J. (2011, February 28). 10 key elements of one of the top Facebook marketing campaigns of the year. *JeffBullas.com.* Retrieved January 8, 2013, from http://www.jeffbullas.com/2011/02/28/10-key-elements-of-one-of-the-top-facebook-marketing-campaigns-of-the-year/

Business Crowdsourcing … The Story of My Starbucks Idea. (2012, April 15). *DigitalSparkMarketing.com*. Retrieved January 11, 2013, from http://www.digitalsparkmarketing.com/2012/04/15/business-crowdsourcing/

Drell, Lauren. (2011, July 13). 6 successful Foursquare marketing campaigns to learn from. *Mashable.com*. Retrieved January 11, 2013, from http://mashable.com/2011/07/13/foursquare-marketing-campaigns/

Facebook.com: One billion fact sheet. (2012). Retrieved January 8, 2013, from http://newsroom.fb.com/ImageLibrary/detail.aspx?MediaDetailsID=4227

Greene, Nicholas. Ten successful social media case studies and campaigns. *SocialMediaStrategiesSummit.com*. Retrieved January 8, 2013, from http://socialmediastrategiessummit.com/blog/ten-successful-social-media-case-studies-and-campaigns/

Griffith, I. (2012, October 1). How social media and digital marketing has impacted global branding. *Smart Insights*. Retrieved January 10, 2013, from http://www.smartinsights.com/online-brand-strategy/international-marketing/how-social-and-digital-marketing-has-impacted-global-branding/

Horner, T. (2012, October 19). Tips for handling negative comments and trolls on social media. *JeffBullas.com*. Retrieved January 11, 2013, from http://www.jeffbullas.com/2012/10/19/tips-for-handling-negative-comments-and-trolls-on-social-media/

Indvik, L. (2012, March 7). How brands are using promotions to market on Pinterest. *Mashable.com*. Retrieved January 10, 2013, from http://mashable.com/2012/03/07/pinterest/-brand-marketing/

Layfield, T. (2010, August 24). The top 10 best social media marketing campaigns of all time. *Acquisitionengine.com*. Retrieved January 8, 2013, from http://www.acquisitionengine.com/top-10-best-social-media-marketing-campaigns-all-time/

Learn social media by example: Dunkin Donuts campaign. (2010, January 25). *Thoughtpick.com*. Retrieved January 10, 2013, from http://blog.thoughtpick.com/2010/01/learn-sm-by-example-dunkin-donuts-campaign.html

Lee, A. (2011, November 25). Qantas social media campaign on twitter backfires. *iStrategyConference.com*. Retrieved January 11, 2013, from http://www.istrategyconference.com/blog/?category=Social-Media&pid=684&title=Qantas-Social-Media-Campaign-on-Twitter-Backfires%E2%80%8E

Massey, P. The role of crowdsourcing in social media. *Impact.WeberShandwick.com*. Retrieved January 11, 2013, from http://impact.webershandwick.com/?q=role-crowdsourcing-social-media

Mortimer, Niland. (2010, September 2). Sure it's bankrupt, but Iceland has killer social media skills. *CBSNews.com*. Retrieved January 11, 2013, from http://www.cbsnews.com/8301-505125_162-44640117/sure-its-bankrupt-but-iceland-has-killer-social-media-skills/?tag=bnetdomain

Qantas apologises after giving tickets to blackface fans. (2011, August 29). *mUmBRELLA.com*. Retrieved January 10, 2013, from http://mumbrella.com.au/qantas-apologises-after-giving-tickets-to-blackface-fans-55889

SourceMetrics.com: Social media marketing campaign success and failure stories. (November 22, 2012). Retrieved January 8, 2013, from http://blog.sourcemetrics .com/social-campaign-success-and-failure-stories/

Stelzner, M. (2012, April). 2012 social media marketing industry report. *Social Media Examiner.* Retrieved November 20, 2012, from http://www.socialmedia examiner.com/SocialMediaMarketingIndustryReport2012.pdf

Swallow, Erica. (2011, July 6). 7 Twitter marketing campaigns to learn from. *Mashable.com.* Retrieved January 10, 2013, from http://mashable.com/2011/07/ 06/twitter-campaigns/

Takktakk.com: Iceland Wants to Be Your Social Media Campaign. Retrieved January 10, 2013, from http://www.takktakk.com/presents/icelandwantstobeyourfriend/

Takktakk.com: In which a project leaves home. (2012, January 22). Retrieved January 11, 2013, from http://takktakk.is/blogging/

Target calls on fans to help raise money for needy schools. (2012, July 26). *Retailing-Today.com.* Retrieved January 9, 2013, from http://retailingtoday.com/article/ target-calls-fans-help-raise-money-needy-schools

Taylor, D. (2012, September 20). Twitter epic fails — how not to run a marketing campaign. *Business2Community.com.* Retrieved January 10, 2013, from http:// www.business2community.com/twitter/twitter-epic-fails-how-not-to-run-a-marketing-campaign-0285301

Van Grove, J. (2009, June 3). Dunkin Donuts' Facebook campaign turns your profile pic into prizes. *Mashable.com.* Retrieved January 10, 2013, from http:// mashable.com/2009/06/03/dunkin-donuts-facebook-campaign/

Wasserman, T. (2012, February 26). 5 clever social media campaigns to learn from. *Mashable.com.* Retrieved January 10, 2013, from http://mashable .com/2012/02/26/clever-social-media-campaigns/

Wasserman, T. (2012, March 23). 5 interesting pinterest marketing campaigns. *Mashable.com.* Retrieved January 10, 2013, from http://mashable.com/2012/ 03/23/pinterest-marketing-campaigns/

Representation of the Brand

In This Essay

- Representation of the brand is how a company chooses to portray itself to potential customers
- Branding is tied to memory and brain processes
- Social media allows representation of brands in personalized ways
- A company can measure its branding success through social media metrics

Introduction

Social media is a public format where people can make personal connections to the wider world by expressing feelings, preferences, opinions, and ideas in writing, pictures, audio, and video. Whether they are blogging, tweeting, podcasting, or webcasting, people are using social media to communicate and socialize. They are also making themselves available to marketers.

Since the early days of online bulletin boards in the late 1970s, people have shared information and opinions online with groups of both like-minded and opposite-thinking peers. Usenet, AOL, Tripod, Mosaic, and Geocities were just a few of the early names in what has come to be known as social media.

The late 1990s produced blogging, instant messaging, online education, and Google. Millions of computers (and people) were connected to the Internet. Early 2000 saw information-sharing take new and different forms such as Wikipedia. Music went online with iTunes and early social sites such as Friendster and MySpace started. Facebook in 2004, YouTube in 2005, and Twitter in 2006 grew to major social media platforms with lightning speed, and spawned new social media terms such as "like," "unfriend," and "tweeting." Smartphones with cameras and video recorders made it easy for people to capture the moment and share it instantly with close friends or everyone all over the world.

For marketers, social media is important to brand representation and customer engagement. It offers endless opportunities to reach customers and potential customers in personal ways, to build and extend the brand, and to create unique experiences to captivate an audience. From the warehouse to the CEO office to the press room, social media holds the keys to customer hearts and minds. To ignore or discount social media jeopardizes brand management. It is viewed as a friendly, trusted and respected source of value and entertainment.

Everyone has a favorite social media. Although levels of participation vary, an informal poll of family, friends, and co-workers would reveal few, if any, who are not involved in some type of social media. Most people participating in social media are sharing what they like, including their favorite places to eat, their favorite brand of shoes, what soft drinks they prefer, what style of furniture they want in their living room—everything imaginable is one recommendation away in social media.

Representation of the Brand

Brand: *Name, term, symbol, sign, or design used by a firm to differentiate its offerings from those of its competitors.*

The phrase *brand representation* refers to any way a company communicates about its **brand** to an audience. (The audience is typically a market or customers.) Traditional marketing represents the brand through print and publication media such as sales ads, television ads, and newspaper and magazine advertising. Social media marketing represents the brand through much wider and diverse media, including social media platforms such as Facebook and Pinterest and mobile media such as cell phone and tablet apps.

Traditional marketing has a lag time between the origin of the communication and its actual delivery. Social media marketing often happens in real time with instant results that can be challenging to track and analyze. Twitter streams about brands and customer experiences with them are fast and can involve a lot of different people. While good input in social media about a brand is desirable, bad input can spread faster than marketers and brand managers can respond and can quickly get out of control. More than one celebrity has made Twitter mistakes that have swayed opinions of fans.

Representation of a brand in social media involves a deep level of commitment to engagement with customers. This requires listening to, understanding, and responding to customers in new ways through new avenues. It also means opportunities to develop sales channels and customer service channels, and to shape customer experiences with the brand. Companies ignore, or worse, misunderstand, social media to the detriment of their bottom line. Through social media, customers have the ability to share their opinions about companies and their products and services to a wide audience. How the brand is represented in social media greatly affects brand management.

Branding, Brand Management, and Brand Extension

All marketers develop brands to influence customers to buy their product or service. Branding and brand management focus on developing a unified message about a product or service. Brand extension uses an established brand to develop new avenues or extensions of a product or service, such as an athletic shoe manufacturer branching out into athletic apparel and gear or a cookie retailer creating specialized coffee and ice cream.

Studies of neuroscience, consumer behavior, and marketing show that many consumers make decisions about brands based on memory. Neuroscience shows that the brain's pain centers are related to price and payment, and the reward or pleasure centers are activated by charitable giving. Marketers can use this information to craft better messages around brands to get customers to act in desired ways. Offers of discounts for purchasing with credit or layaway plans and low price ad campaigns reduce customer anxiety about spending a lot to get what they want and may influence their buying decisions. Charities seeking funds can motivate donors and sponsors to feel good about giving to their causes through their branding messages.

Using a strong brand to develop other offerings makes sense because it builds on memories of desired products or services to sell new offerings, and makes it easier and more economical than creating a totally new brand. Related product lines and complementary services are brought to market faster and at lower cost than what would be required to introduce a new line or service, thus preserving resources and creating higher profit margins.

Brand extension is a part of brand management, which includes using various methods to make a brand memorable to customers and distinguish it from other brands. Goals of managing a brand include precisely defining the brand, creating customer loyalty, and convincing customers the brand is better than other brands. How the brand is represented affects the outcomes of these goals.

Strong emotion, sentimentality, evoking memories of important experiences, and stimulating visuals create a lasting impression of a brand in customers' eyes and memories. From a scientific point of view, branding leads to the creation of networks of brand-related associations in the brains of consumers. These associations influence purchasing decisions. Brand management adds to and strengthens these associations in customers' minds, making representation of the brand an ongoing process.

Real time: *The actual time during which a process or event happens.*

Representing a brand in social media is challenging because of *real time* customer input. Customers chat, share information, rant, or rave about products and services they like or dislike and give much more feedback than is captured in controlled surveys or questionnaires. This volume of data is a rich source of marketing information when harnessed and used to improve products, customer service, and customer engagement. The information provides the opportunity to shape and refine a brand with the direct input of the customers who want and use the brand.

Social Media Habits and Successful CEOs

Chief Executive Officers (CEOs) are viewed as responsible for their companies' products and services and are often scrutinized in social media. They have an impact on representation of their brand or brands whether they embrace that role or not. Some highly engaged and successful CEOs use social media to complement and hone their brands instead of staying in the background and running things from "behind the curtain." CEOs who take this upfront role do not view social media as a risk, but rather use it as a tool and an asset to enhance their leadership roles. Social media presences and communications create transparency that is viewed favorably by customers.

CEO leadership, not only of company employees but also of brand management, is highlighted in social media. Engaged and connected

CEOs such as Richard Branson of Virgin Group use social media to talk directly with large numbers of customers, inviting and shaping direct and open dialog about their brand. Tony Hsieh of Zappos shares corporate strategy and Marc Benioff of Salesforce.com shares his personal views through Twitter with customers and employees alike.

Embracing social media opens wider leadership avenues that enhance brands and let CEOs share deeper insights that develop brand loyalty. CEOs who are open to social media, a new and quickly-evolving technology and marketing tool, are viewed as more effective and more involved with both customers and employees. They are viewed as better able to lead, and are trusted more than their peers, standing out as examples of innovative leaders rather than anonymous mysterious executives.

Social media both enables and requires an openness to employees, customers, suppliers, and investors, and it affords CEOs and other business leaders the opportunity to expand their leadership. Executives who blog, tweet, and post to social media display a human side to the sometimes sterile business role they play. Brand representation in social media by top executives creates good feelings all around by virtue of participation in a wider cultural phenomenon and places them one step ahead of companies whose CEOs do not use social media.

There are many ways to represent and enhance a brand in social media. Engaging in social media as part of brand management requires investment of time and money. Social media strategy can be administered as a stand-alone business plan or it can be incorporated into sales and marketing or customer relationship management.

A Different Way to Represent the Brand

The main goal of branding is to influence customers to choose the brand. Neuroscience shows that customers are more likely to choose a brand that (1) is more distinct in the marketplace, (2) has ongoing branding efforts that repeat the brand's core message, and (3) exists in an engaging, participatory branding environment. Representing the brand in social media offers all of these options to build the brand in customers' memories and thought processes. The more the brand message is repeated and the more opportunities customers have to interact with the brand in participatory ways such as liking a post, commenting on information, and experiencing the brand in social media, the stronger the brand image is cemented in their minds. This is different than traditional brand marketing that relies on static media such as expensive television commercial air time and print ads with more limited customer reach. Representation of a brand in social media is an invitation to customers to "come and play" and be part of the brand instead of just buying the brand.

Market researchers and neuroscience are starting to understand all the ways people remember, recognize, and connect to brands. Social media offers a wealth of data to help understand how brands connect with customers and how customers want to connect with brands. Personalization and proactively reaching out to customers during brand interaction are two common ways to induce customers to choose a brand. Rich visuals, interactive customer service, responsive communications, attractive content, and valuable information are attributes of social media that customers do not get from static media such as magazine advertizing.

Customer actions in social media result in other interactions and are perceived as adding value. The process has a high "What's in it for me?" aspect, creating memorable experiences associated with the brand. If a customer "repins" a page from a catalog with a beautiful sweater onto her "my style" board at Pinterest, she is going to recall that pleasant experience more readily than she would remember browsing sweaters in a store.

Social Media Metrics

Connecting with customers the way they engage with the brand is key to successful brand representation. Social media metrics are available with current statistics about highest usage and types of usage. That information is valuable when planning any brand introduction in social media platforms. For example, YouTube's highest weekly activity occurs on Mondays, Facebook's most active day is Tuesday, and Twitter's least active day is Friday. It pays, therefore, to launch Facebook campaigns on Tuesdays, and YouTube campaigns on Mondays, and Friday is not the day to start a Twitter branding campaign. The brand representation team should be flexible and responsive enough to adapt its programs to the social media it is targeting. If it is not, social media branding efforts will not be as productive as possible and may risk failure.

Other important social media metrics include times of day and week that customers are on social media. The traditional 9-to-5 Monday-through-Friday workweek should not be the goal of Internet branders, as many potential customers are online in the evenings, weekends, and early mornings. To get noticed, a brand needs to be in social media when its audience is there.

Having the message available when customers are there to see it is only part of the social media recipe for success. Good rankings in search engine results has a big impact on customer engagement. Recent studies show that customers are influenced to buy when they find a brand higher in the search engine results list. The first page of search engine results matters, and being on the upper half of the first page matters even more.

Chasing Traffic

The main goal of brand representation on social media is attracting traffic. A large volume of visitors drawn to and interacting with brand-related content equals successful brand representation. Traffic, the visitors to a website, blog, or social media account, means people are being exposed to the brand. The more exposure, the more the brand comes to mind when people see anything related to it, and the more the branding message becomes trusted and well received.

Traffic is generated in social media in a variety of ways. In some social media, such as Pinterest, traffic is generated by visitors sharing content and introducing the brand to each other. If content is being shared by visitors and customers, it is an indication that interest in the brand is being generated. Any changes in traffic, such as sudden high traffic or even a slow increase in traffic, are opportunities to interact more with customers.

Brand representation and traffic are intertwined and are opportunities to engage customers, build a brand, and attract more business. Traffic to a website is favorable, but traffic involving the brand on social media such as Facebook, YouTube, and Pinterest can go viral, or be viewed by large numbers of people in a very short time without much extra effort on the marketer's part. In addition to attracting customers, viral posts also attract media attention and business opportunities. Going viral is usually unexpected and unplanned, but the phenomenon should be optimized if it does happen.

Using Social Media Data

Social media is valuable to brand representation in many ways, among which is the opportunity to accumulate data. Knowing how people talk about the brand and how they interact with the brand in social media tells a marketer the best places to buy ads, the best search terms and tags to use, and what kinds of keywords to use. It reveals the best marketing paths to take and the ways customers want to interact with the brand.

Data from social media is only valuable if it is put to good use. The data alone will not do much. Marketers can use social media data to plan a marketing strategy, to dialog with customers about their experience with the brand, and to extend the brand in ways customers want. These steps will result in better customer engagement and better brand representation.

The numbers in social media reveal a lot, but using those numbers to plan a branding strategy is what gets results. If customers are talking about a product on Twitter and Facebook and using it in ways not related to the company's branding efforts, the company needs to take notice and expand their promotions. That will attract more customers and give existing customers a wider experience with the brand.

Necessary Steps

Social media and branding go hand in hand. There are immediate steps a company can take to represent its brand in social media. One of the first things to do is decide which social media programs are best for the brand and focus branding messages for social media there. A brand ambassador can represent the brand on social media platforms to present a more personalized, humanized aspect of the brand. Additional brand-related content and experiences of interest to customers should accompany the brand in social media. The brand should be represented consistently in terms of image and tone across all the social media platforms used.

Marketers should evaluate their brand in social media for sound, language, "flavor" (for example, foreign accent such as the Geico gecko, or male or female point of view), and visual cues. Are all of these aspects consistent with the brand's message to customers? Although different social media platforms operate with different objectives, a brand's message should be consistent through all the social media where it is represented.

It is important to remember that social media is more than text. Visual media including photos and videos are proven to generate more interaction such as shares and comments that get attention for the brand. Marketers should ask questions in social media and make direct requests for engagement.

Conclusion

Representation of the brand is any way a company chooses to present the brand. In social media, that can mean blogging, tweeting, posting on Facebook, pinning on Pinterest, or developing a channel on YouTube. The best social media vehicle for a brand will vary depending on the target audience. Representing a brand well with social media means presenting a consistent message across all social media used, and incorporating visuals with photos and videos.

Branding, brand management, and brand extension all have a scientific basis tied to memory and brain processes. Some successful CEOs engage in social media to represent their brands and generate trust, respect, and recognition. Social media provides a different way to represent a brand in personalized ways with customers. Social media metrics such as traffic spikes and user habits should not be ignored because they supply valuable information concerning how best to use social media for a particular brand. Social media data provides information about search terms, keywords, tags, and opportunities to extend the brand. Social media can be used to participate in the customer interaction that builds brands.

SOURCES OF ADDITIONAL INFORMATION

American Marketing Association. http://www.marketingpower.com/Pages/default.aspx
Association of National Advertisers. http://www.ana.net/
Direct Marketing Association. http://www.the-dma.org/index.php
Harvard Business Review. New Research on Why CEOs Should Use Social Media. http://blogs.hbr.org/cs/2012/07/new_research_on_why_ceos_shoul.html
Management Study Guide. http://www.managementstudyguide.com
Marketing Research Association. http://www.marketingresearch.org/
National Association for Retail Marketing Services. http://www.narms.com/
Pew Internet. Social Media and Political Engagement. http://pewinternet.org/Reports/2012/Political-engagement/Summary-of-Findings.aspx

BIBLIOGRAPHY

Arnold, J., Becker, M., Dickinson, M., & Lurie, I. (2012). *Web marketing all-in-one for dummies*. Hoboken, NJ: John Wiley & Sons, Inc.

Baskin, J. S. (2011). *Histories of social media*. San Jose, CA: Society for New Communications Research.

Charles, A. (2012). *Social media: The leadership secret of the successful CEO*. Retrieved February 17, 2013, from http://chiefmarketer.com/social-marketing/social-media-leadership-secret-successful-ceo

Cohen, H. (2012). *11 tips to increase Facebook marketing effectiveness.* Retrieved February 17, 2013, from http://heidicohen.com/facebook-marketing-improve-results-based-on-the-numbers-research/

Cohen, H. (2012). *Social media branding: 10 tips you need to know.* Retrieved February 17, 2013, from http://heidicohen.com/how-to-brand-on-social-media-10-tips-you-need-now/

Dessi, C. (2012). *Your world is exploding: How social media is changing everything—and how you need to change with it.* CreateSpace Independent Publishing Platform.

Gilliss, A. (2012). *Social media for small businesses: Another argument for CEOs to blog and tweet.* Retrieved from http://thebeltongroup.ca/blog/2012/05/social-media-for-small-businesses-another-argument-for-ceos-to-blog-and-tweet/

Kabani, S., & Brogan, C. (2012). *The zen of social media marketing: An easier way to build credibility, generate buzz, and increase revenue.* Dallas, TX: BenBella.

Kerpen, D. (2011). *Likeable social media: How to delight your customers, create an irresistible brand, and be generally amazing on facebook (and other social networks).* New York: McGraw-Hill.

Levey, R. H. (2012). *Consumer social media data difficult, rewarding to analyze: Q&A.* Retrieved from http://chiefmarketer.com/database-marketing/consumer-social-media-data-difficult-rewarding-analyze-qa

Macarthy, A. (2012). *500 social media marketing tips: Essential advice, hints and strategy for business: Facebook, Twitter, Pinterest, Google+, YouTube, Instagram, LinkedIn, and More!* [Kindle Edition].

Madia, S. A. (2011). *The social media survival guide for political campaigns: Everything you need to know to get your candidate elected using social media.* [Kindle Edition].

McGovern, G. (2012). *Customer experience: Serving the customer, building the brand.* Retrieved from http://www.cmswire.com/cms/customer-experience/customer-experience-serving-the-customer-building-the-brand-017806.php

McHale, R. (2012). *Navigating social media legal risks: Safeguarding your business.* Upper Saddle River, NJ: Pearson Education, Inc.

Nhotsavang, M. (2012). Socially *savvy CEOs are one step ahead of their peers.* Retrieved from http://www.scgpr.com/41-stories/savvy-ceos

Odell, P. (2012). *Duncan Hines SVP marketing shares social media strategy: Q&A.* Retrieved from http://chiefmarketer.com/promotional-marketing/duncan-hines-svp-marketing-shares-social-media-strategy-qa

Peacock, M. (2012). *Get recognized: Search results contribute to brand awareness.* Retrieved from http://www.cmswire.com/cms/customer-experience/get-recognized-search-results-contribute-to-brand-awareness-017094.php

Peacock, M. (2012). *Social media campaigns don't match consumer engagement patterns.* Retrieved from http://www.cmswire.com/cms/customer-experience/social-media-campaigns-dont-match-consumer-engagement-patterns-016269.php

Quinton, B. (2012). *Why your brand should get active in Pinterest—and how.* Retrieved from http://chiefmarketer.com/social-marketing/why-your-brand-should-get-active-pinterest-and-how

Schubarth, C. (2012). *CEOs who know social media get more respect.* Retrieved from http://www.bizjournals.com/sanjose/blog/socialmadness/2012/04/ceos-who-know-social-media-get-more.html

University of North Carolina. (2011). *The brief history of social media.* Retrieved from http://www.uncp.edu/home/acurtis/NewMedia/SocialMedia/SocialMedia History.html

Walvis, T. H. (2008). *Three laws of branding: Neuroscientific foundations of effective brand building.* Retrieved from http://www.palgravejournals.com/bm/journal/v16/n3/full/2550139a.html

Preparing for a Long-Term Social Media Campaign

In This Essay

- Long-term social media campaigns are valuable marketing techniques associated with emerging new social media management careers that emphasize skills in communication and marketing

- Selecting the appropriate social network is important for a successful long-term social media campaign

- Establishing a coherent and consistent brand should be the first step when engaging in a long-term social media campaign

- A long-term social media campaign can increase brand awareness and sales, as well as allow for detailed analysis of customer data through low-cost or free social media analytics

Preparing for a Long-Term Social Media Campaign

What Is a Long-Term Social Media Campaign?

Social media campaigns can be short-term or long-term. A short-term social media campaign might involve one or a small number of social media activities such as creating a business Facebook page and opening a Twitter account. A long-term social media campaign involves strategically planning social media activities tied to business goals, such as developing a three- to five-year plan for establishing a strong social media presence; integrating social media into sales, marketing, and customer service; creating unique customer experiences with social media; and managing your *brand* and customer relationships through social media tools and channels.

Brand: *Name, term, symbol, sign, or design used by a firm to differentiate its offerings from those of its competitors.*

Trend: *A statistical measurement used to track changes that occur over time.*

Social media is no longer a new or emerging *trend*. It is here to stay, evolving quickly as an integral part of successful sales and marketing. Jan Zimmerman and Deborah Ng revealed some impressive social media statistics in *Social Media Marketing All-in-One for Dummies*. They reported that there are more than 120 million active Internet blogs, 4 billion YouTube videos streamed daily, and 900 million active Facebook users. Every year, new social media companies are created and new social media terms enter the vernacular. Every company that serves customers who use social media needs an active and engaging social media presence to keep those customers. Integrating social media with business operations keeps business up to speed with the competition and expands the return on investment of marketing and advertising budget and efforts. If a business' competition is engaging its customers with social media and the business is not, how long can it realistically expect to keep those customers?

Various professionals and entrepreneurs plan long-term social media campaigns. Entrepreneurial businesses might have only the owner or partners to plan social media campaigns along with all their other operations, or they may work with a social media consultant. Small businesses benefit from dedicating an experienced manager or business consultant to be responsible for the company's social media. Large national and international organizations with more resources dedicate whole departments to managing long-term social media strategy under the direction of senior management. Social media management careers have developed quickly along with the evolution of social media. Titles for people in these careers include social media manager, social media strategist, community manager, social media consultant, blog editor, brand ambassador, digital marketing manager, and new media developer.

Most social media experts agree that the foundation of a long-term social media campaign is a company's brand and its audience. Those two things can help a business decide which social media channels to use in its campaign and set its social media objectives. Tracking social media results is important to achieve the best results and should be a part of planning for a long-term campaign.

Who Plans a Long-Term Social Media Campaign?

Although social media is financially economical compared with traditional advertising methods, it involves a substantial investment in setup and maintenance time to develop and sustain a long-term social media campaign according to Michael A. Stelzner in the "2012 Social Media Marketing Industry Report." Whether it is just an individual with the latest social media books from the library and a computer, or a large team of experienced social media managers and gurus, whoever is involved in long-term planning for social media must draw on a balance of technology and public relations and marketing skills and experience, or find the equivalent resources, to plan and implement social media successfully.

Social media management and related positions are new and evolving career paths. The role of a social media manager varies widely between small and big organizations and types of industries. It is a position based in marketing and management, and most social media managers coordinate with other members of marketing and management teams. There is a big communications aspect in social media management. Ideal candidates have business, marketing, and communications educations and backgrounds, are knowledgeable about new media and technology, and are skilled collaborators.

Those involved with planning long-term social media campaigns must know how to find and reach target customers in the world of social media, understand how social media platforms are connected and how to capitalize on it, and know what attracts interest and sells with social media. There is a large amount of management involved in planning social media campaigns. Coordinating staff and social media tools and activities is best done with project management and effective scheduling. Tracking results and adjusting processes based on data is another important aspect of social media management.

Although social media is still evolving, it is an important marketing channel that requires skilled management for successful implementation and maintenance. While some aspects of social media may be handled by interns or junior administrators, long-term social media planning requires a higher level of management. Job postings for social media managers describe specific skill sets such as the ability to understand and use social media to meet business objectives, the ability to effectively communicate with internal and external business audiences, and the ability to implement an integrated marketing plan. Businesses look for highly motivated communicators and those with a passion for writing and social media. They need people with a professional presence in social media, experience managing social media such as a business blog or online community, and a thorough understanding of social media platforms and tools.

Search engine optimization: *The process of affecting the visibility of a website or webpage in a search engine's search results through targeted keyword phrases.*

Responsibilities of social media managers and other positions responsible for managing social media include building a company's social media presence, regular reporting of the company's social media campaigns, project management for social media campaigns, and cross-selling through social media. Knowledge of keyword and *search engine optimization* strategy and analysis, HTML, and content management, as well as business development, are important in these roles. Social media managers work with various business focuses. Some may run campaigns focused on lead generation and fan acquisition. Others may be responsible for customer relations development, customer retention, or customer loyalty programs.

Social Media Channels

Social media channels or networks are online technologies for user-generated content. According to the "2012 Social Media Marketing Industry Report," the top five social media networks in 2012 are Facebook, Twitter, LinkedIn, blogs, and YouTube, in that order. Google+, introduced in 2011, is already used by 40% of marketers which demonstrates how quickly emerging social media channels take hold. Facebook is used by those with little to no social media experience and by those experienced in social media alike. It is the social media network where a majority of marketers, 92%, focus their social media activities, and where 76% plan to increase their efforts in the near future. Twitter is a close second to Facebook, with 69% of marketers planning to increase their Twitter activities.

One or several of the top five social media channels may be the right social media venues for a company to plan a long-term social media campaign, depending on its target customers. Increased traffic is one of the most reported effects of weekly investment in social media activities, with marketplace insight a close second. Deciding on social media channels for long-term social media campaigns depends on a variety of factors, including social media objectives, target customer audience, experience level of the social media managers or marketers involved, and the existing sales and marketing initiatives. It is worth taking the time to research where and how your customers and prospective customers are using social media when planning your long-term campaign.

Social media channels included in the "2012 Social Media Marketing Industry Report" were Google+, blogs, Facebook, LinkedIn, YouTube,

Twitter, forums, and social bookmarking/news, photo-sharing, geolocation, and daily deals websites. Social media marketers reported the top three other types of marketing besides social media were search engine optimization, email marketing, and event marketing, in that order. Social media channels enable businesses to connect with customers and prospective customers through information, visual media such as photos and video, and interactions such as "likes," "shares," and comments.

Content that features a business's brand and engages, influences, and augments its customers' and visitors' experiences can increase sales, create customer loyalty, and build brand recognition. In *The Social Media Bible*, Lon Safko describes social media as resting on the four pillars of communication, collaboration, education, and entertainment. He explains that social media is about prompting action and interaction from the audience. When planning a long-term social media campaign, remembering these categories of audience engagement can help focus a campaign's goals. Be specific about what is being communicated, how you want the audience to interact with the company through social media, what the opportunities for education are, and how to make it all entertaining. Considering social media goals along with these foundations can help planners choose channels that are the best for their campaigns.

Analyzing your competitors and how they are using social media is another effective way to choose social media channels for long-term social media campaigns. If a company's competitors are all on Pinterest, that is a good indication of where its customers spend their time.

Start with the Brand

No matter what social media channels a business chooses for its long-term social media campaign, it should focus on the brand. Social media is not just a playground for users. It is also an effective, economical marketing tool for businesses to promote their products and services, increase sales, save money on advertising, and interact with their customers more quickly and effectively than with traditional forms of print, television, and telephone communications and marketing. New companies and entrepreneurs who have not yet fully established their businesses can use social media to introduce their products and services and start building awareness of their brands much more quickly than ever before. However, it is important to remember that all social media efforts must support the brand, even newly established brands. As with traditional marketing, communication and calls to action are important in social media, and these should relate directly to the brand.

In *Unleash the Power of Social Media Marketing*, Joe Praveen Sequeira cautions that long-term social media goals can be easy to define but hard to achieve. Marketing expert Heidi Cohen explains that it is very important to extend your brand in social media. She suggests taking the advice of marketing consultants Al Ries and Jack Trout and making a goal to establish a word in customers' minds that conjures your brand. She advises brainstorming words that people associate with your brand, building the brand's story, developing related interests that customers can associate with the brand, and using these to incorporate your brand in social media. Brand consistency is important in social media to build recognition and engagement and to avoid confusion and complication.

Heidi Cohen advises marketers to consider how to represent their brands in video, photography, audio, and live formats when planning their social media presence. Associations with brands such as sounds, language, voice, visual cues (such as Chanel's CC logo or Target's red bull's eye), mascots, and distinct employee appearance must be extended through social media for consistency and strong brand support. Logos, company colors, and mottos or themes in bricks-and-mortar stores or offices should match print and television advertising as well as social media presences on channels like Facebook and Twitter. Heidi Cohen explains that even with a limited or no budget for branding, companies who are in business have brands even if they are not consciously spending money to develop them. She suggests companies take control of branding, even if there is no marketing budget for it, by being aware of things like employee dress and behavior, company printed and online materials, and local and national advertising, and work to make them all consistent. Colors for the website should be consistent with colors for advertising and printed materials such as business cards and sales brochures. Employees should treat customers the same way when dealing with them face-to-face as when dealing with them in e-mail or by telephone.

Identify Long-Term Social Media Objectives

Long-term social media objectives should relate to the business's brand and sales and marketing strategy. If a company sells women's shoes, long-term social media objectives might include increasing shoe sales overall by 5% within two years with Facebook, catalog, and in-store sales promotions, while offering customers fun and interesting style advice about different shoe styles. A Facebook posting schedule aligned with sales and marketing campaigns, along with a blog about shoes in general, all using the logo or company colors, creates brand consistency with social media.

Before a business can identify long-term social media goals, it needs to know what social media its customers use the most, and what social media its competitors use. This information can be collected with market research and analysis, or through customer surveys. If you know your competitors send out notices of special sales to their Twitter followers every month, or if you know your customers are on Facebook and Pinterest, it makes sense to include those social media channels in the long-term plans, rather than exploring less popular avenues or trying to jump into a brand new channel.

If a company has a website or a customer service call center, it can use them to gather information for social media planning by surveying visitors and callers. In *Unleash the Power of Social Media Marketing*, Sequeira suggests analyzing the company's social profile when preparing a social media campaign by defining all the information available to the public about the business to identify gaps and opportunities social media can fill. In *Social Media Marketing All-in-One for Dummies*, Zimmerman and Ng suggest using Google Insights to get an idea of how and where customers search on your website, and then use that information to plan social media. For instance, if customers are searching for red shoes on your website more than other colors, you may plan to feature red shoes in your Facebook cover photo and Tweet about apparel and accessories to wear with red shoes.

How Big Brands Plan Social Media

Small companies and entrepreneurs operate on the same social media playing field as big brands, with the same range of opportunities. While the beauty of social media is the economy, cost-effectiveness, and ease-of-use to create customer engagement that drives sales and brand building, there is not one set formula for preparing a social media campaign. Social media campaigns always start with a strategy, but that strategy may take six weeks, six months, or more than a year to formulate and implement.

Large international brands like Coca Cola can afford to experiment with social media based on analytics to bring a social media campaign to the public, as they did with Coke Zero's "Make It Possible" campaign. Fiat prepared a social media campaign around its Super Bowl ad in six weeks. Big brands often start with customer input to formulate ideas for social media campaigns before developing a strategy and implementing it. Twitter feeds after a sale or promotional offer or Facebook comments on posts provide direct customer input and sentiment about the brand that is used to generate future campaigns. This data is available to everyone managing social media campaigns.

Tracking Social Media Results

Analytics, or measuring, tracking, and analyzing the data from a company's social media presence, means the difference between a static social media presence and an active, effective long-term social media campaign. Every social media channel provides the potential to record and track activity on the site. Successful social media marketers analyze this data, noting what works for things like *click-through rates*, interaction levels, purchases, catalog orders, sharing, and commenting. Many social media analytic tools are free to users.

Social-analytics tools such as Google Analytics, HootSuite, Facebook Insights, Twitter analytics, and social media dashboards provide valuable data on customers and potential customers that is not as easily or economically available with traditional marketing. A business can generate reports easily to see how its monthly Facebook posts affect traffic, likes, and comments. By regularly monitor a brand online with tools like Google Alerts, a company can determine when its brand shows up in search engines. The use of Social Mention measures passion, reach, and sentiment about the brand or of Social Pointer to learn where on the World Wide Web a brand is trending.

Click-through rates: *A ratio showing how often people see an on-line advertisement and then click on it to learn more.*

Data mining: *The analysis of large quantities of data to discover patterns within the data.*

Free or inexpensive analytic tools make it easy and cost-effective to manage and build brand awareness through the long-term social media campaign. Regular and consistent use of social media tracking helps a company monitor its brand, tweak its social media campaign if problems occur, and improve its customers' experience of the brand on social media. When preparing a long-term social media campaign, it is important to include analytics, to measure and monitor the social media results. Marketers save money with social media through the fast and inexpensive *data mining* that is not as readily available with traditional print, television, and radio advertising. Besides engaging customers, businesses can really get to know their customers' habits and preferences with social media and target their marketing efforts to the right customers in the right places at the right time.

How to Prepare for a Long-Term Social Media Campaign

To prepare for a long-term social media campaign, there are several things that need to be done up front. Focus on your brand and how you will use social media to promote it. Identify the social media team, resources, and objectives so they are in place when the campaign is ready to begin. Find out what social media customers and competition are actively using to plan what social media channels to use. Establish a social media campaign schedule and research social media dashboard resources such as Goojet, HootSuite, Netvibes, and Pageflakes. Research the company's social profile, all areas the public encounters information about the company, products, and services. Draft a *social media policy* to set expectations and protect your brand by ensuring a consistent response to customers.

Social media policy: *A corporate code of conduct providing guidelines for employees who post content on the Internet either as part of their job or as a private person. Also known as a social networking policy.*

In *Light, Bright and Polite: How Businesses and Professionals Can Safely and Effectively Navigate Social Media*, Josh Ochs advises those planning social media campaigns to be aware of the time social media takes, the money it costs, and the distractions it creates for staff. He suggests drafting a solid plan before taking any action, and researching the true costs in terms of time, labor, and distraction that managing social media presents. Ochs advises social media campaign planners to set clear goals for social media, use a messaging calendar, and thoroughly assess customers to know where they are in the social media universe for the most effective social media development.

Companies large and small are using social media to promote their brands, develop relationships, improve products and services, and build trust. Although social media can have an effect on sales, its main focus is on relationships. Engaging content, valuable information, excellent customer service, and incentives like discounts and free gifts create good will, customer loyalty, and brand recognition. Contests that are fun and interesting, like Burnaby Hospital Foundation in Burnaby, British Columbia, Canada's "Save the Cake" game, which allows users to navigate a birthday cake past obstacles to deliver it to the hospital to celebrate its 60th anniversary. There users can learn about the hospital and make donations, or enter to win an iPad mini.

Contests like these allow customers to participate online and keep them coming back for more. Social networks are rapidly replacing costly and time-consuming focus groups and market research with practically free engagement tools that yield even better, long-lasting results.

In *The Zen of Social Media Marketing: An Easier Way to Build Credibility, Generate Buzz, and Increase Revenue*, Shama Kabani and Chris Brogan caution that the number one reason people fail at social media marketing is that they do not have a brand. A strong brand, or even a new brand with a good plan for development, is essential to social media marketing and a must for long-term social media campaigns. Social media platforms are tools to showcase a brand, and they are only as effective as that brand's identity. If the brand is fuzzy, or if the social media campaign does not clearly focus on that brand, most of the effectiveness of the social media campaign is lost. A strong, consistent message defining the brand is crucial to preparing any social media efforts.

In their social media profile of Chris Geier of K2, a business process management provider, Kabani and Brogan note K2's social media strategies. K2 opened as many social media channels to its community as possible. It was part of the conversation and made conversations open and two-way. It was authentic, especially with negative information. And it managed the intent to interact. Entrepreneurs should start by listening to the conversations their customers and vendors are having, and then develop their social media presence to be part of those conversations.

SOURCES OF ADDITIONAL INFORMATION

Arnold, M. (2012). *Target on Social Media—5 Lessons from One of the World's Most Successful Retail Brands.* Retrieved February 17, 2013, from http://socialmediatoday.com/morgan-j-arnold/752786/target-social-media-5-lessons-one-world-s-most-successful-retail-brands

Centers for Disease Control and Prevention's *The Health Communicator's Social Media Toolkit.* Retrieved February 17, 2013, from http://www.cdc.gov/socialmedia/Tools/guidelines/pdf/SocialMediaToolkit_BM.pdf

Cohen, H. (2012). *Social media branding: 10 tips you need to know.* Retrieved February 17, 2013, from http://heidicohen.com/how-to-brand-on-social-media-10-tips-you-need-now/

Ferris, H. (2012). *Tweet This! Top tips behind successful social media campaigns.* Retrieved February 17, 2013, from http://www.socialnomics.net/2012/11/20/tweet-this-top-tips-behind-successful-social-media-campaigns/

Wasserman, T. (2012). *How big brands create social media campaigns.* Retrieved February 17, 2013, from http://mashable.com/2012/06/18/big-brands-social-media-campaigns/

BIBLIOGRAPHY

Arnold, J., Becker, M., Dickinson, M., & Lurie, I. (2012). *Web marketing all-in-one for dummies.* Hoboken, NJ: John Wiley & Sons, Inc.

Barger, C. (2011). *The social media strategist: Build a successful program from the inside out.* New York: McGraw Hill.

Baskin, J. S. (2011). *Histories of social media.* San Jose, CA: Society for New Communications Research.

Beckis, A. (2012). *Facebook marketing: Your social media campaigns using Facebook's 2012 additions.* [Kindle Edition].

Blanchard, O. (2011). *Social Media ROI: managing and measuring social media efforts in your organization.* Boston, MA: Pearson Education, Inc.

Breakenridge, D. (2012). *Social media and public relations: Eight new practices for the PR professional.* Upper Saddle River, NJ: Pearson Education, Inc.

Dessi, C. (2012). *Your world is exploding: How social media is changing everything— and how you need to change with it.* United States of America; CreateSpace Independent Publishing Platform.

Hinchcliffe, D., Kim, P., & Dachis, J. (2012). *Social business by design: Transformative social media strategies for the connected company.* San Francisco, CA: Jossey-Bass.

Jones, P. (2012). *How to become a social media manager.* United States of America: CreateSpace Independent Publishing Platform.

Kabani, S., & Brogan, C. (2012). *The zen of social media marketing: An easier way to build credibility, generate buzz, and increase revenue.* Dallas, TX: BenBella

Kerpen, D. (2011). *Likeable social media: How to delight your customers, create an irresistible brand, and be generally amazing on facebook (and other social networks).* New York: McGraw-Hill.

Macarthy, A. (2012). *500 social media marketing tips: Essential advice, hints and strategy for business: Facebook, Twitter, Pinterest, Google+, YouTube, Instagram, LinkedIn, and More!* [Kindle Edition].

Madia, S. A. (2011). *The social media survival guide for political campaigns: Everything you need to know to get your candidate elected using social media.* [Kindle Edition].

Mason, C. (2011). *Social media success in 7 days.* Watford, UK: Inspired Press.

Mathos, M. (2012). *101 social media tactics for non-profits.* Hoboken, NJ: John Wiley & Sons, Inc.

McHale, R. (2012). *Navigating social media legal risks: Safeguarding your business.* Upper Saddle River, NJ: Pearson Education, Inc.

Ochs, J. (2012). *Light, bright and polite: How businesses and professionals can safely and effectively navigate social media.* New York: Media Leaders, LLC.

Peck, D. (2011). *Think before you engage: 100 questions to ask before starting a social media marketing campaign.* [Kindle Edition].

Poston, L. (2012). *Social media metrics for dummies.* Hoboken, NJ: John Wiley & Sons, Inc.

Praveen Sequiera, J. (2012). *Unleash the power of social media marketing: Explosive proven strategies to boost your social media marketing campaign.* United States of America: CreateSpace Independent Publishing Platform.

Safko, L. (2012). *The social media bible: Tactics, tools, and strategies for business success.* Hoboken, NJ: John Wiley & Sons, Inc.

Scott, D. M. (2011). *The new rules of marketing & PR: How to use social media, online video, mobile applications, blogs, news releases, and viral marketing to reach buyers directly.* Hoboken, NJ: John Wiley & Sons, Inc.

Singh, S., & Diamond, S. (2012). *Social media marketing for dummies.* Hoboken, NJ: John Wiley & Sons, Inc.

Smith, D. J. (2012). *Promote your business or cause using social media: A beginner's handbook.* Hoboken, NJ: John Wiley & Sons, Inc.

Zimmerman, J. & Ng, D. (2012). *Social media marketing all-in-one for dummies.* Hoboken, NJ: John Wiley & Sons, Inc.

Managing Your Social Media Campaign

In This Essay

- What is a social media campaign?
- Why use social media?
- Start with a brand and a plan
- Keep it simple
- Make it interactive
- It takes a team
- Successfully implementing your social media campaign
- What a business needs to do now with a social media campaign

Introduction

Social media's numbers are impressive. Blogger hosts millions of blogs. Facebook has more than 800 million users. Wikipedia has practically replaced traditional encyclopedias. YouTube. Twitter. Pinterest. Instagram. These social media channels have a loyal base and a growing numbers of users, making them highly desirable marketing vehicles for brands, new products, and customer service. The most successful social media campaigns do not just happen. They are carefully planned, skillfully executed, and well managed by experienced marketers and savvy entrepreneurs alike.

Social media has reach and is economic. It is an inexpensive and easy way to reach customers on Facebook and Pinterest and build an engaging online presence that supports and promotes your brand. The most successful social media campaigns grab customers' interest, engage them in fun and endearing ways, and support the brand with specific goals such as sales, brand awareness, or education. A business can launch a social media campaign with one employee or use a team to share the load, but either way, good management of the campaign will yield the best results. Plan, use the brand, use social media tools, keep it simple, and integrate fun and interactivity.

One of the first steps in managing a social media campaign is planning the focus. What should the social media campaign do? For example, social media can be used to introduce a company, launch a new product line, offer a special sale, get customers to sign up for a newsletter or like the business' Facebook page, provide education, support a charitable cause, or promote services or expertise. Select a targeted focus with an endgame in mind and build your campaign around it.

Even if there is not money in the business' budget for traditional sales and marketing programs, social media campaigns can be used to achieve marketing goals. Using social media campaigns along with traditional marketing gives a better *return on investment* (ROI) for marketing dollars and improves marketing results.

What Is a Social Media Campaign?

A social media campaign is a focused use of electronic communication and social media to advertise, promote, or sell goods and services by engaging customers and potential customers. Vlogs, weblogs, blogs, podcasts, e-mail, sharing and instant messaging are often-used social media routes. Facebook, YouTube, Twitter, Pinterest, and Instagram are just some of the most popular current social media platforms. A well-organized social media campaign uses one or more of these avenues to interact with customers in a wide variety of ways, including offering special incentives, enhancing sales, getting client feedback, building communities, and promoting brands.

Return on investment: *A performance measure used to evaluate the efficiency of an investment. It is usually expressed as a percentage or a ratio where return of an investment is divided by the cost of the investment. Also known as ROI.*

Social media campaigns yield a wealth of economical and easily accessible marketing data. These include advertising, sales available at all times from Internet websites and affiliates; focus groups that provide detailed customer input through blogs, forums, and reviews; and in-depth customer behavior information through web analysis of traffic, purchasing behavior, and response to other business' specific campaigns. This information is more easily aggregated through social media and Internet technology than traditional sales and marketing through radio, print and television are.

Social media campaigns can direct customers back to a central website for information, placing orders, or both. For example, a simple social media campaign might tweet out advance notice of a sale to a company's Twitter followers with their website referenced and direct them to a Facebook page to share photos and post comments about the sale item. A multi-faceted social media campaign might require a social media, sales, and marketing manager to work together to promote a seasonal sale or promote and introduce a new product line, such as a year-end clearance or a limited-edition holiday dinnerware.

Fun is a central theme in successful social media campaigns, along with personalizing the customers' experience with a brand. Making a social media campaign fun for customers and focused on what they want while getting the desired outcome from the customers makes a social media campaign successful. Companies taking full advantage of social media include Victoria's Secret (Facebook), Zappos CEO Tony Hsieh (Twitter), and Blendtec (YouTube). Victoria's Secret acquired more than 18 million Facebook fans by switching to Facebook Timeline early after its introduction to support its visual marketing campaign and gain attention for its brand. Zappos CEO Tony Hsieh regularly tweets on Twitter and brings his personality and the Zappos brand to customers. Blendtec shows customers just how versatile and tough its line of blenders are with its funny videos on YouTube.

Why Social Media? It's Less Expensive!

Social media is different from traditional marketing in several important ways. One of the ways it is different is that it is much less expensive. Social media marketing should not be entirely separate from traditional marketing, but it should be used as part of an overall sales and marketing program. It has created huge changes and benefits in the marketing world for consumers and brands, especially in the areas of expense, getting closer to customers, building loyalty and trust, and creating community.

Social media compares very favorably when traditional marketing is analyzed. Marketing through social media is relatively inexpensive, whereas traditional marketing is costly. Social media is interactive and engaging, whereas traditional marketing is typically a one-way channel. Social media is measurable, whereas traditional marketing is hard to measure. Social media reaches almost 1,000 times as many customers more quickly and less expensively than traditional media. Social media engenders trust because it uses recommendations from friends and users in real time to promote a brand or product.

Social media is not just good for customers. Although it provides a faster, more interactive way for customers to learn about the products and services available, it also provides businesses with data-driven information about their customers and potential customers for a smaller investment than traditional marketing. A website is always available to customers for sales and customer service. It can provide answers to frequently asked questions; showcase product and service photos, videos, and descriptions; and give customers a place to congregate online to share information. A Facebook page provides customers a place on the Internet to spend time with a business' products and services and others who use them, encouraging information sharing, community, and brand loyalty. YouTube gives businesses the opportunity to showcase their offerings and business practices in a highly entertaining and engaging video format. Twitter is a fun, fast way to get information, such as advance notice of special sales, good press about awards and charitable efforts, and other customers' opinions and experiences to customers. All this can be accomplished for much less than the expense of traditional sales avenues such as customer service call centers, television commercials, and radio advertisements.

Although cost is a big factor in implementing a social media campaign versus a traditional marketing campaign such as television and print ads, it is not the only factor. It ranks high on the list with ease of implementation, creating customer engagement, and instilling trust in the brand. Social media campaigns are used by small and large businesses alike to get in tune with customers, get competitive in the market, and manage their brand and their image with customer engagement.

Nevertheless, although it may be free to post a sale on a Facebook page or tweet about a coupon on Twitter, what is behind those free notices/customer communications is actually a lot of work that is not free. There is a cost to developing an advertising plan, support a product line, pay a marketing staff (even if it is only a marketing manager or consultant), and develop and implement ways to reach customers. Social media campaigns are inexpensive and effective ways to reach out to customers as part of an overall marketing strategy or as part of an economical way to promote a brand.

Start with a Brand and a Plan

A social media campaign should start with a brand, whatever the goal. If a business wants more customers to know about and buy the latest product, form the social media campaign around it. If a business has a new blog and wants subscribers, the social media campaign should inform and encourage people to read the blog and then subscribe to it to read it every week. If a business wants to sell year-end inventory quickly this month before the new inventory comes in next month, the social media campaign should let everyone know about special sales and incentives to buy.

A social media campaign plan should revolve around the end goal, or the desired outcome of the social media efforts. Does the business want customers to buy customized widgets? Does the business want customers to know the company is socially responsible? Does the business want customers to "like" the company on Facebook? Decide what should be achieved with social media and determine the best social media methods to use to make it happen.

If the business has a social media manager, that person can work with the marketing department to integrate marketing goals into the social media campaign. For a solo entrepreneur, a social media consultant may help focus social media goals before planning a campaign. Either way, a social media campaign calendar can help organize social media campaign activities and deadlines, especially time sensitive activities such as holiday sales, contests, and coupon offers.

When developing a social media campaign by starting with the brand, marketing and brand development must be integrated with customer relations for a unique form of marketing medium. The social media activity should always promote and build the brand, just as in traditional marketing. The social media campaign plan should include *metrics* and analytics, the measurement tools that make social media so cost-effective and data rich. It is also an area in which social media outshines traditional marketing: ease of measurement. There are many free and low cost social media analytic tools that let a business track clicks, tweets, posts, and conversions in real time, giving the opportunity to modify the campaign if things are not going as planned and helping manage things that succeed. Seesmic Desktop and TweetDeck are free services that allow a business to manage posts and tweets easily from almost anywhere, anytime. Radian6 and SocialMention are paid services that combine social media

Metrics: *A standard of measurement used to gauge a company's performance.*

management with Google analytics so a business can see trends while managing the company's social media feeds all at the same time.

Keep It Simple

Two advantages and benefits of social media are measurability and economy. Any social media campaign can be as simple or complex as the implementers want it to be, but it is best to keep it simple to retain the attractive ease of use and inexpensive implementation.

Focusing the social media campaign's elements all in the same direction make it easier to implement and sustain. The target audience, choice of social network, and call to action must be aligned. For example, if the customers are young adults who are interested in budget fashion, the social media campaign should target young adults, be aimed at places online where young adults gather, and have a call to action that tells them about the product/service and how it benefits them, such as "Get cheap chic that goes from street to office to club."

Planning the social media campaign with the ability to measure in real time gives the business data about what is and is not working so the business can address it and modify it as it comes up. Create specific metrics that follow the goals and target audience of the campaign, such as audience size and makeup, clicks, conversions, and sales, and the baseline of where the business started the campaign. Building these into the social media campaign from the start helps optimize the campaign, analyze the campaign as it is implemented, and prevent lost time and missed opportunities later.

Set up data-gathering tools for the specific objectives for which the social media campaign is created. When the business knows if its user numbers are growing, if people are engaging with its content, how many people who clicked on its page ordered something, and how many comments or retweets its campaign generates, it can tell how successful the campaign is in real time. This provides the business the opportunity to tweak its campaign to improve the results. For instance, if the goal is to boost sales of the less popular products, and the business sees early in the campaign that sales are only increasing 2% when they should have increased 10%, the business can offer better deals or monitor customers' reactions and comments more closely to discover why customers are not buying and change things immediately rather than waiting until the campaign is over and then addressing the problem. When something is not performing as expected, the business is quickly aware of it and can adjust the campaign by posting when customers are more active, adjusting the call to action, or adding richer content.

Another way to keep the social media campaign simple is through photographs. Much of social media is visual. Look at Pinterest and Instagram, for example. Regularly posting beautiful photos of the staff, facilities, operations, and products helps connect the business to the customers in a very effective way. Professional photographs make an impression, but casual and personal photos will connect with customers in more endearing ways and let them really get to know the company. Timeline on Facebook, videos on YouTube, product portraits on Pinterest, and staff and facilities photos on Instagram create a visual story for customers that is rich in relationship-building potential and easy to implement at the same time.

If the social media campaign is not simple and targeted, much of the benefit of social media is lost. Ease of use, speed of execution, and economical implementation are the reasons why businesses use social media. However, without a simple, targeted approach, the campaign will cost more and be less effective.

Make It Interactive and Get Results

Social media is a rich and interactive resource for users and consumers, and they expect to participate in it. A one-way communication, no matter how attractive, is not enough to keep users interested when they expect to be able to comment, see videos, listen to music, and meet other users. The social media campaign must incorporate interactive experiences for those it targets and have focused goals. For example, if the campaign is to capture information about how much lingerie the target audience buys, plan frequent posts asking about when they buy lingerie.

Rewarding participation is a huge incentive in social media and can mean the difference between an average social media campaign and a successful one that produces quickly. Social media campaigns can dramatically increase profits, significantly impact growth, and increase effectiveness of marketing and sales efforts. Engaging, seasonal, or themed social media campaigns delight customers and reward them for doing something the business wants, such as commenting on a product, telling their story that involves the product or service, buying a new product or service, or registering for a program.

Social media campaigns recognized by Advertising Age on its 2011 list of 10 best social-media campaigns of the year include a major food industry manufacturer, a small town in Switzerland, and a major credit card. Heinz offered to send its Facebook fans' sick friends a can of soup for US$3 at the start of cold and flu season. Obermutten, Switzerland, posted a video on its fan page with the message that the town would add page visitors' photos to its real message board when they liked the town's fan page, resulting in more than 45,000 "likes." American Express offered US$100 ad credits to the first 10,000 businesses that registered on its Small Business Saturday site, doubling its page fans.

When a social media campaign is interactive, it draws customers and endears them to the brand thus creating loyalty. Be careful to keep the interactivity as simple and fun as possible. More than one or two steps will lose users who do not want to stay on a page very long or who are just online during a lunch break or on the train home from work.

It Takes a Team

There are many job titles in sales, marketing, and social media. The most effective social media campaigns do not just happen or go viral all by themselves. They are carefully planned, executed, and managed by experienced teams with focused goals. A marketing manager or director may be responsible for social media campaigns integrated with overall sales and marketing strategies and objectives, but probably does not have the time or capability to launch social media campaigns and will rely on others to do so. Social media marketing managers and consultants can plan and manage teams for campaigns. Social media specialists in Facebook, Twitter, YouTube, Instagram, or Pinterest can post regularly to those platforms. Webmasters can tweak fan pages, landing pages, and special sales offers pages on e-commerce sites. Senior marketing coordinators may be responsible for ensuring that the customer service call center knows about the latest sales being promoted through social media and that the social media specialists have the right scripts to post on the right dates. Special teams can be formed for different campaigns, using those with the most experience in the areas of social media the campaigns will use.

Social media is a perfect medium for small operations because it leverages the power and reach of the Internet in the most cost effective ways. Even if the business is a small start up, it can put together a social media campaign team to manage and execute an online campaign. Work closely with one or two people in your company to plan your campaign. If it is just one or two people in a business, get an intern from a local community college or high school to help with the social media plans, or hire a temporary employee to help launch a campaign. Look for a business mentor with experience in social media. If truly operating solo or on a budget, use the latest books and trade publications about social media to get ideas and learn how to run a social media campaign.

Successfully Implementing Your Social Media Campaign

Successful social media campaign implementation requires an organized effort, whether as an individual or as an experienced team of social media and marketing professionals. Start by getting a team and resources together. Then plan the social media campaign around the brand, whether the goal is to sell, educate, add value, build trust, increase brand awareness, or learn more about how customers use the products or services. The brand is how customers know the business and it should be the center of all social media efforts.

Be sure to include interactivity and engage customers in every social media campaign, whether it is Facebook, Twitter, YouTube, or any other social media platform. Keep it simple, fun, and meaningful for customers so they will not abandon the transaction before completing it and will accept the direction you plan. Integrate the social media campaigns with current sales and marketing efforts and themes, and analyze the activity in real time. Use the tools available for social media such as Bit.ly to shorten URLs you want to mention in tweets, RSS feeds, analytics, dashboards, iPad and smartphone applications for social media, and any tracking media that makes it fast and easy to monitor the campaign in realtime.

Once the social media campaign is launched, keep a close eye on it in real time and be prepared to make adjustments as you go along. Do not just launch and leave the campaign hanging. Have an end strategy for concluding the campaign or repeating it weekly, quarterly, or annually. Study the return on investment and impact on goals.

What You Need to Do Now with Your Social Media Campaign

One centralized social media campaign or a strategy for launching social media campaigns on a regular basis with focused objectives is needed. Either way, there are a few things that should be done right now with the social media campaign to optimize it. Register names to use on social media, share good content, add social media sharing buttons to all online presences, and check the current *search engine optimization (SEO)* to ensure they are current and correct and the pages load quickly.

Search engine optimization: *The process of affecting the visibility of a website or webpage in a search engine's search results through targeted keyword phrases. Also known as SEO.*

Register any name the business plans to use on social media including company name, brand name, and product names. Do this on Google, Twitter, Facebook, YouTube, Pinterest, Tumblr, and any other social media sites that might be used. This will help build the Internet and social media presence.

Share good content. Experts and experienced social media professionals agree that sharing good content is the best way to get followers online. Provide value, humor, socially conscious material, or inspirational content to get people interested and engaged in the company and brand. Let people get to know the company, staff, and products personally while providing value. Keep a fresh supply of good content in the works for the online presence and social media campaign to attract and delight customers.

Add social media share buttons to all online presences, especially new ones, so customers can instantly share content and offers with their social media contacts and networks. This is the whole reason for social media, to allow and encourage users to like and share information about the company and brand, so make it easy for them.

Check the current SEO so that the company website title and tags are optimized and the web pages load quickly and easily for visitors, especially landing pages and e-commerce pages. This is worth a professional audit by a social media marketing company. A business does not want to lose customers or waste efforts if the website does not work well.

These four activities alone will optimize the social media presence, and will put the business on the right track when managing the social media campaign.

SOURCES OF ADDITIONAL INFORMATION

Bitly. https://bitly.com

Inblosam LLC Analytics App. https://itunes.apple.com/us/app/analytics-app/id30368911?mt=8

BIBLIOGRAPHY

Arnold, J., Becker M., Dickinson, M., and Lurie, I. (2012). *Web marketing all-in-one for dummies.* Hoboken, NJ: John Wiley & Sons.

Arnold, M. J. (2012). Target on social media—5 lessons from one of the world's most successful retail brands. Social Media Today. Retrieved March 10, 2013, from http://socialmediatoday.com/morgan-j-arnold/752786/target-social-media-5-lessons-one-world-s-most-successful-retail-brands

Barger, C. (2011). *The social media strategist: build a successful program from the inside out.* New York: McGraw Hill.

Baskin, J. S. (2011). *Histories of social media.* San Jose, CA: Societies for New Communication Research.

Bennett, S. (n.d) Marketing 101—social media vs traditional media. Mediabistro. Retrieved March 10, 2013, from http://www.mediabistro.com/alltwitter/social-vs-traditional-media-marketing_b25389

Cohen, H. (2012). Social media branding: 10 tips you need to know. Personal blog. Retrieved March 10, 2013, from http://heidicohen.com/how-to-brand-on-social-media-10-tips-you-need-now/

Curtis, A. (2011). The brief history of social media. University of North Carolina at Pembrook. Retrieved March 10, 2013, from http://www.uncp.edu/home/acurtis/NewMedia/SocialMedia/SocialMediaHistory.html

Dessi, C. (2012). *Your world is exploding: how social media is changing everything—and how you need to change with it.* Self-published.

Ferris, H. (2012). Tweet this! Top tips behind successful social media campaigns. Socialnomics. Retrieved March 10, 2013, from http://www.socialnomics.net/2012/11/20/tweet-this-top-tips-behind-successful-social-media-campaigns/

Kabani, S., and Brogan, C. (2012). *The zen of social media marketing: an easier way to build credibility, generate buzz, and increase revenue.* Dallas, TX: BenBella Books.

Kerpen, D. (2011). *Likeable social media: how to delight your customers, create an irresistible brand, and be generally amazing on Facebook (and other social networks).* New York: McGraw Hill.

Macarthy, A. (2012). *500 social media marketing tips: essential advice, hints and strategy for business: Facebook, Twitter, Pinterest, Google+, YouTube, Instagram, LinkedIn, and More!* Self-published.

Madia, S.A. (2011). *The social media survival guide for political campaigns: everything you need to know to get your candidate elected using social media.* Buffalo, New York: Full Court Press.

McHale, R. (2012). *Navigating social media legal risks: safeguarding your business.* Upper Saddle River, NJ: Pearson Education.

The Next Web. (2012). Five steps to optimize your social media campaign in real time. The Next Web. Retrieved March 10, 2013, from http://thenextweb.com/socialmedia/2012/10/22/five-steps-to-optimize-your-social-media-campaign-in-real-time/

Peacock, M. (2012). Social media campaigns don't match consumer engagement patterns. CMS Wire. Retrieved March 10, 2013, from http://www.cmswire.com/cms/customer-experience/social-media-campaigns-dont-match-consumer-engagement-patterns-016269.php

Peck. D. (2011). *Think before you engage: 100 questions to ask before starting a social media marketing campaign.* Hoboken, NJ: John Wiley & Sons.

Safko, L. (2012). *The social media bible: tactics, tools, and strategies for business success.* Hoboken, NJ: John Wiley & Sons.

Sahota, P. (2012). 5 companies who show social media who's boss. Socialnomics. Retrieved March 10, 2013, from http://www.socialnomics.net/2012/03/28/5-companies-who-show-social-media-whos-boss/

Signh, S., and Diamond, S. (2012). *Social media marketing for dummies.* Hoboken, NJ: John Wiley & Sons.

Wasserman, T. (2012). How big brands create social media campaigns. Mashable. Retrieved March 10, 2013, from http://mashable.com/2012/06/18/big-brands-social-media-campaigns/

Benefits of Social Media Teams

Benefits of Social Media Teams

Leaders of small and large organizations alike must understand what social media is and how to use it in their businesses and industries not only to be competitive, but also to stay in business. Customer engagement is now a business necessity that creates opportunities for good public relations, customer-centered business processes, and new avenues to profits. Those who ignore social media do so at their own peril, missing emerging customer relationship–building trends and failing to realize its benefits in their businesses.

Although social media is still evolving, it is also rapidly maturing and is no longer a new or untried concept or practice. It is an essential part of modern business, still developing with communications devices such as cell phones and laptop and tablet computers but firmly embedded in traditional business practices like customer service and sales and marketing. Social media has a large emotional component because of user-generated content and seems to be beyond the control of business, unlike the one-way channel in traditional print and television advertising, introducing risk. Taking advantage of opportunity and managing and minimizing risk is where businesses realize the benefits of social media teams to collaborate on best practices and new trends and share the workload of managing social media processes and activities. Social media teams can respond to and interact with customers more quickly and directly through social media than management and marketing could do with traditional media such as newspaper press releases or customer service call centers.

Even a one-person operation will benefit from a social media team to promote its brand and engage its customers. To understand the full benefits of social media teams, entrepreneurs, executives, and managers need to know what social media teams are, who works on social media teams, how they collaborate and work to initiate and maintain social media, and how to develop social media teams.

What Is a Social Media Team?

A social media team is a group of individuals tasked with implementing and maintaining social media for a company. They work under the direction of a lead who sets strategy and expectations and coordinates social media schedules and calendars. The lead may be a social media manager or strategist, or may be a senior marketing professional. Social media teams benefit from a mix of sales, marketing, customer service, and administrative members to coordinate and perform all social media tasks and activities on schedule. A social media team may also be an outside agency hired to handle some or all of a company's social media and work closely with key personnel from the company.

Successful social media teams integrate business goals when developing social media. For example, if an annual business goal is to increase revenue by adding 10,000 customers per year, the social media team would work to not only add fans and followers, but to promote sales, coupons, and contests that convert those online customer prospects into buying customers.

Social media teams work under the direction of a senior leader who may have a title such as director of social media, social media manager, or social media strategist. Teams may include a community manager, a blog editor, a blogger, channel specialists and monitors, a search engine optimization specialist, a photographer/videographer, a web producer or web master, and a web analytics specialist, among other titles.

Community managers represent the company's brand in social media channels and respond quickly to emerging issues. They set the tone for a company's social media presence through voice and personality. Blog editors and bloggers work together to produce content-rich posts relevant to the company's social media and corporate goals. Channel specialists are experts in specific social media channels such as YouTube, Facebook, Twitter, and Pinterest. They know how channels work, how to initialize and maintain a presence on them, and how to monitor and analyze their effectiveness. A search engine optimization specialist will help all team members get their social media message to the top of search engine results lists with key words and key word phrases, driving traffic to the site.

Much of social media is visual, and digital photos and videos enhance user experience, draw traffic and add a new level to social media effectiveness. When users click on your content, it helps your search engine ranking, and photos and videos get a much larger click rate than plain text, making photos and videos essential to successful social media management. A web producer or web master can update and improve a website in response to coordinated social media such as Facebook and Twitter links. A web analytics specialist can research and recognize online behavioral patterns, report in detail on how the social media is attracting and driving traffic and help the team to better target social media efforts to get the best results.

Who Needs Social Media Teams?

Any business or organization that has social media goals and objectives to meet benefits from social media teams. In *Social Marketology*, Ric Dragon describes social media as having two main focuses: creative campaigns and *reputation management*, both ideally managed with teams. He also describes social media projects such as maintaining a brand beachhead; monitoring and responding to brand equity; community-building to become part of the conversation about a brand, service, or industry; and crisis management. These social media projects require teams to navigate and manage them successfully.

Reputation management: *The process of building a company or brand's reputation then maintaining a positive reputation or overcoming a negative one.*

As Nancy Flynn explains in *The Social Media Handbook: Rules, Policies, and Best Practices to Successfully Manage Your Organization's Social Media Presence, Posts, and Potential*, effective social media development depends on an experienced social media team actively engaged in managing and monitoring a company's social media presence. These are best administered through a group of knowledgeable, experienced people on a social media team actively engaged in managing and monitoring a company's social media presence. It is more than one person can perform, even for an experienced senior executive or seasoned social media expert.

In *Socially Elected: How to Win Elections Using Social Media*, Craig Agranoff and Herbert Tabin point to the effectiveness and persuasiveness of social media managed by social media teams in both of Barack Obama's presidential campaigns. They discuss how Obama's successes with social media have spurred other politicians to follow his lead into social media. Politicians use Facebook to announce intentions to run for office and post videos on YouTube to connect with voters and get their messages out. Agranoff and Tabin say that social media is an integral part of political campaigns and call social media a game changer in politics. Politicians and their social media teams harness voter emotion and enthusiasm for an organized purpose in many of the same ways that businesses use social media to promote their brands and persuade customers to buy from them.

Who Works on Social Media Teams?

Emergent social media job titles have developed with emerging and evolving social media trends and platforms. Marketers still need a solid foundation in sales, public relations, communications, and advertising, but now they also need to know about community building, engagement, how to create *buzz*, Internet and online technologies, and social media analytics.

Buzz: *When discussing the Internet, excited attention relating to a new or forthcoming product or event.*

Larry Null, in *Social Media Management*, talks about how social media manager positions as full time career opportunities have only existed since around 2010. It has become common for social media managers who are experienced marketers to lead social media teams, although they may alternatively be led by sales and marketing executives or community managers. They lead a team of coordinators and specialists to both strategize social media development and complete ongoing activities such as posting, blogging, and tweeting once social media is initialized. Developing social media jobs include social media marketers who create buzz around a brand or a promotion; user experience professionals who ensure products and services work as expected and create customer satisfaction rather than frustration; and data analytics professionals who monitor and report on numbers, metrics, statistics, and data generated from social media activity.

Mike Christian outlines various positions in social media in *Social Media Jobs Guide*, such as marketing support specialists, customer communications specialists, content promotion coordinators, online advertising specialists, and public relations managers. He discusses how many companies are developing their online presence through multiple social media channels, and how their social media teams are using tools such as social media *dashboards* that make it easier and more automated to manage these multiple platforms and activities. For example, social media dashboard tools take a company's various social media accounts and consolidate them into one place to see daily likes, comments, and shares easily, and to manage these activities from one place instead of going into each platform individually to manage and monitor activity.

Dashboard: *A web page which collates information about a business.*

Sharing the Workload

One of the biggest benefits of social media teams is the ability to share the workload of maintaining a social media presence. A key to successful social media management is participating in the conversations and communities that are building online. If you start a blog but do not post regularly with content that is relevant and valuable to your audience, they will stop reading your blog. If you want a strong, engaging social media presence for your company, brand, or cause, you need a strong, engaging social media team that regularly interacts, participates, monitors, and maintains that presence and keeps it fresh and relevant for your customers or audience.

In *The Zen of Social Media Marketing*, Shama Kabani and Chris Brogan explain that access and prominence are two of social media's strongest benefits, especially for small business, allowing companies almost instant access to customer habits and preferences and a place of prominence in customers' eyes and minds if they create a social media presence. It is important to have a social media team to develop the means to take advantage of these new media rewards.

Kabani and Brogan also stress the importance of what you do with social media, explaining that it takes much more than just putting up a Facebook page and expecting customers and fans to flock to it. Social media requires participation and activity to work. It is based on engagement, and engagement is not static. It does not operate in a vacuum. Social media teams create that engagement with targeted activities online on Twitter, blogs, YouTube, forums, Facebook, and Pinterest. They invite people, ask questions, use photos and videos, post valuable content, link from other relevant sites and forums, use paid advertising, and pay attention to how people find a web page and what they do when they are there. The value of social media teams is in sharing the many tasks and activities involved in creating engagement.

Social media teams must have a shared purpose and clear vision to operate successfully, and need direction and accountability to perform the many daily, weekly, and monthly tasks and activities involved in social media. Coordinating with the sales and marketing promotions calendar to let customers on Facebook and Twitter know of upcoming special sales and deals requires a good administrative specialist who is organized, collaborative, and interested in Facebook and Twitter. Creating a social media strategy for a team of diverse social media specialists requires a strong marketer with excellent management and communication skills. Monitoring a variety of online input from diverse audiences with social media tools like dashboards and analytic software requires someone with excellent technical and online skills, a keen interest in social media, and a love of numbers and trends. These and other social media management roles have developed to work collaboratively within the framework of creating and maintaining social media experiences.

Developing a Social Media Team

Marketing expert Heidi Cohen says that companies require strong teamwork from an integrated social media team for successful social media development. She advises building a social media team with experienced professionals in the areas of social media content marketing, social media engagement, and social media analysis. Those experienced in social media content marketing include writers, editors, graphic designers, and those who work with new technology such as search engine optimization specialists and social media technology specialists to help navigate the technology of channels like Facebook and Twitter. Social media engagement specialists are drawn from social media experts used to working with social media platforms and audiences such as community managers, customer service specialists who are used to resolving problems and keeping customers happy, and sales and legal specialists who know the products or services and the legal aspects of operating in social media. Social media analysis specialists are especially important on social media teams for monitoring and reporting so trends are spotted and hot spot issues such as excessive negative comments are dealt with as they come up, as well as reporting return on investment. Cohen explains that social media team development depends on the size of the organization and the company's social media and business goals, and that many social media team members perform multiple functions.

Nate Riggs, online marketer and social media strategist for Bob Evans Farms, Inc., suggests building a social media marketing team that includes listening analysts, content engineers, conversational marketing agents, and team captains. He emphasizes how important listening is in social media, and that social media teams must include members who know keyword strategies, search techniques and RSS, and how to use them to "listen" to or monitor social media activity. He describes content engineers as experts of written, photo, video, and audio content strategy and execution. Conversational marketing agents, also called community managers, focus on engagement in various platforms and manage it through a wider view than other social media team roles. Riggs describes team captains as having an analytic role, tracking and reporting on metrics and having project management abilities and responsibilities.

Every social media team is different, depending on the business and the size and scope of the social media projects it supports, but should include a variety of specialists with knowledge and experience in social media technologies and applications. Social media teams need to be aligned with business goals and are often embedded in sales and marketing.

SOURCES OF ADDITIONAL INFORMATION

Structuring a Social Media Team. www.ragan.com/Main/StructuringaSocialMedia Team.pdf.

How to Build an All-Star Social Media Team. www.salesforce.com/uk/social-success/social-media-how-to-guides/how-to-build-all-star-social-media-team.jsp

BIBLIOGRAPHY

Agranoff, C. & Tabin, H. (2011). *Socially elected: how to win elections using social media*. Pendant Publishing.

Arnold, J., Becker, M., Dickinson, M. & Lurie, I. (2012). *Web marketing all-in-one for dummies*. Hoboken, NJ: John Wiley & Sons, Inc.

Barger, C. (2011). *The social media strategist: Build a successful program from the inside out*. New York: McGraw-Hill.

Beckis, A. (2012). *Facebook marketing: your social media campaigns using Facebook's 2012 additions*. [Kindle Edition]

Bingham, T., Conner, M. & Pink, D. (2010). *The new social learning: A guide to transforming organizations through social media.* San Francisco: ASTD & Berrett-Koehler.

Bradley, A. & McDonald, M. (2011). *The social organization: How to use social media to tap the collective genius of your customers and employees.* Boston, MA: Harvard Business School Publishing.

Breakenridge, D. (2012). *Social media and public relations: Eight new practices for the pr professional.* Upper Saddle River, NJ: FT Press.

Burns, M. (2012). *You're a what?! Decoding today's job titles.* Retrieved February 17, 2013, from http://www.thedailymuse.com/job-search/youre-a-what-decoding-todays-job-titles/

Chandler, S. (2012). *Own your niche: Hype-free internet marketing tactics to establish authority in your field and promote your service-based business.* Gold River, CA: Authority Publishing.

Chase, L. & Knebel, K. (2011). *The social media sales revolution: The new rules for finding customers, building relationships, and closing more sales through online networking.* New York: McGraw Hill.

Christian, M. (2012) *Social media jobs guide: How to get a job working in social media!* [Kindle Edition].

Cohen, H. (2012). How *to build your social media team.* Retrieved February 17, 2013, from http://heidicohen.com/how-to-build-your-social-media-team/

Deckers, E. & Lacy, K. (2012). *Branding yourself: How to use social media to invent or reinvent yourself.* Indianapolis, IN: Que Publishing.

Dessi, C. (2012). *Your world is exploding: How social media is changing everything—and how you need to change with it.* Las Vegas, NV: CreateSpace Independent Publishing Platform.

Dragon, R. (2012). *Social marketology: Improve your social media processes and get customers to stay forever.* New York: McGraw Hill.

Falls, J. & Deckers, E. (2011). *No bullshit social media: The all-business, no-hype guide to social media marketing.* Indianapolis, IN: Que Publishing.

Flynn, N. (2012). *The social media handbook: Rules, policies, and best practices to successfully manage your organization's social media presence, posts, and potential.* Hoboken, NJ: Pfeiffer an Imprint of Wiley.

Gattiker, U. (2012). *Social media audit: Measure for impact.* New York: Springer.

Harrin, E. (2010). *Social media for project managers.* [Kindle Edition]

Hinchcliffe, D. & Kim, P. (2012). *Social business by design: Transformative social media strategists for the connected company.* San Francisco, CA: Jossey-Bass.

Holloman, C. (2012). *The social media MBA: Your competitive edge in social media strategy development and delivery.* West Sussex, UK: John Wiley & Sons, Inc.

Jones, P. (2012). *How to become a social media manager.* Scotts Valley, CA: CreateSpace Independent Publishing Platform.

Kabani, S. & Brogan, C. (2012). *The zen of social media marketing: An easier way to build credibility, generate buzz, and increase revenue: 2012 edition.* Dallas, TX: BenBella.

Kerpen, D. (2011). *Likeable social media: how to delight your customers, create an irresistible brand, and be generally amazing on Facebook (and other social networks).* New York: McGraw-Hill.

Kerpen, D., Braun, T. & Pritchard, V. (2012). *Likeable business: Why today's customers demand more and how leaders can deliver.* New York: McGraw Hill.

Macarthy, A. (2012). *500 social media marketing tips: essential advice, hints and strategy for business: Facebook, Twitter, Pinterest, Google+, YouTube, Instagram, LinkedIn, and more!* [Kindle Edition]

Madia, S. (2011). *The social media survival guide for political campaigns: Everything you need to know to get your candidate elected using social media.* [Kindle Edition].

Mason, C. (2011). Social media success in 7 days. Watford, UK: Inspired Press.

Mattern, J. (2011). *You're a social media whatsit? An overabundance of social media job titles.* Retrieved February 17, 2013, from http://socialimplications.com/youre-a-social-media-whatsit-an-overabundance-of-social-media-job-titles/

McHale, R. (2012). Navigating social media legal risks: safeguarding your business. Upper Saddle River, NJ: Pearson Education, Inc.

Meerman Scott, D. (2011). The new rules of marketing & PR: How to use social media, online video, mobile applications, blogs, news releases, and viral marketing to reach buyers directly. Hoboken, NJ: John Wiley & Sons, Inc.

Mergel, I. & Greeves, B. (2012). *Social media in the public sector field: Designing and implementing strategies and policies.* San Francisco: Jossey-Bass.

Meyerson, M. (2010). *Success secrets of social media marketing superstars.* Irvine, CA: Entrepreneur Media, Inc.

Morgan, J. (2011). *Report: The state of corporate social media.* Retrieved February 17, 2013, from http://www.cmswire.com/cms/enterprise-20/report-the-state-of-corporate-social-media-011192.php

Nicholls, S. (2011). *Social media in business: Succeeding in the new internet revolution.* London: Bookinars.

Null, L. (2011). *Social media management.* Scotts Valley, CA: CreateSpace Independent Publishing Platform.

Padron, K. (2012). *How to create a perfect social media team.* Retrieved February 17, 2013, from http://socialmediatoday.com/katrinapadron/435909/how-create-perfect-social-media-team

Porterfield, A., Khare, P. & Vahl, A. (2012). *Social marketing elearning kit for dummies.* Hoboken, NJ: John Wiley & Sons, Inc.

Qualman, E. (2012). *Socialnomics: How social media transforms the way we live and do business.* Hoboken, NJ: John Wiley & Sons, Inc.

Reinders, A. & Freijsen, M. (2012). *The e-factor: Entrepreneurship in the social media age.* Dallas, TX: BenBella.

Riggs, N. (2010). *A simple framework for building your social media marketing team.* Retrieved February 17, 2013, from http://contentmarketinginstitute.com/2010/08/a-simple-framework-for-building-your-social-media-marketing-team/

SalesForce.com's *How to build an all-star social media team.* Retrieved February 17, 2013, from http://www.salesforce.com/uk/socialsuccess/social-media-how-to-guides/how-to-build-all-star-social-media-team.jsp

Sweeney, D. (2012). *Building a great social media team.* Retrieved from http://socialmediatoday.com/deborah-sweeney/508431/building-great-social-media-team

Smith, D. (2012). Promote your business or cause using social media: a beginner's handbook. Scotts Valley, CA: CreateSpace Independent Publishing Platform.

Smith, N. & Zhou, C. (2011). *The social media management handbook: Everything you need to know to get social media working in your business.* Hoboken, NJ: John Wiley & Sons, Inc.

Turner, J. & Shah, R. (2010). *How to make money with social media: An insider's guide on using new and emerging media to grow your business.* Upper Saddle River, NJ: FT Press.

Weber, L. (2011). *Everywhere: Comprehensive digital business strategy for the social media era.* Hoboken, NJ: John Wiley & Sons, Inc.

White, C. (2011). *Social Media, Crisis communication, and emergency management: leveraging web 2.0 technologies.* Boca Raton, FL: Taylor & Francis Group.

Widman, J. (n.d.). *Multiple photo posts increased clicks 1290% - Facebook case study.* Retrieved February 17, 2013, from http://www.convinceandconvert.com/facebook/multiple-photo-posts-increased-clicks-1290-facebook-case-study/

Market Segmentation

In This Essay

■ Social media allows businesses to engage with their consumer base, build brand loyalty, and connect with niche markets

■ Social media marketing is a long-term, highly strategic process

■ The key to targeted marketing remains the one-on-one relationship

■ Businesses segmenting the market should focus on one of three business-related considerations: profit, behavior, or benefit, as the primary targeting tool for direct to consumer marketing and tracking

■ As technology advances, companies must use new and varied platforms, networks, and devices to connect with their target audience

Targeting Markets Through Specific Social Media Trends

Two main innovations are altering the current face of marketing: the evolution of online communities and continuing improvements in technology. The proliferation of the Internet has fostered the growth of social media and modified the initial purpose of their attendant cliques. Simultaneously, advancements in analysis software have enabled marketers to compile detailed descriptions of Internet users: the sites they visit, the purchases they make, and the recommendations they make to others. Marketers can take advantage of these advancements to target users and create communities that are loyal to their own brands.

Properly respected and used, the cliques that sprout up around an organization's online presence can be more than just a conglomeration of potential and actual purchasers of products. Each of these communities is akin to a living organism, a growing, evolving, and interconnected web of creators, producers, users, and sharers. Complying with the dictates of the social media culture, astute businessmen can fashion these specialized communities into the best, most efficient targeted marketers of any organization's products.

History of Targeted Marketing

Targeted marketing as a segment of business strategy is almost 100 years old. In 1915, Ernest Elmo Calkins showed examples of periodicals of the day to disparate groups of readers. His landmark textbook, *The Business of Advertising*, advocated sorting consumers into categories for more effective ad campaigns (Turow, 1997).

By the 1920s, product differentiation accelerated the process of targeted marketing. Businesses creating product lines that ranged in price wanted to spend their advertising budgets in the most efficient manner by featuring these products in ads on radio stations and in magazines that served consumers at the appropriate income levels. Research companies facilitated the process of matching the appropriate medium to the appropriate consumer through analysis of the purchasing and recreational habits of the consumers of specific radio stations and periodicals. The rise of computing power and the widespread adoption of cable television throughout the 1970s further spurred this narrowcasting of advertising (Turow, 1997).

Throughout the latter part of the twentieth century, the marketing strategy comprised targeting consumers as specifically as possible. The goal was to persuade consumers that a particular product would enhance their personal lifestyle. As marketers emphasized the shared interests, income, and beliefs of their segment of the potential customer pool, communities of like-minded consumers were born. Discerning marketers endeavored to create a "must-see, must-read, must-share mentality" that would inspire a feeling of kinship in far-flung partakers of media (Turow, 1997).

Meanwhile, the Internet was growing in popularity. Social media allowed Internet users to build online communities that paralleled their real-life relationships. As the consumer base began to shift its attention to social media, marketers followed.

Social Media Marketing

Social media describes the creation and fostering of relationships, the ability to participate in conversations, and the tribal identity that has arisen through the use of online networks. It is based on trust, and authenticity and transparency are bywords. In a world where consumers have grown skeptical and resistant to blatant advertising attempts by marketers, where users have become accustomed to controlling their own access to messages, businesses are realizing that they must evolve along with their customers. They must do more than tout a product. They must provide content that is relevant and ideas and concepts that resonate with the influential people online. They must minimize time-wasters, or they face the prospect of watching their base slip away. As consumers exercise their ability to tune into messages that they find interesting and click away from irrelevant postings, companies are being held to a higher standard of partnership with their customers (Chaney, 2009).

Social media marketing is "one of the most efficient forms of marketing in the world" (Quinn, 2012). Social media evolved as a means for friends to connect with friends, sharing information that they deemed relevant. Successful marketers provide content that users want to pass on to others. The biggest mistake marketers make is to excessively tout their products instead of eliciting excitement in consumers through creative use of material. The content that marketers post must be consumer-oriented, not business-oriented (Garland, 2010).

The goal of consumer-focused marketing is to discover what people are already engaged in, then introduce these potential consumers to those products that will make their lives easier or richer. Online social media marketing enhances this process by allowing businesses and consumers to interact directly. However, the nature of social media has irrevocably altered the traditional relationship between business and consumers. No longer do businesses merely feed data to consumers. Social media allows consumers to respond, and business and consumers then engage in a two-way conversation (Chaney, 2009; Lambert, 2009). Marketers who consciously replicate the methods used in social media to build connections simultaneously build *brand loyalty* (Quinn, 2012).

Brand loyalty: *A situation when a consumer is reluctant to switch from consumption of a favored good.*

The Nature of Online Communities

Consumers log on to the Internet for many reasons. Most times, they want to find information, learn about a concept they find interesting, solve a problem, or be entertained or inspired (Garland, 2010). When they seek information, they expect to find it. Businesses that provide expertise become assets to an online community, and these engagements lead networks to develop an alternative purpose to building connections with friends (Galagan, 2010).

Social media has come to foster an atmosphere of community and trust through making connections. Marketers who post content on a regular basis build long-term relationships with users (Chaney, 2009), as frequent updating tends to keep members engaged and provides them with information to share with others. Due to the nature of social media, these online conversations tend to be informal. News items posted by businesses that are told in the first person give an aura of immediacy, lending credence to the corporate story (Cavicchia, 2012).

Conversely, customer feedback provides valuable information to marketers (Brogan, 2010). Social media gives a voice to each member of a community, and businesses that listen to those voices discern ways to serve their customers in a way that meets their needs (Brynko, 2011). As Dell Computers advises, "Customers are in control. Work with them and learn from them" (Chaney, 2009).

Marketers must remember that each social network has its own structure. Engaging in a social network without sufficient understanding of its underlying structure may result in a strategy that results in a negative outcome for the corporate brand. People expect businesses to have a profile on LinkedIn for professional credibility. Facebook combines business and personal in "business casual," and Twitter is "after-hours social networking events" (Chaney, 2009).

Clustering

Each social network created a cluster of relationships. To successfully inform the launch of a new product, marketers need to elicit the inherent cliques in a network to identify the primary influencers and target them (Hansen, Shneiderman, and Smith, 2010). Data mining evidences the connections between users, showing the so-called superstars at the center of many links (Galagan, 2010). From there, spokes jut out to the next level of influence (Hansen, Shneiderman, and Smith, 2010). Interconnectivity between members of the community, spurred by tagging efforts (Russell, 2011), creates a web of sharing.

Marketers must identify tribe leaders, gate keepers, decision makers, and thought leaders in their industry, and follow all of them. The goal is to be seen as a peer in customers' eyes, as one who shares a stake in the successful outcome of a brand with the members of the community. To this end, collaboration with network superstars is an important part of the marketing process (Jackson, 2012). Experienced marketers focus their efforts on determining who is being followed and how often their posts are shared (Lambert, 2009) to maximize their marketing efforts.

Research in this area includes a focus on the aspects of soft partitioning, noting the multiple categories into which users may be placed, and longitudinal partitioning, which follows the evolution of clusters over time. Marketers may apply different algorithms to portray alternative clusters, depending on the emphasis placed on the sub-categories in which users are placed (Hansen, Shneiderman, and Smith, 2010).

Also of significance to marketers is the psychology of the social network (Hansen, Shneiderman, and Smith, 2010), how users influence each other, and the ways in which marketers can harness the interconnectedness of the members of a community. Social networks encourage collaboration. They provide a means to carry on a conversation between users who share an interest in a particular topic. The lack of central planning and the eagerness to share knowledge and expertise provides an excellent opportunity for marketers willing to post meaningful content and allow the community to exercise its creative voice (Brogan, 2010).

Educate, Entertain, Inspire

Social media marketing involves a long-term, highly strategic process. Social networks were established to allow connections between users, and that is still considered to be their primary purpose. Marketers must accept the restrictions of this marketplace to be successful. Posting content online is only effective if it is part of an overall strategy to build relationships with customers. Marketers must prove their worth before making their pitch. They must educate, entertain, or inspire their audience before that audience will be receptive to any claims regarding the efficacy of any product (Garland, 2010).

In the initial phase of establishing an online presence, businesses can provide free valuable information to consumers in exchange for the opportunity to build a database for ongoing marketing campaigns. Once a marketer has determined the level of interest for a particular brand, users' desire for expert information about that product can be satisfied through consistent updates and helpful tools (Garland, 2010). Fulfilling that need builds brand loyalty, as postings are opt-in opportunities rather than ads that are force-fed to unwilling recipients (McEntee, 2003).

Posting content on social media networks increases the perceived expertise of a business (Doherty, 2010). If a business abides by the 90/10 rule, in which 90% of content comprises useful, relevant information, consumers will accept overt advertising in the remaining 10%. More acceptable are native ads, which are inserted into the stream of posts as though they comprise mere content. Native ads illustrate the benefit of convergence, in which the lines between useful information and advocacy of a product are blurred (Holmes, 2012).

The key to successful targeted marketing remains the one-on-one relationship. Social media makes such relationships possible (Garland, 2010). Marketers can use social media in four ways (Williams, 2012) that build on each other to establish connections with network users:

- Create a social media community. Marketers who assist the members of a network through providing useful information gain influence.

- Enable conversation by providing apps and tools that assist in navigating the networks. Connections between social media lead to acceptance of the brand.

- Participate in online discussions. Provide expertise where it is warranted and requested.

- Add a widget. These apps personalize brands.

Targeted Marketing B2B

Marketers must employ alternate means of communicating with each of the three types of Business to business (B2B) customers (Brogan, 2010) using the Internet:

- Private customers, who prefer to remain anonymous to other members of the network community. This type of customer is amenable to private email newsletters.

- Newcomers, who are searching the web for prospective business partners. These customers need general information in the form of blogs and podcasts, along with specific-to-their-industry content that shows expertise in the field they need.

- Clean slate customers, who are currently merely browsing. Useful content that is interesting and invites further investigation is intriguing to them.

Online, marketers have the incredible ability to follow businesses and individuals on networks and to join industry groups. They can respond to news stories with information that prospective customers may find valuable. Joining groups that reflect their ideal customer, as well as groups that encompass other personal and professional interests of the marketer, provide unprecedented access to people who will be receptive to sharing the information they post (Hensley, 2011).

Targeted Marketing DTC

Once marketers segmented consumers by demographics, but further research has exposed the fallacy in using this method as the primary targeting tool for direct to consumer (DTC) marketing. Although demographics still plays a part, it has become secondary to other considerations. For Till and Heckler (2008), segmentation of the market should focus on one of three business-related considerations: profit, behavior, and benefit.

Different customers provide different profit opportunities to a particular business, due to their volume of business, their indifference to discounts, their brand loyalty, or their connections to other potential consumers. Alternatively, customers may be targeted based on some behavioral characteristic that corresponds to a particular attribute of the brand. Benefit segmentation describes a factor inherent in the brand that attracts customer attention.

Once segmentation has narrowed the concept of the ideal customer, demographics provide secondary characteristics of the target market. Demographics include such attributes as "age, income, household size, education, gender, and marital status" (Till and Heckler, 2008). Further identification of the target market includes geographical location and psychographics (Till and Heckler, 2008). Geography refers to any size location from a local neighborhood to the east coast to a particular country. Psychographics is the distillation of values, lifestyles, and attitudes of the target audience

(Yankelovich and Meer, 2006). Identifying a target audience with specificity allows an astute marketer to create a compelling brand that speaks to all members of that audience (Till and Heckler, 2008).

Perceptive marketers will allow a target audience to self-identify in a group of potential consumers through advertising a free service or product. Motivated consumers will respond to this form of behavioral marketing (Walmsley, 2007), and a marketer can use that interest to amass data about shared characteristics of those who participated (McEntee, 2003).

More focused on consumer attributes than benefits to business is the Sproles and Kendall Consumer Style Inventory (CSI) Model (Azizi and Makkizadeh, 2012). The CSI Model is based on 12 personality styles, which inform consumer choice and brand loyalty, and can be used as segmentation tools. Different factors tend to dominate depending upon the price of a product. Consumers emphasize price sensitivity and brand loyalty when purchasing functional items, but defer to deeply held beliefs when deciding between life-altering choices (Yankelovich and Meer, 2006).

Although not a primary characteristic, age does tend to have an effect on consumer preference. Snyder (2002) has identified distinct market segments based on the belief systems of older adults. Research on values-based behavior segmentation shows that it is statistically accurate, and that values stay constant over time. Marketing can attract or repel an older audience based on the values emphasized.

Alternatively, tweens (children between the ages of approximately 9 and 12) are extremely brand conscious. They are also greatly influenced by peers because of the formulation of identity that occurs at this stage of life. Tweens respond to marketing that amuses or entertains, or appeals to their technological abilities (Martin and Prince, 2012; Passman, 2012).

In between these age extremes, young consumers relate to brands that appear to be socially and environmentally responsible. They prefer to purchase products that have the potential to improve the planet. Marketers connect with these consumers by posting creative, humorous, original content on social media in an authentic, consistent manner (Carter, 2011).

Targeting marketers need consumer data for more than extant products. They rely upon the ability to discern consumer characteristics to fuel product innovation, price, and distribution channels, as well. Analysis of the consumer decision-making style (CDMS) provides key insights when developing market strategy (Yankelovich and Meer, 2006).

The Importance of the Brand

Above all, the marketer must be passionate about the *brand*. It is this passion that entices customers to try a product (Brogan, 2012), passion that supplies the perceived connection to the individual behind the brand. For this reason, completing a profile prior to launching an effort on social media is vital (Chaney, 2009). Instilling a brand with characteristics, especially actual personality traits, will bring that brand to life for consumers. An interesting personality creates an emotional connection with consumers (Till and Heckler, 2008).

In addition, the more complete the profile and the more detailed and descriptive the summary and specialty profiles are, the more credibility will be granted to any expertise presumed by the business (Hensley, 2011). Facts and knowledge create an intellectual connection with consumers (Till and Heckler, 2008) that complete the business' persona in the mind of the consumer.

In creating that persona, simplicity is the watchword for astute marketers. A brand must be simple, focused, and immediately recognizable to stand out from the crowd of brands that face the modern consumer on a daily basis. More than three characteristics will tend to muddle the brand, whereas demonstration of a meaningful difference in a brand gives its customers a reason for pride. A brand that evokes pride in its followers earns undying loyalty (Till and Heckler, 2008).

Brand: *Name, term, symbol, sign, or design used by a firm to differentiate its offerings from those of its competitors.*

Blogs as Marketing Tools

Once a brand has been established, *blogs* allow the unfolding of the corporate story commensurate with the marketing strategy. Through their encouragement of rebuttal, sharing, and additional content, blogs foster collaboration between a business and its customers, both existing and potential (Brogan, 2010). Socially oriented widgets and plug-ins uplift the blogging experience to almost social media niche-level status. Used as an integral part of a marketing strategy, blogs can provide a ready, engaged audience for a business.

In addition, the dominant bloggers in an area of focus are a part of the larger community that the marketer hopes to influence. These bloggers can assist in the creation of a community of followers tied to and loyal to a particular brand. The followers are then empowered to provide feedback, partake in the conversation and share ideas. Members of a successful

Blogs: *A website on which an individual or group records opinions, information, etc., on a regular basis. Short for web log.*

business community's blog become the voice of that brand, spreading the word about that brand far more effectively than any ad campaign could, providing the best use of a company's advertising budget (Chaney, 2009).

The focal point of any marketing strategy is the persona that exemplifies the ideal consumer of the brand. Once this persona has been created, blog posts and content can then be targeted towards that imagined representative of the community. All content related to the brand needs to be of the highest caliber, posted daily, with keywords "optimized and topically relevant." Consistent communication is vital to keeping the community and its purpose in the forefront of consumers' interests. The business must provide sufficient content for users to consume and react to, and encourage active engagement by the members of the community (Chaney, 2009).

Niche Social Networks

As social media has matured, niche social networks have sprung up (Chaney, 2009). These micro-networks, or Nings, generally focus on a specific topic. Some of these Nings are industry- or trade-specific, which can provide a wealth of information for B2B marketers about issues within the industry, including identification of the leaders and the structure and strength of business relationships (Lambert, 2009). The future of targeted marketing is in the niche networks, as the size of the audience has given way to who is participating in the conversation (Chaney, 2009).

The best niches for data mining by marketers share key elements. The users are passionate about their niche topic, the topic is sufficiently specific to maintain focus among the members of the community, and there is a plethora of material from which to create content (Garland, 2010). Once marketers have investigated the available niche networks, they are poised to develop their own, including such types (Chaney, 2009) as:

- Product-related niches are designed to enable members to interact with their peers, discover new ways of doing business, and learn ways to use software more efficiently and effectively. These communities provide a mix of educational content, articles from experts, and discussion forums to allow member interaction.

- Employee communities give employees a voice and an ownership stake in the company.

- Vendor/partner communities facilitate communications between the business and its partners, provide for the sharing of best practices, strengthen partner relationships, and provide a channel for customer service and support.

Technology

As technology has grown more sophisticated, marketers have been able to target users of the Internet based on the manner of their connection to the virtual world: their location, their choice of default language, and the times of the day and the week they logged on (Walmsley, 2007). In addition, the same technology that drives search engines provides marketers with a wealth of information to be exploited (Brogan, 2010). Embedded links connect networks to allow the convergence of otherwise unrelated information into meta-data (Brogan, 2010).

Marketers benefit from other advances in technology, in the increase in the types and power of different platforms and networks. Where once businesses were confined to text to create their online brand, they now have use of video and podcasts to tell their corporate story (Brogan, 2010).

Social Analysis

Social networks contain a great deal of information about competitors and consumers that can be discover through the use of social analysis tools and software (Brogan, 2010). The behavior of any particular member of a network can be plotted, from the identities of each group of which he is a member to his status in each of those communities. The interaction between users helps to pinpoint the key influencers for DTC marketers (Galagan, 2010). B2B marketers benefit from discovering the launch of new products and changes in corporate structure that can provide new leads for businesses (Lambert, 2009).

The logistics of any particular community can also be tracked to determine how focused it remains. Tags, comments, and images offer insight into shifting demographics and trends. A business that discerns that a community is fracturing may offer information and content that enables the extant self-correcting mechanism of social networks to be activated (Hansen, Shneiderman, and Smith, 2010).

The ability to discern patterns in seemingly unrelated information is the science of big data (Schwab, 2012). The myriad uses of big data are just now beginning to be tapped. Marketers are still striving to turn gigabytes of information into actionable policy on behalf of their companies. The next generation of technology, social media command centers, will assist in furthering this goal through their dedicated interfaces for tracking statistics in real time (Holmes, 2012).

Return on investment: *A performance measure used to evaluate the efficiency of an investment. It is usually expressed as a percentage or a ratio where return of an investment is divided by the cost of the investment.*

Consumer conversations and connections, not ad campaigns, are increasingly determinant of which content is shared. Marketers are employing analysis software and techniques to determine which content is relevant and engaging and to predict potential customer profiles. Compilations of data, analysis of statistics, and measurements of usage will be the determining factors in *returns on investments* (ROI) (Zoratti and Gallagher, 2012). However, marketers must carefully balance knowledge of their customers with the appearance of attaining too much information. Members of a community want to be known as individuals, but they do not want marketers to appear to be too interested in their online activities (Javelin Strategy, 2013).

Strategy Is Still Key

Relocating the advertising budget to the online venue does not mean that a business has the option to ignore the marketing knowledge that makes a business successful in the real world. Before attempting to embark on an online venture, any business must still determine the attributes of its ideal customer base (Chaney, 2009). Marketers must investigate which websites and networks are attractive to Internet consumers, and the manner in which those consumers interact with the local community (Lambert, 2013).

This behavioral targeting combines an "understanding of the brand, consumer insight and a fluency with the new media ecosystem" (Walmsley, 2007) to allow for strategic planning on an entirely different level than has been done in the past. Brian Halligan, CEO and co-founder of HubSpot, Inc., reminds businesses that, "The key to success is to measure often and evolve fast" (Brynko, 2011). Using this metric, even a once-staid industry has managed to engage younger consumers by urging them to purchase life insurance to provide for their families in case of a zombie attack. This strategy was successful due to the research and decision-making performed before the onset of the ad campaign (Passman, 2012).

Social Media Trends

Consumers are turning to social media to provide them with more answers than ever before. The impact on decision-making of opinions of online friends and influencers is increasing (Ganju, 2013), as is the tendency of users to rely on online networks for serious news.

As makes sense for information supposedly relayed by friends, informality is becoming the new tone (Cavicchia, 2012). The traditional hierarchical social order is being dispersed, replaced by a 'network culture' (Galagan, 2010), or 'tribe' (Jackson, 2012). From this culture, organic creative thought springs, such as the idea of "cash mobs," or using the purchasing power of flash mobs to help small businesses. The revolutionary aspect of this phenomenon is using social media to unite online communities with those in the real world (Robison, 2012). "Hyperlocal" is a new watchword, as consumers tether online connections to real-world business neighbors (Cavicchia, 2012).

Other connections will be made through augmented reality glasses that interface virtual reality with the real world. Increasingly, this sort of technology will become a factor in developing mobile apps and creating ad campaigns (Schwab, 2012).

Due to increased mobility, convergence has assumed a vital role in telecommunication technologies, as traditional online networks upgrade their services to provide meaningful content to mobile users (Technology Times, 2012). Mobile interfaces must be streamlined and fast-loading, while exploiting the technologies of GPS, near field communication (exchanging information by touching smartphones), and ambient location functionality (Holmes, 2012).

The invention and acceptance of mobile devices has been a game-changer for both users and marketers (Brynko, 2011). Visual platforms have assumed much more prominence in this arena, yet the ability to compress ads onto a greatly reduced viewing mechanism has proved elusive. (Holmes, 2012). Technology may eventually catch up in this area, but by that time, targeted marketing may have move on, as overt ads give way to the proliferation of native ads.

This unobtrusive content posts in-stream, and appears to be user-generated, except for the discretely placed necessary disclaimer (Holmes, 2012). As Chaney (2009) says, "In social media terms, the word 'community' is a better representation because we no longer 'target audiences,' but we 'participate in communities.'"

SOURCES OF ADDITIONAL INFORMATION

Blogger. www.blogger.com

Nextdoor. https://nextdoor.com

Top Five Niche Social Networks. http://computer.howstuffworks.com/internet/ social-networking/information/5-niche-social-networks.htm#page=0

BIBLIOGRAPHY

Azizi S., and Makkizadeh, V. (2012, April). Consumer decision-making style: the case of Iranian young consumers. *Journal of Management Research*, 4.2, p. 88. Retrieved January 13, 2013, from http://www.macrothink.org/journal/index .php/jmr/article/view/1222

Brogan, C. (2010). *Social media 101: tactics and tips to develop your business online.* Hoboken, NJ: John Wiley & Sons, Inc.

Brynko, B. (2011, July-August). SIIA NetGain: road trip for innovation. *Information Today*, 28.7, p.15. Retrieved January 10, 2013, from http://internet2807 .blogspot.com/2012/02/siia-netgain-road-trip-for.html

Business Wire. (2013, January 3). Financial services analyst firm recognizes top ten trends in banking, payments, mobile and security for 2013. *Javelin Strategy & Research Inc..* Retrieved January 10, 2013, from https://www.javelinstrategy.com/ news/1382/92/Financial-Services-Analyst-Firm-Announces-Top-Ten-Trends- in-Banking-Payments-Mobile-and-Security-for-2013/d,pressRoomDetail

Carter, B. (2011, August). Marketing to tweens and teens: insights, strategies and tactics. *The Licensing Journal*, 31.7, p. 1.

Cavicchia, M. (2012, Winter). Reporter, professor shares insights on the future of communications. *Bar Leader*, 36.2, p.13.

Chaney, P. (2009). *The digital handshake: seven proven strategies to grow your business using social media.* Hoboken, NJ: John Wiley & Sons, Inc.

de Mesa, A. (2005, October 11). Marketing and tweens. *Bloomberg Businessweek.* Retrieved January 13, 2013, from http://www.businessweek.com/ stories/2005-10-11/marketing-and-tweens

Doherty, K. (2010, July). A powerful marketing strategy to build your practice. *Acupuncture Today*, 11.7. Retrieved January 10, 2013, from http://www .acupuncturetoday.com/mpacms/at/article.php?id=32227

Galagan, P. (2009, September). Letting go: some examples of social media used successfully for informal learning do not come out of learning departments. *T+D*, 63.9, p. 26. Retrieved January 10, 2013, from http://www.questia .com/library/1G1-212767597/letting-go-some-examples-of-social-media- used-successfully

Galagan, P. (2010, May). Ready or not? Whether we like it or not, whether we use it or not, social media is changing the way we work. T+D, 64.5, p. 29. Retrieved

January 10, 2013, from http://www.questia.com/library/1G1-226163062/ ready-or-not-whether-we-like-it-or-not-whether-we

Ganju, N. (2013, January 8). Word of mouth. Business World. Retrieved January 10, 2013, from http://www.businessworld.in/en/storypage/-/bw/word-of-mouth/ 717568.37523/page/0

Garland, D. (2010) Smarter, faster cheaper: non-boring, fluff-free strategies for marketing and promoting your business. Hoboken, NJ: John Wiley & Sons, Inc.

Hansen, D., Shneiderman, B, and Smith, M. (2010). *Analyzing social media networks with NodeXL: insights from a connected world.* Burlington, MA: Morgan Kaufmann.

Hensley, R. (2011, March). LinkedIn tips for CPAs. *Journal of Accountancy*, 211.3, p.44. Retrieved January 10, 2013, from http://www.journalofaccountancy .com/Issues/2011/Mar/20103310.htm

Holmes, R. (2012, November 29). The can't-miss social media trends for 2013. *Fast Company*. Retrieved January 10, 2013, from http://www.fastcompany .com/3003473/cant-miss-social-media-trends-2013

Jackson, D. (2012, December 18). Social media trends for small businesses in 2013. *Social Media Today*. Retrieved January 10, 2013, from http://socialmediatoday. com/socialbarrel/1085906/social-media-trends-small-businesses-2013

Lambert, G. (2009, November-December). Harnessing free-flowing competitive intelligence through social media sites. *Law Practice*, 35.7, p. 26. Retrieved January 10, 2013, from http://www.americanbar.org/publications/law_ practice_home/law_practice_archive/lpm_magazine_articles_v35_is7_ pg26.html

Lazar, B. (2010, May). Drafting social networking policies. *Information Today*, 27.5, p. 20. Retrieved January 10, 2013, from http://socmedethics.files.wordpress .com/2011/02/drafting-social-networking-policies.pdf

Lippert, B. (2013, January 10). Keep tabs on social media trends in the new year. *Social Media Today*. Retrieved January 10, 2013, from http://socialmediato- day.com/benlippert/1142296/keep-tabs-social-media-trends-new-year?utm_ source=feedburner&utm_medium=feed&utm_campaign=Social+Media+To day+(all+posts)

Martin, N., and Prince, D. (2012, July). The tween consumer marketing mode: significant and recommended research hypotheses. *Academy of Marketing Studies Journal*, 16.2, p. 31.

McEntee, M. (2003, February 1). Health screening: a tool for today's marketers. *Medical Marketing & Media*, 38.2, p. 52.

Passman, A. (2012, December 24). Zombies breathe life into Gen Y marketing. *Credit Union Journal*, 16.51, p. 11. Retrieved January 10, 2013, from http://www.cujournal.com/issues/16_50/zombies-breathe-life-into-gen-y- marketing-1017044-1.html

Quinn, D. (2012, October 11). Op-Ed: A target audience-social media and marketing. *Digital Journal*. Retrieved January 10, 2013, from http://digitaljournal .com/article/334631

Robison, D. (2012, March 29). National trend 'mobs' local businesses with cash. *NPR*. Retrieved January 11, 2013, from http://www.npr.org/2012/03/29/149555396/national-trend-mobs-local-businesses-with-cash

Russell, M. (2011). *Mining the social web*. Sebastopol, CA: O'Reilly Media, Inc.

Schwab, S. (2012, December 6). Five Social Media Trends for 2013. *Social Media Explorer*. Retrieved January 10, 2013, from http://www.socialmediaexplorer.com/social-media-marketing/social-media-predictions-2013/.

Snyder, R. (2002, March-April). Market Segmentation: successfully targeting the mature population. *The Journal on Active Aging*, p.10. Retrieved January 13, 2013, from http://www.aahf.info/sec_news/section/pdf/marketsegmentation2.pdf.

Technology Times. (2012, December 31). Wateen CEO projects vitality of mobile marketing. *Technology Times,* 4.1. Retrieved January 10, 2013, from http://www.technologytimes.pk/2012/12/31/wateen-ceo-projects-vitality-of-mobile-marketing/

Till, Brian and Heckler, Donna (2008). *The Truth About Creating Brands People Love*. Upper Saddle River, NJ: FT Press.

Tsai, W. (2011, Fall). How minority consumers use targeted advertising as pathways to self-empowerment: gay men's and lesbians' reading of out-of-the-closet advertising. *Journal of Advertising*, 40.3, p.85.

Turow, J. (1997, November). Breaking up America: the dark side of target marketing: media that target specific groups of people are efficient ways to sell products. *American Demographics*, 19.11, p. 51.

Walmsley, A. (2007, February 28). Andrew Walmsley on digital: Behavioural change assails planning. *Marketing,* p. 15. Retrieved January 10, 2013, from http://www.tmcnet.com/usubmit/2007/02/28/2376718.ht.

Williams, J. (2012, February 29). Reaching Your Target Market Through Social Media. *Search Engine Journal*. Retrieved January 10, 2013, from http://www.searchenginejournal.com/reaching-your-target-market-through-social-media/56091/.

Yankelovich, D., and Meer, D. (2006) Rediscovering Market Segmentation. *Harvard Business Review*. Retrieved January 13, 2013, from http://d.yimg.com/kq/groups/10114558/1535182291/name/Week6.pdf.

Zoratti, S., and Gallagher, L. (2012). *Precision Marketing*. London: Kogan Page.

Choosing the Right Media for Your Social Media Campaign

In This Essay

■ A variety of social media platforms are available to be used for marketing campaigns

■ Twitter, Facebook, and LinkedIn are three of the largest social media websites and offer many advertising and marketing opportunities

■ Other websites and tools that can be used in social media campaigns for analytics and advertising

Overview

As of 2011, there were 2 billion social media users worldwide, according to University of California at Berkeley's Berkeley Center for New Media. With the growing popularity of social media, many companies have begun establishing a presence on social networking–related sites. Although being part of the social media network and blogosphere can be a valuable way to promote a company's products and services, certain social media outlets may prove a better fit than others for spreading the word. Different social media outlets offer different methods of posting, tracking results, and reaching out to prospective new clients. However, before a business begins to create a Facebook page or signs up for a Twitter account, creating a well thought-out, comprehensive social media plan can help ensure that the company's social media efforts provide the best possible return on investment.

Introduction

Social media sites offer new ways to connect and share information, and Internet users are embracing those new outlets to correspond with friends, family, and business acquaintances in great number.

A fall 2012 telephone survey conducted by the Pew Research Center's Internet & American Life Project found that 46% of adults who use the Internet in the United States post self-created videos or photos online; 41% of adults repost photos or videos they have found on sites where images are shared; 56% of Internet users either repost images or post original visual items; 32% do both.

Social media sites in particular seem to have illustrated a proven effect on consumers. According to a 2012 survey from parent-centric public relations company Child's Play Communications:

- 92% of mothers who use social media outlets were buying products because of social media recommendations. Mothers focus on Facebook more than any other social site (64% spend the most time on that particular social media outlet). However, the respondents also said blogs had the greatest influence on what items they ended up purchasing. Eighty percent of mothers use blogs as a resource.

- Twitter is a popular outlet—approximately 70% of small businesses use the site—but Facebook remains the top social media choice. Ninety percent of small businesses report they use Facebook, according to marketing service provider Vertical-Response Inc.

- Half (50%) of small businesses are on LinkedIn. Thirty-two percent are active on Google+. Only 29% were on Pinterest as of fall 2012.

- Whatever social media site they choose, many small businesses are posting frequently. Roughly a third said they published items on a daily basis—32% to Facebook and 29% to Twitter.

Blogs
Background

Blogging began in 1994. The verbiage morphed somewhat over the years. *New York* notes that by late 1997, the term "Weblog" was in use, thanks to blogger Jorn Barger; programmer Peter Merholz turned "Weblog" into "blog" a few years later in 1999. By the time the millennium rolled around, blogs had become a very profitable pastime. By 2005, 32 million

Americans were blog readers, and that same year, blog ad sales equaled approximately $100 million, according to *New York*. Today, blogging remains a popular way to frequently update site content and draw new visitors to websites. The pay-off can be big. A recent survey of attorneys showed that not only are more lawyers writing blogs, but also they're experiencing an increase in business as a result.

Business Use

Sites such as Blogger, WordPress, and Weebly allow users to set up free blogs that are easy to maintain using the site's content management system. Users can choose their blog design from a set of templates and can easily upload posts, photos, and other items to their blog. They can also review user statistics to monitor their blog's success and proof the blog to see how it will appear on a mobile phone using tools like Blogger's Mobile BlogSpot. To ensure the level of privacy users desire, most blog providers allow a user to limit blog readership to a specific audience or to open it to the general public. Because users can comment on blog posts, creating a blog allows companies to directly interact with their readers. Organizations can pose specific questions to readers to obtain their opinion on new products or services, ask for customer service improvement suggestions, and more.

Podcasts
Background

Podcasts, which Apple, one of the largest podcast providers, defines as "an episodic program delivered via the Internet," can be video or audio files and are usually downloaded to a computer or device to access. In addition to Apple, other outlets, such as NPR, offer podcasts. They are often transmitted using RSS, also referred to as Really Simple Syndication. The feeds offer blog and podcast producers a way to transmit frequently updated items, and users can subscribe to RSS feeds to automatically receive new content. Some services, including Apple's iTunes program, will regularly check and download updates that have been released since the last time a user logged in to download a podcast.

From the time of its introduction, podcast technology was an almost instant hit with listeners. In 2005, Apple's 4.9 version of iTunes debuted the iTunes Podcast Directory. Within two days of the release, iTunes customers had subscribed to more than one million podcasts (Apple Inc., June 30, 2005). Apple's iTunes store now features thousands of free podcasts. Users can search for new shows by popularity, subject, or title.

Getting Started

Podcasts are fairly easy to create. Business owners can use a number of programs, including Apple's GarageBand or QuickTime, and distribute their podcasts via a website or an outlet like the iTunes store.

A podcast should include keywords that accurately describe the podcast content to help listeners find it. Clear key terms imbedded in the podcast's *metadata* will help it show up in a top position in user searches.

Metadata: *Data that describes other data, or information about a certain item's content.*

Twitter
Background

Approximately 15% of adults who are online used Twitter as of February 2012, according to the Pew Research Center; 8% used the site daily. Pew reported that Twitter was steadily gaining followers, up 2% from May 2011. The amount of online adults who tweeted or read tweets on a daily basis increased even more. The number doubled from 2011 to 2012 and has quadrupled since 2010, when only 2% of Internet users accessed Twitter on a daily basis, according to Pew, which cites smartphone use as a possible reason for the increase.

Like Facebook and blogging sites, Twitter offers some potentially profitable promotional opportunities for companies in a variety of industries. The attorneys who reported finding that blogging could help lead to new clients, according to the American Bar Association's 2012 Legal Technology Survey, also seem to be turning to Twitter to promote firm services. In 2011, 7% of firms told ABA they had a presence on Twitter; in 2012, 13% were actively using the site, more than twice the 5% that said they had a Twitter account in 2010. As with blogs, larger firms of 100-plus attorneys were more likely to maintain a Twitter presence.

Getting Started

Twitter accounts are fairly simple to set up and maintain. Users need to sign up at Twitter.com by creating a username and password. Once signed up, they can follow other users, close friends, celebrities, or other publicly available accounts, as well as encourage friends and others to follow their posts.

Messages, or "tweets," must be 140 characters or less. Because brevity is an issue, including links to photo or websites in a tweet often requires users to create a shortened link using a website like bitly.com or tinyurl.com.

The general information section on Twitter highlights some of the business-related uses tweeting can provide: businesses can "quickly share information with people interested in their products and services, gather real-time market intelligence and feedback, and build relationships with customers, partners and influencers."

Other business-related uses include the ability for companies to send paid promoted tweets, which can help them reach users who are searching for certain terms on Twitter. The promoted tweets appear first on the results page and can also be customized by geographic location to allow locally based companies to reach specific audiences.

Promoted trends are another option businesses can use to market goods and services. Topics that are trending involve subjects that a large number of Twitter users are talking about. Trending items appear on a trend list on the site; paid placement near the top of the list is another option available to market products and services.

Companies can also purchase placement as a promoted account, which will be featured as a suggestion for Twitter users to follow.

Facebook
Background

Since debuting in 2004, Facebook's popularity has steadily increased. As of the fall of 2012, Facebook was the most popular social media website. Because of this, Facebook has not had to invest in much advertising. While approximately 60% of American adults use social networking sites, Facebook has managed to draw 66% of adults who are online, compared with other social media outlets (Pew Research Center's Internet & American Life Project, 2012). The social media site's popularity extends from personal interactions to business use, as well.

Fifty percent of Facebook users who have liked certain brands said they thought a company's Facebook page was more useful than its actual website, according to a 2012 survey from market research company Lab42. Because it provides a simple and free way to frequently post information, Facebook has helped companies that may not have a mega-million dollar marketing budget promote their work and reach new customers. Ninety percent of small businesses reported being active on Facebook, compared to 70% that said they used Twitter (Vertical-Response, 2012).

Regular updates appear to be the norm. Roughly one-third of respondents post to social networking sites on a daily basis; in regard to Facebook, 32% of small businesses post daily, according to VerticalResponse. Businesses may also benefit from offering deals via Facebook. Of the Facebook users who have liked a brand on the site, 77% said they were able to obtain savings by giving the brand a virtual thumbs-up. Lab42's survey found this incentive was a key reason for clicking on the like icon.

Getting Started

Businesses can create a page, which is slightly different than a social profile, to promote themselves by selecting from a list of categories—including local business or place; company, organization, or institution; brand or product; and cause or community. A company will need a Facebook account to create a page. Once the page is created, the company post items to the page under the name of the business.

According to Facebook, an unlimited number of business pages can be created. To build an audience, page owners can invite friends to their page or can add a "like" button to a website to encourage visitors to support their business.

Only officially denoted page managers can enter changes for Facebook business pages; however, page owners can add as many administrators as needed though an option on their Facebook page.

LinkedIn

Background

LinkedIn is a career-based social networking site founded in 2002 and launched in May 2003. Users post a profile resembling a resume containing detailed information about jobs they have had, volunteer work, education, and other attributes; they can link to and share their profiles with other professionals in the online networking community.

LinkedIn is a global site. In September 2012, 63% of members were located outside the United States. LinkedIn members reside in more than 200 territories and countries, according to LinkedIn. Membership has continued to expand since the site's launch; LinkedIn said it was getting two new members per second as of September 2012. The site also claimed to be the world's largest professional network, hosting more than 187 million members. As of August 2012, 20% of adult Internet users were using LinkedIn, according to the Pew Research Center's Internet & American Life Project. Interestingly, LinkedIn users are predominantly male with 63% men and 37% women making up the user demographic. (According to the Pew Research Center, social networking outlets typically have more women than men.)

In some industries, LinkedIn use outnumbers use of other social media entities. Eighty-eight percent of attorney firms, for example, are on LinkedIn, according to the American Bar Association's 2012 Legal Technology Survey. Only 55% of firms said they were on Facebook. Individual attorneys appear to be using LinkedIn even more than the firms they work for, with ABA reporting 95% of individual attorneys using LinkedIn.

Getting Started

Basic profiles are free to create. Users can purchase a premium subscription, which offers expanded profiles and additional ways to connect with people outside their network.

Many of LinkedIn's features are geared toward individuals who are either looking for a job or trying to network. However, several aspects of the site can help businesses with their Public Relations (PR) and Human Relations (HR) efforts.

Business can purchase ad space on the site and opt to target their ad toward certain industries, job titles, and other parameters by choosing what type of page on the site they would like the ad to appear on.

LinkedIn also offers employers the opportunity to promote jobs in a listing area on the site, and companies can recruit employees with specific qualifications through its LinkedIn Recruiter service.

Augmented Reality

Background

App: *Online, down-loadable programs or mobile applications for smartphones or tablets. Short for Application.*

Augmented reality devices offer a computer-generated, enhanced view of the user's environment. The technology can include inventive new items, such as the augmented reality glasses UK-based TTP (The Technology Partnership) has created, which, as *The Guardian* reported in September 2012, reflect and beam an image taken from a projector in the glasses' arm toward the eye or GPS data used in cars and smartphones. The glasses are not in production. However, some augmented reality items have already debuted, such as the Starbucks Cup Magic *app*. Calling augmented reality "a trick that uses digital information to enhance your real world environment," Starbucks premiered the app in November 2011. The Cup Magic app let Starbucks patrons point their phone to one of the coffee chain's holiday cups and create and send a video of an animation imposed on the cup to friends, family or other acquaintances. Starbucks also released a similar Valentine's Day-themed app in Febuary 2012.

Other companies have also created augmented reality apps, according to CNET. In 2011, The Krystal Co., a Chattanooga, Tennessee-based hamburger restaurant released one where its mascot danced; billboards in the U.K. for Domino's allowed customers to access an augmented reality menu to order pizza with their smartphones.

Getting Started

Although creating an augmented reality app requires an additional programming effort that is separate from creating a website, as creating an app of any kind may require hiring an external developer, businesses may benefit from the technology's "wow factor," or the properties of the technology that pleasantly surprise viewers.

Interest in augmented reality has grown in recent years, due in part to the increase in cell phones that come outfitted with GPS capabilities, according to market data provider Research and Markets.

Augmented reality's popularity is expected to increase further, according to Research and Markets "Offers Report: Augmented Reality: Global Market Analysis and Forecast 2012–2017," with the release of new products from Sony, LG, Samsung, Apple, Google, and other companies. The report also forecast that growth would occur as the result of new networks and increased use of cloud storage capabilities that help centralize and streamline storage and connectivity.

Google+

Background

Launched in 2011, the full impact and future potential of Google+ was still being gauged as of fall 2012. In September 2012, Google's Senior Vice President of Engineering Vic Gundotra posted a note on his account saying that Google+ had more than 400 million users. However, various media outlets ran articles in early 2012 citing a 2012 study that found Google+ users average just 3 minutes per month on the site—compared to 7.5 hours per month on Facebook, according to digital business analytics provider comScore.

According to data compiled from various sources, including Google, students have embraced the format and comprise 20% of Google+ users (siteimpulse, 2012). Software engineers are 2.65% of Google+ users. Regionally, a large number of Google+ users are located in India. Although the United States is the top Google+ country, India ranks a close second. Three of the top 10 Google+ cities are Hyderabad, Calcutta, and Bangalore (the number one Google+ city).

Getting Started

To create a Google+ profile, a person is asked to just enter a few piece of key information, including name, gender, and birthday at https://plus. google.com. Google requests permission during registration to personalize content you are shown based on your account information. This along with knowing subscribers' gender and age, can help companies better tailor their campaigns to reach specific audiences.

Google offers several suggestions for businesses to use Google+ to market and reach customers. Companies can use the social networking site to build a personal connection with new and previous customers. A company can increase its presence in Google searches by uploading pertinent photos, videos, and information about their products/services.

Groupon

Background

Groupon is the byproduct of a website called The Point, which offered functionality for people to launch a campaign to incite action or solicit donations. Since premiering in 2008, Groupon has offered a daily deal featuring a discount on local restaurants, activities, and services. The company, which is headquartered in Chicago, served 48 countries and employed approximately 10,000 employees at the end of 2012. In the years since Groupon's launch, other deep discount promotional sites, such as LivingSocial and Lifebooker, have also begun offering similar deals.

Getting Started

In addition to opportunities to advertise on the site, Groupon gives local businesses the chance to market their products and services to new customers by offering a deal through the site. According to February 2012 data from Foresee Daily Deal Commentary promoted on Groupon's site, 91% of its daily deal customers have conducted business with the merchant again or plan to do so.

However, deal sites have received some criticism in the media for possibly not providing stellar results to all companies.

A November 2012 San Francisco Chronicle article highlighted two businesses that reported either experiencing a loss per order or breaking even—and often not gaining the marketing value they had hoped for in the promotion.

Eighty-two percent of respondents in an October 2012 survey conducted by small business listing service Manta said they did not plan on offering a daily deal promotion in 2012, and just 3% felt daily discounts had earned them repeat customers.

Yelp!

Background

Local business review website Yelp.com was founded in 2004. Users can search for reviews on local service providers or post about their experience at local establishments. The user-generated reviews clearly struck a chord with Yelp's audience. By the third quarter of 2012, Yelp was averaging

84 million monthly unique visitors, according to the site, and more than 33 million local reviews had been added.

Getting Started

Businesses can take advantage of the site's access to more than 84 million unique monthly visitors to promote services and products. The site offers advertising opportunities for companies ranging from large corporations to small local businesses hoping to reach various neighborhoods. Ads can be purchased for certain search pages, so when users search for a term such as "soup," a local soup restaurant's ad will appear. Businesses can also place ads on pages where related businesses are profiled.

Business owners also have another, less conventional way of promoting their goods and services through the site. Although negative Yelp reviews, which come from site users and are not advertising-related, can cause issues for businesses, businesses also have the chance to perform some proactive public relations and respond to and counter any criticism.

In addition, business owners can set up a free account to connect with customers. To maintain the integrity of its content, ad space that is purchased on the site is clearly marked to avoid any confusion with the site's reviews.

Geolocation Tools

Background

Geolocation tools, such as the Foursquare app launched in 2009, offer users the chance to identify and broadcast their location. Facebook users can check into venues with them; Twitter also allows users to identify their position.

The functionality is a popular option; Foursquare, for example, has 25 million users worldwide.

Getting Started

Social media phone applications like Foursquare and Facebook include the functionality, allowing users to easily view suggested locations and choose their spot.

According to the Cooperative Association for Internet Data Analysis, geolocation tools can help businesses better focus their pricing and services to suit their local market. Businesses may benefit from setting up a Facebook page and ensuring there is only one official listing on the site, giving its exact address.

Foursquare offers its users an award, a "mayorship," for being the user who checks in most frequently over a 2-month period. Businesses may also benefit from promoting check-in goals or posting signage on-site that encourages customers to check-in online.

However, some users may be hesitant to use geolocation tools because they do present some privacy concerns. Being able to automatically identify a user's location and broadcast it through social media could put security at risk. While the tools can help users locate friends who are nearby, for example, they can also alert associates who have access to their profile that they are not at home.

Social Bookmarking

Background

Social bookmarking, also sometimes called tagging, helps users add, edit, and share online bookmarks by identifying them by certain terms, which helps them appear in searches. Popular social bookmarking sites include Delicious, founded in 2003 and relaunched in 2011, and Diigo, which bills itself as a social information network.

Saved bookmarks may be viewed publically or privately and can be emailed to other users.

Getting Started

Using most social bookmarking tools involves simple steps like adding a button to your browser to save links.

Individual bookmarking options may vary. Diigo, for example, lets users highlight portions of pages they would like to revisit, instead of just bookmarking the entire page, and uses sticky notes to add notes to pages.

Many social media sites offer businesses practical marketing applications. Adding relevant keyword tags to your company's blog posts can help improve the chance they will appear in searches and help promote company content through social bookmarking sites.

However, social bookmarking sites can also help companies conduct research and track their industry position. Businesses can use sites like Delicious to streamline the process of following industry news, including any mentions the company gets in the press (Red Giant Consulting, 2010).

YouTube and Vlogs
Background

Vlogs—or video blogs—offer many of the same benefits as blogs, with a stronger visual component.

The trend began in 2000, according to the book *Naked Lens: Video Blogging & Video Journaling to Reclaim the You in YouTube*, when Adam Kontras began showcasing his move from Ohio to Hollywood to launch a show business career.

Because camcorders and Internet use had by that time become popular and reasonably priced, and Internet access speed and downloading videos became a faster endeavor, vlogs grew in popularity.

In 2005, the vlog medium experienced strong growth, due in part to the founding of video site YouTube. On its launch, YouTube quickly became a popular destination, and by 2006, viewers accessed 100 million videos a day (Reuters, July 2006).

Getting Started

Vlogs let companies present a personalized view of their work and products to engage customers. Sites like YouTube, Blip.tv, and Vimeo, which allow users to offer a link to a video with a brief description, have helped vlogs gain viewers. Fans can post comments to interact with the vlogger; some also offer viewers the option of signing up for an RSS feed to keep updated on new posts.

YouTube offers a guide to setting up your own channel, which can serve as a portal for a company to post videos about its products and services, and then they can promote them to their customers by posting links to the videos on social media outlets like Facebook and Twitter.

File-Sharing Tools
Background

File-sharing tools like SlideShare and YouSendIt let users upload, and share PowerPoint presentations, Word documents, and PDF files publicly or privately. SlideShare boasted 60 million monthly visitors and 130 million pageviews as of 2012. According to YouSendIt, the service has millions of registered users in 193 countries.

Getting Started

YouSendIt offers free service or subscription plans to store and send a larger quantity of files. Businesses may specifically benefit from You-SendIt for Enterprise, a file-sharing solution designed to encourage business collaboration.

SlideShare PRO offers analytics tracking, the ability to create a custom look and feel for your SlideShare channel to fit your current branding, and other business-friendly options.

Companies can also find a number of tips on using SlideShare on the site itself. One posted presentation, for example, from digital marketing agency Spiderhousepr offers a dozen suggestions on maximizing your professional SlideShare presence, including keeping presentations short and incorporating your business name and URL early on in the presentation.

Pinterest

Background

Pinterest lets users create a virtual pinboard, to which they can add photos and other items of interest and share them with other registered users. According to a 2012 report from the Pew Research Center's Internet & American Life Project, women use Pinterest more often than men.

Getting Started

Once registered, the promotional opportunities are endless. Because the site is a visually driven social media outlet, companies that post frequent product or other images may experience a higher response rate from other users reposting the content.

You can also add other users as contributors to let them pin items to your board—and companies can easily add prices to the items they highlight. The site also hosts a library of information about how companies can use Pinterest to grow their business.

E-commerce Sites
Background

Sites like etsy.com, which has featured jewelry, books, and other creative goods from sellers since 2005; Amazon, the Seattle-based company that has sold online goods since 1995; and online marketplace eBay have helped individuals and small businesses find a sales outlet.

Getting Started

E-commerce sites can be a cost-effective way for small businesses or individual retailers to reach customers and sell goods.

Costs are generally reasonable but vary by site. For example, eBay lets sellers list a certain number of items for free each month, and charges for any additional auction items. An account must be created in order to set up sales. Some e-commerce sites also require that you ship items within a set time period.

SOURCES OF ADDITIONAL INFORMATION

Apple, Inc. www.Apple.com

Blogger. www.blogger.com

Delicious. https://delicious.com

Diigo.com. (2012). About Diigo (site information). Retrieved Nov. 25, 2012, from http://www.diigo.com/about

Groupon. (2012). About us (informational section on Groupon.com). Retrieved Nov. 25, 2012, from http://www.groupon.com/about

Twitter. (2012). About Twitter (informational section on Twitter.com). Retrieved Nov. 25, 2012, from https://twitter.com/about

Vimeo. http://vimeo.com

Wordpress. http://wordpress.org

Yelp. (2012). About us (informational section on Yelp.com). Retrieved Nov. 25, 2012, from http://www.yelp.com/about

BIBLIOGRAPHY

Amazon. (2012). Best sellers in novelty apps (Amazon ranking). Retrieved Nov. 24, 2012, from http://www.amazon.com/Best-Sellers-Appstore-Android-Novelty-Apps/zgbs/mobile-apps/2478858011

Ambrogi, R. (2012). ABA survey shows growth in lawyers' social media use. LawSites blog post on the American Bar Association Legal Technology Survey Report: Web and Communication Technology. Retrieved Nov. 24, 2012, from http://www.lawsitesblog.com/2012/08/aba-survey-shows-growth-in-lawyers-social-media-use.html

Apple. (2012). Podcast informational section on apple.com. Retrieved Nov. 24, 2012, from http://www.apple.com/itunes/podcasts/fanfaq.html http://www.apple.com/pr/library/2005/06/30iTunes-Podcast-Subscriptions-Top-One-Million-in-First-Two-Days.html

Arthur, C. (2012). UK company's "augmented reality" glasses could be better than Google's. *The Guardian*. Retrieved Nov. 24, 2012, from http://www.guardian.co.uk/technology/2012/sep/10/augmented-reality-glasses-google-project

Blogger.com. (1999-2012). Blogger tour (instructional section). Retrieved Nov. 24, 2012, fromhttps://www.blogger.com/tour_start.g

Brenner, J. (2012). Pew Internet: Social networking (full detail). *The Pew Internet & American Life Project* (highlights from recent research). Retrieved Nov. 24, 2012, from http://pewinternet.org/Commentary/2012/March/Pew-Internet-Social-Networking-full-detail.aspx

CAIDA. (2011). CAIDA's geolocation tools comparison. Retrieved Nov. 24, 2012, from http://www.caida.org/projects/cybersecurity/geolocation/

Child's Play Communications. (2012). How moms are using social media right now—and how you can make the most of it. Retrieved from http://www.childsplaypr.com/news/news_details.cfm?ID=102

Delicious.com. (2012). About (site information). Retrieved Nov. 25, 2012, from http://delicious.com/about

Dewey, C. (2012). Thanksgiving breaks instagram records. *The Washington Post*. Retrieved from http://www.washingtonpost.com/lifestyle/holiday-guide/thanksgiving-breaks-instagram-records/2012/11/26/52ae5cf2-3811-11e2-a263-f0ebffed2f15_story.html

eBay. (2012). Sell in 4 easy steps (site information). Retrieved Nov. 25, 2012, from http://pages.ebay.com/sellerinformation/howtosell/quickstartguide.html

Elliott, S. (2012). Study suggests a "7 Percent Solution" for mobile marketing. *The New York Times*. Retrieved from http://mediadecoder.blogs.nytimes.com/2012/08/29/study-suggests-a-7-percent-solution-for-mobile-marketing/

Etsy. (2012). Press (press kit). Retrieved Nov. 25, 2012, from http://www.etsy.com/press/

Facebook. (2012). Facebook help center (site information). Retrieved from http://www.facebook.com/help/

FourSquare. (2012). Can a business have more than one mayor? (site information). Retrieved Nov. 25, 2012, from http://support.foursquare.com/entries/196696-can-a-business-have-more-than-one-mayor

Gruber, T. (2010). 5 ways to use delicious.com. Tamara's Tech Marketing Tip Blog, Red Giant Consulting. Retrieved Nov. 25, 2012, from http://www.redgiantconsulting.com/2010/06/30/5-ways-to-use-delicious-com-in-your-business/

Kaminsky, M. S. (2010). *Naked lens: Video blogging & video journaling to reclaim the you in YouTube*. Organik Media. Retrieved Nov. 25, 2012, from http://books.google.com/books?id=grhR1eYswPkC&pg=PA37#v=onepage&q&f=false

Klein, K. E. (2012). Coupons not always good deal for sellers. *San Francisco Chronicle*. Retrieved Nov. 25, 2012, from http://www.sfgate.com/technology/article/Coupons-not-always-good-deal-for-sellers-4038343.php#ixzz2DIlCav00

Lowensohn, J. (2012). Starbucks' augmented reality app gets all lovey dovey. *CNET*. Retrieved from http://news.cnet.com/8301-17938_105-57372047-1/starbucks-augmented-reality-app-gets-all-lovey-dovey/

Manta. (2012). Small businesses are saying Ho Ho Ho this holiday season and predict an increase in sales (press release). Retrieved Nov. 25, 2012, from http://www.manta.com/media/holiday_survey_10302012

Morrow, C. (2011, April 11). 25 Slideshare marketing tips For B2B—Presentation transcript. Spiderhousepr. Retrieved Nov. 25, 2012, from http://www.slideshare.net/spiderhousepr/25-slideshare-marketing-tips-for-b2b

Rainie, L., Brewer, J., & Purcell, K. (2012). Photos and videos as social currency online. *The Pew Research Center's Internet & American Life Project* (report overview). Retrieved from http://pewinternet.org/Reports/2012/Online-Pictures.aspx

Rainie, L., Smith, A., Lehman Schlozman, K., Brady, H., & Verba, S. (2012). Social media and political engagement. *Pew Internet & American Life Project*, 9. Retrieved Nov. 25, 2012, from http://pewinternet.org/~/media//Files/Reports/2012/PIP_SocialMediaAndPoliticalEngagement_PDF.pdf

Research and Markets. (2012). Research and Markets' offers report: Augmented reality: Global market analysis and forecast 2012–2017 (press release). Retrieved Nov. 25, 2012, from http://finance.yahoo.com/news/research-markets-augmented-reality-global-100100118.html

Reuters. (2006). YouTube serves up 100 million videos a day online. *USA Today*. Retrieved Nov. 25, 2012, from http://usatoday30.usatoday.com/tech/news/2006-07-16-youtube-views_x.htm

Siteimpulse. (2012, February 14). Google+ facts and figures (infographic). Website-Monitoring blog. http://www.website-monitoring.com/blog/2012/02/14/google-facts-and-figures-infographic/

Smith, A., & Brenner, J. (2012). Twitter use 2012. *Pew/Princeton Survey Research Associates International*, 2–6. Retrieved Nov. 25, 2012, from http://www.pewinternet.org/Reports/2012/Twitter-Use-2012.aspx http://www.pewinternet.org/~/media//Files/Reports/2012/PIP_Twitter_Use_2012.pdf

Thompson, C. (2006). The early years. *New York*. Retrieved Nov. 25, 2012, from http://nymag.com/news/media/15971/

VerticalResponse small business social media survey. (2012). VerticalResponse press release. Retrieved Nov. 25, 2012, from http://www.verticalresponse.com/about/press/small-business-social-media-survey-results-infographic

Wasserman, T. (2012, February 28). Google Plus users spent just 3.3 minutes there last month *CNN*. Retrieved Nov. 25, 2012, from http://www.cnn.com/2012/02/28/tech/social-media/google-plus-comscore/index.html

Womack, B. (2012, February 27). Google+ users are spending just 3.3 minutes per month on site, ComScore says. *BloombergBusinessWeek*. Retrieved Nov. 25, 2012, from http://www.businessweek.com/news/2012-02-27/google-plus-users-are-spending-just-3-dot-3-minutes-a-month-on-site-comscore-says

Zuckerberg, M. (2012). The things that connect us (blog post). Retrieved Nov. 25, 2012, from http://www.facebook.com/photo.php?v=3802752155040

Internal Social Media Interfaces

In This Essay

- Internal social media, although not shared with the outside world, are important to many businesses
- Internal social media use all of the same components as external social media
- Internal social media is a way to get employees to consider themselves truly invested in a company

Overview

The key word in the phrase *social media* is usually assumed to be *social*, in the sense that collaboration among a wide range of users is considered to be the compelling reason for its use. In general this assumption is true. However, the *media* part of the process should not be overlooked. The tone, ease of use, and intended purpose of the interfaces that make social media possible are crucial aspects of the success or failure of any social media initiative.

Focus on media functionality is especially important when it comes to a business or organization's internal social media systems (also known as *enterprise social media*).

Internal social media systems use the same tools and basic technologies as public social media applications such as Twitter and Facebook. Rather than working across the wider Internet, however, they are built within an organization's internal network. In addition, their use is generally restricted to employees or organization members.

Despite these differences, the goals of internal social media are basically the same as the goals of the larger Internet social media. They similarly enable collaboration among users who may be divided geographically or across time zones, and they encourage engagement and communication. In terms of granting access, a business's internal social media networks are likely to be more restricted than Twitter or Facebook, for example, but open access to all users within the business's network also is a characteristic internal social media.

Internal social media platforms have many effective applications for outward-bound marketing. These range from inspiring employee advocacy to *crowd-sourcing* feedback and concepts for marketing campaigns, or perhaps deputizing all employees as part of an unofficial sales force. Although internal social media can be leveraged for inward-bound marketing *to* the employees or members of an organization, this in practice is often restricted to use by the organization itself (i.e., internal marketing of ideas and new policies). Certain characteristics of internal social media networks make effective inward-bound third-party advertising a challenge. These networks are usually closed, not allowing access outside of the company or organization, and the interface often involves proprietary software or heavily customized systems.

Crowdsourcing: *Obtaining services, ideas, or content by soliciting contributions from a large group of people especially the online community.*

Social Media in Its Simplest Form

Any company that uses an intranet or internal e-mail system is already using the most basic form of social media.

Despite its drawbacks as a social media tool, e-mail has proliferated as a means of internal communication in organizations of all sizes. Employees working in offices without access to other company-endorsed social media tools often turn to lengthy e-mail strings to collaborate and share ideas. Intranet networking speeds often make e-mails essentially instant and quoted forwarding keeps records of "comments" left by co-workers. E-mail is also harnessed as a primitive social media platform when users share and comment on PDF or Word documents.

The drawbacks of e-mail as a social media tool are obvious: The interface is designed at its core to be task-oriented and one-way in its messaging. Thus, collaboration is extremely slow as everyone must wait for the next response wave before changes are implemented. E-mail also eschews one of the main tenets of modern social media: The democracy of voices. When e-mail is used as a social media tool, it assumes a central authority through which all responses must pass and be evaluated.

As a result, when companies come to consider adding social media tools to help increase collaboration in the office, they usually eschew e-mail for more modern and robust solutions, whether they be so-called "freemium" services (which offer a basic level of the service free of charge, usually ad-supported, alongside a premium, ad-free level for a monthly charge, usually offering additional features), the common public social media tools such as Twitter or Facebook, a custom application built by a vendor, or a proprietary system created in-house.

Components of Internal Social Media

All internal social media interfaces have several components in common.

Chat

Instant messaging is a core component of any social media interface, including internal social media. Chat usually has both a public (viewable by either a specific group or by all users of the network) and a private aspect reserved for smaller groupings. E-mail is often integrated into the interface as well if the e-mail is retrievable from a remote server via IMAP (Internet Message Access Protocol) or retrievable over a standard Internet connection via POP3 (Post Office Protocol).

File Sharing

Collaboration in a business environment requires the easy access to documents associated with a project. Internal social media (ISM) systems allow documents to be organized and tagged, and allow for simultaneous real-time access and modification. More robust ISM platforms will also include a *content management system* (CMS) of some sort.

Content management system: *Software that manages maintenance of assets such as articles or images, tracking modification and recording metadata about changes such as user access and dates of revision.*

Project Home Page

Serving as a central place for general announcements and status updates, the project home page is also usually used to advertise the project and its progress to the wider network. It also commonly provides a dashboard of useful information such as which users are currently online and the most recent changes logged to the project documents and other materials.

Mobile Versions

For social media applications to be useful they must have a version available for both iOS and Android devices so they can be accessed on smartphones and tablets. Employees require the ability to respond to queries and solve problems from any location, often after hours or on weekends. Even when working with proprietary ISM networks, employees generally require a smartphone to access the system's complete list of features.

Common Internal Social Media Tools

Companies have many choices when it comes to implementing off-the-shelf social media tools within their organizations.

Tracky.com

Advertised as a social media interface that "bridges the gap between your personal and professional circles," Tracky is a free application available for the desktop and mobile phones. The main attraction of Tracky for businesses is that it reduces clutter by bringing all of the tools an employee might use for collaboration, such as e-mail, chat, event web pages, and file shares, together in one interface. Still considered to be in the testing phase as of this writing, Tracky is free with an option for a premium service for a monthly fee. Tracky also offers corporate-scale plans.

Basecamp

One of the more mature project-management/social media platforms available, Basecamp was launched in 2004. Basecamp is not a free service but it does offer a free trial of its project-management software. Its main attraction is its maturity and support.

CoLab

CoLab is a proprietary internal social network created by the ad agency Possible. Built entirely in-house, it incorporates the standard features of ISM: collaboration tools, chat and messaging tools, file sharing, and project home pages.

Chatter

Chatter was released by Salesforce.com in June 2010 and is billed as a real-time collaboration tool, pushing news out to users proactively instead of waiting for people to log in or check their messages. Chatter is available as both a free basic service and a premium service for a monthly fee. One potential negative regarding Chatter is that it designates moderators who have the authority to delete posts or users from a project. Many users feel that ideally social media tools should be fully decentralized, with no central authority.

Yammer

Launched in 2008 and purchased by Microsoft in 2012, Yammer is one of the most popular nonproprietary ISM platforms. Yammer uses the Internet domain included in organizational e-mail addresses to restrict use to members of that organization. The basic plan is free to use, but it offers two fee-based plans that offer more features.

Other

As internal social media continues to gain popularity, more companies are creating both custom ISM platforms and off-the-shelf offerings. In addition to the ISM products discussed above, other examples include software developed by SAP, Cisco Systems, and Jive Software, as well as products such as Socialtext and Socialcast.

ISM Marketing Strategies

Internal social media works particularly well for the execution of three kinds of marketing: inbound, outbound, and viral.

Inbound Marketing

Inbound marketing means the staff itself is the target audience. The message is crafted by either the organization (making announcements, describing strategies, or launching new product lines) or a third-party advertiser from outside the organization.

Internal social media is frequently used to market new policies, ideas, or products internally to staff. Announcements made via ISM systems encourage employees to share and discuss the new information, trade experiences, and analyze announcements. This takes a process that traditionally has been one-sided (announcements made via memorandum or e-mail blast) and transforms it into a collaborative moment where employees feel empowered to comment and interpret the information. This also allows management and other executive-level officers to respond immediately to questions, criticisms, or other feedback, further enhancing the employees' sense of ownership and empowerment.

Advocates The goal of inbound marketing is to create advocates for the new product or policy among the employees. Whether or not the employee is a member of a sales team, when the employee becomes an advocate, it means he or she will carry that advocacy both inside and outside the company. Internally this can speed the adoption of new tools, procedures, or projects among employees. Externally this can result in spreading positive word-of-mouth as employees take the excitement and conviction of new projects home with them and onto other social media networks.

Internal social media is perfectly suited to the creation of advocates among employees because it encourages the feeling of ownership that is essential to advocacy. Because employees are able to instantly share thoughts and information, they come to understand concepts more quickly and will often adopt new tools or applications more easily because they can see their colleagues doing so in real time.

Outbound Marketing

Reaching potential customers, whether they are individuals or businesses, is the goal of outbound marketing. Using internal social media for outbound marketing is more challenging than it is for internal marketing, but it is worth the effort for several reasons.

Deputies Internal social media is often by definition closed to the outside world and restricted to the members of an organization—the employees of a company, for example. Opening up an ISM network transforms it into a public forum, which is usually undesirable, and there are existing tools that can easily be used when a company seeks to make a public announcement.

By using internal social media, however, companies can deputize employees to perform this role. Employees can be extremely influential outside the company promoting the products and services it offers. Often the employees most engaged and excited by internal social media are equally engaged and active on public social networks such as Twitter and Facebook, and may be extremely influential within their social groups. The sense of ownership and engagement that an ISM grants employees can empower them as unofficial ambassadors or even sales-people outside the company's offices.

Beyond the simple promotion of products, employees are becoming the public faces of a company. Employees who go home at night and use social media to discuss aspects of their business life may make a good im-pression on potential customers, who then seek out the company solely because this employee impressed them. This new reality of the digital age makes internal social media essential both as a way to engage employees and as a way to deputize them as a de facto extension of the sales force.

Influence A key component of transforming employees into either depu-ties or advocates is measuring the influence of individual employees on the internal staff and on the external world. Some tools for carrying out this process do exist on the public social media networks such as Twitter, but they are not reliable. Klout, for example, is inconsistent in its ratings and often rates people as influential in subjects they admit they have no expe-rience with and have never tweeted about. Klout has often awarded high scores to robots as well, and its algorithm remains an obfuscated secret.

However, Klout remains one of the only tools available for measuring the influence of a particular social media user. Internally, an organization can attempt to create its own tools for measuring influence. Identifica-tion of influential employees both within and outside of an organiza-tion allows targeting of these employees for education on new products or initiatives. It also highlights likely starting points for possible viral marketing.

ISM and Exterior Marketing Internal social media platforms have prov-en to be invaluable in the coordination and planning of traditional customer-oriented marketing campaigns as well. The project-based focus of ISMs makes it possible for the sales or marketing team to create and collaborate on new projects. The rollout of a marketing strat-egy can be monitored in real time, and customer reaction and cam-paign impact can be recorded and measured immediately. Crises can be managed in real time as well, and slight adjustments to strategy and tone can be made on the spot.

Most important, customers can see that their concerns or comments receive responses from real individuals who are invested in the product, service, or campaign. This level of engagement will inspire customer interest and loyalty.

Additionally, marketing campaigns can then be reviewed by other employees, who may have invaluable insight to offer. It does not require a trained marketing professional to make valuable contributions to a campaign. Any employee may have a good idea to suggest, or may have had an experience that would be pertinent to the planning and execution of a marketing campaign. All participants are encouraged to feel engaged to a social media platform with which they are connected. This sense of engagement cuts across cultural divisions that often create barriers to information sharing in the offline world.

Personal interaction and open sharing of ideas are among the main benefits of an internal social media network. Although a designated marketing team plans and implements a marketing plan, the entire company can review and comment on the work, and the marketing team can then distinguish between useful and non-useful ideas. In this way the full talents of the staff can be brought to bear on a problem or project.

Viral Marketing

Even when confined within an internal social media environment, viral marketing is an excellent tool for pushing concepts and products. Viral marketing does not have to be provocative or off-color to be successful; it merely has to be *shareable*. This can be achieved through the use of humor, or through eye-catching design elements. The goal is to inspire employees to voluntarily pass a link or document among themselves, thereby pushing and advocating the ideas contained within the shared item.

The defining characteristic of viral marketing is the perceived lack of effort behind it. If a marketer pushes too hard with attempts to create a viral spread for a campaign, users will resist. As a result many viral marketing attempts never gain traction because not enough influential employees become aware of the media in question. It may also be the case, of course, that the media in question is not of sufficient interest to inspire sharing.

On the other hand, when something "goes viral" the phenomenon in some cases may evolve as part of what is known as a "long tail" process. This happens when the marketed product or idea sits unnoticed for periods of time and then suddenly is discovered and explodes into a successful viral payload. Although the passage of time may negate the timeliness of the marketing effort, less time-sensitive materials may become effective days or weeks after initial submission to the network.

Viral marketing's major drawback is the necessary subtlety of the approach, which can inhibit the actual message that is being promoted. Sometimes viral marketing attempts that are extremely successful in terms of reaction and reach are complete failures because very few of the people viewing the media take away the intended conclusions.

Challenges to ISM Marketing

Leveraging enterprise social media systems for marketing is either an internal function (the company using its own network to promote new initiatives, products, or announcements and to shape employee participation in bringing products and services to market) or an external function, usually in the form of advertising. Advertising is only a strategy when the ISM in question is a retail, third-party product being used in conjunction with a free license. In such cases the advertising is directed inward at the organization itself as the ISM system uses advertising as a revenue vector for itself.

For example, the popular off-the-shelf ISM application Yammer was purchased by Microsoft in early 2012. Speculation about the future of Yammer included possible integration with Office or other Microsoft products, or the possibility that the "freemium" version of Yammer would become ad-supported to make the product self-sustaining if not profitable. This is the only proven way for an internal social media platform to become a marketing vector *into* a company or organization that has installed a third-party ISM solution.

There are significant obstacles to both internal and external leveraging of ISM networks for marketing purposes of any kind, however.

Company Policies

External access to ISM networks for the purpose of pushing advertising to end users may violate the internal policies of the company. Although this may simply push a company toward a paid licensing arrangement with the ISM of choice, it does reduce the marketing impact that social media usually represents.

If the enterprise social media network in question is a proprietary or heavily customized application, it is unlikely that the interface will contain a channel for pushing advertising at all.

Employee Resistance

More important and damaging to both internal and external marketing approaches on social media networks inside organizations is employee resistance. This resistance manifests in two primary patterns: Resistance to learning and using a new application, and resistance to the advertising/marketing methods themselves.

Resistance to a New Application

Many employees already use several social media applications both within and outside an organization's network, and often are already using them to organize and collaborate on work. Services such as Tracky allow people to form and join networks based on the Internet domain of their e-mail addresses, requiring no official participation from the organization itself. As a result these employees may feel that they cannot split their attention between these existing tools and a whole new system that is being introduced.

Another reason employees may resist migration to a new ISM system is the difficulty in transferring the material and archives of a lengthy project from an older collaborative ISM network to the new one. Few ISMs provide easy tools for migrating files and messaging logs to a competitor's system, and this can become a very lengthy chore if the project has been in place for some time on another platform.

Finally, employees may resist a new social media application earmarked by their organization for fear of losing control of their projects. Social media encourages ownership and engagement and this often results in very possessive attitudes toward projects that may be collaborative but are ultimately owned by the company. Although employees might know this intellectually, emotionally the project feels like a private domain and they may resent being forced to use a social media interface they did not select.

Resistance to Third-Party Inbound Advertising

Many employees consider advertising or other forms of overt marketing to be the mark of a "free" or amateur social network, and they may claim that it is distracting and detracts from the work experience. The inevitable attempts by established public social media services such as Facebook and Twitter to monetize their market share has inspired a mild backlash. On Facebook, users continuously monitor the privacy settings and spread word of sudden changes that leave their private comments public or that opt them into advertising programs. On Twitter, users identify promoted tweets and corporate-sponsored accounts, and many tweets are tagged as attempts at viral marketing within moments of being posted.

Many employees feel that ad-supported software in general is amateurish. A company that is perceived as not willing to pay a small licensing fee to have a premium version of an application, or to have a custom or proprietary application built, is seen in a negative light as well. If a chosen ISM interface is ad-supported, employees often cite this as a reason for not wanting to migrate from their established collaborative systems (which are also likely free and possibly ad-supported), because they will see little benefit in terms of additional service or capabilities.

Outsider Syndrome in Internal Marketing

Often a major impediment to an organization's ability to push concepts and products via enterprise social media internally is the perception that this is exactly what they are doing—pushing. If the upper management of an organization is not regularly participating on an ISM, employees who do use the network to collaborate and communicate regularly may perceive any messages suddenly dropping down from above as unwelcome intrusions and as obvious attempts to push them in one or more directions.

It is crucial for managers and executives to participate in enterprise social media systems so they will be perceived as legitimate members of the community and not outsiders seeking to use the network for their own purposes. While employees understand on an intellectual level that these systems are installed and maintained so they can perform work for their organization, they often become emotionally possessive of the projects they work on, and can view attempts to leverage the ISM as an attack that must be resisted, or at the very least as an unwelcome intrusion into their sphere of influence.

A digital "open-door policy" must be maintained, where employees can see a direct presence by management on the ISM, with managers and other executives at least superficially available for messaging and other communication. This avoids the "outsider syndrome" that can poison attempts to educate, influence, and guide employees as advocates or deputies in internal and external marketing attempts.

Treating Employees as Customers

One of the key differences between external and internal social media marketing strategies is that internal social media requires the company to treat its employees as customers. Using the same techniques and tools used to reach and engage external customers, the organization reaches out and engages with employees. The goals are remarkably similar: To form a community that employees feels they have a stake in, to foster trust and communication, to distribute news and product information, and to solicit useful feedback.

Emotion plays an important role in this process. Employees must feel an emotional connection to the company that is similar to the emotional connection that a successful marketing campaign can inspire customers to feel about a product or service. This makes employees view their employer as more than just a job and a paycheck. It leads employees to see their company as an integral part of their lives and identity, which leads to them becoming, over time, advocates or deputies in the service of the company's products or services.

To be successful, this transformation must be voluntary, and thus the tools must be inviting and useful. Motivation to use the tools must be real and internally motivated, not a result of commands to do so. Employees must have a real sense of engagement, and feel that their ideas are heard and considered. To foster an instant and inviting community, it is vital that all employees feel welcome to take part in internal social media applications.

As social media of all kinds become increasingly integrated in daily life, touching all aspects of the way people communicate, shop, and travel through the world, it will also affect their lives at work. Companies and organizations will need to pay attention to social media tools for both internal and external marketing purposes, keeping audiences of both employees and customers in mind.

A business's internal social media platform offers benefits in terms of marketing ideas, policies, and products, whether externally to customers or internally to employees. Employees will become advocates and thus the whole staff will become an auxiliary sales force. For any company seeking to remain competitive and successful, development of an internal social media strategy is essential.

SOURCES OF ADDITIONAL INFORMATION

Apcoworld. www.apcoworldwide.com
Internal Social Media Products. www.snapcomms.com
Social Media Today. www.socialmediatoday.com

BIBLIOGRAPHY

Anand, R. (2010). *Recruiting with social media: Social media's impact on recruitment and HR.* Boston, MA: Pearson Education.

Bradley, A. J. (2010, May 17). Why isn't e-mail (and other channels) considered social media? [web log post]. Retrieved December 4, 2012, from http://blogs.gartner.com/anthony_bradley/2010/05/17/why-isnt-e-mail-and-other-channels-considered-social-media/

Browne, T. (2012). *The social trade show: Leveraging social media and virtual events to connect with your customers.* Boston, MA: Pearson Education.

Brzozowski, M. J. (2009). WaterCooler: Exploring an organization through enterprise social media. *Proceedings of the ACM 2009 International Conference on Supporting Group Work.* New York, N.Y.

Brzozowski, M. J., Sandholm, T., & Hogg, T. (2009). Effects of feedback and peer pressure on contributions to enterprise social media. *Proceedings of the ACM 2009 International Conference on Supporting Group Work.* New York, N.Y.

Brzozowski, M. J., & Yardi, S. (2012). *Revealing the long tail in office conversations.* Retrieved October 2012 from www.hpl.hp.com.

Chui, M., Manyika, J., Bughin, J., Dobbs, R., Roxburgh, C., Sarrazin, H., Sands, G., & Westergren, M. (2012, July). *The social economy: Unlocking value and productivity through social technologies.* McKinsey Global Institute. Retrieved December 7, 2012, from http://www.mckinsey.com/insights/mgi/research/technology_and_innovation/the_social_economy

Crumlish, C., & Malone, E. (2009). *Designing social interfaces.* Sebastopol, CA: O'Reilly Media.

Davenport, T. H., & Beck, J. C. (2001). *The attention economy: Understanding the new currency of business.* Boston: Harvard Business Press.

Eikenes, J. O. (2009). *Social navigation: Engaging interfaces in social media.* Paper presented at Nordes '09: Engaging Artefacts, Oslo, Norway. Retrieved from http://www.nordes.org.

Eklund, P., Goodall, P., Wray, T., Bunt, B., Lawson, A., Christidis, L., Daniel, V., & Van Olffen, M. (2009, June). Designing the digital ecosystem of the virtual museum of the Pacific. *Proceedings of Digital Ecosystems and Technologies, 2009 (DEST '09)*. 3rd IEEE International Conference, Istanbul.

Evans, D. (2010). *Social media marketing: The next generation of business engagement*. Hoboken, NJ: John Wiley & Sons.

Flynn, N. (2012). *The social media handbook: Rules, policies, and best practices to successfully manage your organization's social media presence, posts, and potential*. Hoboken, NJ: John Wiley & Sons.

Fuggetta, R. (2012). *Brand advocates: turning enthusiastic customers into a powerful marketing force*. Hoboken, NJ: John Wiley & Sons.

Gibson, S., & Jagger, S. (2009). *Sociable! How social media is turning sales and marketing upside-down*. Detroit, MI: Knowledge Brokers.

Greenberg, P. (2011, November). Social everything comes of age: Enterprise 2.0 and social CRM form the core of social business. *CRM Magazine, November 2011*. Retrieved January 27, 2013 from http://www.destinationcrm.com/Articles/Columns-Departments/Connect/Social-Everything-Comes-of-Age—78085.aspx.

Kain, E. (2012, April 26). Five reasons you shouldn't care about your Klout Score. *Forbes*. Retrieved December 6, 2012, from http://www.forbes.com/sites/erikkain/2012/04/26/5-reasons-you-shouldnt-care-about-your-klout-score

Kopytoff, V. G. (2011, June 26). Companies are erecting in-house social networks. *New York Times*. Retrieved December 8, 2012, from http://www.nytimes.com/2011/06/27/technology/27social.html?pagewanted=all&_r=0

Kurkinen, E., Sullivan, H., Häkkinen, M., & Lauttamus, M. (2010, May). Optimizing mobile social media interfaces for rapid internal communication by emergency services. *Proceedings of the 7th International ISCRAM Conference*, Seattle, WA.

Larson, K., & Watson, R. T. (2011). *The value of social media: Toward measuring social media strategies*. Paper presented at the Thirty-Second International Conference on Information Systems, Shanghai, China.

Leistner, F. (2012). *Connecting organizational silos: Taking knowledge flow management to the next level with social media*. Hoboken, NJ: John Wiley & Sons.

Pantouvakis, A. (2012). Internal marketing and the moderating role of employees: An exploratory study. *Total Quality Management & Business Excellence, 23;2: 177-195*.

Parekh, R. (2012, September 17). Internal affairs: Social media at the office. *AdAge*. Retrieved December 8, 2012, from http://adage.com/article/digital/internal-affairs-social-media-office/237207/

Postman, J. (2009). *SocialCorp: Social media goes corporate*. San Francisco, California: Peachpit Press.

Schaefer, M. W. (2012). *Return on influence: The revolutionary power of klout, social scoring, and influence marketing*. New York, NY: McGraw Hill.

Stanton, E. (2012, July 31). Yammer: Why Microsoft spent $1.2 billion [web blog post]. Retrieved December 8, 2012, from http://www.catchfiremedia.com/2012/07/yammer-why-microsoft-spent-1-2-billion/

Preparing for Paradigm Shifts

In This Essay

■ Social media platforms have come and gone in the past, and will continue to do so

■ Causes of the demise of a social media platform

■ Users are currently more interested in innovation than stability in a social media platform

Overview

The world is rarely static. Even well-established technologies continue to evolve, and they may become barely recognizable compared with their original incarnations. Take, for example, the telephone, which is a permanent and unremarked-upon fixture in the most places in the world. It began as an expensive and exotic piece of equipment that many people resisted as intrusive and somehow coarse. It slowly became a standard piece of business equipment and then an item that almost every home possessed. The blocky landlines of the 20th century have evolved into wireless mobile phones and inexpensive Internet calling options. While the phones of today might have little resemblance to the hand-cranked machines people once used to reach a live operator, the base technology and function remain the same.

Similar evolutions in capability, attitudes, and usage happen with almost every piece of technology, and social media tools are no exception. The Facebooks and Twitters of the future will be different than they are today. Social media, like any other technology, will undergo evolutions in its capabilities, in its interface, and in how it is used, both privately and in business.

Life Expectancy of Social Media Sites

The process of evolution in the social media realm has led to the extinction of several once-popular platforms. Looking at how and why these services failed can be instructive.

MySpace

Until early 2008, the most visited social media website in the world was MySpace. Launched in 2003 and bought by News Corp. in 2005, MySpace was the dominant presence in the nascent social media niche, had plenty of capital, and was growing at a steady pace. This all seemed to stop overnight when Facebook was launched in 2008. Although MySpace still exists and is functioning as a company (ranked as the 161st most-visited website in the world), it has been in steady decline, losing traffic and laying off employees. From a high of 1,600 in the beginning of 2009, its employee count dropped to about 200 people by 2012.

This means that MySpace's journey from launch to irrelevancy took approximately seven years. The speed of this transition is startling considering the dominant position MySpace enjoyed heading into 2008. Under traditional models Facebook should have had a very difficult time breaking into the market and building up a competitive user base. Instead, within months Facebook had established itself as a serious competitor for MySpace, and within a year was clearly in the dominant position, where it has remained. (In 2012 Facebook announced the creation of its billionth user account.)

Several factors contributed to MySpace's precipitous decline.

Site Design MySpace was designed to be highly customizable. Users were able to change almost every visual aspect of their pages, including background images, color schemes, and incidental icons. Music could easily be incorporated via embedded players. Although this might be assumed to be an advantage, the appeal of such a high level of customizable material was also found to be irritating to many people when visiting MySpace pages,as many pages were customized in garish, amateurish ways that were displeasing to the ear and eye. Facebook allows very little customization, which results in a consistent visual look for every page, whether they are personal, corporate, or artist pages. Although some people may consider this visually dull, it translates into a consistency that makes viewing and extracting information from the pages easy. Limiting the customization also served to emphasize the sense of community, which ultimately is the reason people participate in social media.

Lack of Developer Access MySpace attempted to wield a high-level of control over the applications developed for its platform. Almost no third-party application development took place because MySpace itself attempted to provide all new features. This slowed the addition of embedded applications and often angered the user base. One example of this lag concerns the launch of the YouTube video service, which was immediately popular with MySpace users because YouTube allowed for the easy embedding of video content in their pages. MySpace had its own video service, however, and banned YouTube in an attempt to force members to use its internal service. Considering the internal service inferior, the MySpace user base rebelled and eventually the company was forced to allow YouTube on its platform.

In contrast, Facebook has embraced outside development and as a result is able to offer a wide range of add-on services such as games and applications. This fosters a sense of being served by a community instead of being leveraged as an advertising base.

Change of Internet Aesthetic It is impossible to ignore the stark contrast in look and feel between MySpace and Facebook. Whereas MySpace allowed for great customization and addition of features to its user pages, resulting in a varied look and varied user experience, Facebook offers a very clean, consistent look and each page offers a limited scope of features. In some senses MySpace represents an earlier view of the Internet as a wide-open wilderness with few rules and lots of chaotic, disorganized content, whereas Facebook has a more modern view of the Internet as a communication tool that is being curated for personal experience. The rise of alternative tools for the sharing of music and video means that any add-on capability in a site such as MySpace is viewed as second-rate, so sites increasingly specialize in the *"Web 2.0"* version of the Internet. Facebook represents this aesthetic.

Web 2.0: *The second generation of the World Wide Web that includes features such as blogs, wikis, and social networking.*

Friendster

Launched before MySpace, Friendster also once enjoyed a seemingly dominant leadership position in the social media world, gaining more than 3 million users within a few months of its 2002 debut. Although Friendster is still in business as of 2012, it has radically altered its market focus and purpose. It is popular mainly in Asian countries, where it has attained a cultural momentum and where the majority of its 115 million users live. In 2011, Friendster's management shifted the focus of the site from social networking among users to entertainment, music, and gaming. This transformation jettisoned most of the data users had uploaded to the site, including photos and blog entries, and engendered some backlash from old account holders. However, the change did increase traffic and membership. Although Friendster is still a successful website, it is no longer a social media platform.

Technological Failure Unlike MySpace, there is general agreement on why Friendster fell from its dominant position in the social media milieu. Friendster's problem can be summed up in one word: technology. Both MySpace and Facebook were built using AJAX (Asynchronous JavaScript and XML) platforms that provided reliable, fast pages that could be dynamically reloaded without having to reload the entire page. Friendster user pages were served as single monolithic *HTML* pages, which needed to be reloaded en masse if one piece crashed or did not display correctly. This made the Friendster website slow and often frustrating.

Additionally, Friendster did not increase server capacity to match user demand, which resulted in frequent crashes that took the site offline and led to data loss and a host of lesser glitches. These problems, which remained uncorrected for more than two years beginning in 2004, may have been the result of unexpected success as millions joined the service and the company was unprepared to outlay the cash necessary to keep up with storage and web server demands.

HTML: *An authoring language used to create documents on the World Wide Web. Short for HyperText Markup Language.*

Bandwidth: *The data transfer rate of a network or Internet connection.*

The old web design tools and unreliable performance of Friendster gave it an outdated appearance even as it was the most-used social media site in the world. MySpace, and later Facebook, offered a service better-suited to the dynamic behavior of users on social media sites, which requires very high *bandwidth* and disk storage in order to be fluid. As most social media use is simultaneously casual and linked to other aspects of users' lives, it must also be simultaneously instantly responsive to user requests (as its casual nature makes waiting seem unjustifiable) and 100 percent reliable (as users are storing emotionally charged photos and missives on its servers and grow angry and upset when they are lost or corrupted).

Other Life Expectancy Factors

Size It remains to be seen how much a social media platform can scale up. Facebook announced its one billionth account in October 2012, although there is some speculation that this total includes phantom accounts that were created but never used, duplicate accounts, and accounts left dormant by former users who did not know how to cancel their membership. Even with these doubts, Facebook has the most active users of any social media platform, and the question of whether a social media platform can be too large remains unanswered.

Part of the appeal of social media is the sense of community, and the size of that community is certainly a factor. With an increase in population comes a decrease in perceived intimacy. Part of Facebook's initial strategy to gain market share was to pursue a by-invitation-only membership dynamic that required potential users either to be part of an organization (initially, select universities beginning with Harvard, where Facebook was originally created and deployed) or to be specifically invited by the company. This created false scarcity and intrigue and undoubtedly made the service desirable, especially to its initial target market of 18- to 25-year-old users.

Facebook eventually dropped the invitation-only model and has become ubiquitous and corporate. Its members span all generations and fields and there is no bar to creating an account. It is conceivable that a new service may market itself as a "cool" alternative to Facebook, or simply a more intimate alternative. Google+, while not enjoying the initial success that had been expected, plays on the issue of intimacy by allowing users to create different "circles" to differentiate among close friends, family, work acquaintances or business contacts, and the general public, making it possible to post certain content to certain people. Although Facebook could implement a similar system, it appears reluctant to do so, possibly because this might compromise the sources of its revenue: advertising and the sale of user data.

Demographics The speed with which social media platforms have proliferated makes it difficult to confirm any definite overall demographic patterns concerning users. When it comes to the end-of-life scenarios for

MySpace and Friendster, however, it appears that demographic characteristics did play a role. MySpace and Friendster both had user bases dominated by older Internet veterans, adults who had joined the services at their inception. Facebook and Twitter began as services marketed to—and in the case of Facebook, initially exclusive to—a younger demographic. The initial user base for Twitter and Facebook did not overlap all that much with the user bases enjoyed at the time by MySpace and Friendster. Rather than taking users away, this initial, younger user base established the momentum and credibility of the new websites.

The migration of younger, Internet-savvy users to a new service is often due simply to the novelty of the new platform and a perception that the older platforms are behind the times. This dynamic was at work in the demise of Friendster, where technological failings made it appear that the website was not keeping up with advances. Younger users are more apt to have the latest in mobile technology and to expect instant access to their data, having grown up with high-speed Internet and ubiquitous Internet connectivity. The loss of the younger demographic is a clear sign that a new social media platform has emerged to attract them, which is what happened when Facebook, originally started as a service for college students, drew users away from MySpace. The initial limited user base established Facebook as the "new thing" used by the younger demographic and gave Facebook the momentum it carefully managed as it opened the service to wider and wider markets.

Staying Ahead of the Curve

Market dominance: *The measure of the strength of a brand, product, service, or firm, relative to its competitors.*

The evolving dynamics of social media platforms have little precedent in either business projections and models or marketing guidelines, which makes it difficult to predict when a particular platform will cross the line from sustained growth and/or *market dominance* into decline. As seen with MySpace and Friendster, the transition from dominance to decline can be precipitous, sudden, and permanent. On the other hand, Facebook and Twitter have each remained dominant in their niche for a longer period than either MySpace or Friendster achieved, and both have gained "household name" status similar to Google.

One pattern has been established in the life span evolution of social media platforms: When a platform rises in popularity to supplant a previously dominant service, usually it will not have been identified as the "next big thing." Both Twitter and Facebook (and Pinterest as well) arrived with little fanfare beyond casual curiosity, but they quickly gained momentum and market share, especially among younger users who had no history with or connection to established sites.

Several services have the potential to approach Facebook or Twitter levels of popularity and to perhaps also become dominant social media platforms.

Google+

Although Google+ has failed to attract the user base expected, it remains a potential replacement for existing social media platforms. It has the resources of Google behind it and it offers several features that Facebook does not, including the ability to form "hangout" groups with people online and the ability to place connections in groups and specify which groups can see which posts.

Highlight

Highlight has the potential to be the "next big thing" because it takes a different approach to social media and the relationships it creates and supports. Highlight scans the immediate physical location for other Highlight users and then alerts a user to their proximity, displaying a photo and basic information as well as any shared relationships or interests. It is actually designed to bridge the gap between the social media platform and the real world, inviting interaction. However, many feel that part of the appeal of social media platforms has been their partial anonymity and the distance between people who are interacting digitally, which may inhibit adoption of Highlight.

Path

Path's approach to social media differs in terms of scale and intimacy. Path users are limited to a maximum of 150 friends or connections with whom they can share photos, tags, and other material. The focus is on the quality and intimacy of the connections, not the scale. Path hopes to attract users who seek a trusted, intimate circle of connections for social media—families and close friends. Path could also be applied to businesses, with small groups being formed for specific projects or even entire small businesses, where information would be distributed only to appropriate recipients automatically. However, this can also be accomplished on other social network platforms (notably Google+) simply by creating a specific group. This overlapping feature may cause many users to reject Path as an unnecessary additional application.

Pinterest

Pinterest gained a large user base in a short time. This service is distinguished from other social media platforms by its visual focus, where users "pin" images to their pages and can follow other users who have similar visual tastes. Pinterest, launched in 2010, reached 10 million users more quickly than any other social media platform, and as of 2012 had totaled more than 12 million unique user accounts. The reductive visual aspect of Pinterest—it removes most text and boils everything down to images—presents an appealing interface that is less cluttered than Facebook or Twitter. However, Pinterest has already gained a reputation as a vector for advertising as many Pinterest accounts are actually merchant accounts posting photos of products. This perception may blunt users' enthusiasm if they begin to feel the service is really just an advertising channel.

Riffle

Similar in visual focus and design to Pinterest, Riffle is a social media platform for books based around sharing reviews and book recommendations. Still in the testing phase as of this writing, Riffle seeks to differentiate itself from established book-focused social media platforms like Goodreads (which, in existence since 2007, has a healthy membership but little potential to become the 'next big thing') by its focus on recommendations, as opposed to the stats-centric Goodreads. The use of book covers as pinnable images makes it look, superficially, like Pinterest.

Viddy

Viddy concentrates exclusively on video content. It focuses on ease of use, removing the complexities of video format, codecs, and processing to create video files tailored for uploading and sharing with simple effects and editing tools. Like Instagram, Viddy is built on a premise of shared experience and comments. Viddy relies on ubiquitous broadband Internet. However, video files, even heavily compressed, are large and can exceed the limits of a standard cell phone data plan in a short time. For Viddy to be the "next big thing" there would have to be either a giant leap in broadband bandwidth, a huge drop in costs of that bandwidth, or a technological breakthrough in video codec compression technology.

Airtime

Created by Napster founders Sean Parker and Shawn Fanning, Airtime is a video-based social media service. Users post videos and comment on them in real-time, or post videos in response. Airtime combines a video chat service with the ability to search for videos posted by people with similar interests and tastes. Airtime has similar limitations related to bandwidth as Viddy—it relies on ubiquitous, affordable data connections to grow beyond casual home use.

Challenges to Reaching Critical Mass

Despite being creative and popular offerings, none of the services discussed in this essay have attained the critical mass of users required to launch themselves into a dominant position in the social media field. Both Twitter and Facebook, the top names in the field in 2013, launched with fewer features and less publicity, and yet surged quickly to impressive market share in their respective niches. When trying to predict the coming paradigm shifts in social media, it is educational to analyze why new products in the field do not catch on. For the preceding examples we can identify three areas where new social media platforms have failed: Their reliance on high-speed Internet bandwidth, a lack of unique design and functionality, and their separation from real-world tools that can be mapped and thus improved through Internet connectivity (making them too abstract).

Bandwidth Reliant

Many of the newer social media platforms, especially those focusing on video, rely on high-speed data plans. Although high-speed Internet access is reasonably affordable in the home and can be shared with many devices through a wireless router at little cost, roaming charges and limits on the amount of data (measured in megabytes [MB] or gigabytes [GB]) when outside the home are a prohibitive factor to the adoption and use of these tools. Facebook and Twitter, because of their minimalist web designs, consume minimal bandwidth. While both Facebook and Twitter offer the ability to embed and share video, the choice is up to the user whether to click on the shared links or not.

Twitter in particular is sensitive to the bandwidth issue. The website and associated mobile apps have few graphics and concentrate so completely on Twitter's core service (succinct, character-limited public and private messaging) that the bandwidth used is minimal. The hard limit of 140 characters in a tweet is in itself ideal for both awkward mobile keyboards and limited bandwidth.

Many social media competitors appear to be designed more for the larger screens of computer desktops or tablets and for the faster in-home data connections, with colorful animations and graphics alongside their data-hungry services. Although versions of their services designed specifically for mobile devices assist with data consumption concerns, this also means a different experience when accessing the service from a mobile device as opposed to a home computer. Users prefer uniformity of experience and resist having to learn separate ways of interacting with a service.

Too Imitative

Some social media platforms launched in the wake of Facebook and Twitter do not offer new or innovative services, but rather improved or enhanced versions of what is already available. Google+, for example, essentially offers the same features Facebook does, with several enhancements, such as the ability to form contacts into different groupings and have posts appear only to selected groups. However, these options have not been enough to lure users away from Facebook. Many users assume Facebook, in competition with Google+, will eventually add this functionality, and they are willing to wait rather than go through the trouble of migrating their contacts and interactions to an unfamiliar platform.

Since all social media currently operate on a "free-to-use" system sometimes supplemented by ads, there are only two compelling reasons to switch services: (1) a large number of peers and contacts adopts a new service, and (2) an innovative new feature proves irresistible. In the absence of those factors, slight improvements in existing features are not enticing enough to drive migration. In the world of fee-based products and services, price competition serves to distinguish items that may otherwise be similar. When everything is free, as in the social media realm, price-comparison shopping is of no use.

Inadequate Real-World Tools

Often the simplest explanation for the failure of a social media platform is that it does not offer a service that users actually want or need. Another common problem occurs when potential users do not find familiar real-world parallels to a service's tools.

For example, Facebook is a digital and Internet-connected adaptation of the traditional membership directories, called *Face Books*, that college organizations such as fraternities and sororities maintained. In the pre-digital age these Face Books were print items kept in the organization's house or office. The social media platform Facebook began as a digital and connected version of these Face Books, originally specific to the Harvard University campus (when first launched Facebook was accessible only to those with a Harvard e-mail address). Facebook combined a recognizable, real-world tool with enhancements that demonstrated clear advantages over the existing tools, thus driving adoption.

Some social media platforms, such as Facebook and Pinterest, do a good job of clearly mapping to real-world tools. These services offer users an easily understandable digital metaphor that clearly implies benefits and capabilities beyond existing physical tools or services. Others, such as Highlight, may be offering users a service they simply do not want. Although the ability to discover nearby people with similar interests may appeal to some, the social downsides to such a service are easy to imagine. One key to the success of social media platforms is the perceived insulation users have from other users. The assumption, however inaccurate, that postings will be seen only by intimate friends in their digital circles often grants social media users a false but distinct sense of security.

Not If, But When

The question of a paradigm shift in how people use and interact with social media platforms is one of when, not if. Social media as a distinct modern phenomenon has already demonstrated several phases of evolution and transformation. As bandwidth accessibility and processing strength in mobile devices improve, social media platforms will have to enhance the services they offer and include new services, even as the ways in which people use the platforms change and shift.

In the past these shifts in usage and offered services have been difficult to predict. Old patterns of evolving markets and technology do not apply to the Web 2.0 era. Gone are the days when individual or small-business-sized developers (such as Mark Zuckerberg developing Facebook in his dorm room) can create applications in short periods of time and gain market share in just a few days or weeks after launch. Users of social media platforms have also proved to be surprisingly tolerant of "bugs" and regard a lack of features as a design decision rather than a failure of the product. In short, the expectations for social media confound traditional concepts of customer demand and feature offerings. Consumers of social media services value a perception of exclusivity over quality and are more interested in innovation than stability. This is a new and different satisfaction dynamic.

It may be instructive to look at emerging competitors to social media leaders such as Facebook and Twitter, but comparisons should be made with caution. These dominant platforms overtook their more established predecessors with little warning, fanfare, or buildup. A similar "overnight success" might one day usher in the next new paradigm just as quickly and with just as little warning. In other words, it is unlikely that any currently established social media platform is representative of the next market shift.

SOURCES OF ADDITIONAL INFORMATION

Marketbeat. blogs.wsj.com/marketbeat
Mashable. mashable.com/category/social-media/
Social Media Examiner. www.socialmediaexaminer.com
Social Media Today. www.socialmediatoday.com
Social Media Week. www.socialmediaweek.org

BIBLIOGRAPHY

Abrams, J. (2010). What were the key mistakes that Friendster made? [web log post]. Retrieved December 3, 2012, from http://www.quora.com/Friendster/What-were-the-key-mistakes-that-Friendster-made.

Advisers urged to get on social media bandwagon. (2012, November). *Financial Adviser*. Retrieved January 28, 2013, from http://www.ftadviser.com/2012/11/07/ifa-industry/technology/advisers-urged-to-get-on-social-media-bandwagon-UgBnuKykbQ3N5LUTbQXqSM/article.html.

Anderson, A., Kleinberg, J., Huttenlocher, D., & Leskovec, J. (2012, February). Effects of user similarity in social media. Paper presented at Web Search & Data Mining (WSDM) 2012 Conference, Seattle, Washington.

Are your social media campaigns really working? (2012, November). *PC Quest*. Retrieved January 28, 2013, from http://pcquest.ciol.com/content/techtrends/2012/112110705.asp.

Associated Press. (2012, May 15). Poll: Half of Americans call Facebook a fad [web log post]. Retrieved December 3, 2012, from http://drhiphop85.com/2012/05/15/poll-half-of-americans-call-facebook-a-fad

Asur, S., Huberman, B. A., Szabo, G., & Wang, C. (2011). Trends in social media: Persistence and decay. Barcelona, Spain: 5th International Association for the Advancement of Artificial Intelligence (AAAI) Conference on Weblogs and Social Media.

Brands, not celebrities, hog social media in India. (2012, November). *Financial Express*. Retrieved January 28, 2013, from http://www.financialexpress.com/news/brands-not-celebrities-hog-social-media-in-india/1026368/0.

Chan, A. (n.d.). *Social media: Paradigm shift?* Retrieved December 3, 2012, from http://www.gravity7.com/paradigm_shift_1.html

Deahl, R. (2012, November). Riffle readies for launch. *Publishers Weekly*. Retrieved January 28, 2013, from http://www.publishersweekly.com/pw/by-topic/digital/Apps/article/54611-riffle-readies-for-launch.html.

Eileen, F., & Reuber, A. R. (2001). Social interaction via new social media: (How) can interactions on Twitter affect effectual thinking and behavior? *Journal of Business Venturing, 26(1)*, 1–18.

Government approves guidelines for use of social media by government agencies. (2012, August). *Telecom Tiger*. Retrieved January 28, 2013, from http://www.telecomtiger.com/PolicyNRegulation_fullstory.aspx?storyid=15412&section=S174.

Gupta, H., Nicholson, D., & Newman, P. (2012). Usage, impediments and attitudes towards social media in UK building societies. Paper 159 presented at the 16th Pacific Asia Conference on Information Systems (PACIS) 2012, Ho Chi Minh City, Vietnam.

Kietzmann, J. H., Hermkens, K., McCarthy, I. P., & Silvestre, B. S. Social media? (2011). Get serious! Understanding the functional building blocks of social media. *Business Horizons, 54*, 241–251.

Longino, C. (2006, January 10). So that's why MySpace blocked YouTube [web log post]. Retrieved December 3, 2012, from http://www.techdirt.com/articles/20060110/0735214.shtml

Madrigal, A. C. (2012, April 18). The jig is up: Time to get past Facebook and invent a new future. *The Atlantic*. Retrieved December 3, 2012, from http://www.theatlantic.com/technology/archive/2012/04/the-jig-is-up-time-to-get-past-facebook-and-invent-a-new-future/256046

Malhotra, A. (2012, November). How are offline media brands leveraging online? *Pitch*. Retrieved January 28, 2013, from http://pitchonnet.com/blog/2012/11/08/how-are-offline-media-brands-leveraging-online/.

Maney, K. (2009, February). Short & tweet. *Upstart Business Journal*. Retrieved January 28, 2013, from http://upstart.bizjournals.com/executives/features/2009/02/11/Twitter-CEO-Evan-Williams-Q-and-A.html?page=all.

Richard, H., Rohm, A., & Crittenden, V. L. (2011). We're all connected: The power of the social media ecosystem. *Business Horizons, 54*, 265–273.

Segall, L. (2012, May 16). Seven startups Facebook should buy. *CNN Money.* Retrieved December 3, 2012, from http://money.cnn.com/galleries/2012/technology/1205/gallery.startups-facebook-should-buy

Self, W. (2012, March). Twitter is just a new home for old bores. *New Statesman.* Retrieved January 28, 2013, from http://www.newstatesman.com/digital/2012/03/twitter-just-new-home-old-bores

Social media: counting crowds. (2011, February). *New Media Age*, February 17, 2011.

Srivastava, P. (2012, November). Simon Ashwin feels Facebook is not social media. *Pitch.* Retrieved January 28, 2013, from http://pitchonnet.com/blog/2012/11/06/simon-ashwin-feels-facebook-is-not-social-media.

Sutter, J. D. (2012, May 18). What's the next Facebook (or is there one)? [web log post]. *CNN What's Next.* Retrieved December 3, 2012, from http://whatsnext.blogs.cnn.com/2012/05/18/whats-the-next-facebook-or-is-there-one

Tabone, J. (2012, November). Seeing risk in social media. *CA Magazine.* Retrieved January 28, 2013, from http://www.camagazine.com/archives/print-edition/2012/nov/upfront/news-and-trends/camagazine68449.aspx.

Valisno, J. O. (2012, November). New cooking show uses social media. *Business World* [Philippines].

Diminishing Returns of Social Media

In This Essay

■ Social media marketing can be hampered by diminishing returns in the value of the social media interactions

■ Social media campaigns focused solely on marketing or with repetitive, high-volume postings can experience diminished returns and even damaged reputations, and these problems can be avoided by personalizing and humanizing the social media presence

■ Social media outlets as a whole must maintain a sense of legitimacy and popularity and also address user complaints promptly

Overview

Marketing via social media, like anything else, is subject to the law of diminishing returns, which states that past a certain point of optimum efficiency and effectiveness increased effort will yield decreased results. This law is a basic tenet of economic theory, though in pure economics it is more concerned with the specific increase or augmentation of one aspect of production with all other aspects remaining the same.

Many people continue to fall prey to the idea that new technology renders obsolete all existing knowledge or wisdom. In short, dazzled by the apparent infinite nature of the Internet and its component resources, they believe that old sobering laws such as the law of diminishing returns somehow do not apply to new, Internet-based ventures. Sometimes this is assumed based on the belief that because no physical items are passed over the Internet, the laws and behaviors of previous nondigital eras cannot be effectively applied. This is *fuzzy logic*, however, that confuses physical attributes with behavioral or market-based reactions.

Fuzzy logic: *A system of logic in which statements do not have to be entirely true or entirely false.*

It is important to remember when attempting to leverage social media for marketing and Public Relations (PR) purposes that you are not only competing with direct competitors attempting to do the same thing on the same network (e.g., Twitter), but also with other entities that are *not* direct competitors but who are nonetheless attempting the same leveraging, as well as with users who participate in these networks not to be exposed to marketing or advertising, but to connect with friends and acquaintances. As a result, attempts to use these networks for marketing, promotion, or conversion, while usually well-tolerated, are not always effective.

When discussing diminishing returns in regards to social media, there are two overall spheres to consider: campaign-specific diminishing returns and the diminishing returns of social media as a marketing vector in general.

Campaign-Specific Diminishing Returns

Within the realm of social media platforms, individual marketing efforts can fall victim to diminishing returns separate from the effectiveness of social media marketing in general. Campaign-specific diminishing returns do not necessarily have any impact or influence on the diminishing returns of social media as a whole, although in some cases there may be relationships between the two spheres: for example, if a symptom of diminishing returns affecting social media in general makes a specific strategy used in a campaign ineffective.

Within a specific campaign, the main reason for diminishing returns on a marketing investment is market saturation in various forms.

Market Saturation

One main way in which social media marketing suffers from diminishing returns is in the volume of marketing pushed through a particular network. A typical cycle for social media marketing contains three main stages, none of which are generally recognized or well-understood:

- **Initiation.** In this stage the brand, company, or individual is a relative newcomer to the social media platform. They enjoy status as a novelty. In this stage there can be an initial rush of links, "friends," likes, or other successes as measured by the particular meter of the platform in question. Because all the content being sent over the platform is new, the reactions can be largely positive and there can be a rapid growth in connectivity and interaction.

- **Augmentation.** Encouraged by initial success, the strategy is widened and more resources are put into it. An example of this for Twitter marketing would be a company or individual beginning to tweet several times a day, repeating a key message or splitting tweets into several core marketing messages, after an initial positive reaction to a handful of promotional tweets.

- **Collapse.** As the *signal-to-noise ratio* within the campaign itself degrades, users on the social media platform pay less and less attention to the content being pushed out. A lack of original content, a perception of being purely a marketing account, and the unmanageable volume of the messages specific to a branding attempt or marketing campaign conspire to make users ignore the marketing efforts or become openly hostile toward them. Collapse is then accelerated as more pressure is put into the system in the form of an increased volume of postings.

Signal-to-noise ratio: *(informally) The ratio of useful information to false or irrelevant data in a conversation or exchange.*

It is important to remember that while the Internet's capacity is nearly infinite, the capacity of a member of a social media platform to pay attention to and absorb incoming content is limited.

Marketing Blindness

Staying on-message is often a tenet of marketing applied to social media: every post, tweet, or update must include your marketing message in some way. While creativity can be present in the tone and format of the marketing, each interaction must have a component designed to convert a contact into a customer or at minimum spread awareness of the product, company, or message.

This strategy can be initially effective because of the novelty of the interaction. A new presence on a social media platform, especially one designed to be appealing and to encourage interaction and communication, can enjoy distinction from the established community simply by being new and different. Social media users are tolerant of marketing messages in their communities to a higher extent than many other Internet users, and interactions that are viewed as "personal" rather than "robotic" frequently receive little or no objection.

Click-through rate:
A ratio showing how often people seeing an on-line ad end up clicking it.

However, over time, a similarity of messages means that posts, tweets, or updates become predictable. Members of the social media platform deal with a high volume of messages and other content on a daily basis and instinctively ignore unnecessary information. Just as television viewers learn to fast-forward through commercials on recorded programs or to ignore banner ads on websites (which is easily done because most banner ads are of standard size and placement, creating a naturally-occurring blind spot), social media users quickly identify repetitive content and quickly eliminate it from their daily feeds or update digests. This is often done without any awareness on the part of the user aside from a dramatic drop in *click-throughs*, conversions, or other evidence of interaction and penetration.

This is clearly a diminishing return, as increased efforts such as higher volume of posting will only accelerate this phenomenon. Continued escalation of pressure can ultimately poison a brand or account name, resulting in no interactions except when they involve new members of the platform.

Violation of Sense of Ownership

Upsell: *A sales strategy where the seller provides opportunities to purchase related products or services, often for the sole purpose of making a larger sale.*

Social media users have a high sense of ownership of the services and platforms they use. Often they are unaware of or unconcerned about the privacy/marketing transaction they engage in when using free services such as Facebook or Twitter, which seek to leverage their personal information for advertising and *upsell* purposes, and the users come to believe that they have an ownership stake in the platform and should therefore have some say in how it is used.

Although these perceptions are not accurate, they do affect the way posts, tweets, or updates are perceived. Excessive volume of marketing-centric content can result in a perception that the account is not being used in the proper spirit of the platform. This can permanentlyharm the reputation of the account if it is branded as "spam" by influential users on the platform or simply silently committed to spam folders and consequently ignored. Again, this is often invisible to the content poster, who may see no reduction in the number of connections (friends or followers) but see a sharp drop off in the results of their marketing efforts.

Similarly to marketing blindness, violating this sense of shared ownership or community is also a diminishing return, as increased efforts or volume only exacerbate the perception and worsen the reaction.

Strategies to Overcome Diminishing Returns

Being aware of the pitfalls of overly aggressive marketing campaigns using social media is the first and most important step that can be taken. Avoiding a flood of similar marketing messages and saturation of the signal can prevent problems altogether. In the event that a social media identity is already compromised with user belligerence or disdain, there are some strategies that can be used to mitigate these perceptions, and these strategies can also be used at the beginning of establishing a social media presence for the purpose of marketing.

Multiple Personalities

One approach that can be very effective is to split your presence on these social media platforms into two or more accounts or personalities. Each of these presences can then have a focus. One account can be used exclusively for marketing messaging: sales announcements, new service or product announcements, coupon distribution, etc. The other account can be more general and personal, offering interesting (but market-related) links or reading material. A step further would be to have a branded account that does no marketing whatsoever, but simply provides interesting or humorous content.

Content is generally king on social media platforms. Aside from the personal or professional connections established through them, users seek news about their field or area of interest, entertainment, and advice or tips. An account that provides this to them will be accepted into the community and promoted by users to each other as a valuable source, which can be very effective in passive marketing because every post, tweet, or update is branded even if it does not specifically reference a product, service, or marketing message.

The Rule of Thirds

The subject of content leads us to a second strategy for marketing and brand management/awareness enhancement: the rule of thirds.

This rule states that all participation in a social media platform should involve three components. The exact ratio of these components can vary depending on circumstances, but in general the posts or updates sent to the social media platform should be spread among these three general categories.

Marketing It is generally acceptable, even expected, for the social media interactions from a business to be pure marketing. In fact, at acceptable levels marketing is welcomed by other members of the platform, assuming they were interested enough in the first place to forge a connection. The level of acceptable marketing varies from community to community and even from individual member to individual member, so care should be taken initially. When establishing a presence on a social media platform, it is best to err on the side of caution and limit pure marketing messages until a sense of the acceptable is gained.

In addition to marketing, however, social media users expect and demand other content that goes beyond marketing. This additional content is a core part of the social media culture and should never be neglected in favor of increased marketing volume.

Brand: *Name, term, symbol, sign, or design used by a firm to differentiate its offerings from those of its competitors.*

Education/Entertainment Social media users react strongly to posts that have an educational or entertainment slant and these sorts of posts are received positively. Entertainment and education, in the form of links to interesting videos and blog posts (among many other possibilities) that are not created by or hosted by the source are in fact the most effective tools for building a following, whether it be friends, contacts, or followers. Entertaining or educational posts also garner the highest level of forwarding or reposts and are thus essential for building a social media presence and *brand*.

Personal Simultaneously, a large proportion of all social media communication should be personal, in the sense of not being a marketing message and not simply linking to other content or users. This can take the form of activity announcements, general observations (humorous or otherwise), or discussions of various subjects of personal interest. Social media users value the perception of personal insight that such posts convey, and they also serve to humanize corporate or business accounts.

Damaged Identities

Diminishing returns, if unchecked, can eventually damage a social media identity beyond repair. Once users begin abandoning a newsfeed or Twitter stream of an account viewed as purely a vector for marketing material, continued or increased volume begins to have a result opposite from its intention, driving more and more audience away. At a certain point, even changing the overall tone and content of the account will not be able to save it if it has become permanently shunned by the members of the community.

At this stage, which becomes apparent when actions or new strategies do not result in any increase in audience or reach whatsoever, the only alternative is to abandon and/or delete the account and start over with a new identity. Care must be taken, however, to avoid being perceived as attempting deception, or the new identity and brand may be poisoned before a new social media strategy can be established.

Strangely enough, many people are much more forgiving of large corporations than smaller businesses when it comes to perceived abuse of social media platforms. This may be in some part because corporations are made up of a large number of employees and it is easy to imagine "rogue" marketers making mistakes the company as a whole regrets, while smaller businesses are clearly acting on strategies devised by the small number of people running the marketing approach. As a result, and somewhat unfairly, a large corporation has a much better chance of recovering from a damaged identity on a social media platform than a small business.

Diminishing Returns of Social Media in General

It is important to remember that social media as a phenomenon has existed only since the early 21st century and has only been a mature and recognizable segment of Internet culture since approximately 2008, when Facebook became the dominant social media website and Twitter first reached the popular consciousness. It is tempting to imagine that social media has always and will always exist, yet there is absolutely no evidence that this will be the case. The question of the longevity of social media as it exists today is outside the scope of this chapter, but the possibility that social media as a *whole* might experience a downward spiral of diminishing returns is certainly a possibility. The two sides of the question are what circumstances would need to exist to set this decline in motion and whether the process could be reversed.

Causes

Social media platforms exist from two points of view. On the one hand their creators and/or corporate owners see them as businesses, designed to generate revenue. The transaction between themselves and the users of the platform is frequently one of personal information in exchange for services. Revenue is then generated through a combination of advertising and the sale of the personal information collected, which is often very specific and, at least presently, skewed heavily toward high-income individuals. Facebook, for example, is a service predicated entirely on the premise that people will gladly give away data points about themselves that previously required a great deal of effort and expense to gather.

From the users' point of view, however, social media platforms are seen as publicly-owned utilities designed to foster communication and networking. That this is untrue does not seem to factor much into this impression. As a result, there is often conflict between these two perceptions. When Facebook adjusts privacy settings to gain a bigger advantage in collecting personal information about its users, there is often an intensely negative reaction from the user base at the perceived injustice, even though this is, in fact, the entire purpose of Facebook from a business perspective.

The hidden nature of the transaction between user and service common to social media is a new scenario. In the past there was little mystery to the customer/service relationship. For example, even though the telephone was also a social tool in that it allowed long-distance communication between geographically separated people, the money paid to the phone company was clearly in exchange for the service. With modern social media platforms not only is the payment—privacy and user data—invisible, but it is often actively obscured by the service because of its unpopular nature, which helps foster an unrealistic expectation of ownership on the part of the users that may ultimately contribute to the diminishing returns of social media as a marketing vector.

Loss of Implied Consent Because of this imagined communal ownership of the platform, many users of social media assume there is an implied consent regarding marketing targeting them and their connections. While there is usually limited acknowledgment that some marketing is appropriate, the exact volume of the material is often debated. Users do not hesitate to complain if they feel that the purpose of a social media platform is being shifted from communication and interaction toward marketing or spam.

As a result of the largely imagined conflict between an acceptable volume of marketing and too much such material, users may begin to abandon a social media platform despite a healthy user base and popularity. At this point, efforts to maximize the value of a shrinking population will only result in increasing numbers of users coming to a similar conclusion and abandoning the platform, forming an endless loop of diminishing returns. Most likely, users will abandon the platform for a newly launched service that has not yet reached a significant level of exposure.

Legitimate marketing methods using social media are also compromised by "social spam." Social spam generally manifests as malicious or unwanted links embedded in posts or tweets using a link-shortening service such as Bitly or Google URL Shortener. This transforms the link's web address into a random-looking series of letters and numbers, making it impossible to predict the target of the link without actually clicking on it. URL shortening is very common among all users of social media, especially for services like SMS texts and Twitter, which drastically limit the number of characters available to users in each post. If a social media platform is infested with social spammers, acceptable marketing becomes drowned out in the noise or lumped in, fairly or not, with the undesired spam content.

Social media platforms can combat this simply by being reactive to their user base. Taking complaints seriously and offering adjustments to privacy policies or acceptable use policies can often be sufficient to calm unhappy users, who then feel that they have reasserted their control over the process.

Privacy Issues Closely related to implied consent are fears of privacy invasions. Although the purpose of most social media is to mine private data for both marketing and connection purposes (to sell to advertisers and to make it convenient for users to make social connections with people with similar interests), users of social media frequently assume they have not actually given up any reasonable expectation of privacy. As a result, any change to existing privacy policies can trigger complaints and dissatisfaction.

As an example, in 2010 Facebook announced plans to share phone numbers and home addresses of its members with application (App) developers to make online transactions easier and simpler. This sparked a backlash throughout the ranks of Facebook's user base. After some impotent attempts to explain the move's safety and utility, Facebook announced it would indefinitely shelf the plans to release this information. Although Facebook was completely within its rights, under its own terms of service, to implement this change in policy, it was wary of driving away its user base over a privacy issue and fundamentally acknowledged the user base's implied consent over its actions.

A perceived erosion of privacy in an attempt to mine user profiles for salable marketing information can eventually devolve into diminishing returns in a manner similar to the ownership issues previously discussed. As users leave a service to escape what they perceive as unfair privacy violations, the attempts to leverage the remaining population in turn cause more users to exit the service, eventually leaving the platform essentially dead.

Similarly, companies can combat this cycle by addressing privacy concerns promptly and by strengthening privacy protections, if only in the short-term. Quick action on these concerns can be crucial toward preserving an existing user base and building up new members.

Solutions

The main way to combat the cycle of diminishing returns in social media platforms is to maintain the user base. Eroding populations not only destabilize social media platforms, they make it increasingly difficult to monetize the remaining populations. A shrinking user base simultaneously makes the private data available to the service less desirable (and thus less lucrative) and makes it more difficult to attract new users to the service.

The "Studio 54" phenomenon concerns people's reluctance to join services that do not already have a significant user base. When the infamous nightclub Studio 54 opened in New York in 1977, the owners would frequently refuse to admit people despite having only a handful of people inside the club, thus creating the illusion of high demand and popularity. Similarly, social media platforms that do not have many users must combat this perception through advertising and by keeping all accounts on the books whether they are active or not. Advertising and invitation-only strategies can work in the early stages of building a user base, but once a social media platform has been established it is difficult to combat the perception that a dropping user base indicates a dying or dead community. This sort of diminishing return is being experienced by MySpace today. Once a dominant social media platform, it is now perceived as a "ghost town" despite still having a large number of active users.

Keeping a user base sufficiently populated not only battles perceptions of irrelevance or abandonment, but also keeps enough resources active in the platform to keep it financially viable. A user base can be maintained in a variety of ways:

- Addressing concerns over privacy or spam promptly

- Keeping inactive accounts listed as active

- Offering new services or premier services to existing users

- Partnering with users by giving certain "power users" official recognition

- Re-orienting the focus of a social media platform to align with most of the remaining users. While MySpace is considered irrelevant in many circles today, it has successfully rebranded itself as a social media platform specifically oriented toward musicians and independent bands and record labels. While its user base remains tiny compared with its previous height, its tighter focus has kept it viable.

Unlike traditional communication or networking services, social media platforms must be managed as a resource as well as a source of revenue. Because most are offered at no monetary cost to users and the customers themselves are, in a sense, the product, social media is extremely vulnerable to the phenomenon of diminishing returns in both acute, marketing campaign-specific situations and overall as a cultural phenomenon. While an overall collapse of social media as a popular segment of online culture and the modern lifestyle is unlikely, individual campaigns remain extremely vulnerable to diminishing returns as the signal-to-noise ratio of the content drops below acceptable levels.

Social media platforms are made up of individuals, but collectively they form a "hive mind" which will have definable opinions and coherent standards of what is acceptable and unacceptable, and the challenge is in defining these standrads for the particular platform in question. Although outliers will always exist, a consensus is usually attainable on social media platforms regarding acceptable behaviors, by both individuals and corporations and organizations using the network—as well as by the network itself.

A successful marketing campaign using social media platforms will do so without abusing the network to the extent that users reject the messages entirely or possibly even abandon the account. Careful monitoring, quick response to user reactions, and a mix of nonmarketing content in addition to on-message campaign material will keep diminishing returns from coalescing into an unavoidable cycle.

SOURCES OF ADDITIONAL INFORMATION

Social Media. http://mashable.com/category/social-media/
Social Media Platforms. http://www.myprgenie.com/articles/social-media-platforms
Social Media Resources. http://www.engage121.com/resources
Social Media Today. www.socialmediatoday.com

BIBLIOGRAPHY

Adhikari, R. (2011). Facebook does about-face following privacy backlash. Retrieved on January 28, 2013, from http://www.technewsworld.com/story/71672.html

Backstrom, L., Huttenlocher, D., Kleinberg, J., & Lan, X. (2006). Group formation in large social networks: membership, growth, and evolution. Proceedings of the 12th ACM SIGKDD international conference on knowledge discovery and data mining. *ACM*.

Charney, D. (2010). Social media could be harming your company: make sure you have clear policies in place regarding social media in the workplace. *EHS Today* 3(12), 8.

Di Giovanni, M. (2011). Filene undertakes study to determine social media value. *Credit Union Times*, 8.

Dumenco, S. (2012). What took us all so long to figure out the fatal flaw in Zuckerberg's Law? You know, there are actually limits to human attention spans. Retrieved on January 28, 2013, from http://adage.com/article/the-media-guy/zuckerberg-dismiss-law-diminishing-returns/235415

Fournier, S., & Avery, J. (2001). The uninvited brand. *Business Horizons*, *54*(3), 193–207.

Gross, W. (2011). Social media and the law of diminishing returns. Retrieved on January 28, 2013, from www.netlocations.com/nlblog/2011/11/social-media-and-the-law-of-diminishing-returns.

Hutkin, B. (2012). The online marketing law of diminishing returns. Retrieved on January 28, 2013, from www.mumsbusiness.com.au/2012/11/14/the-online-marketing-law-of-diminishing-returns

Kim, W. (2012). Man with a plan: advice from the Reddit co-founder on how to make social media work for you. *Popular Mechanics*. Retrieved on January 28, 2013, from http://www.popularmechanics.com/technology/gadgets/news/reddits-alexis-ohanian-on-good-social-media-karma-11000798

Kumar, V., & Reinartz, W. (2012). Relationship marketing and the concept of customer value. *Customer Relationship Management*, 21–31.

Marshall, G. W., Moncrief, W. C., Rudd, J. M., & Lee, N. (2012). Revolution in sales: the impact of social media and related technology on the selling environment. *Journal of Personal Selling and Sales Management*, *32*(3), 349–363.

Martinez, J. (2010). Measuring your social marketing: in his new book, social media metrics, Jim Sterne explains the right way to gauge your success. *CRM Magazine,* 19.

McIlwain, A. (2011). Do you make these social media mistakes? *Senior Market Advisor,* September 2011.

McKeon, M. (2010). The evolution of privacy on Facebook. Retrieved on January 28, 2013, from http://mattmckeon.com/facebook-privacy.

Melson, E. (2012). Social media & the law of diminishing returns. Retrieved on January 28, 2013, from writersadvancebootcamp.com/socail-media-the-law-of-diminishing-returns.

Murray, A. (2012). Don't stay stale: change up your social media campaign. Retrieved on January 28, 2013, from www.socialmediadelivered.com/2012/11/15/dont-stay-stale-change-up-your-social-media-campaign

Opsahl, K. (2010). Facebook's eroding privacy policy: a timeline. Retrieved on January 28, 2013, from https://www.eff.org/deeplinks/2010/04/facebook-timeline

Peterson, T. (2012). Farmers Insurance director of social media says people want to connect with faces, not products, on Facebook. *DM News,* 13.

Pollitt, C. (2011). Social media's point of diminishing returns—a small business conundrum. Retrieved on January 28, 2013, from http://www.kunocreative.com/blog/bid/57145/Social-Media-s-Point-of-Diminishing-Returns-A-Small-Business-Conundrum

Rice, R. E., & Atkin, C. H. (2013). *Theory and principles of public communication campaigns. Public communication campaigns.* Thousand Oaks, CA: Sage Publishing.

Shakarian, P., & Paulo, D. Large social networks can be targeted for viral marketing with small seed sets. arXiv preprint arXiv:1205.4431. Retrieved on January 28, 2013, from http://arxiv.org/pdf/1205.4431

Shalako, L. (2012). The law of rapidly diminishing returns: social media. Retrieved on January 28, 2013, from http://shalakopublishing.blogspot.com/2012/06/law-of-rapidly-diminishing-returns.html

Silpayamanant, J. (2012). Social media marketing and diminishing returns. Retrieved on January 28, 2013, from http://silpayamanant.wordpress.com/2012/06/11/social-media-marketing-and-diminishing-returns

Social experiment: you're on Facebook and LinkedIn. You Blog. You Tweet. But are you getting business benefit out of your social media strategy? (2011). *Inside Business,* 6.

Social media: counting crowds. (2011). *New Media Age,* 25.

Tobin, J., & Braziel, L. (2008). *Social media is a cocktail party.* Cary, NC: Ignite Social Media.

Consistency Among All Social Media Outlets

In This Essay

- Maintaining consistency in social media marketing and branding is a difficult but important task

- Avoiding controversial subjects and using humor judiciously help contribute to a positive social media presence and ensure a consistent tone and message

- Managing challenges to a consistent marketing message

- Different social media venues have different cultures and sensibilities

Overview

It is ironic that the ease with which social media is engaged often undermines its effectiveness both in simple communication and in terms of being an effective *marketing channel*. Since most public social media platforms have been designed to make it as easy as possible to create accounts and engage the network, it is easy for companies and individuals to set up multiple accounts, each representing a particular strategy at its time and each out of date or unused. It is also easy to have multiple active accounts broadcasting contradictory messages or messages at cross-purposes on both the same social media platform as well as concurrently on separate platforms.

The issue of consistency of message, of visual approach, and of tone is crucial to establishing a successful presence on any social media platform. Users of social media tend to be participants in more than one network simultaneously, and inconsistent messages or presentation will be noticed and remarked on. Once noticed, this perception undermines any future attempts at communicating an effective marketing message.

Marketing channel:
All sources used by marketers to get the product to the consumer.

Keeping brand messaging and customer contacts consistent is not simply a question of language choice and keeping information in line from one message to the next. There are many factors that need to be considered. A social media marketing presence must be planned in advance and carefully implemented to not only ensure consistency but also to be able to measure effectiveness and make adjustments to message and branding as needed.

The concept of consistency in a marketing context is not new. The term *integrated marketing communication* was coined in the 1990s to describe marketing plans that sought to have a consistent and cohesive approach via all avenues. Although social media as such did not exist at the time, the concept itself is very much the same today: use the available tools—now including social media platforms—in a way that is consistent across the spectrum of media and formats in order to deliver the same message over every channel for maximum impact.

Consistency of Message

The most important aspect of consistent use of social media is maintaining a consistent message across all social media platforms in use while still conforming to each community's aesthetic and expectations.

The first step toward this goal is to narrow contact with each platform to a single, official account or presence. Having several Twitter accounts, Facebook accounts, or Pinterest boards simply invites either duplicated content, which is counterproductive, or different voices and information produced by each. If earlier accounts were created for earlier, defunct campaigns or as dormant points of contact, they should be removed if possible or clearly deprecated and unused—marked as defunct and unofficial so there is no confusion as to which accounts are the official brand accounts—if deletion of the account is not possible.

In terms of message, consistency should involve not just the details of a product and service in regards to pricing, availability, special offers, and other database factors, but also what is *not* included in posts and updates. While a certain amount of personality should be striven for in social media engagements, there should be a consistent omission of political, religious, and off-color content or opinions unless these are consistently part of the brand's identity. It is tempting, sometimes, for a company to create and maintain a social media account for the owner or CEO where he or she interfaces more directly with customers and might pursue a more personal approach. However, it is crucial that even accounts which have a specific face attached to them maintain a consistent message that falls within the lines of the company's overall social media strategy.

Seizing the Moment: Deprecated

Often inconsistent social media mistakes occur when a marketing team attempts to co-opt a current event or sudden fad into their marketing. This sort of loose, ill-defined strategy is not only inconsistent because it relies on random events to occur that coincide with a marketing goal, it also means that approaches and language are not always vetted before they are launched into the world.

An example of a marketing team attempting to ride a current event and failing miserably was the Kenneth Cole Twitter fiasco of 2011. Noting the demonstrations in Egypt which eventually saw the ouster of President Mubarak, the Kenneth Cole corporate Twitter account sent the message "Millions are in uproar in #Cairo. Rumor is they heard our new spring collection is now available online at http://bit.ly/KCairo" and was signed "KC," implying that Kenneth Cole himself had either written or approved of the message. The negative reaction was swift and universal, forcing Kenneth Cole to issue an apology and remove the offending tweet.

The attempt to use an unfolding current event in a dynamic way might have seemed bold, but in reality it was viewed as simply offensive and inconsistent with the balance of Kenneth Cole marketing.

The lesson here is that social media marketing campaigns must be planned as part of a consistent approach, and sudden diversions from this plan, no matter how ingenious they might seem in the moment, can turn disastrous in terms of branding and consistency of message.

Variety of Formats

With only one point of contact on each platform, it is much easier to ensure that every communication is consistent in terms of content. However, it is also important to not simply copy and paste the same content from one account to another.

For one thing, having consistent information in duplicated formats makes the communications seem robotic and possibly auto-generated. Although users of social media platforms are generally tolerant of marketing incursions into their networks, they are also very quick to dismiss such messages if they are perceived as robotic. The entire point of a social media platform is interaction, and the automatic generation and distribution of identical posts, tweets, or updates makes a company's presence seem automated and detached. It is essential that each post be consistent in terms of message, but varied in terms of approach.

This can often be easily accomplished simply by re-casting the language of each post. Even minor variations in sentence structure or other aspects of the content can imply human interaction. This is often necessary when adjusting a post from another platform to Twitter or other size-restricted platforms, but it should be pursued for all the social media platforms utilized in your campaigns. The focus for consistency should be on the content, message, and visualization, not on the format and wording.

Consistency of Tone

In addition to consistency of message, there must also be a consistent tone to the messages passed through social media platforms. Tone consistency is a much greater challenge to achieve because of the subjective nature of the concept and the fact that many successful social media marketing strategies will incorporate a variety of content, as discussed below.

Although the tone of purely sales-driven or "official" communication—involving product descriptions, sales announcements, and other content directly related to the business—is relatively easy to manage because it consists naturally of "dry" information such as pricing or special offers, social media content that is meant to engage the community on a more humorous or educational basis is often difficult to bring into line regarding tone.

Attempts at humor are especially difficult. Humor is subjective and what seems like a mild joke to most may be perceived as inappropriate or offensive to some. The use of humor itself should also be carefully considered as it relates to the corporate or personal image being promoted. Although humor—whether simply a wry tone in a post or a joke or humorous link being passed on—is received very well on most social media platforms and can be very effective in establishing a positive image in users' minds, there are two main considerations when contemplating the use of humor in social media:

Appropriateness of Venue. Although general social media platforms such as Twitter and Facebook are very tolerant of humor in most forms, industry-specific social media platforms and smaller, more niche-oriented platforms may have a much different culture and be less tolerant of humor, even general, inoffensive humor.

Appropriateness of Culture. Many social media platforms are international and cross cultural borders. Even if the interactions to these sites are translated as appropriate, the root of the humor being quoted may not translate well to another culture.

As a result of these limitations, humor must be very carefully vetted and considered before being used, even if a humorous tone is consistently maintained across all social media interactions.

Consistency Across Media

The substance of content being transmitted over social media platforms is not the only consideration regarding consistency. Although the message must be consistent in detail and tone, the look of each message must also be consistent, incorporating a standardized look.

Textual

While many social media platforms do not allow or tolerate much font diversity, text messages can be disseminated as graphical attachments. In those cases font, font size, and layouts should be consistent from one platform and message to another. Having a disparate collection of stylistically unrelated fonts on each piece of a campaign can result in none of the postings being perceived as part of an identifiable individual account.

The wording of messages should also be consistent. Although there will likely be different versions of any post, tailored to the space requirements and other factors of each social media platform, certain keywords and phrases should be used consistently while the balance of the message can be varied as needed to prevent a "robotic" tone or perception.

Visual

Even more important is the visual design of non-textual elements. Logos and other graphics, if used, should be consistent from one message to another and one platform to another. Linked websites should also have the same design and graphics. Color schemes should be similar between all social media interactions, if appropriate.

Updated logos and other design changes should also be swapped in immediately to avoid having a variety of color palates and inconsistent design styles in the visual approach, and if multiple accounts are used on one social media platform, it is vital that they all follow a consistent design guideline. Even subtleties such as font choice can have a jarring or a cohesive effect on the overall reception of a marketing campaign.

Challenges to Consistency

Consistency across social media platforms may seem to be a simple concept, easily achieved. However, social media–based marketing campaigns differ from other marketing campaigns or promotional efforts because they are open-ended and without a precise end point. Once a social media presence is established in the service of a brand or company, it remains even if the accounts are allowed to go dormant or even, in some cases, deleted. This open-endedness also manifests in account proliferation.

Unofficial Accounts

Control over employee accounts on social media can be problematic. Employees clearly have the right to their own private presence on social media platforms; as a result it is impossible to prevent employees from creating such accounts. Preventing employees from polluting a marketing message with unscripted posts and tweets that are linked back to the brand or company can be prevented by advising employees not to incorporate any official branding into their account names or interactions. Even so, some employees will take it upon themselves to evangelize for their company or its products. Such actions may be perceived as the honest enthusiasm of an excited employee that it is, but amateurish attempts at marketing may backfire and implicate the entire company.

Additionally, it is often difficult to even identify which accounts may in fact be employees. There is very little attempt in the social media world to verify accounts. Twitter and Facebook do make these attempts with celebrities and some corporate or brand names, but even if the employee accounts are prevented from including a direct reference to a company or product in the account name in order to prevent confusion, there is still no way to prevent employees from discussing company strategy, products, or other aspects publicly on social media networks. This can lead to inconsistency in the marketing messages put out on these platforms.

Although organizations cannot prevent employees from posting content to social media, it is advisable for them to draft clear guidelines for their employees for posting content both as representatives of the organization using branded channels and as private individuals posting to their own accounts. It is important for employees to understand that they should not under any circumstances claim to represent the company or organization unless they are specifically and explicitly doing so as part of an overall social media plan.

Multiple Accounts

Marketing efforts on social media platforms can also be diluted, blunted, or rendered inconsistent when multiple accounts are maintained on a single platform, such as multiple Twitter accounts with variations of the organization name, or separate Facebook accounts with company branding. This is frequently the consequence of separate marketing teams for different products or aspects of one product, or older accounts from previous social media attempts that remain active either through separate marketing teams, distribution lists, or scheduled posts. When a new marketing effort involving social media platforms is planned, existing accounts should be shut down, or inventoried and incorporated actively into the new effort, complete with a graphical revamp to match the visual design of the rest of the campaign.

Tools Aiding a Consistent Approach

There are several tools available that can help make any social media presence more consistent. The key aspect to any marketing effort involving a social media presence is in planning and organization. Instead of treating social media as a "live wire" communication channel where raw, unedited materials are dumped into the channel, social media channels should be carefully orchestrated and every aspect of the communication passed through them—visuals, text, links—should be part of a cohesive plan with a consistent voice, look, and purpose.

Scheduling

One aspect of social media that can be incredibly useful for any sort of social media campaign is pre-scheduling of posts and tweets. A service such as Sendible (www.sendible.com) can be used to coordinate posts between multiple accounts on many popular social media platforms, including Twitter and Facebook.

Scheduling allows for a layer of editorial approval to be inserted between pushed social media posts and tweets and their public display. A marketing team can thus author several posts and schedule them, and an editorial team can review each one and check them for consistency of information, tone, and visual feel (if applicable). Messages that are not sufficiently consistent can then be removed from the queue and either deleted or sent back for revision, or simple changes can be made directly to correct inaccuracies or minor deviations from the design specs.

Looking Forward

As important as consistency is generally regarded to be, the new thinking regarding consistency in social media approaches has less focus on absolute consistency and more focus on what is termed *coherence*. The coherence approach seeks to take into consideration the different facets and aspects of different marketing channels, both in a macro and micro sense.

For example, a coherent approach to marketing would take into consideration the vast difference between a television ad and a Twitter account and seek to have an approach for each that kept consistency of message while eschewing consistency of format, style, or visuals (especially when the online channel in question, such as Twitter, has virtually no visual aspect at all). Humor may be appropriate on some platforms but not on others, and some platforms will obviously allow for a huge amount of detail to be communicated whereas others must be boiled down to the most basic bullet points of the marketing message.

The advantage to a coherent as opposed to a consistent approach is obvious: each channel is leveraged for its specific advantages. Although this may lead to some inconsistency in format, the core ideas remain consistent while the individual approach is specific to the platform being utilized.

For some marketing professionals, the movement toward a coherent approach signals a maturing view of social media platforms in general. Instead of a "everything but the kitchen sink" approach, used because no one truly understands social media or, perhaps, no one trusts that it will be a permanent marketing tool, a coherent approach understands better how people use social media platforms. They use these platforms differently than they use other media—differently from how they watch television and differently from how they read magazines and books. As a result, there is no "one size fits all" approach to marketing, and simply editing marketing copy down to 140 characters for use in a tweet is not sufficient for a marketing campaign, no matter how consistent the final result is with the balance of the campaign materials.

Include Offline Activities

The key component to many coherent marketing approaches is the integration of offline activities and online channels such as social media. This real-world activity has become a staple of online marketing approaches, whether it be meet-ups for socializing among members of an online community or contests that involve real-world items created or curated by users. Many marketing strategies that seek to incorporate social media neglect a real-world or offline component, imagining that the online communities formed via social media platforms are somehow purely digital. Consistency is often seen as part of the problem, as offline activities make it difficult to guarantee a consistent look and feel as compared with online content.

Conclusion

Marketing campaigns must always seek to be greater than the sum of their parts. The *signal-to-noise ratio* of the world in general and the Internet specifically is very low, and a single message is often lost in the tumult. For the same reason that any successful piece of individual marketing must repeat the key information and tag line several times in order to be memorable. Marketing messages must be repeatable to a very high degree and comprehensive in their choice of medium in order to raise their message above the din and tumult of competing messages. As time has gone by, the channels available for advertising have grown. Where once a single campaign in print magazines, augmented by radio or television buys, was sufficient, there is now no single dominant

Signal-to-noise ratio: *(informally) The ratio of useful information to false or irrelevant data in a conversation or exchange.*

medium for advertising, and thus a multifaceted approach has to be undertaken that includes both more traditional channels such as print, radio, and television alongside newer concepts such as social media and other Internet-related marketing.

This varied approach carries with it the danger of an unfocused and inconsistent message actually harming a brand or company. Inconsistency in branding dilutes brand identity and can be confusing and irritating to consumers. Modern marketing campaigns must be taken as a whole—social media components cannot simply be "dropped in" without a coherent, planned integration with the other media and approaches.

Understanding of social media in a marketing environment is evolving quickly. Social media did not exist 10 years ago and only recently has it been taken seriously as a marketing tool—or taken seriously in any context. Where once the idea of communicating in 140-character tweets was open for mockery, today books are written on the subject of how to effectively use Twitter to promote your brand. The understanding of social media will continue to evolve, as will the platforms themselves and how users make use of them in their daily lives, leading to an ever-changing, always challenging venue for marketing.

SOURCES OF ADDITIONAL INFORMATION

Facebook. www.facebook.com
Pinterest. www.pinterest.com
Twitter. www.twitter.com

BIBLIOGRAPHY

Belan, K. (2012). Five substantial shifts in branding that might be revolutionary. *Popsop*. Retrieved January 27, 2013, from http://popsop.com/59780.

Belch, G. E., & Belch, M. A. (2003). *Advertising and promotion—An integrated marketing communication perspective* (6th ed., pp. 16–18). New York: McGraw Hill.

Bennett, S. (2012). Simplicity, consistency and social media—How to brand your small business. Retrieved January 27, 2013, from http://www.mediabistro.com/alltwitter/smb-branding_b28231.

Bhagat, R. N., Dutta, M., & Dutta, B. K. (2012). Social media promotion: Role of IMC in rising above the clutter. Roorkee, India: National Conference on Emerging Challenges for Sustainable Business 2012.

Burton, S., & Soboleva, A. (2011). Interactive or reactive? Marketing with Twitter. *Journal of Consumer Marketing, 28*(7), 491–499.

Dahlen, M., Lange, F., & Smith, T. (2010). *Marketing communications: A brand narrative approach.* Hoboken, NJ: John Wiley & Sons.

Glauberman, S. (2012). Many platforms, one voice: How to maintain a consistent social media persona. Retrieved January 27, 2013, from http://contentmarketinginstitute .com/2012/05/how-to-maintain-a-consistent-social-persona.

Henley, N., Raffin, S., & Caemmerer, B. (2011). The application of marketing principles to a social marketing campaign. *Marketing Intelligence & Planning, 29*(7), 697–706.

Hurley, L. (2012). If content is king, consistency is queen. Retrieved January 27, 2013, from http://www.thesocialnetworkingnavigator.com/social-media-strategy/ if-content-is-king-consistency-is-queen.

Kanter, B. (2012). One simple secret to social media success: Post consistent content your audience loves. Retrieved January 27, 2013, from http://socialmediatoday .com/kanter/597356/one-simple-secret-social-media-success-post-consistent-content-your-audience-loves.

Kaplan, A. M., & Haenlein, M. (2011). The Britney Spears universe: Social media and viral marketing at its best. *Business Horizons.*

Olenski, S. (2012). Integrated marketing communications—Then and now. *Forbes.* Retrieved January 27, 2013, from http://www.forbes.com/sites/ marketshare/2012/05/31/integrated-marketing-communications-then-now

Peck, D. (2011). *Think before you engage: 100 questions to ask before starting a social media marketing campaign.* Hoboken, NJ: John Wiley and Sons.

Ripam, T., Pandit, Y., & Fleit, C. (2012). How to be a more coherent marketer. Retrieved January 27, 2013, from http://www.strategy-business.com/article/ 12202?gko=f9a77

Smith, P. R., & Zook, Z. (2011). *Marketing communications: Integrating offline and online with social media.* Kogan Page.

Welker, K., Guo, F., & Shamdasani, S. (2011). Designing web marketing that works for users: Finding best practices through evaluation and conversation. *Internationalization, Design and Global Development,* 407–416.

Taking Advantage of Interactivity

In This Essay

- Many people use social media to talk about and review products and services, making social media the new "word of mouth" method for learning about these products

- Social media encourages interaction, and brands can benefit from having potential customers interact with them by using concepts such as gamification

- Social media interactions can help consumers identify with and remain loyal to a brand, and giving consumers a sense of control adds to a company's credibility

Overview

A primary component of social media marketing is the ability of a customer to take an active part in developing user-generated content, thus putting them in control of the online experience. By understanding how this interactivity works, it is possible to design a social media marketing strategy that creates loyalty among customers through the use of active engagement and gamification methods of marketing.

The marketing company Bunchball specializes in gamification, describing it as an implementation of "game mechanics across websites, social networks and mobile applications [so] businesses can engage their users in a more meaningful way and reap tangible business benefits, such as increased customer loyalty and increased time spent on site" (Bunchball, 2012).

By developing a marketing plan based on the concept that users beget more users by spreading the word and increasing the success of a product just by using it, a business can capitalize on its social media presence.

This concept assumes that social media sites such as Facebook, Flickr, and YouTube exist primarily for the purpose of interaction and the sharing of information.

Gamification of Social Media

The concept of gamification, or developing active methods of engaging customers with a brand or company's products, has been around for many years. One example is from the early 1990s "Friends and Family" campaign from the cellular phone company MCI, where rewards were offered to spread the word about a specific project.

Before the 1990s, credit card companies were using point systems to encourage customers to use their cards in exchange for rewards when their points reached a certain level (Samuel, 2011). The fact that consumers have been exposed to this concept in offline environments for quite some time means it is not necessary to introduce or explain the concept before implementation.

New Rules of Engagement

Web 2.0: *The second generation of the World Wide Web that includes features such as blogs, wikis, and social networking.*

Use of the Web as an interactive environment, often referred to as *Web 2.0*, has created a virtual water cooler where customers can rate products on sites like Amazon, review an actor's performance by creating a YouTube video critique, or even create their own websites that focus on specific topics or trends that are relevant to their social network.

Consumers in their teens, 20s, and 30s are no longer passive viewers of information provided by corporations, businesses, and government organizations. Simply posting a link to another website from a Facebook page immediately creates a new Web experience for other users viewing that page.

This level of instant engagement has the potential to directly affect the Web experience, and is being used by businesses to encourage spreading the word about products and services. Wikipedia is one of the most well-known examples of a user-generated content (UGC) website that allows anyone in the world the ability to write or edit any topic on the site (Rosen, 2010).

A 2007 study stated that "out of more than 1,200 Net-Geners and iGeners [those under age 22], 39% spent one hour per week working on their MySpace pages, with another 22% spending two to three hours per week" (Rosen, 2007).

This usage has continued to increase as social sites evolve to allow for advocacy of social causes, networking beyond private social circles on sites such as LinkedIn, and targeted paid advertising that seeks to reach niche markets. As of May 2010, a CNN report stated that Twitter users tweet more than 50 million times per day (Parks, 2011).

A 2008 survey by Synovate in partnership with Microsoft entitled "Young Adults Revealed" was conducted to find out exactly how much young adults engage with online brands on a daily basis. Twenty-eight percent of 12,603 people between 18 to 24 years of age from 26 countries said they had talked about a brand on an online forum. Twenty-three percent added brand-related content to their instant messaging (IM) service, with 19% using branded content on the personal home page of their favorite social sites (Synovate, 2008).

The New Word of Mouth

Word of mouth has always been held in high esteem as a reliable way to receive information about products or services. Using social media to communicate is the better than word of mouth, giving the customer the power to search for what they want (Qualman, 2011).

Many brands work to develop quality content on social media sites in order to build and sustain a loyal following. This approach is the opposite of traditional marketing techniques that follow a top-down dissemination-of-information approach.

> People tend to believe the content on websites that contain information they are interested in or invested in (Choi, Watt & Lunch, 2006).

Building Trust Through Interactivity

By attracting and maintaining engagement with loyal customers through social media, a business or brand's information and updates can be quickly and easily supported and shared through a customer's use of social sites. Products such as Skittles and Starbucks have a history of creating a great customer experience online and have benefitted greatly from this marketing approach. Celebrities including Ashton Kutcher, Amitabh Bachchan, Paulo Coelho, and Lady Gaga have used Twitter and other social sites to gain support from fans, which translates into more moviegoers, more concert tickets sold, or the purchase of goods backed by them.

A former advertising executive from MySpace and other social sites views this viral loop as "the *most* advanced direct-marketing strategy being developed in the world right now" (Penenberg, 2009).

Creating a Feedback Loop

By creating a feedback loop between product and customer, a company or individual can alter customers' purchasing behavior by providing them with information about their actions or decisions and then giving them the opportunity to change those actions, encouraging them to buy a product or try it for the first time.

An offline example of a feedback loop is the thermostat of a building, which is designed to turn on when the building temperature drops to a predetermined number, thus firing the furnace or heater to maintain a stable interior temperature. Another example is the miles per gallon display for the Toyota Prius, which has been known to convert drivers into hypermilers that become overly focused on trying to get every last mile out of a tank of gas (Goetz, 2011).

In 2011, Thomas Goetz explained a feedback loop as having four stages:

TABLE 1 Stages of a Feedback Loop

Description of Stage	Behavior
Stage One: Evidence Stage or Data Collection Stage	A behavior needs to be measured, captured, and stored.
Stage Two: Information Relay to the Individual/Relevance Stage	The collected information must be transformed from a raw-data format into compelling information. It then needs to be relayed to the individual in a context that makes it emotionally resonant.
Stage Three: Consequence Stage	In this stage the information being relayed must clearly illuminate one or more paths one wishes the individual to take.
Stage Four: Action Stage	This stage clearly defines a moment when the individual can change their behavior, make a choice, and act on it.

After the four stages are complete, the action is measured for success and the feedback loop is run again, with each action simulating a new desired behavior that gets the individual closer to the goal or purchase.

When using social media to market or gain widespread support for a product, the use of online games, incentive programs, and reward systems are a few of the ways these stages can be implemented without being blatantly obvious to the consumer.

David Wiesenfeld, of Brand Advertiser Solutions, stated in September 2009 that "in the future, your children will likely conduct the majority of their shopping online." Gamification and interaction with brands is something that has become automatic and assumed as the Web and social media sites evolve.

Creating Advocacy for a Brand

By linking a game or memorable advertisement with a brand, it becomes more likely that a consumer will remember the brand itself. Joe Stagaman, EVP, Advertising Effectiveness Analytics for Nielsen, said "a memorable commercial is important, but won't be effective if viewers don't make a connection between the ad and your brand."

According to a Nielsen October 2012 study, the top five characteristics of ads that exhibit strong brand linkage among consumers are:

1. **Brand Cues Early and Often, Visual & Verbal**: The brand's representation should be pervasive throughout the advertisement, depicted with auditory cues that mention the brand as well as with visual cues, such as the actual product or brand logos.

2. **Leverage Brand Icon:** Using a recognized icon is a tried-and-true technique that both injects the brand into the advertisement and makes the story about it.

3. **Integrate Brand into Storyline:** A storyline creates a scenario to which your audience can relate. Adding brand elements into the scenario allows the audience to connect with the brand.

4. **Establish an "Ownable" Creative Concept:** From a signature character to a theme that spans across a campaign, some creatives are truly unique to the brand.

5. **Message as Brand Cue:** A storyline is an effective way to deliver brand messages in a meaningful and memorable way.

Case Study Example: Foursquare

The social website Foursquare.com provides a mobile app that allows a person to share where they are at any given time. At the same time it provides recommendations and deals that are customized based on where the user, their friends, and people with similar tastes have been. This is designed to encourage a customer to do specific things or take pre-designed steps through the site to earn higher levels and badges (Priebatsch, 2010).

Brick and mortar businesses are able to use Foursquare to broadcast local updates that connect with users in their area, encouraging them to check-in at their store or share updates with their friends. Virtual companies or brands can create Foursquare pages that allow customers to comment on products and events, connect via social media sites, and use other engagement tools. When a person checks in, they can browse tips, specials, and related products based on their location (Foursquare, 2012).

Turning Interaction Into Purchases

By turning users into fans, a company can increase sales and productivity for its products (Bunchball, 2012). The following are some examples of successful campaigns that rely on gamification.

Wendy's Fry-for-All Facebook Campaign

Designed to promote awareness for their Natural Cut Fries product, this social media marketing campaign used the company's Facebook page to encourage interactivity in a game called "Fry-for-All."

All players posted a small box of virtual fries to their personal Facebook page and as a reward, received an order of free Wendy's Natural Cut Fries. By encouraging friends to pick a fry from their box, all participants were entered into sweepstakes for larger prizes, such as iPads and Nintendo Wii systems. Boxes that were emptied resulted in a coupon for free fries being unlocked, enticing the customer to move on to the next level for an even larger box of fries.

This direct product engagement created a feedback loop for a new product launch, encouraging loyal customers to purchase multiples of the same item as well as securing new customers through friend referrals (Bunchball, 2012).

Curiosity—What's Inside the Cube?

As of November 2012, nearly half a million people have played a game that requires poking a giant virtual cube with the promise of seeing the center. The game *Curiosity—What's Inside the Cube?* is owned by the independent game studio 22Cans and has been described as delivering an almost obsessive experience to users (Tanz, 2012).

Rewards include virtual coins for efficient poking, which allows for even faster poking, with some players spending their time carving personal designs into the cube for the simple anticipation of someone else finding it on the vast canvas. A launch trailer for the game stated that "whoever chips away at that last block will have their life changed forever," evoking a feeling of anticipation and desire that is similar to the thought of winning the lottery.

The company 22Cans was founded by well-known game designer Peter Molyneux, known for past successes with games such as *The Entrepreneur, Populous,* and *Black & White*. Although he created the disappointing game *Milo* in 2010, which was unsuccessful in its promise to deliver "a real, living being in a computer" to users, gamers continue to be mesmerized by his creations (Tanz, 2012).

Club de Noveleras

Created in 2011 by L'Oreal USA with the Telemundo Communications Group, a social media marketing campaign was fashioned to connect Telemundo telenovela fans with beauty brands from the United States.

Designed to capitalize on the growing economic power of Hispanic America, this social media marketing campaign relies on online and offline methods of connecting with consumers, including a fan opt-in website called *clubdenoveleras.com* that offers beauty tips and social engagement with telenovela stars (Elliot, 2011).

The website includes branded content with prizes from each featured company. Fans sign up on the site and are rewarded points for making comments, viewing photo galleries and videos, and sharing content with friends on Facebook. In addition to the online marketing campaign, an off-line sister campaign with ten Telemundo markets provided opportunities for fans to try the products and meet Telemundo stars in person (Bunchball, 2012).

The Future of Interactivity

In the book *Socialnomics*, Eric Qualman believes that what an individual posts on social media sites about their actions, lifestyle, and behavior choices actually "contributes to your individual brand or social tattoo".

In the same way, it is possible for a company or brand to produce interactive games and other elements online that evoke a desire for people to not only choose to use and be associated with a product, but to also take ownership of it as they would their unique personality traits and actions viewed as desirable by friends and associates.

Much easier, responsive, and more intimate than e-mail, social media sites provide a multitude of ways people can update their status in relationships, jobs, or other endeavors. These updates tie directly into their purchasing behavior, making this valuable information from a marketing perspective.

When Tony Blair, former prime minister of the United Kingdom, was asked what he believed to be the most challenging aspect of his job, he said:

> The way in which information is exchanged so quickly has forever changed the way in which people want to consume information. They demand that things be condensed into 20-second sound bites. With complex problems, this is exceedingly difficult, but to be an effective communicator and leader you need to be able to condense complex items down to the core and be able to do this quickly (World Business Forum, 2008).

By becoming comfortable with the idea of relinquishing some control of a brand image and, instead of trying to control all aspects of it, shifting into a marketing model that allows manipulation by customers through social media, a company can use this method of marketing to their advantage.

If 90% of opinions on social media are positive and only 10% are negative, the positive will overwhelm the negative, and the 10% will not cripple the brand's reputation. In fact, negative comments have been proven to add credibility. Numerous studies have shown that products with zero negative comment are consistently outsold by products that have a few negative comments (Qualman, 2011).

With Facebook adding millions of new users each month, with over 30 million people joining in May 2010 alone, it has overtaken Google as the most visited site in the world (Partridge, 2011). Marketing campaigns that use social media sites as a core strategy have proven successful with far-reaching effects as more and more of these sites are seen as a primary and trusted way to share information with each other.

SOURCES OF ADDITIONAL INFORMATION

How Gamification Can Create Social Media Buzz. www.entreprenew.com/video/224177

22cans. www.22cans.com.

BIBLIOGRAPHY

Abernathy, J. (2012). *The complete idiot's guide to social media marketing*. New York: Alpha.

Brogan, C. (2010). *Social media 101: Tactics and tips to develop your business online*. Hoboken, NJ: John Wiley & Sons, Inc.

Bunchball. (2012). Bunchball case studies. Retrieved November 11, 2012, from http://www.bunchball.com/blog-categories/case-study.

Choi, J., Watt, J., & Lunch, M. (2006). Perceptions of news credibility about the war in Iraq: Why war opponents perceived the Internet as the most credible medium. *Journal of Computer-Mediated Communication, 12*(1).

Elliot, S. (2011, April 5). A growing population, and target, for marketers. *The New York Times*. Retrieved November 7, 2012, from http://www.nytimes.com/2011/04/05/business/media/05adco.html?_r=2.

Foursquare. (2012). Case studies of Foursquare brand platforms. Retrieved November 10, 2012, from http://business.foursquare.com/case-studies-brands/.

Foursquare. (2012). Introducing Local Updates from businesses—keeping up with the places you love has never been easier!. Retrieved November 2, 2012, from http://blog.foursquare.com/2012/07/18/introducing-local-updates-from-businesses-keeping-up-with-the-places-you-love-has-never-been-easier/.

Goetz, T. (2011, June 19). Harnessing the power of feeback loops. *Wired*. Retrieved November 8, 2012, from http://www.wired.com/magazine/2011/06/ff_feed-backloop/.

Halligan, B., & Shah, D. (2010). *Inbound marketing*. Hoboken, NJ: John Wiley & Sons, Inc.

Harfoush, R. (2009). *Yes we did! An inside look at how social media built the Obama brand*. Berkeley: New Riders.

Keane, M. (2008, October 29). Hulu celebrates first anniversary, gains popularity by serving fewer ads. *Wired*. Retrieved November 12, 2012, from http://blog.wired.com/business/2008/10/hulu-turns-one.html.

Kelsey, T. (2010). *Social networking spaces: From Facebook to Twitter and everything in between*. New York: Apress.

Martin, S. (2012). *The ten, make that nine, habits of very organized people. Make that ten: The tweets of Steve Martin.* New York: Grand Central Publishing.

McCorvey, J. (2010). How to use social networking sites to drive business. *Inc.* Retrieved October 26, 2012, from http://www.inc.com/guides/using-social-networking-sites.html.

Mooney, C. (2009). *Online social networking.* Detroit: Lucent.

The Nielsen Company. (2009). Nielsen Global Online Consumer Survey 2009. Retrieved November 4, 2012, from http://blog.nielsen.com/nielsenwire/wp-content/uploads/2009/07/pr_global-study_07709.pdf.

Nielsen Wire. (2008). Effective ads marry message with impact. Retrieved November 4, 2012, from http://blog.nielsen.com/nielsenwire/consumer/effective-ads-marry-message-with-impact/.

Parks, P. (2011). *Online social networking.* San Diego: Reference Point Press, Inc.

Partridge, K. (2011). *Social networking.* New York: The H. W. Wilson Company.

Penenberg, A. (2009). *Viral loop.* New York: Hyperion.

Priebatsch, S. (2010). Building the game layer on top of the world. TEDxBoston. Retrieved November 8, 2012, from http://youtu.be/Yn9fTc_WMbo.

Qualman, E. (2011). *Socialnomics.* Hoboken, NJ: John Wiley & Sons, Inc.

Rigney, R. (2012, November 9). Why are half a million people poking this giant cube? *Wired.* Retrieved November 9, 2012, from http://www.wired.com/gamelife/2012/11/curiosity/.

Rosen, J. (2009, March 11). Be it twittering or blogging, it's all about marketing. *The New York Times.*

Rosen, L. (2007). *Me, MySpace, and I.* New York: Palgrave Macmillan.

Rosen, L. (2010). *Rewired.* New York: Palgrave MacMillan.

Samuel, R. (2011). Gamification: A new name for an old trick. Retrieved November 10, 2012, from http://rajsamuel.squarespace.com/samosa_babble/2011/8/11/gamification-a-new-name-for-an-old-trick.html.

Shih, C. (2009). *The Facebook era: Tapping online social networks to build better products, reach new audiences, and sell more stuff.* Boston: Pearson.

Smith, T. (2001). *Loyalty-based selling.* New York: Amacom.

Synovate. (2008). Young adults eager to engage with brands online, global research from Microsoft and Synovate reveal. Retrieved November 11, 2012, from http://www.webwire.com/ViewPressRel.asp?aId=79517.

Tanz, J. (2012, October 19). How a videogame god inspired a twitter doppelgänger— and resurrected his career. *Wired.* Retrieved November 11, 2012, from http://www.wired.com/gamelife/2012/10/ff-peter-molyneux/all/.

Twitchell, J. (2004). *Branded nation.* New York: Simon & Schuster.

Wiesenfeld, D. (2009). In the future your kids won't shop the way you do. *Nielsen Wire.* Retrieved November 2, 2012, from http://blog.nielsen.com/nielsenwire/consumer/in-the-future-your-kids-won%E2%80%99t-shop-the-way-you-do/2009.

World Business Forum. (2008). Radio City Music Hall, New York.

Increasing Online Discoverability

In This Essay

- Search engine optimization (SEO) is very helpful in increasing online visibility

- One of the ways to optimize search engine results is to make use of keywords

- Linking to other websites can assist in increasing online visibility

- Web analytics can let a business see how much traffic is coming and going from the website

- Content is very important to creating a useful website

Introduction

For many businesses, overall success depends on online success. This means that the online presence, whether it is a website, a blog, or an e-commerce shop, is a critical aspect of marketing. The goal, as with most marketing tools, is to increase exposure to the target market.

Online marketing can be as challenging as traditional marketing, but there are many ways to increase the likelihood that a website will be reached by potential customers. Marketing success depends on reaching customers where they are, and where they are is increasingly online. According to *Forbes* magazine, in the United States alone, the number of Internet searches made every month has reached 12 billion.

Consumers search the Internet for products and information. When they find a reliable online source, they return to that source. The development of this trust translates into online accountability, which has wide-ranging benefits for the company. According to the book *The Art of SEO: Mastering Search Engine Optimization*, online search activity drives offline sales. As the book's authors explain, "Search marketing has a greater impact on in-stores sales lift than display advertising—three times greater, in fact."

However, before consumers can trust a website, they first have to find the site. No matter how good a website may be in terms of usability and content, the site is useless if it remains out of reach of consumers. Improving the odds that a site will be discovered begins with improving the site's rankings in search engine results. Effective strategies exist to help boost a website's ranking in search engines such as Google, Firefox, and Bing. However, getting to the top of the search-engine results mountain is no small task.

Understanding Search Engines

Understanding how search engines operate is the first step toward taking control of a website's discoverability. A search engine, the tool that allows Internet users to access information, depends on software programs called *spiders* to gather data from the web. As their name suggests, these programs crawl the Internet, from website to website, searching for information relevant to a particular search. As part of their information-gathering process, the programs index information to make it ready for retrieval when an Internet user conducts a search. The search engine then scans its index file to connect the searcher with the websites most relevant to the search terms used.

Although all search engines use the spider method, each search engine has a unique way of interacting with the information gathered. Search engines use various methods to match search terms with the stored information, which is why Internet users should conduct their searches with more than one search engine. This will ensure that the searcher reaches as much information as possible.

Another way to access information on the web is through directories. The listings of open directories are compiled by human editors rather than computer software. Paid inclusion directories are similar to open directories, but the people or businesses who pay for inclusion have priority in having their website listed (nonpaying users do get listed but lower in the results).

Knowing how search engines gather and rank information is pivotal to online success. This knowledge makes it possible to optimize a website's rankings within the major search engines.

Search Engine Optimization (SEO)

Search engine optimization (SEO) tactics are associated with the use of keywords within website content. Although content development is a major aspect of SEO, experts in the technology field emphasize that SEO involves much more than keywords. SEO, in fact, encompasses a wide-ranging strategy.

According to Nick Burcher, author of *Paid, Owned, Earned: Maximizing Marketing Returns in a Socially Connected World*, many factors contribute to where a website appears in search results: "Technical optimization is based on how a site is structured and set up. The site coding and programming language used, the site structure, the way a site is hosted, the load speed, the URL formats, the tagging and a whole range of other technical aspects which contribute to how a site shows up on a search engine, and more importantly, where it shows up in the search engine rankings" (Burcher, 2012). SEO is not only a matter of the site's content. Optimizing a site's rankings also depends on how the site is set up. It should be easy for "spiders" to access and index the website's information for search engine retrieval.

According to the authors of *The Art of SEO*, plans regarding search optimization should be discussed during the website development phase. Important factors include decisions about content management system, site architecture, and content development, all of which are integral parts of any website's foundation. Including SEO strategy as part of the website development process makes good sense because the site's overall purpose and goals will help guide SEO decisions and strategies from the beginning.

The first priority in the development process is to build a website that is well organized and easy to navigate. Then specifics related to the site's content can be addressed. Editorial optimization, therefore, is the second element of a successfully optimized website. Unlike the site's underlying technical architecture, its content is more often changing than not.

What will appear in the list of websites on a search engine results page depends on what terms a user has entered into the search box. Search engines scan a website's content, or articles, for words that match or are similar to words used in the search terms. These keywords have become a main emphasis in content creation, because the more keywords a search engine encounters when crawling the site, the higher the site will appear on the results page.

This does not mean, however, that content creators should target an audience of spiders and cram keywords everywhere. The search engines have caught on to this process of keyword stuffing and this strategy can backfire. As Neil Patel writes at Copyblogger.com, "Stuffing all of your keywords into the first 200 words of your articles will definitely send up red flags, not only from search engines but from people as well." Keywords are important, but the best SEO content creation strategy is to write relevant content with keywords placed strategically throughout an article.

According to Patel, the most effective placement areas for keywords are the following:

- H1 tags
- Title tags
- H2 and H3 tags

- The first paragraph
- Image tags
- Anchor tags

Keywords should be used in a way that makes sense within the content rather than being just thrown in where they do not fit organically in hopes of improving search results.

There are several million keywords, and choosing those that are most relevant to site goals is essential. The Google keyword tool can help find words that are popular for specific subject areas. A content writer can type in a particular category, the name of the website, or even a general category, and the Google keyword tool will offer suggestions based on input. Results are ranked based on popularity, global monthly searches, and local monthly searches. This will help pinpoint popular keywords used in a local or global scale. Content developers can choose the word, or words, most appropriate to their specific audience and apply them in strategic areas throughout their website content.

In addition to technical and editorial optimization, according to Burcher, the third pillar of SEO is linking. Search engines aim to provide the most relevant results; thus, the results listed higher up on search engine results pages are usually the websites that have the most inbound and outbound links to and from other websites. In other words, how many other websites think the information on a particular website is important enough to share on their site? Also, does the website in question offer other relevant content from outside sources?

Exchanged information is a sign that the information is relevant to the search terms used. The website that has (1) the best organization, (2) the most valuable information (with strategically placed keywords), and (3) many incoming and outgoing links is the site that ranks highest in search engines.

Web Analytics

The phrase *web analytics* refers to the diagnostic information that describes how users interact with a particular website. On what page or pages does the user click? Which information is shared, and which is not being shared? According to Andrew Maier, in his article "Complete Beginner's Guide to Web Analytics and Measurements," web analytics answers the question, "What action(s) do people take after they give us their attention?" Furthermore, Avinash Kaushik, author of *Web Analytics 2.0: The Art of Online Accountability & Science of Customer Centricity*, states that using web analytics is: "the analysis of qualitative and quantitative data from your website and the competition, to drive a continual improvement of the online experience that your customers, and potential customers have, which translates into your desired outcomes (online and offline)."

When these tools were first used in the early 1990s, only large companies had access to them because they were very expensive. However, now that they are widely available and free, anyone can use web analytic tools to boost online efficiency. According to Kaushik, "[Among] the biggest changes in recent years was the introduction of a free robust web analytics tool, Google Analytics... Google analytics' biggest impact was to create a massive data democracy. Anyone could quickly add a few lines of JavaScript code to the footer file on their website and possess an easy-to-use reporting tool. The number of people focusing on web analytics in the world went from a few thousand to hundreds of thousands very quickly, and it's still growing" (Kaushik, 2010). Web analytics tools have become so popular, in fact, that choices about what tools to use can be overwhelming. An online search using the terms "free web analytics tools 2012," for example, returned 334 million results.

In his 2010 article "11 Best Web Analytics Tools," Lou Dubois, a social media editor for NBC Universal's WCAU-TV, offers help in searching through the myriad of analytics tools. He lists the best tools as including (but not limited to) the following:

- Google Analytics: Service offers information on which site the user has come from and what they have done while visiting the website.

- Yahoo! Web Analytics: Service with offerings similar to those of Google Analytics with good multisite raw data information gathering.

- Crazy Egg: This service offers heat maps for the data collected. It permits website owners to track a visitor's every click allowing the owner to see which parts of the site are getting the most traffic.

- Compete: This analytics tool allows the tracking of which keywords were used to find the website, as well as which keywords are sending users to the competition.

- Google Website Optimizer: Tool that allows the analysis of which content on the site leads to the most clicks.

- Optimizely: This tool allows the website owner to measure and improve the website through *A/B testing*. There is no programming involved and the tool is very user friendly.

- KISSinsights: This analytics tool offers a customizable feedback form for visitors. Site owner can manage questions easily, and customer responses are provided in short comment form.

- 4Q by iPerceptions: Service that allows a website owner to understand what people are doing while on the site. This involves a survey that asks users what they came to the website to do, did they actually accomplish this task, and were they satisfied?

- ClickTale: This tool records every click visitors make on a website from the second they land on the site until they leave. Offers heat maps, customer behavior reports, and traditional conversion analytics.

- Facebook Insights: Service for e-commerce businesses that have a Facebook presence. There is detailed information on follower counts, the number of "likes" and comments a post receives, and more.

- Twitalyzer: Service that measures the impact and levels of engagement Twitter followers are having on a particular account. Information used to analyze impact is based on number of followers and retweet levels.

A/B testing: *An experimental approach to website testing in which two versions of a website are compared. The two versions of the website are identical except for one variation that might impact user behavior.*

Although web analytic tools may seem practically limitless, Dubois goes on to say that having the necessary people on board to translate this data is essential to putting all that information to good use. The data collected from these tools should be used to implement real change on a website to help meet e-commerce goals.

What Makes an Effective Website?

According to a "25-Point Website Usability Checklist" at the website User Effect (www.usereffect.com) and used as a companion to Kaushik's *Web Analytics 2.0* book, the first principle for keeping users at a website is quick loading time. The importance of this factor continues to increase as more Internet users get online via broadband connections. User Effect's checklist puts ideal loading times at less than 100 kilobytes per millisecond. Other important factors include adequate contrast between text and background, and easy-to-read font size and spacing. The goal is to make the reader's experience as comfortable as possible. Plug-ins such as Flash should be used sparingly. The company logo should be prominently displayed within the website, and the tagline should clearly state the business goal. This allows the visitor to know what the website is about within a few seconds, which is an important rule of thumb for the home page. The company logo should be a clickable image that leads the visitor to the home page. A website does not have much time to make an impact before a visitor decides to stay or leave a page. If the home page is not clear, concise, and appealing to the eye, there is a good chance a visitor will leave within seconds.

Contact information is important. The fanciest graphics and add-ins will be worthless if the "about" page is not well-written. The "about" page should include a description of the business, including purpose and vision, and contact information. Using text, as opposed to images, when listing contact information is better so that this information can be picked up by search engines.

There should be a clearly outlined search box within the website. The in-site search box serves the same purpose as a general search engine but this is site specific. It helps the user find particular information needed inside the website by typing in keywords. In addition to a search box, site-wide consistency with style is important. Consistency between layout and headings should be maintained to avoid confusing the visitor. Site copy should be clear, concise, and jargon-free.

Content Is King

The content created on any website should be determined by the audience the site is trying to attract. According to the authors of *The Art of SEO*, determining the audience for a website involves "an understanding of what you have to offer visitors to your site, both now and in the future." This goes beyond having a relevant library of articles, videos, and photo gallery; it also involves creating something that competitors are not readily providing. For instance, several similarly themed websites may all have solid how-to articles in their content base, but for one site to move ahead of the others its information has to be innovative. The authors of *The Art of SEO* explain that to successfully out-rank competitors, a website must offer something that particular niche market has not yet seen. The site "must bring something new and unique to the market. Perhaps it can offer a solution to a problem that no one else has been able to solve before. Or perhaps it covers the same content as its competition, but it is the first to release a high-quality video series on the topic. Or perhaps it focuses on a specific vertical niche, and establishes itself as a leader in that specific niche."

In *The Art of SEO*, the authors stress the importance of having a clear focus for the website. Ideally, during the website development phase, a company's leaders will determine site goals, and SEO tactics will merge with long-term business goals.

Mikal Belicove, writing at the Entrepreneur.com blog, says that content has been elevated over "search engine marketing, print relations and even print, television, and radio advertising as the preferred marketing tool for today's business-to-business entrepreneur." He describes content marketing as the creation of original content, with the goal of generating business leads. Another aim is to boost a business's brand visibility. The popularity of content marketing has to do with its relatively low cost, as well as its ability to generate qualified leads while simultaneously engaging prospective consumers.

Social Media Marketing for Online Visibility

Sharing the content that websites put so much effort into creating is the next step toward enhancing online visibility. This is where social media comes into play. According to Dave Evans, author of *Social Media Marketing: An Hour a Day*, social media "is text, words, pictures, video, and the like created with the intention of sharing." Social media is based on real and authentic dialogue between people who share common interests. The sharing, of course, takes place across the web. Examples of popular social media sites include Twitter, Facebook, Flickr, and YouTube. Using social media as a marketing tool is "about what your community of supporters can do to help you build your business" (Evans, 2008). Social media allows marketers to provide valuable, solid information to a consumer base and then entice them to share that information with their social networks.

Successful social media marketing depends on a site's ability to influence a group. The way to increase influence across social media is to listen to the target consumer group. Marketers must be sensitive to the online pulse. To measure the mood of the online social sphere, marketers follow the "content trail" of ratings, reviews, and comments. Content developers are guided by this trail. "Listening to and responding to your customers by paying attention to their conversations is a great way to use social media to influence these discussions" (Evans, 2008). It is the responsibility of a business owner who is using social media to provide consumers with an experience that they actually want to talk about and share.

An invaluable aspect of social media for the marketer is the feedback loop, whereby consumers can respond immediately to content. Dave Evans writes that it is "through this feedback loop—and your measurement of it—that you learn where and how to influence the social conversations that are important to you." However, this process is not only about collecting important data or feedback from clients. Real influence on an audience comes from taking real action based on their comments. As consumers grow more bold in expressing their opinions via the web, the strength of the Internet feedback loop continues to grow. Small business owners, especially, can become beholden to the comments features of certain sites, and may be discouraged from taking action in the social media world for fear the feedback loop will backfire on them.

Protecting Social Media Reputation

Although many businesses go into social media seeking additional marketing leads, there may come a time when business owners receive negative feedback. Online visibility may not always come in a positive light. There are several ways business owners can protect their online reputations.

According to the U.S. Small Business Administration website (www.sba.gov), the first step in monitoring online reputation is to listen to what's being said. Reading comments on social media outlets such as Yelp and joining relevant online forums is essential. For most people, the first instinct is to respond to negative comments; however, this may not be the right move to make. In some instances, leaving obviously contrived comments alone might be the best course to take. If a reasonable complaint does come in on a forum, it is the business owner's responsibility to respond. Social media participants are not patient and have come to demand immediate responses.

When addressing a reasonable complaint, the Small Business Administration advises the following: "Even if you don't have an immediate answer, tell the commentator that you hear them, acknowledge their complaint, and promise to investigate further." If the matter has been investigated and it was found that the business was at fault, a sincere apology should be issued. There are occasions when a conversation with a complainant should be taken offline. Sometimes a situation can be better managed and resolved by phone or email. Generally speaking, good business sense is good business sense, whether online or offline, and respectful communication with customers is always important.

A New Way to Do Business

The Internet has revolutionized how businesses connect to and influence their consumer base. Consumers use the Internet to communicate with and interact with businesses. To increase online visibility, businesses must be willing to meet consumers where they are, and they are using social media.

It is important for businesses using social media marketing to test their strategies. This will help an e-commerce business assess what is working and what is not working. According to Kaushik, of *Web Analytics 2.0*, "Testing is great because you can get the most important person's opinion: the customer's." Analytical tools such as Compete (www.compete.com) offer important data on how a website is performing, but they also offer information on the competition. Competitive intelligence analysis can determine what is working for a particular as well as, for example, which keywords are achieving good search rankings for the competition.

There are several strategies for optimizing a website's online visibility. More than one strategy may apply for a particular segment, but no business should ignore Internet marketing. According to a *Los Angeles Times* article, "How the Internet Has Changed Companies' Marketing Plans," businesses spent US$36.5 billion on Google ads in 2011. Online marketing allows businesses to tap into audiences that they would not have been able to reach otherwise.

The web has changed how businesses market to and communicate with their audiences. Internet marketing offers the opportunity to engage a wider audience. Traditional marketing via radio, TV, and print may provide large audience counts, but measuring who was really paying attention is not possible with these outlets. Tracking success through web analytics is just one advantage of online marketing. With a website, a business owner can see how much time visitors spend at the site, and what they are doing while at the site. For instance, an analytics program can track which links users followed.

SOURCES OF ADDITIONAL INFORMATION

ClickTale. www.clicktale.com
Crazy Egg. www.crazyegg.com
Google Analytics. www.google.com/analytics

BIBLIOGRAPHY

Beesley, C. (2012, October 11). Seven tips for dealing with criticism of your business on social media [web log post]. Retrieved December 7, 2012, from http://www.sba.gov/community/blogs/7-tips-dealing-with-criticism-your-business-social-media

Belicove, M. (2011, October 20). Why content marketing is king [web log post]. Retrieved December 7, 2012, from http://www.entrepreneur.com/blog/220587

Burcher, N. (2012). *Paid, owned, earned: Maximizing marketing returns in a socially connected world.* Philadelphia, PA: Kogan Page Limited.

Burgess, S., Sellitto, C., & Karanasios, S. (2007). *Effective web presence solutions for small businesses.* New York: IGI Global.

Dubois, L. (2010, December 31). Eleven best web analytics tools. Retrieved December 7, 2012, from http://www.inc.com/guides/12/2010/11-best-web-analytics-tools.html

Enge, E., Spencer, S., Fishkin, R., Stricchiola, J. (2010). *The art of SEO: Mastering search engine optimization.* Sebastopol, CA: O'Reilly Media.

Evans, D. (2012). *Social media marketing: An hour a day.* Indianapolis, IN: John Wiley & Sons.

How do search engines work? (2009, May). Retrieved December 7, 2012, from http://www.spcollege.edu/SPG/WSPCL/librarians/mairn/lis2004/3b_how_do_search_engines_work.html

How the Internet has changed companies' marketing plans. (2012). Retrieved December 7, 2012, from http://www.latimes.com/features/aranet/business/ara-8066600101-20120521,0,1440360.adstory

Kaushik, A. (2010). *Web analytics 2.0: The art of online accountability & science of customer centricity.* Indianapolis, IN: Wiley Publishing.

Maier, A. (2010, July). Complete beginner's guide to web analytics and measurements. Ux Booth. Retrieved February 23, 2013, from www.uxbooth.com/articles/complete-beginners-guide-to-web-analytics-and-measurement/

Patel, N. (2012, April). Five steps to getting more targeted website traffic with SEO copywriting [web log post]. Retrieved December 7, 2012, from http://www.copyblogger.com/seo-copywriting-tips/

Steiner, C. (2010, January 12). The latest tricks for getting found online. *Forbes. com.* Retrieved December 7, 2012, from http://www.forbes.com/2010/01/12/search-engine-optimization-tactics-entrepreneurs-technology-seo.html

Thurow, S. (2008). *Search engine visibility* (2nd ed.).Berkeley, CA: New Riders Publishing.

Building a Relationship

In This Essay

- The Internet is no longer a static experience. This helps social media marketing strategies build relationships with consumers and potential consumers

- There are many ways to develop and share social media marketing content on the Internet, such as YouTube videos, Facebook pages, and LinkedIn groups

- Many companies, such as Whole Foods and Pepsi, have used social media marketing to increase awareness of their brand and more directly involve consumers in their marketing

Overview

Social media marketing has grown to become one of the most important ways an individual or business can build relationships with current and potential customers. It has also become a successful platform for *crowdsourcing* and *customer relations management* (CRM).

Social networking sites such as LinkedIn, Facebook, Pinterest, Twitter, StumbleUpon, and YouTube have become significant places on the Internet to socialize and collaborate with others who have similar interests and goals. According to Kenneth Partridge (2010, p.4) in the book *Social Networking*, "time spent on social networking and blogging sites is growing at more than three times the rate of overall global Internet growth."

Social media sites are used as a tool to further develop personal and professional relationships by using existing friendships and connections as the foundation for building new partnerships and customer bases.

Crowdsourcing: *Obtaining services, ideas, or content by soliciting contributions from a large group of people, especially the online community.*

Customer relations management: *A model for managing a company's interactions with customers, clients, and sales prospects using technology.*

Websites such as Facebook began as social networking sites that focused on interactivity between friends, whereas sites such as Pinterest and YouTube concentrate on videos, images, and visual appeal to connect with like-minded individuals.

All social media sites rely on creating a sense of community as a way to build online relationships (Breitbarth, 2011). Many have begun to bridge the divide between personal and professional content, with some sites providing users with the ability to create separate personal and professional profiles or pages for an even greater ability to connect online. This also offers a powerful sales channel for businesses.

The Growth of Social Media

The history of social networking sites and their use as a marketing platform began in 1995 with websites such as Classmates.com, a site that targeted people who wanted to communicate and reconnect with friends and acquaintances from their elementary, middle, high school, and college years. This was followed by Sixdegrees.com in 1997, which allowed users to create their own online profiles and accumulate a list of online friends.

Several similar websites, such as Friendster, MySpace, and Facebook (which launched in 2004) followed (Parks, 2011). As of October 2012, Facebook continued to outpace the growth of other sites, with approximately 1.01 billion people using Facebook each month (The Associated Press, 2012).

Creating an Interactive Experience

The phenomenon of social networking and social media marketing is often referred to as Web 2.0, or the second generation of the World Wide Web. This refers to the shift from using the Internet as a vehicle for gathering research and information to an experience that is less static, allowing a user to engage in customized interactive experiences with the websites they visit.

This has resulted in the Internet becoming more social and directly responsive to consumer needs. Users have access to many ways to use the web, depending on personal preferences. Many businesses have capitalized on this interactivity by working to create a strong social media presence as a way to connect with customers (Parks, 2011).

Types of Social Media Marketing Sites

As online marketing and networking has evolved, social media websites have become extremely specialized in how they deliver an engaging, interactive experience to their targeted user. Social media sites can be generally divided into the following types:

Business Networking Sites This type of social media site is primarily used to update employment information and make business connections. Business networking sites are also used as places for job applicants to seek employment and for businesses to find new employees through job postings. As of August 2012, LinkedIn was the world's largest business and professional networking site, with more than 175 million professional users and 20 locations around the world (McCorvey, 2010). It is estimated that new members join LinkedIn at approximately two per second, as of the second quarter of 2012 (LinkedIn.com, 2012).

There are also business networking sites that cater to specific niches. Some examples are:

Proskore: Launched in 2011 this site boasts approximately 200,000 members worldwide. It measures professional reputation by looking at a user's background and social media influence to generate a score that helps generate new business from other network members (fastpitchnetworking.com, 2012).

Plaxo: This social media site provides an online address book that accumulates a user's contact information, keeping it updated to provide a valuable communication resource for online social media networking (plaxo.com, 2012).

Industry Specific Sites There are also various industry-specific sites geared towards helping users narrow their search when looking for contacts, connections, or services within a specific field (McCorvey, 2010). These sites often provide information and resources for topics that are relevant to the industry they accommodate.

Some industry specific site examples are I-Meet, which targets event planners, and ResearchGATE, an online community for researchers in the fields of science or technology.

Social Networking/Community Sites The common element of social networking sites is a customizable profile that allows users to build relationships with people who share similar friends and interests, rather than focusing on providing information feeds (McCorvey, 2010).

As of October 2012, Facebook was the most popular social networking site for all ages, allowing sharing updates, photos, events, and many other activities (http://searchengineland.com, 2012).

MySpace targets youths and teens, allowing members to tinker with music, themes, and HTML code (McCorvey, 2010). Twitter is considered a micro-blogging site, encouraging users to carry on quick conversations using 140 characters or less (seomoz.org, 2012).

Other examples include Friendster, a social gaming website, and Foursquare, a free app that caters to mobile phone users, allowing them to share and save the places they visit.

Video/Image Sites YouTube is the most popular video/image site, claiming more than 800 million monthly users. It allows people to create accounts, upload videos, and subscribe to other user's channels (youtube.com, 2012).

Pinterest, launched in 2009, gives users the ability to "pin" images, videos, and other objects to a webpage and share these pins with others (pinterest.com, 2012).

Social News Sites This type of site promotes discovery while allowing businesses access to a wider audience. Digg, for example, is a social news site that collects news and information from hundreds of websites submitted by users. This provides content visibility to masses of users, beyond what a small site can achieve on its own (Halligan & Shah, 2010).

StumbleUpon gives users the ability to like or dislike content, and then shows web pages with content that similar members have followed based on the feedback given (stumbleupon.com, 2012).

Using Social Media to Establish Credibility

Social media sites are a way to introduce new products and services to potential customers, with the additional ability to target customers according to how and where they shop online. In the book *Inbound Marketing* by Halligan and Shah (2010), the authors explain that by developing social media pages and profiles that serve as a hub for collaborating and connecting with others, marketers and business owners can establish credibility as an expert source of information in their field. This approach, along with providing access to website subscriptions, email newsletters, and RSS updates, keeps users actively engaged and updated with the businesses and organizations they favor.

Using social media marketing allows information to spread quickly and easily using methods such as tweets (Twitter), shares and Likes (Facebook or Digg) to show interest in a news story. The speed at which this information can be shared has extended everyone's reach across the marketplace, tipping the traditional balance of power.

The marketing playing field has been more level than it was before the development of social media marketing, moving beyond paid ads on websites to the use of sophisticated social media marketing campaigns, offering a single person the use of the same online marketing tools as a multi-million dollar company with a massive marketing budget. The ability to reach an audience through blogs, social media sites, tweets, videos, links, and keywords makes these marketing methods accessible to anyone with Internet access.

Becoming an Expert in Your Field

Social media marketing is a way to create content that is extremely valuable to a defined *target market*. Creating quality content results in the creation of links to it that increases traffic to a social media website or blog. This sharing of information allows a content producer to establish himself or herself as an expert through social media connections. If a piece of content spreads virally through social media, it can have a profound impact on the success of a company, service, or brand (Halligan & Shah, 2010).

Target market: *The clients or customers sought for a business's product or service.*

In the book *Linchpin* (Godin, 2010, p. 57), the author believes that "every interaction you have with a coworker or customer is an opportunity to practice the art of interaction. Every product you make represents an opportunity to design something that has never been designed, to create an interaction unlike any other."

Many entrepreneurs have taken this a step further and developed online businesses that specialize in teaching others how to master social media marketing, thus creating a new marketing business from the concept.

Ways to Develop and Share Content

The following are some of the ways to successfully share content to become an expert in your field:

- **Videos:** Brief videos that are two or three minutes long featuring interviews with others in the field, questions and answers on timely topics, and quick tips spread quickly in social media.
- **Webinars:** Live or recorded presentations using PowerPoint or Prezi on a timely topic that can be offered to fans and followers as incentives to join.
- **Podcasts:** Audio programs similar to radio shows that can inform on a product or give a lesson on an industry topic.
- **Online forums:** Active communities of members that focus on a specific type of business or interest, for example, stage managers, freelance writers, K-12 science teachers, and so on.
- **Online Groups:** A LinkedIn group, Facebook page, or YouTube channel can help connect to an audience and build an expert presence online.
- **Product reviews:** Brief reviews posted on your social media page or linked to your website that provide the pros and cons of popular products and services (Halligan & Shah, 2010).

By sharing relevant content and using that shared information to attract visitors, web credibility increases and a stronger presence in search engine ranking results occurs. This in turn drives more viewers to social media sites where a presence has been established (Halligan & Shah, 2010).

Success Stories

Marie Forleo In 2001, this entrepreneur began using social media marketing to develop a successful business, claiming a worldwide following of more than 50,000 women in 108 countries as of 2012.

Her YouTube channel, MarieTV, and associated website has helped her develop expert status in the field of small business and personal development training for women entrepreneurs. This social media notoriety landed her an invitation to visit Sir Richard Branson in South Africa to mentor other young entrepreneurs (Sommer, 2012).

Marie Forleo's success is an example of how providing free, quality content through social media outlets can be critical to business growth.

Jon Morrow Morrow is a blogger and associate editor for Copyblogger .com. He has gained credibility as an expert specializing in how to get more readers for a blog or website, build an email list, and become an authority in a niche group. His following has been built using Twitter, blogging, and public guest expert appearances. He focuses on his belief that success lies in "helping smart people connect with hundreds of thousands or even millions of people who need to hear their message." He has used social media marketing to promote his products and services through joint ventures with others who promote what he does in exchange for a percentage of every sale (Philips, http://www.naijapreneur.com, 2012).

Building Trust Through Word of Mouth

Using social media as a means to build trusted relationships with customers has transformed the way many companies market themselves, placing their efforts squarely in front of their target market. This allows companies to avoid the time lag associated with print advertising, costly television contracts, and other traditional marketing methods.

As Kenneth Partridge notes in *Social Networking* (2010, p. 67), "satisfied and loyal consumers communicate their positive attitudes towards the brand itself or toward the social application created by the company (be it a Facebook application or group, a Twitter presence, a blog or a YouTube video) to new, prospective customers both online and offline."

Case Studies

Whole Foods Market In 2006, this U.S. food chain began using a blog to create more customer loyalty and to better connect with their customers outside their company website. The blog provides visitors with information on the food industry, recipes, and created videos that move beyond basic coupons and in-store specials. By becoming a source of trusted, engaging information, they are able to offer information that is easily shared via tweets, likes, and comments on posts (Halligan & Shah, 2010).

Barack Obama's 2008 U.S. Presidential Campaign This campaign successfully used social media platforms to beat a better-funded rival. The campaign had less funding for telemarketing, direct mail, television, and radio advertising, so they used technology and the Internet to create new rules for campaign advertising using inbound marketing to connect with tech-savvy young and first-time voters. This allowed Obama to compete and eventually beat his competition even though he had less money.

People were able to connect with Obama by visiting his blog, Facebook page, Twitter, LinkedIn page, and YouTube channel as well as other social media sites. His Twitter account alone had more than 450,000 followers (Halligan & Shah, 2010). Using "register to vote" widgets on his Facebook page helped him to secure more than three million followers as compared with his rival John McCain's 610,000.

Pepsi With a newly designed logo, Pepsi capitalized on the success of the social media marketing used by the Obama campaign by harnessing video and digital content through social media sites to reestablish its position as a youthful brand in 2009 (Partridge, 2011).

Using traditional paid search and display ads online, Pepsi drove Internet traffic to their YouTube brand page and a "Refresh Everything" *microsite*. Banner ads that ran across the top of websites invited people to record their message directly within the banner, with the best videos featured on a branded YouTube channel and microsite for the Refresh Everything campaign.

Microsite: *A separately provided part of a large website with a separate URL designed to meet discrete objectives*

This effort relied on the concept of crowdsourcing (Howe, 2006). Another practitioner of crowdsourcing is Netflix, an online video rental service, which uses crowdsourcing techniques to offer customer video recommendations using software algorithms. The creation of the term is attributed to Jeff Howe in a June 2006 article for *Wired Magazine*, where he is a contributing editor (cbsnews.com).

Customer Relations Management

A strong social media presence allows companies to quickly respond to positive and negative press and comments, allowing the company's voice to be part of the discussion. Tracking brand awareness and building loyalty through social media marketing is another way companies are able to track, manage, and solidify valuable relationships with a customer base.

Users are now able to research companies, products, and services online; ask for feedback and share experiences through social media; and share their uncensored personal opinions about whatever they desire. As a result, social media managers for a company or business must exercise control over the rules of and framework for how a brand participates in social media. The initial launch and subsequent management of social media marketing campaigns must take into account a feedback loop, realizing that the environment is dynamic and constantly evolving (Partridge, 2011).

By providing information such as product comparisons, surveys, and contests that are benefit-based for the customer, companies are able to quickly receive information about shopping habits, allowing them to hyper-target a market with special coupons, free items, and other incentives. Taking part in an online dialog may also lead to new customers (McCorvey, 2010).

Conclusion

Social media puts the customers in control of what sites they visit and where they interact, so they are often the actual creators of the content rather than the company. By understanding the special ability of social media to create opportunities for improved marketing and branding efforts through direct and immediate engagement with a user, companies seeking to establish or solidify a brand can use social media marketing as a cost-effective, measurable way to establish an online presence to build a brand and broaden their reach (Breitbarth, 2011).

Social networking has changed the way the Internet is used and shifted the way commerce takes place around the world both online and offline (Halligan & Shah, 2010). In a 2009 on how the Internet and mobile phones impact Americans' social networks, it was noted that "social networking services, such as Facebook, provide new opportunities for users to maintain core social networks. Core ties can be highly influential in decision making and exposure to ideas, issues and opinion" (Pew Research Center, 2009).

Social media has become a fully integrated way for a company to engage with like-minded individuals to build their brand and constituency. By engaging and tracking what users do with the information provided, social media marketing techniques can be used to analyze market trends, test products, and gauge consumer reactions at a brisk pace.

SOURCES OF ADDITIONAL INFORMATION

Facebook. http://www.Facebook.com
iMeet. http://www.imeet.com
LinkedIn. http://www.linkedin.com
Prezi Online Presentations. http://www. prezi.com
Proskore. http://www.fastpitchnetworking.com
Plaxo. http://www.plaxo.com
ResearchGate. http://www.researchgate.net

BIBLIOGRAPHY

Alsever, J. (2007). What is crowdsourcing? *CBS Money Watch.* Retrieved October 19, 2012, from http://www.cbsnews.com/8301-505125_162-51052961/what-is-crowdsourcing/

Associated Press (AP). (2012). Number of active users at Facebook over the years. *Yahoo.com.* Retrieved on October 26, 2012, from http://finance.yahoo.com/news/number-active-users-facebook-over-years-214600186—finance.html)

Breitbarth, W. (2011). *The power formula for LinkedIn success.* Austin, TX: Greenleaf Book Group Press.

Brogan, C. (2010). *Social media 101: Tactics and tips to develop your business online.* Hoboken, NJ: John Wiley & Sons, Inc.

Culwell, L. (2009). *Million dollar website,* New York: Prentice Hall Press.

Godin, S. (2010). *Linchpin,* New York: Penguin Group.

Halligan, B, & Shah, D. (2010). *Inbound marketing.* Hoboken, NJ: John Wiley & Sons, Inc.

Harfoush, R. (2009). *Yes we did! An inside look at how social media built the Obama brand.* Berkeley, CA: New Riders.

Kelsey, T. (2010). *Social networking spaces: From Facebook to Twitter and everything in between.* New York: Apress.

Kim, W., & Mauborgne, R. (2005). *Blue ocean strategy.* Boston, MA: Harvard Business School Publishing Corporation.

LinkedIn. (n.d.). LinkedIn Media Information. *LinkedIn.com.* Retrieved on October 28, 2012, from http://press.linkedin.com/content/default.aspx?News AreaId=29)

Mashable.(n.d.). Facebook. *Mashable.com.* Retrieved October 20, 2012, from http://mashable.com/category/facebook/

Mashable. (n.d.). *LinkedIn.* Mashable.com. Retrieved October 20, 2012, from http://mashable.com/follow/topics/linkedin/

McCorvey, J. (2010). How to use social networking sites to drive business. *Inc.com.* Retrieved on October 26, 2012, from http://www.inc.com/guides/using-social-networking-sites.html

Mediamind. (n.d.). Case study: Pepsi refresh everything. *Mediamind.com.* Retrieved October 21, 2012, from http://www.mediamind.com/resource/case-study-pepsi-refresh-everything

Mooney, C. (2009). *Online social networking*, Detroit, MI: Lucent.

Parks, P. (2011). *Online social networking*. San Diego: Reference Point Press, Inc.

Partridge, K. (2011) *Social networking*. New York: The H.W. Wilson Company.

Pew Internet & American Life Project. (2009). Social isolation and new technology. *Pew Research Center Publications*. Retrieved on October 22, 2012, from http://pewresearch.org/pubs/1398/internet-mobile-phones-impact-american-social-networks

Philips, T., Jr. (2012). Unusual entrepreneur interview with Jon Morrow of Copyblogger.com. *Naijapreneur*. Retrieved October 25, 2012, from http://www.naijapreneur.com/unusual-entrepreneur-interview-with-jon-morrow

Qualman, E. (2009). *How social media transforms the way we live and do business*. Hoboken, NJ: John Wiley & Sons, Inc.

Rosen, L. (2010). *Rewired*. New York: Palgrave MacMillan.

Search Engine Land. (2012). What is social media marketing? *Searchengineland.com*. Retrieved on October 19, 2012, from http://searchengineland.com/guide/what-is-social-media-marketing

Shih, C. (2009). *The Facebook era: Tapping online social networks to build better products, reach new audiences, and sell more stuff*. Boston, MA: Pearson.

Sommer, C. (2012). When you've got it flaunt it: A case study on Marie Forleo. *Forbes.com*. Retrieved on October 27, 2012, from http://www.forbes.com/sites/carisommer/2012/02/22/when-youve-got-it-flaunt-it-a-case-study-on-marie-forleo/

StumbleUpon. (n.d.). What is StumbleUpon? *StumbleUpon.com* Retrieved on October 27, 2012, from http://www.stumbleupon.com/about

YouTube. (n.d.). YouTube Statistics. *YouTube*. Retrieved on October 27, 2012, from http://www.youtube.com/t/press_statistics

Social Media Marketing Strategies

In This Essay

- Best practices in social media marketing
- Trends in social media marketing
- Producing the kind of products that engage prospects/customers
- Producing enough content or a suitable variety of content
- Budget to produce/license content
- Creating a sustainable process for content creation/management

Best Practices

Social media has become pervasive. Although it began as means for individuals to connect with each other, its role has greatly expanded and has entered the realm of business and government. Social media now offers the opportunity for businesses to showcase their brands to customers, for government agencies to provide information to millions of constituents, and for charities and other causes to reach target audiences and achieve their fund-raising goals.

No entity seems to be complete without a presence on social media sites such as Facebook, Twitter, or LinkedIn, or sites such as Hi5 in Asia. Due to the proliferation of data, businesses must implement new strategies to stand out online. They must put into place new tactics to draw web surfers to their sites. *Search engine optimization (SEO)* has become the new catch-phrase, and avatars are the new salesmen. Managers must make the shift from drawing up short-term ad campaigns to engaging their audience long-term in a way that will make their brands go viral.

Search engine optimization (SEO): *The process of affecting the visibility of a website or webpage in a search engine's search results through targeted keyword phrases.*

This essay addresses what leading social media experts consider the best practices to employ when embarking on an Internet campaign, what new trends are expected, and what types of products or services tend to engage customers. The pitfalls of not producing enough, or enough variety, of content and the hidden cost of free websites are also explored. Finally, the often overlooked necessity of creating a sustainable process for continuous production of content is covered.

There are many differences between traditional ad campaigns and those on the Internet. Social media users tend to be much more engaged in the entire process than the typically more passive audiences focused on in traditional campaigns. From initial search to final click, web surfers drive themselves. They are proactive, and they do not hesitate to give their opinions or share their likes and dislikes with others. They have their own cultures. Organizations that want to build a relationship with consumers of online services must have some understanding of those cultures before they can determine what will be the best use of social media for their purposes.

Online Brand Creation

Most experts agree that the first action for an organization starting an Internet marketing campaign is to decide on a user name or brand name (Zarella, 2009). Adopting a name before deciding whether to expand to the Internet may seem backwards. On many sites, however, once an entity has recorded a user name, it is difficult, if not impossible, to change it. A company that explores the Internet under a quickly-constructed username may find itself stuck with that moniker for a long time. Selecting the name by which an organization will be known is not an easy task. Many names are already taken, even possibly the organization's own name, and the organization must put some thought into how it wants to be known across the World Wide Web.

A brand links all of an entity's interactions across the Internet. It allows a user to recognize an entity instantly, no matter which social medium that user is currently accessing. The brand name must be carefully chosen with the target audience in mind to entice the audience to readily identify with the product. Whether the brand represents a large corporation, a startup business, or an individual, that brand acts as a voice or personification of it (Peck, 2011). For this reason, the executives and management of any organization interested in expanding to the Internet should be involved in all aspects of the first foray into social media (Agresta and Bough, 2010).

Once a brand has been chosen, the next step is to explore the social media available. The executives should log on to Facebook, Twitter, You-Tube, and other social media sites to determine how those sites are being used by others and what types of conversations are being generated there. Following conversations without joining in, or lurking, as it is known, gives a sense of the rules and customs and influential people (Zarella, 2009). Lurking will offer insight into which social media platform will provide the most receptive audience for the product and will help social media managers discover the major players and current trends.

There are a number of social media websites for a reason. Each one fulfills a different need for its users. Each one uses different methods for capturing an audience's attention. Each one has a different ambience. Promoting content on the web is the antithesis of broadcasting to an amorphous crowd. On the Internet, each social medium has its subgroups, and each of these groups has a "socialeader," with a select group of like-minded followers (Oatway, 2012).

These "*socialeaders*" can help promote a company's brand or urge that brand be publically ridiculed. Managers of social media initiatives who fail to take these "socialeaders" into consideration can do their company or their cause major harm from which it may be difficult to recover. Completing the necessary research prior to launch is critical.

Socialeaders: *Those who maximize their own digital influence in a personal or professional capacity.*

Using Social Media

Having gathered identifying data on social media websites and their users, an organization can now answer the following questions (CDC, 2012):

- What is the need/desire that the organization fulfills?
- Who is the target audience for the organization?
- What is the purpose of the organization's Internet presence?

The answers to those questions will determine which of the social media the organization will employ in its campaign. Once that has been decided, the next step is to create an *avatar*. This virtual stand-in for the entity can be modeled on an employee or on the company itself. Whatever avatar is chosen, the organization should fill out the profile as fully as possible to give the audience an opportunity to create a greater connection with the brand (CDC, 2012).

Avatar: *In computing, the graphical image of the user or the user's alter ego or character.*

With the avatar profile complete, the organization is ready to set up an account, a website, or a combination of both. The most important considerations in any campaign are to:

- Post often, daily if possible (blogs, tweets, podcasts, video, and pictures)

- Engage the audience through calls to action (links, likes, sharing, surveys, polls, etc.)

- Keep the brand the same across all social media

- Comment on others' posts to show interest in other users and engagement in the media

 Managers of social media must always be mindful that everyone on the Internet has a voice. All interactions, whether a post, a tweet, or a comment, must be respectful of others. Users are quick to begin campaigns of their own when they feel their views have been unfairly criticized. Managers must also remember that the Internet is forever. All posts should be made only after deliberation, keeping the organization's principles in mind. For these reasons, entities should carefully select their social media managers.

Trends

Virtual World Trends

M-commerce: *The buying and selling of goods and services through wireless handheld devices. Also known as mobile commerce.*

Although the role of social media in marketing has expanded tremendously since its inception, experts foresee social media becoming even more ubiquitous in the future. More e-commerce will be conducted through *m-commerce*, or mobile apps, as the use of smartphones grows (Richardson, Gosnay, and Carroll, 2010).

Smartphones, with their many applications (apps) and constant connection to the Internet, are fostering the expansion of virtual worlds as well. Users can open the portal into a virtual world almost anywhere on the planet. Recognizing this trend, organizations have been quick to exploit virtual worlds to showcase their brands. There are many methods by which an organization can foster brand recognition in a virtual world (Richardson, et al., 2010), including:

- Product placement, such as a virtual store in a game that stocks Pepsi products

- Sponsoring a promotion

- Running a competition

- Creating a branded world, such as Coke Studios (http://www .cokestudio.com.pk/season5/)

- Selling products or services as *microtransactions*, such as the Reeboks that a Second Life avatar may wear

Microtransaction: *An electronic commerce transaction of very low value.*

Akin to virtual worlds are games. In fact, some games, such as World of Warcraft or other massively multiplayer online roleplaying games (MMORPG), have their own virtual worlds. Organizations can heighten brand awareness in these spheres in three main ways (Richardson, et al., 2010):

- Monopolization, in which the world is identified with the brand

- Billboarding, a virtual form of advertising that parallels its real world counterpart

- Utilization, in which characters use a product in a natural way

Although use of all of these techniques will continue to increase, Richardson, Gosnay, and Carroll (2010) envision a future in which brand placement is woven into social media in a more natural way. In this guise, brands would overlay the entire Internet instead of being confined to individual websites. They refer to this effect as a "long media tail."

Aligned with the dominance of the mobile app is the increased availability of code-recognition and product-recognition tools. Smartphones are already able to scan QR (quick response) codes, which relay information about a product or place to the user. According to Agresta and Bough (2010), the next step is location-based applications. Through these apps, a consumer can check in with a business when near one of that business' products. The business then awards him "purchase incentives" for checking in. Agresta and Bough (2010) call this a "transformational opportunity" for businesses.

Real World Trends

Another aspect combining location and trends is anchored in the physical world. Leaders in the social media field have told Advertising Age that the Middle East and North Africa are positioned to have a major effect in the digital realm. Matt Simpson, head of digital at Omnicom Media

Group, EMEA, stated that his company has more social media specialists in that area of the world than they do in the United Kingdom (Hall, 2012). As the Internet trends in that direction, its endemic culture will be altered accordingly.

One concern of the digital world is potential interference by world governments. Governments can restrict access to the Internet based on threat assessments. They may decide to design social policies that end up transforming the virtual landscape. Environmental issues could arise, as ever-increasing consumption of data translates into ever-increasing consumption of energy. As governments familiarize themselves with how interwoven the Internet is with the daily lives of their citizens, more regulation of social media appears to be inevitable (Richardson, et al., 2010).

Producing Products That Engage Prospects/Customers

Primarily, the social media manager of any organization must be responsive to that organization's online audience. The manager must pay attention to the trends the organization's audience is following, and where their interests lie. Charlesworth (2009) advises that there are three considerations to keep in mind when developing a brand across social media:

- Satisfying the need that prompted a consumer to visit a site
- The information the consumer expects to find on the site
- How the consumer expects the information to be presented

Polls and surveys can be very helpful in determining audience interest and expectations, especially if they are paired with some type of reward to increase response. Tying a campaign to a holiday provides its own element of appeal (Agresta and Bough, 2010), and giveaways are always popular.

Tailoring Content to Media

The kinds of products an organization decides to promote in any marketing campaign depends on which social media services it is using. Although many products can be embedded in most types of social media, different types of social media lend themselves to alternate methods of interaction. Also, different types of social media tend to attract different types of users. Organizations should take care to match their products, their users, and their form of social media.

Twitter is good for branding in short bursts. Due to its 140 character message limit, its followers expect a minimal expenditure in time and effort. Twitter is useful for announcing offers and events, alerting followers to new blog posts, and enlightening readers about breaking news stories (Zarella, 2009). Penney Fox, President of Fox Interactive, has determined what what Twitter audiences are looking for. She says that organizations should tweet up to three times a day. Seventy percent of those tweets should comprise information and education about the organization. Twenty percent can be updates in sales, and the remaining ten percent should be news bits about the organization's community or its followers (Warnke, 2012).

YouTube, on the other hand, is much more time-consuming. Users expect to have to expend energy in searching for videos before they can experience them. After that, watching the video itself is a commitment. For this reason, videos should be short (no more than 10 minutes long) and very engaging (Zarella, 2009).

Organizations can assist YouTube viewers by customizing their channel and making a playlist of in-house productions or relevant videos already on YouTube. In-house videos for organizations without much production experience or budget can comprise little more than glorified slideshows with added music and a voiceover (Reynolds, 2011). Those organizations ready to create new video may appreciate these tips from Miller (2008):

- Make sure the video is correctly sized
- Shoot up close
- Use adequate light
- Use two cameras
- Use professional production techniques

Videos are also popular blog products. In addition to embedded video, blogs lend themselves to articles, links to outside videos and other blogs, and contributions from multiple authors. The most effective blog posts should be easy to read and updated regularly. Zarella (2009) maintains that "every company should have a blog, and it should be the center of [its] social marketing efforts."

Call to action (CTA): *In computing, commands designed to trigger a desired action.*

Engaging the Consumer

Whatever product is offered, it should interest the user. A game or a contest, for example, can entice a visitor into remaining on a website. An incentive such as free initial content may prod a hesitant consumer into enrolling in a long-term subscription (Richardson, et al., 2010). A *call to action (CTA)*, such as a button that requires the user to click it to proceed, can propel a user deeper into a website.

Effective CTAs use clear, active language, tell the user exactly what to do, and reward the user for completing the CTA (Boag, 2009). Peck (2011) suggests embedding a "Like" button that, once clicked, converts a visitor into a fan of that website, combined with a portal that allows only fans access to the website.

The key concept in producing an effective product is engaging the consumer. Therefore, one of the most satisfying elements for consumers may be the comments section of a website. Comments allow the consumer to express opinions, satisfaction or dissatisfaction with the organization, and provide a wish list for that organization.

Whenever possible, an organization should offer its followers the opportunity to interact with the content, to share it, to Like it, and to respond to it. Zarella (2009) encourages organizations to allow followers to embed the organization's videos on the follower's own website. When that happens, the fans themselves are actually providing the product, to their own specifications, to their followers.

Producing Enough or a Variety of Content

Once an organization has established a presence on social media sites, it must continually refresh its content. Otherwise, it risks its brand identification going stale and therefore losing its followers. According to the "2013 B2B [business to business] Content Marketing Benchmarks, Budgets and Trends—North America" survey (2013 B2B), the number one challenge B2B marketers say they face is producing enough content to keep their presence up to date in social media (Pulizzi, 2012).

Organizations have many assets at their disposal, both in-house and online, to combat this challenge. The driving factor in social media is the ability to connect with others. Connections imply an exchange of information, which, when done properly, leads the user to identify with the organization's brand. This identification in turn leads the user to desire that the brand be as consistent with his or her worldview as possible. Allowed to interact with the brand, many users will freely give advice and opinions to the entity hosting the brand. In its quest to provide continual content, the entity can use this relationship with its users in a myriad of ways.

In-house Product

The social media manager can keep users updated about new products, new services, new locations, and any other changes in its business model. The more that users know about a brand, the more they will identify with it. Consumers are aware of the vast amounts of information that are available online, and they are availing themselves of that information before making purchases.

Organizational marketing strategies should include willingly giving consumers the data they are seeking. Penn (2009) described it thus: "Information-seeking is not just an activity, it's a way of looking at the world. New info shoppers are proud of the progress they have made in putting facts over pablum."

One method of dispersing information to users is for social media managers to assign articles and products to a team of content providers. This content can be based on a constantly updated list of topics and suggestions. To expedite this task, the social media manager may create a different template for each social media website. The manager can also suggest alternative methods of creating content (video, pictures, and podcasts, among others). Cohen (2012) offers four areas of content that are amenable to continual updating:

- Giving an insider's perspective into the organization and its employees
- Teaching consumers how to use the organization's products more effectively
- Providing news about the organization's industry
- Interviewing experts

Outside Content

The business can also request input from users about potential new products (a web-wide focus group) or ask users to generate wish lists of future products (Zarella, 2009). Consumers already familiar with a product may be asked to create their own content by taking pictures or video with themselves and the product and posting the results (Penn, 2009; Constantinides and Fountain, 2008). Other input from users may come in the form of ratings of products or services provided by the entity. In addition, forums allow users to share their experience and knowledge in conjunction with technical support through the organization.

Another source of content is the open forum, where little to none of the content is provided by the entity itself. All content comes from guests and links to other sources on the Internet, such as feed providers or content syndicators (Monty, 2012). If all else fails, or in addition to all other sources, an organization can subscribe to content specialists who provide industry-specific products for their clients.

Budget to Produce/License Content

Although most basic forms of social media are free to use, organizations should remember that there are costs associated with employing them. For the most effective use of social media, a manager should oversee all aspects of an organization's online presence. Providing content, even text, is not without some cost. Members of the organization must take time from other duties to create the product that is to be posted.

According to the 2013 B2B survey, companies with fewer than 10 employees spend 34% of their budgets on content marketing, which is defined as communicating with customers and prospects without selling. Companies with more than 1,000 employees spend 20% of their budgets on content marketing. Respondents to the survey stated that they spend, on average, 25% of their content creation budget on outside resources (Pulizzi, 2012).

Initial Costs

Before the first piece of content can be uploaded, the website must be designed and implemented. Catherine Wijnberg, CEO of Capetown, South Africa-based Fetola, strongly advises treating an initial foray into social media as the organization would any brand development in the brick-and-mortar environment. An organization that would consider hiring experts for "logo design, copywriting, even assistance with overall strategy" for a real world ad campaign should do the same for its virtual presence (WealthWise, 2012).

Agresta and Bough (2010) suggest reallocating 10 to 15% of the budgets of each current marketing technique towards social media marketing. The authors also advise reducing the real world customer service budget in favor of enhancing the online customer service experience.

Ongoing Costs

Organizations may not have to pay for the space for their content, but they must invest the time and effort in building and maintaining relationships with their followers (Agresta and Bough, 2010). Attracting web surfers to a website, engaging visitors so that they will prolong their stay, and enticing fans into becoming consumers is a long-term process that requires the redistribution of a substantial amount of an organization's resources.

The social media environment is a community environment. An organization with an online presence must allocate human resources to establish and maintain the following elements involved in building a social media community (Agresta and Bough, 2010):

*   Listening to and monitoring relevant conversations
*   Managing the community to keep followers engaged
*   Offering ways for the community to participate and be active
*   Exchanging value with followers
*   Identifying advocates who are passionate about the brand

Agresta and Bough (2010) state that the human resources cost of a social media marketing campaign is often less than a traditional real world ad campaign. In addition, the resources provide a higher return on investment (ROI), due to the relationship that is developed with the consumers. However, the authors caution that an online campaign should be an adjunct to a real world campaign, not a replacement for it. Organizations need to budget for both types of campaigns simultaneously.

Creating a Sustainable Process for Content Creation/Management

Content Management

Any effective process for managing social media content must start with a social media manager. Each organization should appoint one person to oversee the current campaign and keep track of the organization's overall presence on the Internet (Emery, 2012). The social media manager can simplify his task by accessing all of the organization's channels through a dashboard (Contract Flooring Journal, 2012).

The social media manager should be someone who is already a part of the online community in which the organization wants to be a member. The manager should be someone who is accepted by the socialeaders, and feels akin to the other members of the community (Agresta and Bough, 2010). Under that construct, the manager will be able to respond in a timely manner to problems, difficulties, and general dissatisfaction with the organization.

To achieve some measure of control over negative comments that may not be posted on the organization's sites, the manager should initiate a search for the organization's name and product names, then subscribe to the results via Really Simple Syndication (RSS). With a subscription to a feed reader of choice, the manager can easily check the account once or twice a day (Zarella, 2009).

In-house Content

Once appointed, the social media manager should implement an editorial calendar. The editorial calendar will serve as a framework around which the ongoing process of creating content will be structured. From the basics of the editorial calendar, the social media manager can assign specific content. The editorial calendar should comprise at least the following elements (Cohen, 2011):

- Seasonality, including high traffic times for the organization
- Holidays, special events, and contests
- Planned marketing promotions
- Content categories
- Search keywords to help develop content
- Recurring features
- Major content offerings

Every organization has an origin story, a story about the launch of its first product, its best day, and its worst day. These stories combine to form the ethos of the organization. It is the ethos of the organization that can be shared with its followers (Levine, et al., 1999). Every day brings a new story; thus, every day brings new content. That content can take the form of press releases, product brochures, and other products, which can be posted across the social media websites (Richardson, et al., 2010).

Ongoing conversations with followers can fuel new content. The Frequently Asked Questions (FAQ) page can be updated almost constantly based on new inputs. Followers express their interest, or lack thereof, in the current content output of the organization through obeying or disregarding CTAs and sharing opportunities. Users make comments about the organization and its products, both complimentary and not. Both types of comments are useful in providing a direction for the organization's response (Monty, 2012). Discarding methods that do not provoke the correct response and creating content that engages followers is a continual cycle of experimenting, tweaking, and learning (Agresta and Bough, 2010).

Outsourced Content

Engaged followers can be the most prolific content creators. Whenever possible, they should be encouraged to remix and repost the organization's content and to create their own content on the organization's page (Zarella, 2009). Before an organization can request its followers provide something of value, however, it must first provide value to them (Acunzo, 2012). Followers can add to the ethos of an organization, but they cannot create it.

Another method of providing continually fresh data is via RSS feeds. An organization can subscribe to any number of feeds to keep its audience engaged and its content fresh.

Whenever members of an organization become discouraged at the effort required to generate new, engaging, creative content, the social media manager can remind them of the numbers. Customer lifetime value (CLV) is the amount of revenue generated from one customer over the lifetime of the relationship. Most experts agree that the cost per acquisition (CPA) is approximately 10% of CLV. It costs three to five times as much to get a new customer as it does to keep an existing one (Harden and Heyman, 2010).

SOURCES OF ADDITIONAL INFORMATION

Biggest Moments in Social Media Marketing 2012. http://www.mobile marketingwatch.com/infographic-the-biggest-moments-in-social-media-marketing-28891/

Constant Contact Social Media Strategy Resources. http://www.constantcontact.com/social-campaigns/social-media-marketing-strategy-resources.jsp

Corporate Social Media Marketing Strategy for 2013. http://www.clickz.com/clickz/column/2230322/corporate-social-media-marketing-strategy-checklist-for-2013

BIBLIOGRAPHY

Acunzo, J. (2012, September 30). "Three rules for earning quality user-generated content." *The Huffington Post.* Retrieved December 20, 2012, from http://www.huffingtonpost.com/jay-acunzo/three-rules-for-earning-ugc_b_1927546.html

Agresta, S. & Bough, B. (2010). *Perspectives on social media marketing.* Boston: Course Technology PTR.

Baker, R. (2012, July 19). "Technology is key to better customer retail experience. *Marketing Week.* Retrieved December 18, 2012, from http://www.marketing-week.co.uk/news/tech-is-key-to-better-retail-experience/4002836.article

Boag, P. (2009, January 22). 10 Techniques for an effective "call to action" [Web Log Post]. Retrieved December 19, 2012, from http://boagworld.com/design/10-techniques-for-an-effective-call-to-action/

CDC. (2012, July 17). CDC social media tools, guidelines, & best practices. *Centers for Disease Control and Prevention.* Retrieved December 14, 2012, from http://www.cdc.gov/socialmedia

Charlesworth, A. (2009). *The digital revolution.* London: Dorling Kindersley Limited.

Cohen, H. (2011, October 22). How to develop your editorial calendar. [Web Lob Post]. Retrieved December 20, 2012, from http://heidicohen.com/editorial-calendar/

Cohen, H. (2012, October 15). "Content marketing drives social media and sales—are you spending enough? *Clickz.* Retrieved December 19, 2012, from http://www.clickz.com/clickz/column/2186568/content-marketing-drives-social-media-sales-spending

Constantinides, E. and Fountain, S. (2008). Web 2.0: conceptual foundations and marketing issues. *Journal of Direct, Data and Digital Marketing Practice.* Retrieved December 20, 2012, from http://www.palgrave-journals.com/dddmp/journal/v9/n3/full/4350098a.html#top

Contract Flooring Journal. (2012, June). "Only one in 10 UK companies 'serious about social media." *Contract Flooring Journal.* Retrieved December 18, 2012, from http://www.contractflooringjournal.co.uk/archive/newsJun07_2012.html

CyberMedia. (2012, March 29). "Adobe study shows social media impact undervalued by nearly 100 percent." *PC Quest.* Retrieved December 18, 2012, from http://pcquest.ciol.com/content/search/showarticle.asp?artid=132108

Emery, M. (2012, February 23). Social media best practices for increased engagement. *Social Media Today.* Retrieved December 14, 2012, from http://socialmediatoday.com

Hall, E. (2012, June 11). "Year after Arab spring, digital, social media shape region's rebirth; marked by their proven influence in the uprisings, Facebook, Twitter, mobile define 'normal' life—and marketers adjust accordingly." *Advertising Age.* Retrieved December 18, 2012, from http://adage.com/article/global-news/year-arab-spring-digital-social-media-shape-region-s-rebirth/235259/

Harden, L. & Heyman, B. (2010). *Marketing by the numbers: how to measure and improve the ROI of any campaign.* New York: AMACOM.

Levine, F., Locke, C., Searls, D., & Weinberger, D. (1999). *The cluetrain manifesto: the end of business as usual.* New York, New York. Retrieved December 20, 2012, from http://www.cluetrain.com/book/index.html

Mauldin, C. (2011). The new rules of PR and marketing: a teaching unit for college public relations programs. *ERIC: Reports.* Retrieved December 18, 2012, from http://www.eric.ed.gov/ERICWebPortal/search/detailmini.jsp?_nfpb=true&_&ERICExtSearch_SearchValue_0=ED524603&ERICExtSearch_SearchType_0=no&accno=ED524603

Miller, M. (2008, September 2). Tips for producing more effective YouTube videos [Web Log Post]. Retrieved December 19, 2012, from http://www.quepublishing.com/articles/article.aspx?p=1238247

Monty, S. (2012, November 20). The pressures of content creation [Web Log Post]. Retrieved December 19, 2012, from http://www.scottmonty.com/2012/11/the-pressures-of-content-creation.html

Oatway, J. (2012). *Mastering story, community and influence: how to use social media to become a socialeader.* West Sussex, UK: John Wiley & Sons, Ltd.

Peck, D. (2011). Think before you engage: 100 questions to ask before starting a social media marketing campaign. Indianapolis, IN: John Wiley & Sons, Inc.

Penn, M., with Zalesne, E. (2009, January 8). New info shoppers. *The Wall Street Journal.* Retrieved December 19, 2012, from http://online.wsj.com/article/SB123144483005365353.html?mod=dist_smartbrief

Pulizzi, J. (2012, October 24). 2013 B2B content marketing benchmarks, budgets and trends [Research Report]. *Content Marketing Institute.* Retrieved December 20, 2012, from http://contentmarketinginstitute.com/2012/10/2013-b2b-content-marketing-research/

Questia. (2012, September 12). "The age of influence." *Marketing.* Retrieved December 18, 2012, from http://www.questia.com/library/1G1-302172251/age-influence

Reynolds, S. (2011, April 4). "How to use YouTube for effective marketing." *Business Insider.* Retrieved December 19, 2012, from http://articles.businessinsider.com/2011-04-04/strategy/29991843_1_youtube-video-jawed-karim-chad-hurley

Richardson, N., Gosnay, R., & Carroll A. (2010). *A quick start guide to social media marketing.* London: Kogan Page Limited.

Rouse, M. (2012). "B2B (business2business or business-to-business) definition." *TechTarget.* Retrieved December 20, 2012, from http://searchcio.techtarget.com/definition/B2B

Turner, J., & Shah, R. (2010) The top 10 things you must know about measuring ROI on social media marketing. Upper Saddle River, NJ: FT Press.

Udese, C. (2012, July 17). Deciphering social media and online marketing myths in business. *TechTalkAfrica.* Retrieved December 18, 2012, from http://techtalkafrica.com/deciphering-social-media-and-online-marketing-myths-in-business.html/

Warnke, K. (2012, October 12). Business basics: how to use Twitter effectively for your business. *Orlando Business Journal.* Retrieved December 19, 2012, from http://www.bizjournals.com/orlando/print-edition/2012/10/12/business-basics-how-to-use-twitter.html?page=all

Zarrella, D. (2009). *The social media marketing book.* Sebastopol, CA: O'Reilly Media, Inc.

Diversification of Social Media Content Strategy

Introduction

A number of inventions over the course of history have changed the ways people have interacted with each other and information has been presented in the public sphere. The printing press lowered the cost of reading material, allowing people to become more literate and bringing the Western world into the "Age of Enlightenment." This created more space for public debate (Duke University, Unknown).

Although inventions such as the telegraph, telephone, and computer have increased the speed of communication, the one invention that has revolutionized the way in which the world is perceived has undoubtedly been the Internet, and later social media. Arguably one of the most revolutionary aspects of this was noted by Chan-Olmstead and Chang in *Diversification Strategy of Global Media Conglomerates*, "Just as in the oil and automotive industries earlier this century the media is going through a profound transformation" (Chan-Olmstead & Chang, 2003).

The growth of social media has been huge. Jeff Bullas illustrates with an example: "Radio took 38 years to reach 50 million users. Facebook had 200 million [users] in less than 12 months" (Bullas, 2012).

In some respects this is why certain companies have been hesitant to use the Internet. There are many stories of people who thought they had sent a private message only to discover that it had been broadcast to more than the intended audience. This can be avoided, however, by having a corporate social media content strategy that acknowledges both the fluid and flexible nature of social media, how its users interact, and how this can potentially benefit businesses using it (Dutta, 2010).

Understanding Terms

Before analyzing diversification of social media content strategy, it is important to define what these terms mean. In its definition of social media, About.com's Small Business Guide includes some examples:

- Social networks, such as Facebook, Twitter, and Pinterest

- Social sharing websites, such as YouTube and Flickr

- Job search websites, such as LinkedIn

- General interest websites such as StumbleUpon, Reddit, and Digg (Ward, 2012)

Website content can include status updates, videos, photographs, blog posts, and so forth (Ward, Susan, 2012). Although the quality of the content is important, the way in which it is presented and the strategy behind the content is crucial (Hemley, 2012).

Companies and media content providers can use various types of strategies to promote this material, and more detail about these different approaches will be discussed later.

Diversification is defined as trying to increase profitability by marketing new products in new markets. This often requires a company to learn new skills to create a product and to adapt to the new market. The writers Booz, Allen, and Hamilton noted that the concept of diversification is nothing new and has been a business strategy since the 1950s. They define diversification as "A means of spreading the base of a business to achieve improved growth and/or reduce overall risk" (van Kranenburg, 2004).

In the case of social media, it is often not just new skills that need to be learned but an entirely new approach. Those who have adapted quickly have flourished while those who have not can find themselves in a situation that could harm their brand image (Wilson, Guinan, Parise, & Weinberg, 2011).

This essay illustrates the different types of strategy available to a business to ascertain their benefits and acknowledge the potential risks and how to avoid them.

Effective Strategies

When formulating a strategy for social media content, the potential risks and how to avoid them need to be considered (Thompson, Hertzberg, & Sullivan, 2011). One problem with social media content is that interaction on social media sites is not the same as traditional broadcast or print advertising (Hall, 2012). If a website is blanketed with positive statuses about its company, this does not equate with increased exposure if users feel a lack of interaction from the business (Merrill, Latham, Santalesa, & Navetta, 2011).

Increasingly, social media has more user-generated content. Some companies employ people solely to check the accounts of their customers to quickly respond to complaints. This in turn helps maintain a more positive image of the company because customers can see the business is prepared to adapt and respond to feedback (Hemley, 2012).

One example of this is shown by Blendtech CEO Tom Dickson. His "Will it blend?" videos featured him blending a number of items (marbles, iPods, etc.). The iPhone video alone reached 9 million YouTube views, and the company saw a sevenfold increase in blender sales because of the inventiveness and ubiquity of the videos (Dutta, 2010).

When formulating a social media content strategy it helps to know the benefits:

- Low cost platform. Videos can be produced relatively inexpensively, status updates are free, and it is possible to spread a brand message quickly without having to spend a lot of money (Chaney, 2012).

- Helps communicate what a business is. Social media can help to establish a brand's content identity (Divol, Edelman, & Sarrazin, 2012).

- Rapid engagement. The instant nature of a social media website allows one to quickly respond to comments or feedback (Agathou, 2011).

- Unvarnished feedback. Some companies are afraid that social media networks may lead them to get abused online. Although that is a possibility, many websites have controls to help prevent this. Constructive criticism, however, is not something to be afraid of, and responding to criticism quickly can often improve one's brand image (Catone, 2010).

One example of how not to respond to feedback via social media is Irish airline Ryanair's CEO Michael O'Leary. He is known for being outspoken, and sometimes vulgar in his interactions with the media and airline customers. His big personality makes him memorable, but his inability to filter what he says may have a negative impact on the airline and its marketing strategies.

Although some may argue that controversy and "larger than life" characters can establish a brand image in people's minds, a reputation for poor customer service and abuse of people with valid complaints is not an effective content strategy (Talk About Social Media, 2012).

Personal and Private Spheres

One of the issues that often arises from social media is what constitutes private and public spheres. Habermas defined the idea of "the public sphere" as a place where people could interact and offer their ideas (Thompson, 1995).

Increasingly, problems in social media occur not so much in public spheres but in private spheres. This can make social media content problematic. One way to avoid this is to be aware of the different audiences that a company is trying to reach within a social media marketing strategy (Thompson, 1995).

- Personal and private. This usually refers to family and close friends. The content provided usually regards family matters and things that do not have relevance with regard to business or promotion (Goldman, 2012).

- Professional and private. This usually refers to work colleagues. Generally, these are messages sent through private platforms or messaging. Messages, however, can get "leaked," so it is vital that colleagues are aware of the confidential nature of these messages and ensure they are delivered securely (Goldman, 2012).

- Personal and public. This usually refers to social media accounts used to send public messages to friends and family. Companies should be wary of what is posted on these forums, as names can be searchable, so information that could potentially damage one's brand should be avoided (Goldman, 2012).

- Professional and public. This usually refers to messages that are posted in public to promote a business. This can include content such as videos, blogs, articles, and the like (Goldman, 2012).

The difficulty can be in knowing the difference between these spheres and what types of messages are appropriate to each one. For example, a more formal, business-like approach is appropriate to a platform such as LinkedIn, which is oriented toward business, whereas a post on Twitter may be suitable for a less formal and approachable form of message.

One's strategy should look at the potential risks and benefits to ensure it is effective (Goldman, 2012).

A number of social media platforms use *private messaging services.* Unfortunately, despite being private, there is still the chance that information imparted via these services could be leaked and impair the image of the company. This is why the content of any messages sent should be evaluated to ensure that it is appropriate to each of these particular public and private spheres (Goldman, 2012).

Private messaging services: *An e-mail or text message sent from one user to another on a social networking site. They are often more anonymous than e-mails, as the e-mail address and IP address of the senders are not disclosed.*

Various other issues can arise from this. One example is of a bank that is assessing its social media strategy. They note that one of their customers has more than 100,000 followers on a networking site. This particular customer does not have a high credit rating, so he does not have access to the better products that the bank offers. But is their influence on the network enough to give them special treatment (Wilson et al., 2012)?

Another issue concerns the potential abuse of different public and private spheres. A controversial trend in social media spheres is what is known as creating "sock puppets." Sock puppets are fake accounts created by an individual or company to give flattering reviews or feedback (Oxford Dictionary, 2012).

This tactic can often backfire when it is discovered (which it often is), making the perpetrators look foolish at best and manipulative at worst. Although it may be tempting to think that this is purely something small companies do for a bit of quick attention (Herrington, 2012), numerous companies, large and small, have been guilty of this. To avoid the potential fallout, when considering content strategy, resist the urge to deceive people like this. Although such strategies may give a company a spike of attention at first, it could result in a lot more harm than good in the long term (Ward, Lisa, 2012).

A more positive approach is to look at what the purpose is of the social media strategy. This is not the same as saying "I want 100,000 followers by the end of the week." Rather, such a purpose is about reaching a wider audience, engaging with them, and using content in the most effective way to maintain an audience that wants to listen (Odden, 2010).

Different Types of Content Strategies

To create a social media strategy, it helps to know what types of social media are currently being used by businesses. Admittedly, it can be difficult to ascertain as social media networks are changing all the time. Even the websites themselves change in terms of functionality and presentation. Therefore, a sensible business has to be aware of this and must have a system in place that allows them to adapt as required (Wilson et al., 2012).

- Predictive practitioner is the first strategy. This strategy is about engaging directly with customers and asking what they want. This conversation could be about improving the functionality of a product or getting feedback on an advertising campaign (Wilson et al., 2012).

- Creative experimenter is the second strategy. This is often done in the private sphere and on a small scale. These tests are often performed to improve the functionality of a design or to get feedback from employees. Len Devana, who directs social strategy at EMC, emphasized the importance of this testing period. "We need to be free to make mistakes and learn our lessons before exposing ourselves to the outside world" (Wilson et al., 2012).

- Social media engager. This strategy allows a company or individual to use social media to promote their business. In 2011, Ford Motor Co. lent 100 Ford Fiestas to chosen customers, especially young, Web-savvy drivers, with the promise that the drivers would post their adventures and impressions on sites such as YouTube, Flickr, and Twitter. The promotion resulted in 60,000 posted items of content, 4.3 million views on YouTube, and 50,000 sales of the car to new customers (Wilson et al., 2012*).*

- Social media transformer. This approach is about fundamentally changing how a company conducts their business. Cisco Systems has used social media content to hold training sessions and meetings virtually, using videos and live feed rather than physically going out to each company location. An additional benefit to Cisco is that posting training videos online rather than by mail reduces postage costs, saving the company money as well (Wilson et al., 2012).

The development of strategies today should allow companies to be more flexible in the future. "Understanding how company strategies are evolving to use existing social media will not only be of use today but also should guide managers as they adapt to platforms developed in years to come" (Wilson et al., 2012).

Content and Strategy

Defining the right strategy is difficult because the inference from the strategies described above is that businesses remain static, meaning that they remain unchanged and may be viewed as boring or undesirable. Companies need to create a plan to diversify their websites. Diversification, however, has to be handled appropriately and businesses need to be cognizant of what they are doing when they are making changes to their websites (Bullas, 2012).

The content a company places on a social media site is also a key part of the promotion. Sometimes the desire to create something memorable or distinct can mean that the creator loses sight of the original intent of the content. Although videos and blogs can be transmitted to a wide audience, that audience may not particularly appreciate the message, especially if they feel it is not relevant. It is important for a business to stay focused on the customers at all times when creating social media content. It is possible to make relevant content that is appealing to the consumer (Bullas, 2012).

Awareness of the type of content and its purpose helps to focus the strategy. If there is awareness, then it is easier to know to whom the message should be distributed and what tone should be taken with the target audience (Bullas, 2012).

There are three main categories of content:

Traffic: *Visitors to a website, blog, or social media account on the Internet.*

- *Liquid content* refers to the idea that this content "flows." Content that flows creates a buzz on the Internet and draws users to it in large numbers, almost making it contagious because word spreads so quickly. People like this content and share it among their friends, family, and co-workers. This could be content that features a brand message but it also could be something fun that gets attention and brings *traffic* toward one's website (Bullas, 2012).

- *Linked content* is about creating clear brand values and sharing them with people. One example of this could be a video that takes place during a presentation. Giving a speech about one's business is an obvious example of linked content. This video would then be posted around, showing a person discussing his or her beliefs (Bullas, 2012). (An example is Bill Gates of Microsoft discussing his views on how to be more motivated and successful in your business.)

- "Two Step" is content in which one piece of content follows up another. One way this has fundamentally changed promotion is with advertising. Advertising campaigns start a story and then direct users to a website with more information.

The three categories could cross over at various points. If a brand has an emphasis on fun, then liquid content could also work as linked content. The two step is something that, if properly handled, can also bring people into the brand who have had their curiosity piqued.

Application

One problem with diversification is that by definition it is about extending further. There is the danger that in going to the unknown, a business may go too far or may not apply a strategy effectively. Companies should keep this in mind when considering diversification (Thompson, 1995).

In *The Media and Social Modernity,* John B. Thompson outlines his view on how a business should approach social media. "What we need today is not a theory of a new age but rather a new theory of an age whose broad contours were laid down some while ago" (Thompson, 1995).

It is important to assess a diversification strategy based on Booz et al.'s definition. A company needs to look at whether its strategy will result in increased growth or reduced risk. Equally difficult is how to define what that growth or risk is (Thompson, 1995).

The main difficulty is that achievement can be hard to quantify. Although having a large number of followers can look impressive, this may not necessarily translate into greater sales. Given the nature of social media sites, there is the danger that many of them could be spam accounts with no potential for interaction. Thus, the message of any content is lost (Thompson, 1995).

Making It Work

Numerous theories exist about how to make social media work. For some theorists, the strategy is to jump in and get involved. Other social media strategists warn against this approach, believing that this can often lead to short-term fixes and distraction by platforms that initially seem promising but have no real staying power (Stelzner, 2012).

Dave Fleet defines this as "bright shiny object syndrome." Companies often produce content for the latest social media platform, believing that it is important to be the first and be praised as early adopters. "Companies need to consider their audience." Fleet argues, "You need to consider the infrastructure that is in place. It needs to be context specific or there is the danger of employees 'going rogue' and damaging the brand" (Stelzner, 2012).

Fleet also warns against how some companies quantify results. "It is not just about numbers. It is better to focus on a broad overall objective rather than numerical results" (Stelzner, 2012).

Admittedly, lack of quantification makes it difficult to define the overall success of a social media campaign. Although numbers can offer a clear indication of success, one must also consider what other aspects of a strategy are important, such as the feedback from customers. There are a number of different strategies that can be used in both private and public contexts, depending on the platform (Stelzner, 2012).

The diversification of social media strategy depends on a company having a clear idea of what they intend to achieve, the infrastructure and resources needed to deliver it, and a sensible approach that knows how to address different audiences in the right way (Stelzner, 2012).

Conclusion

As a content strategy for a social media presence is being developed, a company may find that it has a checklist of questions that works for the strategy. It can seem contradictory, as a clear objective must be combined with flexibility to react to the changing nature of social media platforms. Assessing both these aspects is vital, however, when determining the success of a strategy.

It is also worth remembering that as a company diversifies, it can grow, so a strategy that may have been effective in the earlier life of a business may not be the right strategy as the business becomes larger. This will often necessitate a change in strategy.

Size is not everything, however, and smaller businesses also need to be aware of their strategy. Although social media is often thought of as

TABLE 1. Questions to Consider when Compiling a Social Media Content Strategy

Purpose	Questions
Content Audience	Who is the content for? Is the content directed at the public or private sphere?
Content Presentation	How is the content presented? Does one go for a light-hearted approach or is it intended to direct a message?
Content Type	What type of content is it? Does it use videos, blogs, articles, or all of the above?
Content Delivery	Who is delivering the message? Remember, people will often associate the content with the company, so it is important to be aware of how it is perceived.
Content Objective	What is the overall social media objective? Is it target- or objective-driven?
Content Feedback	Should employees respond to feedback? Is feedback being actively sought out? Will messages posted online receive a response?
Content Platform	Does one have the infrastructure needed to use a platform correctly?
Content Flexibility	Is the strategy flexible enough?
Content Efficiency	Is social media being used in the most effective way?
Content Assessment	Is the strategy being assessed regularly?

having a global reach, it is also something that can be useful on a local level. It can be used to encourage people to buy from local companies. It can also allow local businesses to network with each other and mutually promote each other's services.

Another aspect of using social media on a smaller scale is that companies can take advantage of their smaller size. This allows the business to engage with customers more personally. Customers often appreciate a less formal level of communication.

In short, there is no right answer for a social media strategy. There is certainly not one that will fit all organizations equally. What is important is that any agreed-upon strategy is properly implemented and assessed. Although this may not result in easily displayable short-term results or figures, research seems to suggest that better long-term results come as a result of a broad approach that balances a community of people and their needs rather than purely counting them as figures. This results not only in better sales in the long term, but also better brand loyalty and a more secure approach to an ever-changing platform for promotion.

SOURCES OF ADDITIONAL INFORMATION

Social Media Examiner. http://www.socialmediaexaminer.com/about/c

The Social Media Sun. http://socialmediasun.com/twitter-content-strategy/

BIBLIOGRAPHY

Agathou, A. (2011, June 27). 9 Ways to build an easy, engaging content strategy. *The Next Web*. Retrieved December 10, 2012, from http://thenextweb.com/socialmedia/2011/06/27/9-ways-to-build-an-easy-engaging-content-strategy/

Bullas, J. (2012, October 23). How to get started with social media marketing. Personal blog. Retrieved December 12, 2012, from http://www.jeffbullas.com/2012/10/23/how-to-get-started-with-social-media-marketing/

Catone, J. (2010, February 21). How to deal with negative feedback in social media. *Mashable*. Retrieved December 9, 2012, from http://mashable.com/2010/02/21/deal-with-negative-feedback/

Chan-Olmstead, S., & Chang, B.-H. (2003). Diversification strategy of global media conglomerates: examining its patterns and determinants. *Journal of Media Economics*, 16 (4): 213–233.

Chaney, P. (2012, October 3). The 4-step social media content trategy. *Practical eCommerce*. Retrieved December 5, 2012, from http://www.practicalecommerce.com/articles/3756-The-4-Step-Social-Media-Content-Strategy

Divol, R., Edelman, D., & Sarrazin, H. (2012, April). Demystifying social media. McKinsey & Company: *McKinsey Quarterly*. Retrieved December 15, 2012, fromhttp://www.mckinseyquarterly.com/Demystifying_social_media_2958

Duke University. The Gutenberg printing press. *Duke University*. Retrieved December 10, 2012, from http://www.cs.duke.edu/~chase/cps49s/press-summary.html

Dutta, S. (2010, November). Managing yourself: what's your personal social media strategy? *Harvard Business Review*.

Feldman, V. (2002). Competitive strategies for media companies in the mobile internet. *Schmanlenbach Business Review*, 54: 351–371. Retrieved December 10, 2012, from: http://papers.ssrn.com/sol3/papers.cfm?abstract_id=349433

Goldman, E. (2012, September 28). Big problems in California's new law restricting employers' access to employees' online accounts. *Forbes.com*. Retrieved December 6, 2012, from http://www.forbes.com/sites/ericgoldman/2012/09/28/big-problems-in-californias-new-law-restricting-employers-access-to-employees-online-accounts/

Hall, D. (2012, April 19). Guess what......social media is NOT replacing traditional journalism [Infographic]. Personal blog. Retrieved December 10, 2012, from http://davidhallsocialmedia.com/2012/04/19/guess-what-social-media-is-not-replacing-traditional-journalism-infographic/

Hemley, D. (2012, June 7). 26 tips for integrating social media activities. *Social Media Examiner*. Retrieved December 11, 2012, from http://www.socialmediaexaminer.com/integrating-social-media-activities/

Herrington, D. (2012, October 8). Social media: from monitoring staff to fake pages—five tips to protect brands. Tech Republic.com. Retrieved December 5, 2012, from http://www.techrepublic.com/blog/cio-insights/social-media-from-monitoring-staff-to-fake-pages-five-tips-to-protect-brands/39749492

Markowitz, E. (2012, Feb. 28). Guy Kawasaki's social media secret. *Inc.* Retrieved December 5, 2012, from http://www.inc.com/eric-markowitz/guy-kawasaki-dont-plan-your-social-media-just-do-it.html

Merrill, T., Latham, K., Santalesa, R., & Navetta, D. (2011, April). Social media: the business benefits may be enormous, but can the risks—reputational, legal, operational—be mitigated? Retrieved December 10, 2012, from http://www.acegroup.com/us-en/assets/ace-progress-report-social-media.pdf

Odden, L. (2010, April). Social media strategy—a definitive guide. Top Rank Blog. Retrieved December 12, 2012, from: http://www.toprankblog.com/2010/04/social-media-strategy-tactics/

Oxford Dictionaries. (2012, September). From sock puppets to astroturfing: the language of online deception. *Oxford Dictionaries blog*. Retrieved December 4, 2012, from http://blog.oxforddictionaries.com/2012/09/from-sock-puppets-to-astroturfing/

Stelzner, M. (2012, November 22). How to set your social media strategy and measure it. *Social Media Examiner*. Retrieved December 7, 2012, from www.socialmediaexaminer.com/set-your-social-media-strategy-and-measure-it

Talk About Social Media. (2012, August 22). Ryanair fails to address social media crisis. Retrieved December 9, 2012, from http://talkaboutsocialmedia.wordpress.com/2012/08/

Thompson, J. B. (1995). *The media and modernity: a social theory of the media.* Stanford, CA: Stanford University Press.

Thompson, T., Hertzberg, J., & Sullivan, M. (2011). Social media and its associated risks. Retrieved December 9, 2012, from: http://www.grantthornton.com/staticfiles/GTCom/Advisory/GRC/Social%20media%20and%20risk/social%20media_whitepaper%20-%20FINAL.PDF

Van Kranenburg, H. L. (2004, May 12–15). Diversification strategy, diversity, and performance among publishing companies. 6th World Media Economics Conference. 1–14. Retrieved December 12, 2012, from http://www.cem.ulaval.ca/pdf/Kranenburg.pdf

Ward, L. (2012, September 17). Social media reviews may be 15% fake by 2014: report. Bizjournals.com. Retrieved December 12, 2012, from http://www.bizjournals.com/nashville/blog/socialmadness/2012/09/social-media-reviews-may-be-15-fake.html

Ward, S. (2012). Social media definition. About.com. Retrieved December 10, 2012, from http://sbinfocanada.about.com/od/socialmedia/g/socialmedia.htm

Wilson, H. J., Guinan, P. J., Parise, S., & Weinberg, B. D. (2011, July). What's your social media strategy? *Harvard Business Review.* Retrieved December 12, 2012, from http://hbr.org/2011/07/whats-your-social-media-strategy/ar/1

Keeping Up with the Competition

Overview

In 2012, the number of Internet users was 2.27 billion, almost twice the number from five years earlier. In 2012, Facebook had more users than the entire Internet had in 2004. Asia's Internet population now almost equals the entire Internet population of five years ago, more than 1 billion. Europe has more than 500 million Internet users, twice as many as the United States (Pingdom, 2012). Today's consumer either purchases or researches products online (Funk, 2012).

Where the Competition Is

According to Nielsen (2012), businesses are paying attention consumers. The first quarter of 2012 saw advertisers spending 12% more on Internet advertising than they had one year prior. Growth was especially high in Europe, with an increase of 12%; Latin America followed with almost 32%; and leading the world, the Middle East and Africa grew more than 35%.

The retail industry is the biggest online ad purchaser in the U.S., spending US$3.4 billion in the first half of 2012. Second is the automotive industry, followed by the financial service industry, and then the telecom, computing products, and leisure travel industries (Marketing Charts, 2012).

Keeping Up with the Competition

Current technology has made a person's online presence measurable (Donaton, 2012). Knowing where the competition is spending advertising money and what strategies they are employing is useful because competitors give a frame of reference of comparable success to measure against (Lebel, 2011). Furthermore, tracking competitors can help marketers focus strategies and create more innovative solutions to business challenges (Shah et al., 2011). Competitive analysis helps identify potential threats to brand recognition and possible opportunities for differentiation of that brand (Lebel, 2011). Knowing how well the competition's strategy is faring allows allows a business to create an even more successful strategy (Lebel, 2011).

It is not enough to determine how many consumers view a competitor's online content, however. A competitor may have higher total audience numbers, but it is the consumers' share of the conversation that shows the true picture of a brand's influence. Discovering where, when, and how often a competitor engages users gives a more complete picture of that brand's immersion in the social media marketplace. Even more indicative of the success of a business is the overall sentiment attached to a particular brand (Lebel, 2011).

According to a survey by Mzinga and Babson Executive Education, only 16% of companies polled measured *return on investment (ROI)* for their social media campaigns. More than 40% didn't know whether the social tools they used had ROI measurement capabilities at all (Shah et al., 2011). The first step for any marketer is to determine the unique selling proposition (USP) of a product, or the benefit to the customer that sets it apart from all similar products, yet many businesses have not even defined their target audience (Funk, 2012; Safko, 2010).

Today's consumers are seeking excitement in their online experience (Safko, 2010). Successful marketers know their audience and create trust in their brand by keeping their content current (Safko, 2010). Marketers

Return on investment (ROI): *A performance measure used to evaluate the efficiency of an investment. It is usually expressed as a percentage or a ratio where return of an investment is divided by the cost of the investment.*

who update their content consistently outperform 75% of the competition (Brogan & Smith, 2009). In addition, marketers who realize that *conversion* is the main dynamic that enhances the brand work to transform users into consumers by providing them some means to express themselves, such as allowing them to tag photos, review books, or recommend products to others (Brogan, 2010). Customer experience may be the most important ingredient in the successful expansion of businesses (Hinshaw, 2010).

Conversion: *The rate at which one currency is transformed into another.*

Providing that experience costs money, however. The highest ROI comes from social advertising that starts with a reasonable online budget, usually 5 to 15% of the total advertising allowance. Ninety percent of those funds are then allocated to core strategies, with only 10% allotted to experimental platforms. To learn how well that money is performing, businesses must establish measurable goals for each social media campaign, constantly test assumptions, and reallocate resources based on the results (Funk, 2012).

E-tail versus Retail

The first goal of any business establishing an online presence is to use traditional media or word-of-mouth advertising to increase awareness of the move to social media (Shah et al., 2011). No online campaign will be successful until consumers are aware that brand information is available on social media platforms. The advertising money spent online is of no use if it doesn't translate into sales. Properly used, social media is a force multiplier. Whether that force is beneficial to a business or not depends on whether that business has learned how to leverage what is available to make their advertising go viral and how to use social analytical tools to compute their ROI so that they can make their message more effective (Blanchard, 2011).

Online consumers are looking for transparency and reliability in online marketing (Safko, 2010). Online consumers trust other consumers more than they do businesses, and they rely on the consumer conversation about a brand more than they do the official voice of that brand to make decisions about what to purchase (Funk, 2012). Potential purchasers look to user-submitted ratings and reviews on products to make purchasing decisions (Funk, 2012; Safko, 2010). Social networks allow consumers to easily share recommendations. Such reviews are meaningful to other users because they come from trusted sources. The tally of comments that a brand receives becomes its "social proof," the Internet version of reliability. Successful businesses increase consumer trust by allowing consumers to use social networks to resolve complaints and satisfied customers to provide feedback to companies and information and encouragement to other customers (Funk, 2012).

The Sales Funnel

Consumers trend through stages when making purchasing decisions. Businesses must be positioned to capture their awareness at each of these stages (Funk, 2012; Safko, 2010):

- Awareness: realization of need
- Search: general, not any particular brand
- Research: specific to one brand
- Buy: ready to purchase
- Post-sale: need customer support, want to share experience

Businesses that allow consumers to interact with them at each stage of the sales cycle generate exposure to the brand. Exposure is a necessary precursor to a purchase. Consumers interact within their own socialnetworks. If a business is not established on that network, either through advertising or through word-of-mouth recommendations, the potential consumer will never be funneled to that business' brand (Lovett, 2011).

Social Media Strategy

Lurk: *In Internet discussion forums, to follow conversations without contributing.*

The awareness and personality of the campaign and the relationships with consumers are vital ingredients for social media success (Funk, 2012). Before a business attempts any online marketing, its first virtual presence must be as a *lurker* (Funk, 2012, Safko, 2010). Lurking provides two benefits: learning the types of users at each platform, and understanding what the overall sentiment towards the business is. Once the marketer knows how the business is perceived, the work to create the best brand possible can begin. Brand storytelling is an effective tool that reaches across platforms, binding consumers together and creating excitement for the product (Donaton, 2012).

Social networking provides an unparalled means for building brand loyalty (Jothi, Neelamalar, & Prasad, 2011). The marketer must determine the best method for reaching customers and the metrics to determine whether the strategic goals have been reached (Brogan, 2010; Safko, 2010). The combination of using social media platforms, paid online Pay-Per-Click (PPC) ads, and effective search engine optimization (SEO) create a greater sense of authority and trust in a brand because consumers encounter it all across the Internet (Dragon, 2012). The blanket coverage of the virtual world strengthens each aspect of marketing and overall brand presentation. The same means of establishing brands holds true globally, as Facebook and Twitter have extended their reach to join Orkut as corporate branding hubs in countries such as India (Jothi et al., 2011).

Once the platform for the social media campaign has been determined, the marketer can claim territory by establishing a brand name (Dragon, 2012). Laying claim to the same brand name across different social networking platforms provides a connection between users of many different sites.

Tactics

With all of the available online options, consumers are looking for experiences that are out of the ordinary (Roberts, 2010). However, they generally tend toward activities and sites that are simple and streamlined, with information that is easily accessible (Brogan, 2010). Preferably, information and content are presented visually. Lon Safko (2010, p. 29) states that "audiences tend to prefer video over audio, and audio over text."

Mostly, however, audiences prefer games (Jothi et al., 2011). The gamification of advertising energizes social media campaigns (Brogan, 2010; Funk, 2012; Jothi et al., 2011; Safko, 2010). More than one quarter of users are attracted to games, quizzes, and other interactive opportunities, and respond more to that form of advertising than to more traditional marketing techniques. Contests help generate engagement (Chipkin, 2012). Competitions run through Facebook and other similar platforms are the latest method marketers are using to establish brand loyalty to exploit this trend (Cuddeford-Jones, 2010).

Social Media Tools

Many online social media tools are available to assist the astute marketer reach the desired audience. Some platforms date almost from the onset of the Internet, whereas others comprise the latest technology. Successful businesses constantly test, analyze, and modify social media campaigns to take advantage of the benefits of each tool and to combine them to spread awareness of a brand.

E-mail is one of the oldest forms of social networking, but it has retained its usefulness. Updated technology, such as social analytics, allow marketers to test how well various messages perform by segmenting e-mail lists and tailoring subject lines, content, and time-of-day mailings to determine which is the most efficacious (Safko, 2010).

Websites are a business' office online. Reputable businesses give their customers enough specifics about their organization for the customers to feel that they are dealing with a trustworthy company (Brogan, 2010). In addition to providing a physical address, contact information, and credentials, websites should provide pages with all of the information customers and potential customers are seeking. These pages not only serve to attract users at each stage of the sales cycle, but each named page offers another site for search engines to display (Safko, 2010).

Constantly updated blog posts on the homepage of a website provide current content for customers and search engines (Brogan, 2012; Funk, 2012; Safko, 2010). In the transition from press release distribution tools to channels of communication between businesses and customers, blogs have reached their true potential (Shah et al., 2011). The ability to carry on a conversation establishes a link between customers and marketers, creating yet another avenue for building brand loyalty.

Facebook is the platform that ties all of the social media platforms together with a reach that spans the Internet (Safko, 2010). All businesses should create at least one page on Facebook filled with sharing tools and blog posts, in addition to purchasing more conventional advertising on it (Funk, 2012; Safko, 2010). Posting pictures is an important aspect of any Facebook experience. "Images," says Susan Black, executive vice president and chief marketing officer of Travel Impressions, "are the lifeblood of successful Facebook pages" (Chipkin, 2012).

Other popular platforms include forums (Safko, 2010). Another of the oldest forms of technology on the Internet, their capacity for interaction with knowledgeable agents ensures that they remain a viable means for creating a trusted community focused on a brand.

Podcasts, audio or video recordings that can be downloaded to any personal computer or mobile device, help convey a sense of authority and expertise to marketers employing them (Safko, 2010). Creating a series of podcasts enhances the sense of authority and encourages followers to subscribe, leaving less opportunity for them to become distracted by a competitor's claims. Akin to podcasts are streaming video or audio, another method of building trust with customers through conversation (Sakfo, 2010).

Successful businesses create a brand presence across many platforms, so that (Funk, 2012):

- The brand is a presence wherever consumers search

- A number of consumer needs can be met, including research, customer service, amusement, and immersion in the brand experience

- Each presence provides consistent amplification, echo, and support for social media campaigns and brand messages across multiple media

- The fixed costs of a social media campaign, including program strategy, policy establishment, planning and staffing, and analytics and technology investment, are further disbursed

Techniques

As more consumers want to educate themselves about a product before making purchasing decisions, search engine optimization (SEO) becomes a more vital business tool. Marketers need to have some understanding of how search engines work to position their content competitively (Safko, 2010). Some key concepts include (Brogan, 2010; Safko, 2010):

- Search engines place much emphasis on URLs, so they should contain keywords

- Meta-descriptions tell users what information is on each page of a website

- Title tags must match content

- Content that is more current ranks higher

- The more sites that link back to a website, the more reputable that site becomes

- Websites should have comprehensive site maps, so that all pages are searched separately

Search engine marketing (SEM) is a corollary to SEO (Safko, 2010). Cost-Per-Click (CPC) or Pay-Per-Click (PPC) ads, which only charge advertisers when users click through to their websites, are targeted to key search terms. Gretchen Howard, a director at Google, states that effective ads "get to the point quickly, convey key product benefits, and use strong calls to action" such as "Buy Now" on a clickable button that transfers consumers to the website page that most directly relates to the ad (Safko, 2010).

Mobile marketing provides a new level of interest for consumers, as it takes advantage of GPS to provide coupons or information about local outlets (Safko, 2010). Another popular use of mobile technology is to create advergames, which can showcase a brand in some manner or construct an entire virtual world around that brand.

Building Social Capital

Any successful social media ad campaign begins with a profile for the brand that customers can identify with (Safko, 2010). Consumers are interested in making connections with other people, and businesses that are able to project personality into their brands become more successful (Lebel, 2011). Next, the business must extend its online presence by joining and participating in groups (Blanchard, 2011; Brogan, 2010; Safko, 2010).

Businesses build relationships through social networks; through being helpful and connecting to consumers (Brogan, 2010). Marketers provide information to consumers and allow them to comment on products and services, which facilitates mutual gain and demonstrates mutual interest, two areas that greatly stimulate customer loyalty (Tsai, 2009). From there, the marketer can build networks that support the social media plan's strategic goals (Cross & Thomas, 2009; Safko, 2010).

Marketers become successful through being transparent, demonstrating a clear and sincere interest in people, and actively appreciating the openness that the Internet provides both businesses and consumers (Brogan & Smith, 2009). Successful marketers, or "digital natives," leverage the natural connectivity of the Internet to personalize their business and turn the ongoing conversations into a business asset.

Businesses that allow interaction with the brand encourage users to become more engaged, increasing loyalty (Lovett, 2011). Content that is posted often, asks open-ended questions, gives users the opportunity to comment and inform, and offers multiple options for sharing creates the tightest bonds between consumers and brands (Brogan, 2010; Safko, 2010). The best practices for social media optimization include (Lovett, 2011):

- Create shareable content
- Make sharing easy
- Reward engagement
- Proactively share content
- Encourage mashup, in which users take content and remix it by adding their own input and voice

Blogs especially provide many opportunities for creating excitement in users through creative post titles, freshly posted content, comments and links to other blogs, images and video, and posts that inform or train (Brogan, 2010; Safko, 2010). Done properly, blogs can be used to promote a brand, set a brand apart from competitors, provide a forum for interested parties, and link traffic from multiple sites (Brogan, 2010). A showcase of the best posts can heighten interest in a blog, as well as provide fresh content for SEO. Really simple syndication (RSS) allows all content to be distributed to all followers as soon as it is published, making the spread of information much more streamlined (Brogan, 2010).

Social Media Campaigns

Social media campaigns must comprise 10 elements: 1) Strategy, 2) Audience, 3) Commitment, 4) Content, 5) Staff, 6) Identity, 7) Metrics, 8) Policy, 9) Crisis management, and 10) Fortitude.

Every social media campaign should start with a clearly defined strategy and measurable goals (Funk, 2012; Lovett, 2011). Further, each campaign should encompass only one theme (Safko, 2010). The campaign's purpose is to harness the power of the network to create more brand awareness and loyalty and, eventually, to increase revenue (Lovett, 2011). Listening to customers is an asset for any business, as is patience (Funk, 2012). Social media campaigns do not always provide an immediate, tangible ROI. However, done well, social media campaigns rank among the lowest-cost, fastest data turn-around, and highest returns of any marketing efforts (Funk, 2012).

Overarching goals for every business that engages in online marketing should include enhancing the brand through engaging consumers, transforming purchasers into loyal advocates (Funk, 2012). One of the methods for accomplishing this is through upgrades to customer service. Satisfied customers provide one means of increasing brand awareness and, potentially, the generation of further leads, which may in turn bring about the ultimate goal of raising revenue. Other methods include generating consumer excitement through sweepstakes and games, or through the prospect of fundraising for a charitable goal (Lovett, 2011).

Social responsibility is a metric that marketers ignore at their peril (Funk, 2012). Research has shown that 75% of consumers believe that social responsibility is an important attribute for a company to have, that 70% are willing to pay more to buy products provided by socially responsible companies, and that 55% of consumers would choose a product that supports a good cause over one that doesn't (Funk, 2012; Malykhina, 2010; Olsen & Livingston, 2010). However, the cause must resonate with the brand for it to resonate with consumers. Espousing a charitable cause is an important part of creating an online community that wants to be associated with a particular brand. In the process of cultivating long-term engagement of consumers, successful marketers elicit ideas of what causes resonate with most their fans and create an online social media strategy that focuses on those topics (Olsen & Livingston, 2010).

Metrics

No social media campaign is complete without knowing whether it gave an effective return on investment (ROI) (Lebel, 2011). Conversion from prospect to sale is the only indicator that makes any difference to the bottom line (Lovett, 2011). At the same time that marketers are fostering connections with consumers, they must keep track of the metrics (Brogan, 2010; Safko, 2010). Fortunately for marketers, almost everything on the Internet can be measured (Blanchard, 2011; Funk, 2012; Safko, 2010). Unfortunately, it is all too easy for businesses to become lost in the morass of available data and lose sight of the core values that comprise customer satisfaction (Hinshaw, 2010).

No business can know whether the advertising dollars spent on Internet marketing are being applied effectively without the technology-based solutions that constitute customer relationship management (CRM)

(Hinshaw, 2010). All conversion events, whether financial or figurative, should be followed closely, amenable to quantification and understood by everyone in the business (Lovett, 2011).

Social analytics can provide instant feedback and valuable data on everything from insights into consumer behavior to the calculation of ROI (Blanchard, 2011). This feature of online data gathering allows for a more dynamic business model, one in which response time can quickly follow any event (Safko, 2011).

The most effective measurement framework is built on the following concepts (Blanchard, 2011; Lovett, 2011):

- Keep track of everything that can be measured
- Separate out everything that must be measured
- Stay current on the best measurement tools
- Tie all measurements back to stated business objectives

Businesses that prioritize data organization and analysis tend to outperform their competition, scoring higher in customer retention, real-time response, and ongoing optimization of resources (Lovett, 2011). Specific data analysis provides specific metrics, revealing not only consumer behavior attributes but also which aspects of a social media campaign were successful, which channels were most effective, and which activities led to the production of revenue.

The five most important metrics for any business attempting to improve its ROI are new leads, enhanced revenue, and new customers, along with which social media effort performed the conversion, the loyalty value of retained customers, and the net promoter score (Funk, 2012). All social media efforts should always remain results-oriented and grounded in sound analytics practices. Best practices to ensure that they stay that way include:

- Using platform reporting of the social media networks to track the fans, followers, on-platform reach, and interactivity of the online community
- Using monitoring software to track the overall sentiment towards the brand
- Using social analytics to measure conversions

- Using measuring tools to assess which comments receive the greatest number of responses, the demographic profile of the users interacting with the brand, and how much activity social plug-ins are generating

Types of Metrics

With the many types of metrics that are available, marketers must know which ones are useful to any particular campaign (Funk, 2012). ROI can take many forms, both tangible and intangible (Lovett, 2011). Some intangible forms of ROI that can be measured with accuracy are return on interaction, return on engagement, return on satisfaction, and return on advocacy. The metrics to measure ROI, in whatever form necessary, include (Funk, 2012):

- Reach: The total audience reached by all social media posts, fans, followers, likes, comments, and shares
- Engagement: The total number of interactions with a post (likes, comments, shares, retweets, and so forth). Total interactions is divided by total number of fans
- Share of voice: Total number of references to a brand divided by the total number of references to all brands and companies in an industry
- Share of media: Tracking of a brand's share of all references to an industry on a particular social networkccc
- Share of sentiment: The fraction of all positive, negative, and neutral sentiment for a particular brand versus all brands
- Net promoter score: On a scale of zero to ten, the likelihood that customers would recommend a brand to others
- Net sentiment: All positive and neutral conversations minus all negative conversations, divided by the total conversations about the brand
- Social influence measurement (SIM): Net sentiment for the brand divided by net sentiment for the industry
- Net brand reputation: Positive sentiment percentage minus negative sentiment percentage, compared against others in the industry

Multiplying Influence

Although the specifics of metrics are comprehensible, applying the numbers to the bottom line can be problematic (Lovett, 2011). A successful social media campaign may be measured only in greater awareness of a brand. Online marketing is a long-term prospect, devoted to building a loyal customer base that in turn multiplies the limited resources of the business to expand the brand far beyond what the business could manage (Brogan & Smith, 2009; Funk, 2012; Safko, 2010).

Successful marketers tap into the desire of the users of social media networks to be involved, to feel that they are doing something "important, interesting, and worthwhile," as Chris Brogan (2010) states it. Encouraging interaction with a product makes that brand much more competitive in the market (Jothi et al., 2012). Discussion can lead not only to dispersal of information but to innovation (Jothi et al., 2012). In addition, the opportunity for communication directly with a company leads to increased customer satisfaction (Jothi et al., 2012).

Online consumers do not want to be force fed advertising (Lovett, 2011). They see themselves as the directors of brand integrity. Marketers desirous of creating a community must comply with the demands of their followers. Many businesses have encouraged consumer activism, valuing the opinions of their fans and rewarding their creative innovations, spurring greater consumer loyalty, which in turn leads to word-of-mouth (WOM) advertising (Bakshy, Hofman, Mason & Watts, 2011; Lovett, 2011).

WOM has long been accepted as an advantageous means to diffuse information to a large group of people (Bakshy et al., 2011). Because WOM is seen as trustworthy, it has the added potential of influencing public opinion, encouraging innovation, and enhancing brand awareness. The five elements contributing to successful WOM are (Funk, 2012):

- Developing a true, interesting story about the brand that will resonate with consumers

- Identifying and cultivating the "influentials," also known as "mavens," or "superfans," the well-connected users in the target market who will spread the word about the brand and who will be listened to

- Finding fun and clever ways to seed the story among the influentials

- Creating tools and apps that make sharing the story easy for all users to do

- Interacting with the community so that the impulse to share develops into an ongoing conversation

To remain effective, a WOM campaign must remain authentic and amateur (Funk, 2012). The marketer creates an environment conducive to passing along the information, but the consumers extolling the brand do so out of conviction and belief in the product. A successful WOM campaign works because the customers are engaged. The marketer able to harness that community effort has not only kept up with the competition but outpaced them (Funk, 2012; Lovett, 2011; Safko, 2010).

SOURCES OF ADDITIONAL INFORMATION

Pay-Per-Click ads. http://www.payperclick.com/
Six Hot Trends in Social Influence Marketing. http://www.businessesgrow.com/2012/08/05/six-hot-trends-in-social-influence-marketing/
Word of Mouth Marketing Association. http://www.womma.org/

BIBLIOGRAPHY

Bakshy, E., Hofman, J., Mason, W., and Watts, D. (2011, February 9) Everyone's an influencer: quantifying influence on Twitter. [Research paper]. *University of Michigan.* Retrieved February 1, 2013, from http://misc.si.umich.edu/media/papers/wsdm333w-bakshy.pdf

Blanchard, O. (2011). *Social media ROI: managing and measuring social media efforts in your organization.* Upper Saddle River, NJ: Que Publishing.

Brogan, C., & Smith, J. (2009). *Trust agents: using the Web to build influence, improve reputation, and earn trust.* Hoboken, NJ: John Wiley & Sons.

Brogan, C. (2010). *Social media 101: tactics and tips to develop your business online.* Hoboken, NJ: John Wiley & Sons.

Chipkin, H. (2012, October 22). In N.Y., marketing execs share social media success stories. *Travel Weekly,* 71.43, p. 10.

Cross, R., and Thomas, R. (2009). *Driving results through social networks: how top organizations leverage networks for performance and growth.* San Francisco: Jossey-Bass.

Cuddeford-Jones, M. (2010, February 18). Competitions: interactive brands gain competitive advantage. *Marketing Week,* p. 20.

Donaton, S. (2012, May). 2012: the year of brand storytelling. *DM News,* p. 46.

Dragon, R. (2012). *Social marketology: improve your social media processes and get customers to stay forever.* New York: McGraw-Hill.

Funk, T. (2012). *Advanced social media marketing: how to lead, launch, and managea successful social media program.* New York: Apress.

Gahran, A. (2011, April 8). How to gain influence on Twitter? Focus. *CNN.* Retrieved January 31, 2013, from http://www.cnn.com/2011/TECH/social.media/04/07/twitter.influence/index.html.

Gainor, B. (2011, September 6). 5 ways Flickr serves as a promotion marketer's best friend. *Promo.* Retrieved January 31, 2013, from http://chiefmarketer.com/social-marketing/5-ways-flickr-serves-promotion-marketers-best-friend.

Hinshaw, M. (2010, September). Controlling touchpoints: branding expert Michael Hinshaw says most companies are not paying enough attention to the customer experience. *American Executive*, 8.5, p. 48.

Jothi, P., Neelamalar, M., and Prasad, R. (2011, July). Analysis of social networking sites: a study on effective communication strategy in developing brand communication. *Journal of Media and Communication Studies, Vol. 3(7)*, pp. 234-242, [Full Length Research Paper].

Lebel, J. (2011, October 14). Keeping up with the competition: metrics that matter. *Likeable*. Retrieved January 31, 2013, from http://www.likeable.com/blog/2011/10/keeping-up-with-the-competition-metrics-that-matter/.

Lovett, J. (2011). *Social media metrics secrets*. Hoboken, NJ: John Wiley & Sons.

Malykhina, E. (2010, March 31) Social responsibility boots brand perception. *Adweek*. Retrieved January 31, 2013, from http://www.adweek.com/news/advertising-branding/social-responsibility-boosts-brand-perception-101965

Marketing Charts. (2012, October 15). 1 in 5 online ad dollars spent by retail Industry in H1. [Web log post]. Retrieved February 1, 2013, from http://www.marketingcharts.com/wp/direct/1-in-5-online-ad-dollars-spent-by-retail-industry-in-h1-24061/

Mohapatra, M. (2012, June 20). First citizen members contribute to 72 per cent of our sales. *Pitch*.

Nielsen (2012, July 10). Global Internet ad spend sees double-digit growth, outpaces other media. *NielsenWire*. [Web log post]. Retrieved February 1, 2013, from http://blog.nielsen.com/nielsenwire/global/global-internet-ad-spend-sees-double-digit-growth-outpaces-other-media/

Olsen, K., and Livingston, G. (2010). Cause marketing through social media: 5 steps to successful online campaigns. *Network for Good and Zoetica*. Retrieved January 31, 2013, from http://www1.networkforgood.org/ckfinder/userfiles/files/CauseMarketingThroughSocialMedia.pdf.

Roberts, J. (2010, March 4). Peer panel: How to keep the customer on your side. *Marketing Week*, p. 28.

Royal Pingdom (2012, April 9). World Internet population has doubled in the last 5 years. *Pingdom*. [Web log post]. Retrieved February 2, 2013, from http://royal.pingdom.com/2012/04/19/world-internet-population-has-doubled-in-the-last-5-years/.

Safko, L. (2010). *The Social media Bible: tactics, tools, and strategies for business success*, 2nd ed. Hoboken, NJ: John Wiley & Sons.

Shah, R., Shah, R., Turner, J., Reece, M., and Tasner, M. (2011). *Supercharge your social media strategies (Collection)*. Upper Saddle River, NJ: FT Press.

Slutsky, I. (2010, September 27). Media mavens: Bay Area young gun introduces savvy way to corner the social-video-campaign market and slays the competition. *Advertising Age*, 81.34, p. 42.

Tsai, J. (2009, June). Everyone's social (already): your customers are increasingly connected—to you, to your competition, to each other—but you're not supposed to be the center of every network. *CRM Magazine*, 13.6, p.34.

Developing Brand Loyalty through Social Media Communication

In This Essay

- Social media marketing offers enormous benefits to businesses but it must be approached with specific goals in mind

- A good social media marketing strategy has clear goals and ways to measure attainment of those goals and adapt if efforts are failing to generate interest

- Customer interaction fostered by social media allows businesses to create loyal, long-term customers

Overview

A restaurant offers free calamari to customers who sign in at the establishment with their smartphones on Foursquare. A computer sales company promotes one-day discounts on Twitter. A company places its products in a game that is played on Facebook. In each instance, a business is using social media to build a relationship with potential consumers. In many cases, such efforts are the beginning of a beautiful friendship in which brand loyalty develops between the business and the consumer. The development of this form of business relationship through social media can be accomplished through various forms of communication. This entry is aimed at explaining why it is beneficial and ways it can be successfully done.

Introduction

The average consumer receives an estimated 3,000 advertising messages a day. That is a great deal of information. Sixty-five percent of Americans say they are "constantly bombarded with too much advertising," according to a survey by Yankelovich, a firm that does marketing of social behavior. So how does a business get through the clutter of all this information and build a profitable brand loyalty with consumers?

A key to breaking through is learning that the communication with consumers must be a two-way conversation. Social media is a premium opportunity to establish a brand and share your vision, as well as your products. Through traditional media (television, radio, and print) and some online media, the interaction is one-way. With social media, there is the potential to be a lucrative two-way relationship. Marketing efforts focused on the social feedback cycle are less about what a marketer has to say and more about the consumer and what the consumer wants to know right now (Evans, 2011). Marketers must now provide good information and be creative to attain their goals.

Metric: *A standard of measurement used to gauge a company's performance.*

Customers who engage with companies through social media spend 20% to 40% more money with those companies than other customers (Phillips, 2012). They also demonstrate a deeper emotional commitment to the companies. Therefore, the first question a business should answer is "What are our goals?" According to an eMarketer Report, 80% of marketers incorrectly begin with tactics instead of goals. When respondents in a 2010 joint DMA-COLLOQUY study were asked to identify the most important measure of social media success, nearly two-thirds selected "don't know." When Deloitte and *MIT Sloan Management Review* asked 3,748 executives from 115 countries and 24 industries about their social-initiative *metrics* in early 2012, the most frequent answer was that they "do not measure" (Everett & Sullivan, 2012). In essence, most marketers don't know what their true end goal is. Before a marketer decides on a social marketing campaign, they should determine their goals and think critically about how long it will take to attain them and what tools are necessary to achieve them.

Developing a Plan

The mere act of writing a short public statement on a business' website from a visitor's perspective spurred significant lifts in transaction activity immediately following its posting. The increased activity continued for as long as two months after the events, compared with a control group of members who received the same marketing prompts but who did not participate (Everett & Sullivan, 2012). In the social media environment, marketers have unique opportunities to develop social media programs that tackle awareness, engagement, and word-of-mouth objectives. Social media applications can fulfill any of these objectives. Marketers must determine issues such as whether the campaign is for a particular product or promotion that will last six months or one year, or whether it is a branding campaign that is complementary to a long-term strategy. Thus, there are two key objectives to consider that are hallmarks of any successful business enterprise: consistency and providing excellent customer service.

The next step is learning how to execute the plan. The development of brand loyalty to a business or product is a process that requires a commitment of time and energy on the part of the business. Large companies spend hundreds of thousands of dollars, if not millions of dollars, annually on businesses to manage their social media content. Smaller business owners must ask themselves whether they want to manage the effort themselves or hire an individual or firm to do it for them.

If a business is not communicating regularly via its social media network, it may not receive the level of hits or interest it desires. It is probably best to start off with a narrow focus, using one or two social networks at first, and then branch out as needed or desired. Ideally, goals should be specific and measurable. For example, one small business might want 1,000 local follows/likes in three months and then a 20% increase every three months after that. Another might want 2,000 user interactions in that time or $10,000 in sales directly attributed to social media (Levin, 2012).

Social media marketing plans, like any relationship, take time to nurture and strengthen to produce a desired result. The most successful implementations of social media marketing are undertaken by organizations that are in fact social at their core, organizations that have made collaborative practices part of their internal organizational culture (Evans, 2011).

What Is Your Strategy?

Hoffman and Fodor break strategies into three types:

- "Dead end." In this scenario, the marketer has only a limited ability to measure his social media efforts (fuzzy) and believes that his efforts are not working (failing). Managers find themselves in this situation as a result of a trail and error strategy and perform arbitrary changes with no way to measure their effect. The manager has little insight or idea what to do because measurement is fuzzy and the effort's effectiveness appears to be failing. The outcome is fairly predictable: the manager will give up on social media efforts or continue efforts that involve random adjustments without data support. This situation is a dead end.

- "Measure and adjust." In this scenario, the marketer has a reasonable ability to quantify his social media efforts, and these measurements lead him to believe that his efforts are not working (failing). Since the components are being measured, there are probably some good clues about what is going wrong. This means the manager can evaluate and adjust the social media strategy accordingly.

- "Naïve optimist." Here, the marketer has only a limited ability to measure his social media efforts (fuzzy), yet believes that his efforts are working (succeeding). We believe most marketers actually start here. They believe using social media is worth the effort, but are not quite sure how best to measure their efforts.

Real time: *The actual time during which a process or event happens.*

Facebook, Twitter, and YouTube are the most frequent social media channels businesses or recreational social media customers use. They have the largest audiences, they are user-friendly, and they can provide large and *real-time* feedback about a product, pro or con. A vast majority of Fortune 500 companies surveyed by the Center for Marketing at the University of Massachusetts at Dartmouth found the use of all forms of social media including Facebook and Twitter, but also podcasting, blogging, and more, to be an effective use of time and resources (Jackson, 2011).

Measuring audience engagement is relatively simple on Facebook and Twitter, as both sites record how many followers or friends a page has. On Facebook, the number of likes on a post is also an easy measuring stick. On Twitter, users can monitor how many times someone retweets their message.

The more detailed approaches to measuring engagement can involve other data-driven methods. The collection method to measure metrics can be as simple as tracking Google alerts. Some service providers will prepare that data for its customers. The more time a person spent on a site means a greater likelihood that he or she will purchase your product. Conversely, the bounce rate is far less desired. It is the percentage of landing page terminations compared with arrivals. A bounce rate of 100% means everyone who landed did not stay. With social media campaigns, a business can measure who is talking, what they are saying, and how often they are saying it through tools such as Nielsen's Blogpulse. Research suggests that marketers should try for at least a 1% visitor-to-conversion rate on untargeted traffic. A 5% rate is considered very good (Evans, 2011).

There are other websites in which consumer feedback and the ability to build loyalty is even more prevalent. Foursquare, Groupon, and LivingSocial have provided businesses direct consumer access opportunities by offering discounts for products, thereby fostering client brand loyalty. "Location-based mobile apps enable businesses to reward loyalty in a very powerful way," according to Sam Ganga, executive vice president for commercial operations with DMI (Wagner, 2012). Location-based mobile apps allow businesses to market to owners of mobile devices who are near an advertising location.

While most companies rely on third-party analytics to capture social media *metrics*, leaders such as Dell and Gatorade have invested in their own social media listening command centers. Within these centers, employees use social media monitoring software, with a dashboard of key metrics such as brand discussions, customer interactions, and media campaign performance. These dashboards emphasize the role of listening as an organizational priority, and better enable companies to spot important trends quickly (Barry, Markey, Almquist, & Brahm, 2011).

Metric: *A standard of measurement used to gauge a company's performance.*

Many companies struggle to calculate a *return on their investment* (ROI) in social media. However, without confidence in clear returns, they have difficulty securing the funds needed to scale their efforts.

Companies that most successfully make the business case for social media use a two-pronged approach. First, they set clear business objectives for using social media at each step. They run small, contained pilot programs, carefully tracking returns to demonstrate whether further investment is warranted. For example, if the objective is to generate leads, the same metrics and measures used to assess the effectiveness of other marketing vehicles can be deployed to gauge the success of a social media pilot campaign. If the objective is to boost customer service, the effectiveness can be measured by service resolutions, relative cost and productivity, call avoidance, and the ratios of

Return on investment: *A performance measure used to evaluate the efficiency of an investment. It is usually expressed as a percentage or a ratio where return of an investment is divided by the cost of the investment. Also known as ROI.*

detractors converted to promoters. Second, the company will cement the case for a social media strategy by considering the broader value of such a strategy. Customers who engage with companies in social media spend 20% to 40% more than customers who do not, so there is real business value in engaging with customers on social media platforms (Barry et al., 2011).

By December 2012, Foursquare estimated that 1 million businesses and 25 million people used the site. The site allows customers to give their feedback about products or services and make testimonials that are viewed by their followers. The feedback can also be viewed on Facebook, which widens the audience and has the potential to increase their reach and also to build loyalty.

Foursquare offers businesses free use of its tools and data. Users can see how many check-ins they are getting each week, and how many of those are being shared on Facebook and Twitter. A business can learn who are its best customers on Foursquare and forge loyalties with them. Foursquare makes the person who has visited a site the most its "mayor." This designation has several advantages. First, a business can learn more about the mayor and some of its top visitors. Second, it creates competition among Foursquare friends to be the person who visits the site the most. The opportunities to create a loyalty among those friends are boundless. Foursquare also sends a business emails with data about how many people are visiting, recent tips, and photos that people have left at your business.

LivingSocial also offers unique opportunities to engage consumers. After a consumer purchases an item, he or she can share it with their family and friends. Customers can win free promotional offers. Businesses can see the gender of their customers, what time of day people check-in, and what portion of check-ins are also broadcast on Twitter and Facebook (McLaughlin, 2011).

Interacting with Customers

App: *Online, downloadable program or mobile application for smartphones or tablets. Short for Application.*

"Social media is the new name for old-world word-of-mouth advertising, and loyal customers are the only source of this free advertisement," said Roli Agrawal, chief executive officer of ReZoop, a mobile business *app* company (Wagner, 2012).

Social media and the marketing forms based on it are grounded in the belief, accurate or not, that the information needed to make a smart choice is available on the Internet (Evans, 2011). Some marketing managers still do not fully appreciate that they are entering a new world of deeper "relationships" with customers. This is a world in which customers are fully in *control* of their online experiences and where their motivations lead them to connect online with other consumers while they *create* and *consume* online content, much of it user- rather than marketer-generated (Hoffman & Fodor, 2010).

In a January 2012 study by Loyalty 360, it was revealed that 84% of Americans are part of at least one retail loyalty strategy (ACI Worldwide, 2012). One example is awarding points for engagement. By providing rewards around engagement online, businesses encourage users to come back to the site outside of advertising campaigns. This benefits the business beyond a tangible purchase, while also benefitting the customers with a tangible reward. This tactic creates much sought-after customer loyalty, providing a long-term financial benefit to the business by creating customers who keep coming back. When done right, these repeat visits by customers result in more revenue per customer over time (Clay, 2012).

Effective social media measurement should start by turning the traditional ROI approach on its head. That is, instead of emphasizing their own marketing investments and calculating the returns in terms of customer response, managers should begin by considering consumer motivations to use social media and then measure the social media *investments* customers make as they engage with the marketers' brands (Hoffman & Fodor, 2010). Handling the measurements this way makes much more sense. It takes into account not only short-term goals, such as increasing sales in the next month via a social media marketing campaign or reducing costs next quarter due to more responsive online support forums, but also the long-term returns of significant corporate investment in social media (Hoffman & Fodor, 2010).

There are several proven strategies for businesses to engage with customers:

- A tweetup is an event where Twitter friends meet face-to-face. Many companies have used tweetups as a way to meet their followers and plant the seeds of a long-term social media strategy.

- Blogs, videos, and live webcasts can help build brand awareness and generate more conversation and consumers. What should you blog about? Anything that interests you. Also, share articles that have helped you or that you have found interesting, and start a conversation that draws viewers to your products or services. You should write a blog post at least once a week. Encourage people to post comments. You can start by writing a blog and sharing with your personal friends to get feedback and build a network. A video or blog that has a large number of comments will pique the interest of others. They will be curious and ask themselves "What's everyone talking about?" You may want to submit a blog or video to Digg or YouTube to gain followers and/or generate interest. A following of visitors will not happen immediately.

Whole Foods Market has a successful blog that has built a loyal following. Their writers cover topics including organics, supporting local growers, Fair Trade, cooking techniques, and green practices (Halligan, Shah, 2010). The content is useful to the personal goals of its readers who continue to return for information that is relevant to them. Over 12,000 other websites link to the Whole Foods pages, which were created in July 2006. In addition, Whole Foods has more than 3 million Twitter followers.

In 2007, the Kellogg Company created an integrated digital media experience for the "Special K Challenge," featuring a support website that offered consumers the opportunity to customize a diet using Special K cereal, participate in online forums with advice from experts, join a Yahoo! email support group, and click-through to Amazon.com to purchase the cereal. Kellogg, which was able to translate those website interactions and click-throughs to market response over 18 months, found that the online ROI for Special K cereal was twice as large as that from television (York, 2008.).

Friend2Friend, a social media software developer, created an app to build fan engagement for the films distributed by Universal Pictures, one of its clients. The apps range from a tab on the web page with video clips, a photo gallery, interactive quizzes, external promotions, and activities they can share with friends (Evans, 2011). For the movie *The Fast and the Furious*, Friend2Friend built an app with a twice-a-week video or a photo-based quiz or poll. Viewers could earn points that they could post on their Facebook pages. Facebook friends could take the quiz, viewing the pictures or videos in the newsfeed and learn more about the film (Evans, 2011).

Only 12% of your friends get to see your Facebook status updates on your personal account, and it is not much better for brands that can expect to get a 16% conversion rate from likes to impressions (Justice, 2012). Thus, a multifaceted social media approach can be useful when building customer loyalty. One of the most successful alternate reality games to date is considered to be *Why So Serious,* which involved millions of players across 177 countries over a period of 15 months. This game, as with most other alternate reality games, was in fact a viral marketing campaign promoting the film *The Dark Knight.* It was the highest-grossing film of the year 2008 in the United States and, according to its producers, a big part of this success was due to the alternate reality game that preceded it (Koivisto & Rodic, 2012). Warner Brothers, which distributed *The Dark Knight,* was willing to engage in a marketing strategy that lasted longer than a year. Find the bloggers who are writing about your topic area, subscribe to their feed, and offer comments. You can build relationships with them and their followers may become your followers.

Marketing managers need to remember that social media is about the smart use of the natural conversational channels that develop between individuals (Evans, 2011). What is particularly important is trust.

Once you are able to build trust, it is invariably easier to sell your product. One theory is there are three stages of the sale: awareness, consideration, and purchase (Evans, 2011). It is the combined effects of various ways to communicate support for a product that make social media such a powerful tool. A company's customers should be its most vocal supporters on social media. They can become the best spokespersons in a campaign to build brand loyalty.

Foursquare's website offers some examples of how businesses have built an audience. New Era, the sports apparel company, offers a 15% discount to customers who have been to their flagship store three times. Astor Wines shares updates alerting customers about free wine-tastings. Happy Paws, a pet resort, offers first-time customers a 20% discount on their next purchase.

Twitter offers a unique method to interact with customers. Some companies have made time-sensitive offers on Twitter, such as the first five people to tweet back get an offer. A competition is another idea. "The first person to respond to this tweet" or "the first person to retweet our special" are other ways to engender brand loyalty. Before conducting any contest, marketers should review Twitter's guidelines to ensure any promotions are within their rules. Another way of interacting with your users is to ask questions on Twitter. Questions are a great way of having people interact in real-life and the same is true on Twitter. Sometimes it can be worth taking an hour of time to think about potential questions to ask to elicit good feedback.

Companies such as Disney, Wal-Mart, and Mattel, who target moms, will find they are disproportionately "Social Butterflies," or people who like to attend online forums and participate in groups, and "Social Gamers," or people who play games that take advantage of friendships in meaningful ways in-game. A key demographic on Facebook, moms (women between the ages of 35 and 55) as a group spend significant amounts of time playing social games. Companies such as Nestlé have found ways to embed their brands into the games that moms play online. For example, the company allows users to grow ingredients of its Stouffer's brand prepared meals within the FarmVille game (Barry et al., 2011).

Social media leaders also think just as carefully about how they can effectively nurture and mobilize "Influencers"—those hyper-connected individuals who have disproportionate online clout through blogging, posts on Facebook, and content creation that cause other social media users to follow them. Companies such as Microsoft, Dell, and Procter & Gamble host events for influencers, provide special online recognition, allow them to try and test products, and host online chats. They invest in the influencers to magnify the effect of their engagement efforts (Barry et al., 2011).

Conclusion

The prevalence of mobile devices allows businesses to engage more customers through social media in new and meaningful ways that can result in long-term brand loyalty. Whether it is a game on Facebook in which a user can earn points for a product, a tweetup, or a deal on appetizers at a restaurant, social media is a useful tool to build alliances with users.

The use of social media should be a tactic considered by any business hoping to build an audience. Some businesses have shown that a consistent approach to engaging those users through these means has proven fruitful.

The key is to be consistent in whatever method of social media you use. One cannot discuss a deal on Twitter and then disappear from the site for several weeks afterward. Businesses should also be mindful of making sure they are interacting with their audience by having conversations with users, requesting and accepting feedback, and being proactive when someone has a complaint about a product or service on social media. The opportunities are boundless.

SOURCES OF ADDITIONAL INFORMATION

Facebook statistics. http://www.socialbakers.com/facebook-statistics/
Social Vibes. www.socialvibe.com
Twitter statistics. http://www.socialbakers.com/twitter/
YouTube statistics. http://www.socialbakers.com/youtube-statistics/

BIBLIOGRAPHY

ACI Worldwide. (2012). Loyalty programs influence 84% of members: ACI Worldwide study. *Loyalty 360*. Retrieved February 17, 2012, from http://loyalty360.org/resources/article/loyalty-programs-influence-84-of-members-aci-worldwide-study

Barry, C., Markey, R., Almquist, E., Brahm, C. (2011). Putting social media to work. *Bain & Company*. Retrieved March 10, 2013, from www.bain.com/publications/articles/putting-social-media-to-work.aspx

Boyd, B. (2011). 5 mistakes companies make with a social media strategy. *Media Connect Partners LLC*.

Clay, K. (2012). Will 2013 be the year of loyalty programs? *Forbes*. Retrieved February 17, 2013, from http://www.forbes.com/sites/kellyclay/2012/12/15/will-2013-be-the-year-of-loyalty-programs/

Evans, D. (2011). *Social media marketing: An hour a day* (2nd ed.). Hoboken, NJ: Sybex.

Everett, M., & Sullivan, J. (2012). The social media payoff: Establishing the missing link between social media and ROI. *LoyaltyOne*. Retrieved February 17, 2013, from http://loyalty.com/knowledge/articles/social-media-payoff

Halligan, B., & Shah, D. (2010). *Inbound marketing: Get found using Google, social media and blogs*. Hoboken, NJ: John Wiley & Sons.

Hoffman, D., & Fodor, M. (2010). Can You Measure the ROI of Your Social Media Marketing. *MIT Sloan Management Review*. Retrieved February 17, 2013, from http://sloanreview.mit.edu/the-magazine/2010-fall/52105/can-you-measure-the-roi-of-your-social-media-marketing/

Jackson, N. (2011). Using social media to build brand loyalty. *The Atlantic*. Retrieved March 10, 2013, from www.theatlantic.com/technology/archive/2011/07/infographic-using-social-media-to-build-brand-loyalty-241701

Jacob, S. (2012). Do you have a long-term social media marketing plan. *KISSmetrics*. Retrieved March 10, 2013, from blog.kissmetrics.com/longterm-social-media-plan

Justice, A. (2012). Long Term Goals for Social Networking. *Social Media Sun.* Retrieved March 10, 2013, from socialmediasun.com/long-term-goals-for-social-networking-2

Kelly, C. (2012). Will 2013 be the year of loyalty programs? *Forbes.* Retrieved March 10, 2013, from www.forbes.com/sites/kellyclay/2012/12/15/will-2013-be-the-year-of-loyalty-programs

Koivisto, E., & Rodic, N. (2012). Best practices in viral marketing. Aalto University School of Economics. Retrieved March 10, 2013, from www.aaltomediamark.org-wp-content-uploads/2012/02/Rodic-No-2012-Best-Practices-in-Viral-Marketing.pdf

Levin, L. (2012). The recipe for long-term social media success. *Under30CEO.* Retrieved March 10, 2013, from under30ceo.com/the-recipe-for-long-term-social-media-success

McLaughlin, J. (2011). How to use Foursquare for small and local businesses. *Sprout-Social.* Retrieved March 10, 2013, from sproutsocial.com/insights/2011/07/how-to-use-foursquare-small-local-business

Phillips, S. (2012). How can social data help drive brand loyalty. *Fresh Networks.* Retrieved March 10, 2013, www.freshnetworks.com/blog/2012/11/how-can-social-data-help-drive-brand-loyalty

Taylor, C. (2012). Does Twitter have half a billion users? *Mashable.* Retrieved March 10, 2013, from mashable.com/2012/07/30/twitter-users-500-million

Wagner, V. (2012). Building loyalty when customers are a moving target. *E-Commerce Times.* Retrieved March 10, 2013, from www.crmbuyer.com/story/76812.html

York, E. B. (2008). Kellogg says ROI on digital trounces TV by 'factor of 2.' *Advertising Age.* Retrieved March 10, 2013, from adage.com/article/news/kellogg-roi-digital-trounces-tv-factor-2/130795

Zarrella, D. (2010). *The social media marketing book.* Sebastopol, CA: O'Reilly.

Transparency of Social Media Marketing

In This Essay

- User perception and the transparency of a social media marketing campaign are at the heart of a successful social media marketing strategy

- Transparency is the availability of social metadata surrounding an information exchange

- There are three different aspects to transparency: identity, content, and interaction

- Transparency causes users to engage in an organization's social media

Overview

Social media is changing the communications landscape, and marketing is changing accordingly. Marketing planning is changing as users move away from traditional media such as newspapers, television, telephones, and letters to obtain news, communicate with family and friends, and conduct business.

Communication is instant in the age of social media. Texting gives instantaneous responses between individuals. Tweeting gives instantaneous responses among group members. Following someone on Facebook allows groups to share experiences through photos. YouTube allows video sharing en masse. Mass communication leads to action. Users have and use many options for sharing and using information.

The scope of marketing is broadened by Internet communications, providing potential customers with a domestic and international influence. However, the Internet takes the exclusive control of the dissemination of information away from its source. In traditional marketing, the source knows exactly what audience it is targeting, but in social media marketing, the information is available immediately and can be sent to a diverse, broad, and technically savvy audience in a matter of seconds. This presents the challenge of making the message appealing and appropriate for a broad spectrum of consumers. Where marketing is concerned, communications via the Internet broaden its scope.

Background

The 60-hour terrorist attack in Mumbai, India, in 2008 came to the public's awareness through Twitter, Flickr, and other social media feeds. Those who reported the Mumbai incident were not trained journalists, yet they produced content that gripped the world's attention and went viral in minutes. U.S. President Barack Obama's election victory that same year attributes its success to social media. Using Twitter, Facebook, and other social media tools, the Obama campaign organized an online community to motivate voters to get out and vote and thus achieved an election victory (Currie, 2009). The U. S. company CareOne Debt Relief Services maintains an online presence through its social media channels. Their embrace of social media resulted in an online community of more than 1 million members (PRWeb, 2012).

In each of these instances, the user is the focus. The sources used this social media-initiated information exchange and influenced a response that positively affected their respective organization or business.

As far as marketing is concerned, social media is a fast-growing means of increasing brand awareness for advertising or public relations purposes. It is a tool for sharing and refining a message or product image and for developing relationships with a target audience (Mastering, 2011).

Peer pressure, an inherent threat in social media, causes concern for the validity of the information exchanged. Because of it, there is a need to evaluate the degree of validity a message carries, especially in the absence of face-to-face interaction and the impersonal nature of Internet communication.

It is a challenge over who controls or disseminates information, especially when the disseminator is external to or beyond the sources' control (Currie, 2009). That validity or transparency and its impact in social media marketing is explored here.

To explore transparency and its implications for social media marketing, there is the need to remember a drawback unique to online communication—its impersonal quality. When communicating online, it is impossible to see the cues and innuendos that prove the trustworthiness of a source in face-face interactions. (Stuart, 2012).

Thus, online social cues and innuendos come from how users evaluate information exchanges (Stuart, 2012). As a result, transparency in social media is increasingly important. It affects a company's message and its perception with users.

Transparency has to do with the message and its credibility. The credibility of the sender also influences transparency. Both influence the perception of the message's receiver. They contribute to the conclusions drawn by researchers and analysts studying these dynamics (Stuart, 2012).

Perception and transparency are at the heart of social media interaction (Stuart, 2012). Can the receiver trust the message? Does the receiver see the message and source as credible? What level of transparency is necessary to accomplish the message's goal—action; for example, purchasing product or supporting a cause. Which social media forum best complements a message and its goals?

Choosing the message forum is the realm of social media marketing. As marketers choose a social media forum, they also need to ensure their choice has the level of transparency appropriate for engendering the trust and credibility necessary for their brand (Mastering, 2011). Once the choice or choices are made, transparency can be measured. Marketers and PR professionals use analytics to evaluate the effectiveness in reaching their audience (Mastering, 2011). To further understand transparency and its impact, a more in-depth explanation is in order.

Transparency: An Overview

Transparency is defined as the availability of *social metadata* surrounding an information exchange (Stuart, 2012). Information can be exchanged between sender and receiver, or between sender, receiver, and observer. The presence of a third party observer is an important factor in measuring marketing effectiveness because the observer is a neutral party that is able to see the interactions of the sender and receiver and have a better understanding of what one is trying to convey and why the other interprets the message in a certain way. The information exchange can be broken into three types of transparency: identity, content, and information transparency (Stuart, 2012).

Social metadata: *Data added to content by people other than the content creator, such as tags, ratings, votes, comments, etc.*

A short primer on transparency terms includes the following (Stuart, 2012):

Information exchange	This is data sent between two users.
Source	This is the user initiating information content.
Receiver	This is the user receiving information content.
Observer	This is the user viewing interaction between sender and receiver and their information exchange.
Metadata	This is the information related to online user behavior, such as demographics, purchases, surveys, click through rates, site views, and so on.
Transparency/ translucence	This is the degree of visibility of an information's source by its unique identification.
Engagement	This is the participation level with a brand/message.

Identity Transparency

Avatars: *In computing, the graphical image of the user or the user's alter ego or character.*

Transparency is not large and unchanging but complex. It has many levels and types. At its core, it has different aspects. These aspects are identity, content, and interaction. As its name implies, *identity transparency* focuses on the uniqueness of the source. Such transparency can be determined from the information exchange. Here, users determine transparency levels. Level ranges include anonymous (lowest level-source unknown), alias (mid-level-user IDs, *avatars*), and real names (highest level-name, personal identifiers) (Stuart, 2012).

Computer users look for behavioral cues and recommendations from their community's responses to determine the credibility of the source of the information they receive. Accountability is also an issue for this type of transparency. A source will behave according to the degree of accountability associated with transparency level. The source will have more to protect, will act according to expected behavior, and will be more accountable and truthful if they are operating with a higher level of transparency (Stuart, 2012).

Content Transparency

Content transparency focuses on how the information exchange originated. It focuses on what behaviors resulted from the information exchange. As with identity transparency, content transparency also has levels. The higher the level, the better the receiver of the information can judge the quality of the source. Quality speaks to the credibility of the source as well (Stuart, 2012).

It also allows users to follow a digital *paper trail* of changes made to content. This helps users attribute the source to its owner(s). The ease of following the trail and the ease of content verification contributes to the source's credibility (Stuart, 2012).

Paper trail: *Documentary evidence of what was done, discussed, etc.*

Quality, developmental changes, and content verification influence reactions to content. Content transparency can affect productivity and can induce stress. It affects productivity, particularly in the community setting. Community members may be more productive based on the productivity of fellow members. By the same token, members can experience stress if their productivity is not on par with fellow members (Stuart, 2012).

Interaction Transparency

Finally, there is *interaction transparency*. Interaction transparency describes the capability of a third party to view the information exchange between the source and the receiver. It allows third parties to observe the details of the information exchange. By observing the relationships among source, receiver, and the information itself, the observer can draw conclusions and quantify the observations for research purposes (Stuart, 2012).

Using These Transparencies

It is interaction transparency that offers the most useful possibilities to marketers and marketing research analysts. Metadata transparency at this level can help planners evaluate buying behavior, judge sentiments, and assess product loyalty by showing the frequency of a computer user's visits to a particular site. Interaction transparency is also the first step in determining the best social media options for branding a product and for reaching the brand's target audience (Stuart, 2012).

Identity and content transparency seem to be the most important factors for consumers in terms of usefulness. It is useful for consumers pending the degree of transparency in a brand's message or product. The greater the level of trust and authenticity receivers attach to the message or product, the more they are inclined to take action (Stuart, 2012).

Symmetrical: *The sender, receiver, and observer of Internet discussions can see the other's identities.*

Asymmetrical: *Only one of the sender, receiver, and observer of Internet discussions can see the other's identities.*

All three types of transparency can be *symmetrical* or *asymmetrical*. That symmetry can be with the source, the receiver, or the observer. The observer or third party can be symmetrical to one or all parties. Observer transparency may be dictated by the goals of observation. The observer may need to be anonymous to gage true behavioral results. This makes participating in the information exchange more complicated only for the observer (Stuart, 2012).

Effects of Transparency

The greater the degree of trust and credibility with the sender, the more reliable the receiver finds the message and the source. A review of the literature suggests that transparency is the lens through which users view information and attach governing factors. Those factors, trust, credibility, and loyalty, determine a user's actions (Stuart, 2012).

Businesses want users to buy their products or services. Organizations want users to support their causes. Governments want citizens to act responsibly towards their decisions. However, these entities do not have the same control over the information exchange as they did with traditional media outlets (Currie, 2009). This means that the way the information about their product or service is conveyed to and received by the users of social media is beyond their control.

The ability of individuals to participate in the information exchange is the strongest appeal of social media. Interaction transparency affects creativity when the source is known. The strength of transparency and its implied accountability can cause the source to act as expected and to observe expected courtesy while online (Stuart, 2012).

Two other factors can result from interaction transparency particularly: popularity and herding. *Popularity* can cause consumer action based on the user's perception gained from its community, experts, and frequent mentions of the source. *Herding* has to do with the group mentality of a community. The first pieces of information visitors to a site are exposed to are usually the photos, songs, or pages most frequently viewed by previous visitors to the site. This is considered herding because people will be exposed only to the most popular content of a site. They will miss out on new information because they are automatically drawn to what others like (Stuart, 2012).

Transparency and Social Media Marketing

Marketing using transparency factors is becoming more important in strategic planning. Marketers do not have the control they once exerted through traditional media. That control appears to be switching to consumers and their peers through networking communities (Dapp, 2011).

Consumers rely on the comments and reviews of their peers, especially when it is someone they know. If the source of the comment is known to the user and it has an authentic reputation, the user will be more likely to be positively influenced by that source and take action.

A trusted website where users remain anonymous can have the same effect as a website where people readily identify themselves. A medical website such as WebMD is a good example. Such a website allows the user to interact anonymously, which implies the source engenders trust. Freeing users to act anonymously can also help users protect their private information in such instances (Stuart, 2012).

Influence does not rest with consumers only; it also rests with trusted experts. These experts have a credible reputation. Product reviews, recommendations by friends and family, and surveys with positive results regarding a product influence buying behavior and product loyalty. Influencing involvement levels with products and messages is increasingly important (Haven, 2007).

In addition, with the instant nature of online interaction, when discrepancies are detected or there is disgruntlement with a product, the reaction is immediate. That reaction can be positive or negative. The higher involvement of consumers requires a higher involvement on the part of marketers.

Increased involvement is shown in CareOne Credit Counseling's attention to its consumers. By addressing comments and complaints through its social channels like Twitter and Facebook, the company has garnered itself 1 million followers. Adopting social media transparency helped CareOne establish itself as a leader in the debt relief industry (New Marketing, 2012).

Implications of Transparency

If a company ignores issues raised by its consumers, the consumers can feel isolated, ignored, or that the company is insensitive to their needs. The feelings can be communicated to family, friends, and network peers. As a result, a company's product and image suffers. The word-of-mouth effect is intensified exponentially in an Internet media outlet. Therefore, companies cannot afford to ignore social media communications (Dapp, 2011).

By investing in social media, companies are able to communicate their message, manage their advertising, and gauge customer feedback more directly and efficiently. The next decision is which social media forum best suits a company's need. This depends on what is being communicated or sold (New Marketing, 2012). For example, companies could use Twitter to share daily tips from their area of expertise, advertise company specials, or share success stories. If the company opts to use Facebook, this is a good forum for potential customers to ask questions and read about the experiences of current customers.

Transparency and Engagement in Social Media Choices

Forum transparency levels greatly influence marketing choices. No one medium can take care of a company's marketing needs. Companies need a combination to succeed. Therefore, it is recommended that a business develop an engagement profile for each product, service, or message and decide the social media tool appropriate for that audience. An engagement profile is a portrayal of the kinds and degree of involvement customers display. Similar to buying behavior, engagement is involvement behavior for a company (Haven, 2007).

Engagement is necessary in social media marketing because online communities are dynamic, active, and vocal. Members converse, recommend, and share opinions. Individuals give more credence to members of their online community than to an organization's representative (Mastering, 2011).

Engagement is the degree of participation a user has with the brand or message of a company. It is a four-fold concept whose components, in increasing levels of degree of transparency, are involvement, interaction, intimacy, and influence (Haven, 2007).

Each level mentioned in Table 1 implies an increased degree of transparency and accountability for the marketing agent. An engagement profile covering these elements then allows a company to make informed choices about its social media options (Haven, 2007).

Table 1. Components of Engagement

Engagement Component	Definition
Involvement	Initial method of participation with a brand (site visits, reviewing product reviews, browsing blog comments, examining articles, etc.)
Interaction	Builds on involvement by tracking the depth of the user's participation with the brand (leaving comments, placing product reviews, submitting blog posts, etc.)
Intimacy	Increases interaction and gages the consumer's care or concern for the brand
Influence	Furthers intimacy by evaluating the probability that the user will persuade another to participate with the brand

Adapted from Haven, 2007.

What choices contribute to engagement? The answer depends on the purpose of marketing communications. Adapting social media to engagement purposes as well as using a number of social media types ensures that the brand's message is communicated to its target audience. The communication is geared to how that target audience consumes their information (Haven, 2007).

Table 2. How to Track Social Media with Engagement

Tracking Method	Description
Expand awareness	Track responses to current marketing venues in use along with responses to brand boosters and determine the most effective venue(s).
Drive business	Track consumer initiated content and how the content plays into buying behavior. Develop strategy that capitalizes on the identified buying positives.
Brand preference	Monitor the degree of and how the consumer interacts with its own brand. Discover what makes them buy or not buy. Then build on those results.
Increase loyalty	Observe frequent buyers, brand boosters, and product zealots. Strategize how to motivate these boosters to cultivate word-of-mouth promotion.

Adapted from Haven, 2007.

A profile further breaks consumers into three types: passive, semi-active, and zealot. Passive users visit websites without participation. Semi-active users are more active. Their visits show average participation. They visit before and after a purchase. They may leave comments or a review. Zealot is a brand booster. They have the greatest degree of participation and are more likely to involve family, friends, and fellow community members. Here is a summary of how to track social media based on the type of consumer engagement based on literature recommendations (Haven, 2007).

CareOne uses Facebook, Twitter, Google+, LinkedIn, YouTube, and Pinterest. Their strategy is to communicate with people who need debt relief services on every possible level. They provide a forum for questions, advice, and complaints. Their strategy resulted in more than 1 million active users visiting their sites (New Marketing, 2012). This translates to strong goodwill and a target audience for their services.

Users are employing social media more and more as search engines. Users can search by hash tags on Twitter or use the search bar on Facebook. An example of this is a typical young user who is trying to decide whether to buy a product. She will touch base with her Facebook friends and see what choices they have made. Then she may check the Facebook pages her friends recommend to thoroughly check those options. (Dapp, 2011). The level of engagement she feels after her search leads her to her purchase.

Social Media Policy, Transparency and Global Communication

Social media is becoming integral to global issues, risk and crisis management, and civic involvement. It is already prominent in some countries. Social media has the force of decentralizing information (Dapp, 2011).

In Germany, which has the reputation of being a technically savvy country, 5% of companies use all types of social media. Twenty-five percent of German companies use at least one form of social media (Dapp, 2011).

This is a stark contrast to user demographics. For example, in the United States, 47% of users over the age of 18 use social media and are online daily. With that amount of usage, there is increasing demand for more content and more information. Facebook hit its 1 billionth member in 2012. Facebook membership constitutes the digital equivalent of the third largest country in the world, after China and India (Dapp, 2011).

Out of necessity, business, civic, and governmental organizations are being pulled by information demands to reevaluate or even develop a social media policy.

Social media marketing is not limited to business use. Civic, political, and governmental issues are coming under public scrutiny as well. This is causing those entities to manage their online presences with greater scrutiny. This is clear as users review these entities with greater scrutiny (Dapp, 2011).

For example, mobile messages helped communicate the need for blood donations in Kenya. The country has 11.3 million mobile phone users, 264,000 landline users, and 3 million online users. Kenyan blood donors opted-in for a system that reminded them by text message when they were eligible to give blood. The efforts resulted in lessening a blood shortage (Currie, 2009).

Social Media Marketing, Transparency, and Social Responsibility

Managing risk and crises through social media is becoming the norm. Prior to the rise of social media as an information dispersal tool, experts handled information dissemination. In a crisis, those with access reported on the crises. That reporting was sometimes done by those trained as well as those untrained in journalism. Information dissemination's goal was making sure information on the crisis was reported, creating awareness (Currie, 2009).

Importance of Transparency and Engagement

For organizations, companies, and governments that manage risk and crisis, social media can be beneficial. It represents an efficient, effective way to manage a company's response to customer inquiries and feedback. It is also a way to get information out to a target audience in a timely manner. It can address information put out by laymen as well as errone-ous information (Currie, 2009).

High transparency, as evidenced by truth and accurate information, encourages high engagement with users. Social media's effectiveness increases when communicators use a "human element or used a conver-sational voice" in relating to their customers (Voss, 2011).

The most effective philosophy on social media use is to think long term. Organizations who build relationships with their target audiences reap the highest engagement and benefits from that engagement (Mastering, 2011). In the same vein, having a goal of two-way communication encouraged greater engagement (Voss, 2011).

Users Want Transparency and Engagement

Organizations, whether business or governmental, cannot let content that directly affects them go unaddressed. Thank you notes, compliments, and direct engagement sent directly to these customers who are producing the content are appropriate. By the same token, the literature suggests organizations especially cannot let negative content go unanswered. Negative content can possibly go viral. If left unaddressed, the damage may be potentially devastating as well as hard to recover from (Mastering, 2011).

In addition, in light of disasters, the public has a need to know and wants information immediately. In the example of the 2007 Mumbai, India terrorist attack, social media feeds enabled traditional news media to monitor, verify, and prepare reports based on feeds from their online communities. In turn, traditional news audiences had a more in-depth presentation and were more engaged as a result (Currie, 2009). Engagement, working hand-in-hand with transparency, makes social media marketing effective. This relates to the business world because companies are able to rely on the input from their customers via social media sites to improve their marketing and their products and in turn, gain new customers.

Conclusion

Social media represents a fast-growing segment of Internet interaction. It is also a dynamic sector for marketing. Successful social media marketing is dependent on a number of factors, most importantly transparency and engagement. Both increase interest in a business or organization.

Transparency is a key factor because it generates trust, authenticity, loyalty, and support for the product or service. How the receiver of a message perceives transparency dictates their engagement. Transparency also enables marketers to draw inferences on audience behavior based on how the target audience participates in social media. That engagement can be measured. Each social media tool has its own means of measuring how effective the tool is in reaching a target audience. Transparent content has sources that are both verifiable and reliable to its users.

Engagement is crucial. Without it, marketing is ineffective. To engage customers, marketers must develop high value content. This content spurs activity from a brand's users. Brand content should support two-way communication. Brand content should have the goal of developing long-term relationships. Both approaches increase engagement.

Social media analysts can adapt their product or service to their audience's needs. They can also clarify or refine their marketing messages. A brand's social media choice does not lie with one tool but with a combination. Communicators have to use the media tools their brand's audience uses. If an audience uses Twitter, Facebook, and a popular blog, then a social marketing plan must also use those tools to be effective.

As companies actively manage their content and use of social media, they will better ensure their message accomplishes its purpose. Whether that purpose is purchasing a product, supporting a cause, or selecting a service, transparency and engagement aids that purpose.

More and more, the receiver and their interaction with information, products, and messages drive the success of marketing strategies. As marketers adapt to accommodate the switch to user-generated content development, transparency and engagement will be a key factor in influencing consumer loyalty and involvement.

SOURCES OF ADDITIONAL INFORMATION

Mashable.com. http://mashable.com/category/social-media-marketing/Slideshare.net.

BIBLIOGRAPHY

Currie, D. (2009). Expert round table on social media and risk communication during times of crisis: strategic challenges and opportunities. Retrieved December 4, 2012, from http://www.apha.org/NR/rdonlyres/47910BED-3371-46B3-85C2-67EFB80D88F8/0/socialmedreport.pdf

Dapp, T. (2011). The digital society. Deutsche Bank Research. Retrieved December 4, 2012, from http://www.dbresearch.com/the-digital-society/PROD0000000000276332.pdf

Haven, B., Bernoff, J., and Glass, S. (2007). Marketing's new key metric: engagement. Retrieved December 4, 2012, from http://www.forrester.com/marketing_new_key_metric_engagement.pdf

Stuart, H., Dabbish, K., Kinnaird, P., and Kang, R. (2012, February 11-15). Social transparency in networked information exchange: a framework and research question. Retrieved December 4, 2012, from School of Computer Science, Carnegie Mellon University, http://www.cs.cmu.edu/~xia/resources/Documents/cscw2012-449.pdf

United Business Media. (2011). Mastering Marketing in Social Media. Retrieved December 4, 2012, from http://promotions.prnewswire.com/rs/prnewswire/images/wp_Mastering_Marketing_in_Social_Media.pdf

United Business Media. (2012, March 3). New marketing effort embraces transparency through social media. Retrieved March 21, 2012, from PRWeb Newswire http://www.prweb.com/releases/3/prweb9283006.html

Voss, P. (2011, December). Transparency through social media: improving the credibility of professionals in the twenty-first century. Retrieved December 4, 2012, from Gonzaga University, School of Professional Studies, http://web02.gonzaga.edu/comltheses/proquestftp/Voss_gonzaga_0736M_10104.pdf

Updating Social Media Efforts

In This Essay:

- Search engine optimization is a technique used by many companies to diversify their social media marketing strategies

- RSS feeds push content into many social media platforms, thereby enabling a wide group of people to see it

- Consumers expect instant updates and gratification in their social media marketing strategies

Overview

As e-mail becomes an antiquated communication tool and the cost associated with traditional marketing campaigns continues to rise, companies are searching for innovative ways to reach out to and communicate with clients and potential customers. Social media marketing has proven to keep customers interested in the companies they endorse, and it allows consumers to stay current with important industry-related news on the same platform that they use to communicate with friends and family.

Considering the origins of social media is an important step in understanding the effects of social media on society. Social media has evolved quickly and without borders because of new information and techniques that are created daily.

Looking at the top contenders in the social media world today is important to begin structuring a personalized social media marketing plan. Following their lead, consider factors related to the target demographic, and determine how to maintain a homepage presence and resonate with consumers.

Although many companies have found a perfect balance of when social media marketing strategies need to be updated and evaluated, it is still a daunting task for companies or industries new to this marketing effort. It is integral to understand social media marketing techniques in the high-stakes technological business world. A company must also be mindful of the needs of the desired demographic.

Understanding the customer's needs is key to perfecting the frequency of updates and determination of what information should be shared with followers. Using various analytical techniques such as Hootsuite (http://hootsuite.com/) and Klout (http://klout.com/home) will enable further identification with a target demographic and help concentrate marketing efforts on the most effective demographics.

Maintaining a constant presence and sharable content are important aspects of a social media marketing campaign. A healthy homepage presence that informs consumers immediately of entertaining and exciting content will allow a company genuine staying power in a global marketplace.

Introduction

According to Alexa.com (2012), the Web Information Company, the top websites in the world are:

- Google
- Facebook
- YouTube
- Yahoo!
- Baidu.com
- Wikipedia
- Windows Live
- Twitter
- QQ.com
- Amazon
- Taobao.com
- Linked In
- Blogspot.com

Each of the top sites in the world integrate social media functions within their platform. The general public is interested in using such functions, and many businesses can promote themselves through social networking efforts.

According to *The History of Social Media (1978–2012)* (Bennett, 2012), social networking originated in 1978 when Ward Christensen and Randy Suess, two computer hobbyists, invented the computerized bulletin board system (BBS) to inform friends of meetings, make announcements, and share information. Social networking has evolved tremendously since then; however, much of the social aspect of the practice is similar to those early years. Using the foundation laid by the BBS, companies and individuals can network with others through the Internet, discussing products, ideas, events, and news.

In a highly criticized *Newsweek* article called "The Internet? Bah!" (1995), author Clifford Stoll proclaims "baloney" on the notion that "Visionaries see a future of telecommuting workers, interactive libraries and multimedia classrooms. They speak of electronic town meetings and virtual communities. Commerce and business will shift from offices and malls to networks and modems. And the freedom of digital networks will make government more democratic."

Although at the time, Stoll disagreed with this possible future and considered the negative implications of the visionaries' ideas, it certainly seems as if the visionaries were correct regarding the future of the Internet and the impact social media has had on society.

Another important event in the evolution of social media was the release of the social networking platform Facebook. According to article *A Timeline of Facebook History: From Fledgling Startup To $114 Billion Giant* (International Business Times, 2012), although the social media powerhouse was not the first contender in the marketplace, the site became viral. Within 4 years of its founding in 2004, Facebook had reached 100 million active users, and 6 months later it overtook top contender MySpace as the Internet's largest social network.

Facebook's popular function, updating the status on the page to inform other users about new locations, products, news, information, and more, has been adopted by many competitors. Followers or friends can see these updates through their *news feed* as a few lines of text or a photo, and if users want to learn more, they can usually broaden the view with a click.

News feed: *In social media, a constantly updating list of stories from people and pages that one follows.*

Although Facebook remains an important tool in the social media world, the introduction of competitors such as Twitter have attracted a healthy respect from corporations, public figures, and social media marketing efforts. Ingrid Lunden (2012) reported that although Twitter has more than 500 million registered users, less than one third of the accounts overall are active. Twitter allows users to share information in 160 characters or less. Although many social networking users tweet regularly throughout the day to satisfy micro-blogging needs, Twitter is a platform primarily used for self-promotion, brand awareness, ranting, and public conversation. Staying atop the twitter feed is a task that requires up-to-the-minute dedication.

Search engine optimization, commonly referred to as SEO, is the process of affecting the visibility of a website or a webpage in a search engine's "natural" or unpaid ("organic") search results. Many social media marketing efforts are invested in using SEO practices. The more certain key terms appear throughout websites and the more pertinent, factual, and previously unpublished information that appears, the higher the ranking will be with major search engines. This allows these sites the opportunity to appear on the first pages of the search.

Most diversified digital marketing plans incorporate a heavy reliance on SEO practices. To add the pertinent, factual, and previously unpublished information needed, many companies have implemented blog campaigns. More recently, multi-author blogs (MABs) have developed (Blog 2012), which consist of posts written by large numbers of authors that are professionally edited. MABs from newspapers, universities, think tanks, interest groups, and other media outlets account for an increasing amount of blog traffic.

What Is Social Media Marketing?

"Social media marketing refers to the process of gaining traffic or attention through social media sites.

"Social media itself is a catch-all term for sites that may provide radically different social actions. For instance, Twitter is a social site designed to let people share short messages or 'updates' with others. Facebook, in contrast, is a full-blown social networking site that allows for sharing updates, photos, joining events and a variety of other activities." (*What Is Social Media Marketing?*, 2012)

Twitter and Facebook, although different, are important to the world of social media marketing. Blogging and RSS feeds are also helpful.

What are RSS feeds? "RSS stands for 'Really Simple Syndication.' It is a way to easily distribute a list of headlines, update notices, and sometimes content to a wide number of people. It is used by computer programs that organize those headlines and notices for easy reading."(*What Is RSS?*, 2012).

Many people get their news exclusively from the Internet. Although it is important to compare information to ensure its accuracy, it is also important for blogs, publications, and the like to publish only verifiable information. This helps to retain customers and improve overall influence as an informational source. The more trust readers have, the more prone they will be to retrieving a greater percentage of their news from a company's source(s). Facebook, Twitter, blogging and RSS feeds follow in the footsteps of one of the initial social media sites, MySpace.

MySpace was in 2005 what Facebook had become by 2012. Many people were involved and major brands started using the platform for marketing. By 2008, MySpace announced it had 76 million unique visitors in one month—more than any site on the web at that time. Then suddenly, MySpace was no longer a main social media platform.

However, according to the article, *5 Reasons why MySpace Is Making a Comeback* (Despres, T. 2012), "…just as it was about to hit the devastatingly hard concrete of social media obscurity, it started to breathe again. Young investors Tim and Chris Vanderhook decided it was time to give MySpace a second chance. Buying the fledgling site for a mere $35 million, the two savvy entrepreneurs quickly partnered with entertainment mogul Justin Timberlake—and people started to listen. And as with everything else he touches, Timberlake started to make MySpace sound good."

By 2012, MySpace had reinvented itself as a place for music fans. Fans can watch videos, interact with their favorite artists, and comment on their friends' music choices. MySpace changed from encompassing all of social media to one prime aspect: the music industry and music-related brands.

Although Facebook continues to rule the social media world, many social media websites of various premises are allowing certain brands to flourish within their platforms.

LinkedIn, which has more than 110 million unique monthly visitors, Google+, LiveJournal, DeviantArt, and Pinterest are also in the top ten most interesting social media platforms on the web. All of these sites are geared toward social networking, and all of them offer businesses and brands the opportunity to market to a certain demographic. A company interested in social media marketing could copy information from its website or main blog and syndicate throughout all of these other networking sites for more views. This method of marketing could possibly get you thousands more unique visitors per month.

Extensive research cannot say how frequently to update any social media source. In *How Often Should I Post on Facebook?* (2012), author CJ Arlotta says "The answer to this question is simple: there is no answer."

Although many members of social media sites view their homepages daily, with 33% looking at the site more than once per day (*Shift*, 2012), it is impossible to know for certain whether these people will see or recognize a particular company's efforts.

Truly, all a company can do is try. Every type of marketing is a numbers game. If a company is promoting specials, promotions, and giveaways through social media, it will be able to better track the response it is getting from its social media efforts. Put a user number or name on each giveaway, coupon, or promotion to track the type of customers interested in a company's social media efforts. This will help better target in the future and build an online presence within a targeted demographic.

The Modern World: Integrating Versatile Social Media Marketing

Keeping an open mind regarding marketing efforts is important to the success of business owners. In travel agent and writer Carrie Finley-Bajak's (2012) article from *Travel Weekly*, Finley-Bajak provides the important knowledge that she has collected on her road of self-taught social media efforts. Some of these efforts involve realizing the importance of quality over quantity; frequently, either personally or through a representative, chatting online simply to be social; and creating a network of digital allies, such as other companies within a company's industry or those that support that industry, and teaming up with them to further brand awareness. With these principals in play, developing a solid diversification plan and ensuring the instant gratification of target consumers is an attainable goal.

Developing a business marketing diversification plan is a good place to start understanding how a marketing plan will work. Although certain industries have demographic norms, a target market can differ greatly from the industry as a whole depending on a company's marketing efforts and diversification.

It is important to take into consideration the various platforms a company is willing to dedicate time to in order to further a marketing plan. The less time a company can devote to different strategies, the smaller their diversification will be.

Concentrating Efforts on Marketing that Works

Shift (Kemp, 2012) describes consumers' expectations for instant gratification. Companies need to provide their services quickly and empathize with the needs of their customers while meeting rising expectations. Kemp explains that "those such as the London Evening Standard, which has blazed a trail with its phenomenal 'dispossessed' campaign, prove the worth of investing in actively improving consumers' lives."

In the social media world, instant gratification typically refers to communication and availability of information. Updating social media marketing efforts on a regular basis and keeping consumers informed at all times allows consumers to feel gratified.

For example, according to *One Aspect of Social Media Marketing...* (2012), "Pool and beach attendants at the Westin Casuarina Resort & Spa on Grand Cayman noticed that many guests asked staff to take their photos lounging by the Jacuzzi or tanning on a lounge chair. The guests immediately posted their photos to the resort's Facebook page.

"So the resort put someone in charge of manning and scanning the page. When a guest's photo popped up on screen, it was quickly followed poolside by a waiter bearing a tropical libation as a thank-you to the guest for the publicity."

Press releases and viral campaigns are another useful way to reach out to customers. Take a look at U.S.-based Ford Motor Company's strategic social media release of the newly redesigned 2010 Ford Explorer.

"When Ford introduced a redesigned edition of the Ford Explorer in 2010, it skipped the conventional auto show unveiling to auto journalists in favor of simultaneous announcements in eight cities—and on

Facebook. The Facebook campaign, created using tools from Buddy Media (now part of the Salesforce Marketing Cloud), featured videos about the vehicle from the product managers and engineers. The Explorer 'reveal' campaign attracted 99 million social media impressions and became the No. 1 trending term and the No. 2 search term for the day on Google" (Carr 2012).

Using Analytics

Hubspot CMO Mike Volpe meticulously clarifies the differences between web analytics and marketing analytics: "Web analytics measure things a webmaster cares about, like page load times, page views per visit, and time on site. Marketing analytics, on the other hand, measure *business* metrics like traffic, leads, and sales, and which events (both on and off your website) influence whether leads become customers. Marketing analytics includes data not only from your website, but also from other sources like e-mail, social media, and offline events. Marketing analytics are also usually people-centric, featuring the prospect, lead, or customer as the unit of focus, whereas web analytics usually regard the page view as the unit of focus in its reports."

According to *Transforming Social Media Data into Predictive Analytics* (2012), many companies are using their social media data to aid in their predictive process. "More than 900 million people worldwide check their Facebook accounts on a monthly basis, followed by Twitter, which has more than 150 million active users. In March, LinkedIn claimed it had more than 160 million users, with two new members joining the site every second."

What Does This Information Mean?

Using research and analytics to maintain an efficient homepage presence, companies are able to provide their followers with targeted social media efforts, further encouraging Internet users to engage in social media. An effective method of using the data would be "to produce targeted ads based on an aggregate collection of customers' shopping behaviors and preferences. At the same time, many companies are treading carefully when using their customers' social data to personalize offers or products (due to consumers increasing concerns with privacy)" (Aquino, 2012).

From 2010 to 2012 the percentage of Americans following any brand on a social network has gone from 16% to 33%. Companies still have substantial room for growth in connecting with customers and fans on social networks (Baer, 2012).

Using this information in marketing essentially allows companies to continue creative campaigns, daily or hourly microblogging, daily blogging, frequent press releases, and many other social media efforts. These efforts will guarantee a continuous homepage presence for followers and potential customers with like interests.

Providing the best possible content promotes a company's likeability and shareability among the general public. Corporations that are competing in the social media-marketing world with compelling, well-written content are well-liked.

> ...Areas such as traditional and local search engine optimization (SEO), social media and content marketing saw the greatest increases in marketing demand this year, 2012, according to August 2012 data from SEOmoz (SEO Social, 2012).

Specifically, according to *SEO, Social and Content Marketing in Top Demand* (2012), "The [SEOmoz] study broke out the three marketing areas into distinct tactics, but SEO, social media and content marketing are not mutually exclusive. All three rely heavily on the production and distribution of content—both written and visual."

Sharing content throughout various social media platforms is an important aspect of the diversified marketing plan. Newly released content should be published on multiple platforms to receive attention from users over the World Wide Web. Articles published on personal blogs can be shared through Google+, Facebook, Twitter, Yahoo!Voices and RSS feeds, thereby reaching millions of potential viewers in just moments. If Internet users see specific content on their homepage on multiple social media platforms, they will be more prone to absorb the information, read further, or share the information with friends.

Author David Grzelak investigated the ideology behind *What Motivates Social Interaction with Brands* (2012) and found "The truth is that for most people, their actions are more self-serving. We recognize or follow a brand on social channels because of what it says *about us*, not for some altruistic reason. We have all been there: 'I'm about to 'like' Kingsford charcoal. My friends will see it. What does that say about me?'"

We know that the general public bears this attitude about brand awareness, so it is important to ensure that positive information about a product is released. Although it is desirable that people of all ages gain interest in the brand and products offered by a company, each age group may require individual attention. Nabisco, for example, uses different marketing techniques for their younger demographic than for their older demographics. They also sell different products to each age group marketed toward the characteristics that each wants in their snacks.

Social networking is described by Amy Bax in *Importance of Social Networking* (2012) as follows: "…with the Internet now integrated into nearly all aspects of everyday business use, many business owners are recognizing the important role that social networking can play in the world of entrepreneurship."

Bax describes the roles of social networking in today's web-based society: to gain contacts, to gain clients, and to increase public awareness. Without these factors, businesses would be operating without the ability to communicate openly with a target marketplace and essentially, would be unable to grow as a corporation at an ideal pace.

Social networking is an important ally in properly maintaining brand representation. Take, for example, the Austrian company Red Bull GmbH. Red Bull is one of the most popular energy drinks in the world, with 4.6 billion cans sold in 2011.

Most of the world is familiar with Red Bull's famed motto: Red Bull Gives You Wings. Red Bull uses a number of Internet-based social media marketing campaigns to publicize their products. Some of these include music videos produced by their in-house label, Red Bull Records. The company also markets a number of celebrity endorsements.

Red Bull engages in a number of viral campaigns, such as the annual Flugtag and a recent event entitled "Red Bull Stratos," in which they aided a man in skydiving from the edge of outer space back to earth. The website, redbullstratos.com, is still live with blog updates that continued to be added at least a month after the space jump that occurred on October 14, 2012.

Despite some criticism regarding their product, Red Bull has forged onward with strong brand representation. They offer a number of giveaways in high profile locations, they appeal greatly to their various demographics, and they are always on the cutting-edge of media attention with their events and social media.

Red Bull uses more than six different Facebook fan pages that appeal to product users as well as individuals interested in their racing team, surfing team, X-fighters sports league, storm chasers team, and music label, to name a few. With more than 35 million Facebook fans, they also engage in brand awareness campaigns outside of the Internet and through various other digital marketing techniques.

Red Bull is currently the most liked brand on Facebook. "Several celebrities like Rihanna and Lady Gaga have more than 50 million Facebook fans, as do services like YouTube and Facebook, but Coca-Cola is the first retail brand to hit this milestone. Disney, Converse and Starbucks, three of the other popular retail brands, each have fewer than 40 million fans on Facebook at the moment" (Flegerman & Seth, 2012).

Following in the social media marketing footsteps of major brands such as Red Bull, Coca Cola, Disney, and Starbucks requires a lot of effort and a lot of research. The major factor that all of these brands have in common is that they use social media marketing appropriately. They cater to their various demographics, they are constantly on the cutting edge of marketing efforts, and their teams are both tech- and information-savvy.

Although it requires billions of dollars to market and network on the same level as multinational corporations, a business can do this on a somewhat smaller scale on its own. By analyzing various diverse marketing plans, working in regular information and blog updates, and narrowing clientele to a target demographic (or multiple target demographics), a business can be on its way to large-scale marketing efforts through digital media.

By reviewing the efforts of major contenders in a similar marketplace, it is easy to see that most brands and blogs are being updated on a daily basis to further promote homepage presence. In these cases, no amount of updating is too much in a fast-paced micro-blogging platform where some individuals update as often as every few minutes every day.

The Internet marketing age has left users for the desire for instant gratification. With this in mind, targeted information is always in need: now. In today's society, no information is "too much," users are increasingly looking for blurbs of smaller information (hence the popularity of microblogging), and the more information and the more quickly it is published, the better off a brand will be.

SOURCES OF ADDITIONAL INFORMATION

7 Things You Should Know about Microblogging. http://www.educause.edu/library/resources/7-things-you-should-know-about-microblogging

20 Social Media Tools You Should Be Using. http://smallbiztrends.com/2012/09/20-free-social-media-monitoring-tools.html

Red Bull Stratos. http://www.redbullstratos.com

BIBLIOGRAPHY

Aquino, Judith. (2012, November). "Transforming social media data into predictive analytics: More organizations are leveraging psychographic data to forecast positive—and negative—results." Retrieved November 30, 2012, from http://www.destinationcrm.com/Articles/Editorial/Magazine-Features/Transforming-Social-Media-Data-into-Predictive-Analytics-85687.aspx

Arlotta, C. (2012, May 29). "How often should you post on Facebook?" *MSPmentor | Managed Services & MSP News Blog*. Retrieved November 18, 2012, from http://www.mspmentor.net/2012/05/29/how-often-should-i-post-on-facebook/

Baer, Jay. (2012, June 6). "11 shocking new social media statistics in America." *Convince and Convert Social Media Strategy and Content Marketing Strategy*, June 6, 2012. Retrieved November 18, 2012, from http://www.convinceandconvert.com/the-social-habit/11-shocking-new-social-media-statistics-in-america/.

Bax, Amy. (2012). "Importance of social networking." Retrieved November 18, 2012, from http://www.gaebler.com/Importance-of-Social-Networking.htm.

Bennett, Shea. (2012). "The history of social media (1978-2012) [INFOGRAPHIC]." *AllTwitter*. Retrieved November 18, 2012, from http://www.mediabistro.com/alltwitter/social-media-history_b18776.

Carr, David F., and Donston-Miller. Debra. (2012). "7 lessons in social business." *Information Week*, February 17, 2012, p. 22. Retrieved November 18, 2012, from http://www.informationweek.com/thebrainyard/news/social_networking_private_platforms/240012640/7-lessons-from-social-business-leaders.

Country. (n.d.). "Alexa top 500 global sites." *Alexa—The Web Information Company*. Retrieved November 15, 2012, from http://www.alexa.com/topsites

Despres, T. (2012, August 1). "5 reasons MySpace is making a comeback." *iMedia Connection: Interactive Marketing News, Features, Podcasts and Video—iMediaConnection.com*. Retrieved November 18, 2012, from http://www.imediaconnection.com/article_full.aspx?id=32367

eBizMBA. (n.d.). "Top 15 most popular social networking sites." *eBizMBA—The eBusiness Knowledgebase*. Retrieved November 18, 2012, from http://www.ebizmba.com/articles/social-networking-websites

eMarketer. (2012). "SEO, social and content marketing in top demand." *Market research on digital media, internet marketing | eMarketer*. Retrieved November 15, 2012, from http://www.emarketer.com/(S(43hyfd452pyph345ldrou545))/Article.aspx?R=1009368

Finley-Bajak, Carrie. (2012). "Social media 101, for agents." *Travel Weekly*.

Flegerman, S. (2012, September 4). "Coca-Cola is first retail brand to pass 50 million Facebook fans." *Social Media News and Web Tips—Mashable—The Social Media*

Guide. Retrieved November 18, 2012, from http://mashable.com/2012/09/04/coca-cola-50-m-facebook-fans/

Grzelak, David. (2012, November 15). "What motivates social interaction with brands?" *Digital Marketing Resources For CMOs (Chief Marketing Officer).* Retrieved November 15, 2012, from http://www.cmo.com/branding/what-motivates-social-interaction-brands

IBT Staff. (2012, May 18)."A timeline of Facebook history: From fledgling startup to $114 billion giant." *International Business Times,* May 18, 2012. Retrieved November 18, 2012, http://www.ibtimes.com/timeline-facebook-history-fledgling-startup-114-billion-giant-699093

Kemp, Nicola. (2012). "Shift." *Business and Company ASAP.* Retrieved November 18, 2012, from http://www.questia.com/library/1G1-309369485/shift

Lunden, I. (2012, July 31)."Twitter may have 500M users but only 170M are active..." *TechCrunch RSS,* Retrieved November 15, 2012, from http://techcrunch.com/2012/07/31/twitter-may-have-500m-users-but-only-170m-are-active-75-on-twitters-own-clients/.

SearchEngineLand. (n.d.). "What is social media marketing." *Search Engine Land: Must Read News About Search Marketing & Search Engines.* Retrieved November 18, 2012, from http://searchengineland.com/guide/what-is-social-media-marketing

Software Garden. (n.d.). "What is RSS: A tutorial introduction to feeds and aggregators." *rss.softwaregarden.com.* Retrieved November 18, 2012, from http://rss.softwaregarden.com/aboutrss.html

Stoll, C. (1995, February 26). The Internet? Bah!. *Newsweek magazine,* 1-2.

Travel Weekly. (2012, July 30). "One aspect of social media is the instant gratification that comes when a message sent generates a response in a New York minute or, in this case, a Cayman five minutes." *Travel Weekly,* July 30, p 4.

Sentiment Analysis

In This Essay

- Sentiment analysis is a complex and useful tool for evaluating preferences and for behavioral study

- Some of the uses of sentiment analysis include focused marketing, assessing competitors, promoting brands, and many other possibilities

- Online services can help analyze users' sentiments toward businesses, products, keywords, or individuals

Overview

Sentiment analysis, also know as *opinion mining*, is the systematic use of methods to identify, classify, and extract subjective information from written sources. Typically these methods are implemented in computer software, and the analysis itself involves the processing of natural language and the use of computational linguistics. The idea behind sentiment analysis is that the attitude of a writer with regard to any particular topic can be determined by assessing the overall contextual polarity of the writing; it detects, reports on, and quantifies opinions and emotions in any given information source. The first work in sentiment analysis was done by Peter Turney and Bo Pang. Turney and Pang analyzed movie reviews and product reviews for polarity at the level of the document as a whole.

Most research on sentiment analysis has occurred since 2000. This is mostly because opinion-based text was not widely available before the advent of the Internet. The World Wide Web has changed the way opinions are expressed, and today online word of mouth is a crucial source of academic, political, consumer, and marketing information. For individual consumers, Internet research can provide a wealth of consumer opinions on any given product. For companies, marketing surveys and focus groups are not as important because a great deal of information is available on the Web; the main hurdle for companies is finding, monitoring, and processing the opinion data.

What is meant by the writer's attitude varies depending on the writing. Appraisal theory looks to judgments and evaluations expressed by the writer to determine attitude, but the affect or emotional state of the writer or the emotion the writer intends to evoke in the reader can also constitute the attitude of the writer.

Emotion has been the subject of academic study in many fields. Although there is no hard and set list of primary human emotions, most authoritative sources agree that love, hate, happiness, sadness, fear, and surprise are the most basic human emotions. Each of these has many sub-emotions and can be experienced in different intensities. These six basic emotions can be expressed in almost unlimited ways using language; deciphering the range and intensities of emotions expressed by language is the challenge of sentiment analysis.

How and When To Use Sentiment Analysis

Writing that may be subject to sentiment analysis can come from any source that contains subjective information. This means that academic and professional articles, business presentations, social media conversations, and even communications like customer feedback can be used. Sentiment analysis allows examination of the roots of problems and successes. For businesses, sentiment analysis equates to more focused marketing, better assessment of threats and boons, and, of course, promotion of their brands and accompanying earnings.

Polarity: *The state in which two opinions or ideas are very different from each other.*

Sentiment analysis works at both basic and advanced levels. Basic analysis consists of classification of a text's *polarity*, and this type of analysis takes place at the sentence level. The question asked here is whether the opinion or idea expressed in any given sentence or feature/aspect is positive, negative, or neutral. It is worth noting, however, that even basic sentiment analysis is much more involved than a simple comparison of the number of positive and negative words and phrases to produce a numerical value.

A slight variation of this method requires a scale of 11 values that are assigned to frequently used words associated with positive or negative sentiment: -5 is the most negative and $+5$ is the most positive. When this scale is used, these valued sentiment words are analyzed alongside the concepts they describe. In this way each concept can be characterized by the attached sentiment words that come with it, and values for the concepts themselves can be quantified.

Another method of sentiment analysis simply attempts to classify sentences as either objective or subjective. This is useful for sentiment analysis because, once classified, the objective sentences can be removed from the analysis. This is a way of distilling the sentiment in a piece of writing.

Sentiment analysis can be fine-tuned. For example, suppose a movie production company produces a film that contains one particularly controversial murder scene in it. The company releases the film only for a test run so they can decide how the final edit of the movie should proceed. They want to analyze the sentiment viewers have not only for the whole film but for the murder scene as well; more sophisticated sentiment analysis can provide this information.

This kind of analysis involves several steps. First, relevant features or aspects of a given concept or product must be determined. In this example, the movie itself is obviously a relevant concept, as is the murder scene. Next, the features or aspects of each relevant feature must be designated, and finally, a determination must be made about whether the opinions expressed on each relevant feature are positive, negative, or neutral.

Although most *data-mining* algorithms work to recognize the in-text polarity of sentiment, for some uses it is important to identify both the kind of sentiment and also the strength of the expressed emotions and opinions. Sentiment analysis functions at these more advanced levels. This type of "beyond polarity" analysis evaluates actual emotional states rather than using a simple positive/negative classification. This type of sentiment analysis might classify sentences or features/aspects as "happy," "sad," "frustrated," "satisfied," or "angry." Recent advances in the field include analysis of images, video, and other media alongside text, and the linking of expressed sentiment with transactional histories.

Data-mining: *The analysis of large quantities of data to discover patterns within the data.*

Most sentiment analysis is actually performed automatically by software tools working to program specifications. Open source programs use banks of words with assigned values to perform analyses on masses of texts. Some focus more on the author and attempt to identify that person's sentiment; others focus on the object of the sentiment and what emotions the topic tends to garner. Dependency grammar (DG), statistics, and natural language processing techniques are all used in sentiment analysis.

Why to Use Sentiment Analysis

Written information can be split into facts and opinions. Obviously, facts are objective and opinions are subjective, and the subjective expression of ideas contains sentiment. Certainly it is useful to gather facts for analysis of buying patterns, for example, but opinions are all that concern sentiment analysis. Algorithms can be used to identify both sentiment and sentiment strength, and this is the basis of sentiment analysis.

One issue that makes automated sentiment analysis complex is the fact that, particularly given the informal nature of most online communication, rules of grammar and spelling are frequently broken in texts subject to sentiment analysis. Emoticons, repeated letters, punctuation used for emphasis (like "hiiii!!!"), and abbreviated words are among the biggest challenges for this kind of analysis because typically these programs rely on standards for grammar and spelling for their part-of-speech tagging functions.

Another challenge for sentiment analysis is that any given expressive text may have multiple emotions and targets for emotions. If, for example, a company wants to know what reviewers thought of their product, they will have to parse through reviews like this:

> I love this computer! I am so over the one I had before, this one is faster and looks nicer. My husband thought it was too expensive, but I thought he was just being cheap. I love the look of the case too. The only thing that's not so good is the charger. I have to use it a lot because the battery dies and I hate how it messes up my desk. But whatever, overall I really like it.

The problems for sentiment analysis in this example are as follows: What are the opinions? How can they be found? Basic Internet queries about a given product will find reviews like the previous example as well as a great deal of other information. For sentiment analysis to be successful, a program must achieve three goals. First, it must locate text that relates to the query. Then it must find text that expresses opinions within the result. Finally, it must order or rank opinion text in a way that is relevant to the query. The first problem for the sentiment analysis is the process of finding suitable texts, and then the problem is the effective retrieval of data.

What is the target or object of the opinions? The one that matters in the previous example is the computer, and possibly the charger and battery; an object can have a number of parts and attributes, and the charger and battery fall into these categories. This reviewer also expressed an opinion about her husband and her husband's opinion about the computer. These details should be parsed out properly because an incorrect analysis of this opinion might lead the company to think the reviewer thought the computer was "cheap" when in actuality it is her husband that she is discussing. These issues constitute obvious challenges for automated analysis.

What are the opinions? Are they positive or negative, and how strong are they? Looking back to the example, some of the opinion words used include "love," "hate," "over it," "(really) like," "cheap," "(too) expensive," "faster," "nicer," and "not so good." It will also matter to the company what the reviewer means by a word like "cheap." In this context it is a negative opinion, but in many cases it could be positive.

Another issue for discerning opinions is analysis of comparative statements. In the example, most of the opinions were directly expressed, but there is also a comparison with the old computer. The comparison indicates that this reviewer thinks the company's computer is faster and looks nicer than the old computer. This preference is an important aspect of the reviewer's opinion.

Spam and false information are other problems for sentiment analysis. Phony opinions designed to mislead can give undeserved positive praise to a company or product, or unfairly negative opinions can be used to hurt a given product, organization, or person. These kinds of misleading opinions are "opinion spam," and detecting this spam is crucial for good sentiment analysis. Spam opinions should not be confused with actual opinions that are of low utility.

One final problem of note for sentiment analysis is that algorithms use relatively simple terms to analyze expressed emotions about products, organizations, and services. The shorter the analyzed text, the less information is available for analysis, as well. Human emotion, however, is not simple, even when expressed in brief terms. Cultural differences, language usage peculiarities, and the ongoing challenges posed by context render the process of transforming a set of words into a simple positive or negative sentiment difficult. To understand this issue, consider how often people who speak the expressed language will disagree about the meaning of a text.

The accuracy goal for sentiment analysis is 70%; in other words, an accurate sentiment analysis tool and human judgments will agree about 70% of the time. This figure is based on the fact that humans disagree approximately 30% of the time about any given judgment or answer to a given query.

Sentiment Analysis Tools

Because location of opinion-based data, organization of the found data, and interpretation of the data all constitute major challenges for companies, automated systems for completing these tasks are required. This need and its momentous value to all kinds of organizations were the impetus for sentiment analysis. Research in academic settings as well as practical venues is ongoing and growing rapidly. As of 2012, in the U.S. alone there were between 20 and 30 companies whose exclusive function was the provision of sentiment analysis and related services.

Most of these services have been oriented toward commercial gain rather than behavioral understanding. Nevertheless, sentiment analysis has other applications and can be used to understand the ways that emotion functions in the informal communication that dominates the Internet. This kind of analysis can also help identify inappropriate or anomalous emotional responses, and to effectively correlate certain emotional speech with potentially dangerous behavior. The key for this sort of analysis is building a program sensitive enough to discern both the strength of expressed emotions and whether the sentiment expressed is appropriately balanced between negative and positive emotions.

Social Mention

Social Mention (Socialmention.com) is an Ottawa-based company that provides a free, automated system that locates opinion-based data in real time. A Social Mention user can register to receive "social media alerts" through the website; these alerts are the reported results of a Google-style trolling of more than 100 social media, news, video, and blog sites for mentions of your company (or of your competitors, a news keyword that impacts your business, etc.).

Social Mention offers several tools to its users. The "Sentiment" tool uses sentiment analysis techniques to assess whether the mentions of your company are positive, negative, or neutral. This is not, however, a scientific study of the mentions and constitutes a basic tool. The "Top Users" tool lets you know who is discussing your query subject the most. Social Mention's "Top Hashtags" feature reports which popular Twitter hashtags, if any, are found in conjunction with your target query.

"Post Rank" is a feature designed to let users of Social Mention know the degree of interest and importance that Internet users attribute to the company in the query. This tool sets out to find indicia of social engagement on a given topic, such as posts about the subject, comments on blogs, articles or other sources of information on the topic, or clicking on a related link. The "Sources" tool allows users to see which search engines provided the Social Mention results reported to the user. Finally, the "Microblogs" search on Social Mention locates tweets on the key word or phrase in question, showing the user who is tweeting about their product or business and what the tweets are saying.

Unrelated to specific queries, Social Mention also has a "Hot Conversations" feature. This feature lists trending topics in real time without regard to a user's specific query. Any given topic might appear in this feed.

The strength of Social Mention is also the weakness: the platform aggregates a huge amount of information into a single stream. This means that it is discovering a great deal of information that can be used by a business owner, public figure, or anyone else who has an interest in a search. However, the actual analysis of the data is left to the user, and the tremendous amount of information can be overwhelming.

Network: *A chain of interconnected individuals or organizations sharing information and/or services.*

Klout

Klout (Klout.com) is a San Francisco-based company that attempts to measure the "influence" of individual people with online presences. It uses social media analytics including the size of a person's *network*, the amount of content created by the person, the number of interactions with that person's content, and supposedly the quality of interactions with the person and his content. Klout mines data from sites like Twitter,

Facebook, and Google+ to assess influence and assign a score based on the data.

Klout, therefore, attempts to use certain principles of sentiment analysis that have traditionally been used to assess opinions about brands, organizations, companies, and products and apply them to individuals. It is not an "opt-in" service so it is possible to have a Klout score without being aware of it. This Klout score can range from 1, the least influential, to 100, the most influential. The score itself is calculated using Twitter data points including following count, follower count, retweets of the user's content, list memberships, the number of spam and inactive accounts that follow the user, the Klout influence of the user's followers and retweeters, and unique mentions of the user. This basic Twitter data is combined with other social network data such as Facebook comments and likes and the number of people in your LinkedIn network; the result is a "Klout Score" that, according to the company, measures online influence.

The Klout business model is somewhat circular in that it requires belief in the validity of the Klout score that it partially manufactures; for example, users are directed to post about Klout and link their networks to Klout to boost their scores. What these actions do, however, is spread Klout's influence by increasing their number of users. The more users believe that value is attributed to the scores, the more actual value accrues as users participate in the system.

Ultimately it is unclear how Klout's algorithms work or how closely they reflect what real world influence might look like. A number of companies have partnered with Klout to receive access to users with high Klout scores; this paid access is intended to provide the companies with ongoing "free" publicity as their businesses become part of the stream of high-influence users and, consequently, are seen by their followers.

SOURCES OF ADDITIONAL INFORMATION

Feelings, Nothing More Than Feelings: The Measured Rise of Sentiment Analysis in Journalism. http://www.niemanlab.org/2013/01/feelings-nothing-more-than-feelings-the-measured-rise-of-sentiment-analysis-in-journalism

How Sentiment Analysis Works. http://www.slideshare.net/mcjenkins/how-sentiment-analysis-works

The Future of Sentiment Analysis. http://www.socialmediaexplorer.com/social-media-monitoring/sentiment-analysis

BIBLIOGRAPHY

Abbasi, A., Chen, H., Thoms, S., & Fu, T. (2008). Affect analysis of Web forums and Blogs using correlation ensembles. *IEEE Transactions on Knowledge and Data Engineering, 20*(9), 1168–1180.

Argamon, S., Whitelaw, C., Chase, P., Hota, S. R., Garg, N., & Levitan, S. (2007). Stylistic text classification using functional lexical features. *Journal of the American Society for Information Science and Technology, 58*(6), 802–822.

Artstein, R., & Poesio, M. (2008). Inter-coder agreement for computational linguistics. *Journal of Computational Linguistics, 34*(4), 555–596.

Balahur, A., Kozareva, Z., & Montoyo, A. (2009). Determining the polarity and source of opinions expressed in political debates. *Lecture Notes in Computer Science, 5449*, 468–480.

Baron, N. S. (2003). Language of the Internet. In A. Farghali (Ed.), *The Stanford Handbook for Language Engineers* (pp. 59–127). Stanford: CSLI Publications.

Barrett, L. F. (2006). Valence as a basic building block of emotional life. *Journal of Research in Personality, 40*(1), 35–55.

Boyd, D. (2008). *Taken out of context: American teen sociality in networked publics.* University of California, Berkeley: Berkeley.

Boyd, D. (2008). Why youth (heart) social network sites: The role of networked publics in teenage social life. In D. Buckingham (Ed.), *Youth, identity, and digital media* (pp. 119–142). Cambridge, MA: MIT Press.

Brill, E. (1992). A simple rule-based part of speech tagger. *Proceedings of the Third Conference on Applied Natural Language Processing*, 152–155.

Chaumartin, F.-R. (2007). UPAR7: A knowledge-based system for headline sentiment tagging. In *Proceedings of the 4th International Workshop on Semantic Evaluations (SemEval-2007)* (pp. 422–425). New York, NY: ACM.

Choi, Y., & Cardie, C. (2008). Learning with compositional semantics as structural inference for subsentential sentiment analysis. *Proceedings of the Conference on Empirical Methods in Natural Language Processing*, 793–801.

Community Research and Development Information Service. (2009). *Cyberemotions: Collective Emotions in Cyberspace.* European Commission.

Cornelius, R. R. (1996). *The science of emotion.* Upper Saddle River, NJ: Prentice Hall.

Crystal, D. (2006). *Language and the Internet* (2nd ed.). Cambridge, UK: Cambridge University Press.

Das, S., & Chen, M. (2001). Yahoo! for Amazon: Extracting market sentiment from stock message boards. *Proceedings of the Asia Pacific Finance Association Annual Conference (APFA)*, Bangkok, Thailand, July 22–25, Retrieved July 17, 2009, from http://sentiment.technicalanalysis.org.uk/DaCh.pdf.

Denecke, K., & Nejdl, W. (2009). How valuable is medical social media data? Content analysis of the medical web. *Information Sciences, 179*(12), 1870–1880.

Derks, D., Bos, A. E. R., & von Grumbkow, J. (2008). Emoticons and online message interpretation. *Social Science Computer Review, 26*(3), 379–388.

Derks, D., Fischer, A. H., & Bos, A. E. R. (2008). The role of emotion in computer-mediated communication: A review. *Computers in Human Behavior, 24*(3), 766–785.

Dey, L., & Mirajul Haque, S. K. (2008). Opinion mining from noisy text data. *Proceedings of the Second Workshop on Analytics for Noisy Unstructured Text Data*, pp. 83–90.

Diener, E., & Emmons, R. A. (1984). The independence of positive and negative affect. *Journal of Personality and Social Psychology, 47*(5), 1105–1117.

Ekman, P. (1992). An argument for basic emotions. *Cognition and Emotion, 6*(3/4), 169–200.

Fox, E. (2008). *Emotion science*. Basingstoke: Palgrave Macmillan.

Fullwood, C., & Martino, O. I. (2007). Emoticons and impression formation. *The Visual in Popular Culture, 19*(7), 4–14.

Gamon, M. (2004). Sentiment classification on customer feedback data: Noisy data, large feature vectors, and the role of linguistic analysis. *Proceedings of the 20th international conference on Computational Linguistics*, No. 841.

Gamon, M., Aue, A., Corston-Oliver, S., & Ringger, E. (2005). Pulse: Mining customer opinions from free text (IDA 2005). *Lecture Notes in Computer Science, 3646*, 121–132.

Gill, A. J., Gergle, D., French, R. M., & Oberlander, J. (2008). Emotion rating from short blog texts. In *Proceeding of the twenty-sixth annual SIGCHI conference on human factors in computing systems* (pp. 1121–1124). New York, NY: ACM.

Grinter, R. E., & Eldridge, M. (2003). Wan2tlk? Everyday text messaging. *CHI 2003*, 441–448.

Hancock, J. T., Gee, K., Ciaccio, K., & Lin, J. M.-H. (2008). I'm sad you're sad: Emotional contagion in CMC. *Proceedings of the ACM 2008 conference on Computer supported cooperative work*, 295–298.

Hopkins, D. J., & King, G. (2010). A method of automated nonparametric content analysis for social science. *American Journal of Political Science, 54*(1), 229–247.

Hu, M., & Liu, B. (2004). Mining and summarizing customer reviews. *Proceedings of KDD 2004*.

Huang, Y.-P., Goh, T., & Liew, C. L. (2007). Hunting suicide notes in web 2.0— Preliminary findings. In *Ninth IEEE International Symposium on Multimedia— Workshops, Proceedings* (pp. 517–521). Los Alamitos: IEEE.

Huppert, F. A., & Whittington, J. E. (2003). Evidence for the independence of positive and negative well-being: Implications for quality of life assessment. *British Journal of Health Psychology, 8*(1), 107–122.

Kim, S. M., & Hovy, E. H. (2006). Identifying and analyzing judgment opinions. *Proceedings of the Human Language Technology / North American Association of Computational Linguistics conference (HLT-NAACL 2006)*, New York, NY.

Krippendorff, K. (2004). *Content analysis: An introduction to its methodology*. Thousand Oaks, CA: Sage.

Kukich, K. (1992). Techniques for automatically correcting words in text. *ACM computing surveys, 24*(4), 377–439.

Liu, B. (2010). Sentiment analysis and subjectivity. *Handbook of natural language processing* (2nd ed.) (N. Indurkhya & F. J. Damerau, Eds.). Boca Raton, FL: Chapman & Hall/CRC.

Liu, B., Hu, M., & Cheng, J. (2005). Opinion observer: Analyzing and comparing opinions on the web." *Proceedings of WWW 2005*.

Liu, H., Lieberman, H., & Selker, T. (2003). A model of textual affect sensing using real-world knowledge. *Proceedings of the 2003 International Conference on Intelligent User Interfaces, IUI 2003*, 125–132.

Mauss, I. B., & Robinson, M. D. (2009). Measures of emotion: A review. *Cognition and Emotion, 23*(2), 209–237.

Mihalcea, R., Banea, C., & Wiebe, J. (2007). Learning multilingual subjective language via cross-lingual projections. *Proceedings of the Association for Computational Linguistics (ACL)*, pp. 976–983.

Mishne, G. (2005). Experiments with mood classification in Blog posts. *Style—the 1st Workshop on Stylistic Analysis of Text For Information Access, at SIGIR 2005*.

Mishne, G., & de Rijke, M. (2006). Capturing global mood levels using Blog posts. In *Proceedings of the AAAI Spring Symposium on Computational Approaches to Analysing Weblogs (AAAI-CAAW)* (pp. 145–152). Menlo Park, CA: AAAI Press.

Nardi, B. A. (2005). Beyond bandwidth: Dimensions of connection in interpersonal communication. *Computer-Supported Cooperative Work, 14*(1), 91–130.

Neviarouskaya, A., Prendinger, H., & Ishizuka, M. (2007). Textual affect sensing for sociable and expressive online communication. *Lecture Notes in Computer Science, 4738*, 218–229.

Ng, V., Dasgupta, S., & Arifin, S. M. N. (2006). Examining the role of linguistic knowledge sources in the automatic identification and classification of reviews. *Proceedings of the COLING/ACL 2006 Main Conference*, 611–618.

Pang, B., & Lee, L. (2004). Sentimental education: Sentiment analysis using subjectivity summarization based on minimum cuts. In *Proceedings of ACL 2004* (pp. 271–278). New York: ACL Press.

Pang, B., & Lee, L. (2005). Seeing stars: Exploiting class relationships for sentiment categorization with respect to rating scales. *Proceedings of the Association for Computational Linguistics (ACL)*, pp. 115–124.

Pang, B., & Lee, L. (2008). 4.1.2 Subjectivity detection and opinion identification. *Opinion Mining and Sentiment Analysis.* Hanover, MA: Now Publishers Inc.

Pang, B., & Lee, L. (2008). Opinion mining and sentiment analysis. *Foundations and Trends in Information Retrieval, 1*(1–2), 1–135.

Pang, B., Lee, L., & Vaithyanathan, S. (2002). Thumbs up? Sentiment classification using machine learning techniques. *Proceedings of the Conference on Empirical Methods in Natural Language Processing (EMNLP)*, pp. 79–86.

Papadopoulos, E. (2001). *The relationship between the Internet financial message boards and the behavior of the stock market* (unpublished doctoral dissertation). University of Hong Kong, Hong Kong, China.

Pennebaker, J., Mehl, M., & Niederhoffer, K. (2003). Psychological aspects of natural language use: Our words, our selves. *Annual Review of Psychology, 54*, 547–577.

Prabowo, R., & Thelwall, M. (2009). Sentiment analysis: A combined approach. *Journal of Informetrics, 3*(1), 143–157.

Read, J. (2005). Using emoticons to reduce dependency in machine learning techniques for sentiment classification. *Proceedings of the ACL 2005 Student Research Workshop*, 43–48.

Riloff, E., Patwardhan, S., & Wiebe, J. (2006). Feature subsumption for opinion analysis. *Proceedings of the Conference on Empirical Methods in Natural Language Processing*, 440–448.

Russell, J. A. (1979). Affective space is bipolar. *Journal of Personality and Social Psychology, 37*(3), 345–356.

Schapire, R., & Singer, Y. (2000). BoosTexter: A boosting-based system for text categorization. *Machine Learning, 39*(2/3), 135–168.

Short, J. C., & Palmer, T. B. (2008). The application of DICTION to content analysis research in strategic management. *Organizational Research Methods, 11*(4), 727–752.

Snyder, B., & Barzilay, R. (2007). Multiple Aspect Ranking using the Good Grief Algorithm. *Proceedings of the Joint Human Language Technology/North American Chapter of the ACL Conference (HLT-NAACL)*, pp. 300–307.

Stone, P. J., Dunphy, D. C., Smith, M. S., & Ogilvie, D. M. (1966). *The general inquirer: A computer approach to content analysis*. Cambridge, MA: The MIT Press.

Stoppard, J. M., & Gunn Gruchy, C. D. (1993). Gender, context, and expression of positive emotion. *Personality and Social Psychology Bulletin, 19*(2), 143–150.

Strapparava, C., & Mihalcea, R. (2008). Learning to identify emotions in text, *Proceedings of the 2008 ACM Symposium on Applied Computing* (pp. 1556–1560). New York, NY: ACM.

Strapparava, C., & Valitutti, A. (2004). Wordnet-affect: An affective extension of wordnet. In *Proceedings of the 4th International Conference on Language Resources and Evaluation* (pp. 1083–1086). Lisbon.

Su, F., & Markert, K. (2008). From words to senses: A case study in subjectivity recognition. *Proceedings of Coling 2008*, Manchester, UK.

Tang, H., Tan, S., & Cheng, X. (2009). A survey on sentiment detection of reviews. *Expert Systems with Applications: An International Journal, 36*(7), 10760–10773.

Thelwall, M. (2009). MySpace comments. *Online Information Review, 33*(1), 58–76.

Thelwall, M., Buckley, K., Paltoglou, G., Cai, D., & Kappas, A. (2010). Sentiment strength detection in short informal text. *Journal of the American Society for Information Science and Technology,* 61(12): 2544–2558.

Thelwall, M., Wilkinson, D., & Uppal, S. (2010). Data mining emotion in social network communication: Gender differences in MySpace. *Journal of the American Society for Information Science and Technology, 21*(1), 190–199.

Turney, P. D. (2002). Thumbs up or thumbs down? Semantic orientation applied to unsupervised classification of reviews. In *Proceedings of the 40th annual meeting of the Association for Computational Linguistics (ACL), July 6–12, 2002, Philadelphia, PA*, 417–424.

Walther, J., & Parks, M. (2002). Cues filtered out, cues filtered in: Computer-mediated communication and relationships. In M. Knapp, J. Daly, & G. Miller

(Eds.), *The Handbook of Interpersonal Communication* (3rd ed.) (pp. 529–563). Thousand Oaks, CA: Sage.

Watson, D. (1988). Intraindividual and interindividual analyses of positive and negative affect: Their relation to health complaints, perceived stress, and daily activities. *Journal of Personality and Social Psychology, 54*(6), 1020–1030.

Watson, D., Clark, L. A., & Tellegen, A. (1988). Development and validation of brief measures of positive and negative affect: The PANAS scales. *Journal of Personality and Social Psychology, 54*(6), 1063–1070.

Wiebe, J., Wilson, T., Bruce, R., Bell, M., & Martin, M. (2004). Learning subjective language. *Computational Linguistics, 30*(3), 277–308.

Wiebe, J., Wilson, T., & Cardie, C. (2005). Annotating expressions of opinions and emotions in language. *Language Resources and Evaluation, 39*(2–3), 165–210.

Wilson, T. (2008). *Fine-grained subjectivity and sentiment analysis: Recognizing the intensity, polarity, and attitudes of private states.* University of Pittsburgh.

Wilson, T., Wiebe, J., & Hoffman, P. (2009). Recognizing contextual polarity: An exploration of features for phrase-level sentiment analysis. *Computational linguistics, 35*(3), 399–433.

Wilson, T., Wiebe, J., & Hwa, R. (2006). Recognizing strong and weak opinion clauses. *Computational Intelligence, 22*(2), 73–99.

Witten, I. H., & Frank, E. (2005). *Data mining: Practical machine learning tools and techniques.* San Francisco: Morgan Kaufmann.

Wu, C.-H., Chuang, Z.-J., & Lin, Y.-C. (2006). Emotion recognition from text using semantic labels and separable mixture models. *ACM Transactions on Asian Language Information Processing, 5*(2), 165–183.

Measuring Social Media Efforts

In This Essay

- The development of tools to measure social media marketing's performance and effectiveness have not kept up with the pace of social media marketing development

- The metrics used to track data depend greatly on what social media platform a business is using

- Strategy is very important when developing a social media marketing plan, or goals will not be properly reached

- Create a social media policy to handle potentially negative reactions to a marketing strategy

Introduction

Since its introduction in 2002, social media has changed the way the world thinks about marketing (Cray, 2012). Various forms of media, such as newspapers, radio, and television, dominated the 20th century (Ulitz, 2012), but social media seems to be the main media of the 21st century.

Social media plays an integral role in the global market, working in concert with other forms of media to strengthen a brand. Although social networking itself is not new—because humans have always socialized as a form of communication with one another—it is now possible to communicate over the Internet. Various social media networks, such as Facebook, Twitter, MySpace, Google+, and YouTube, are used by millions of people every day, and that number continues to rise.

The adoption of social media has become the fastest rising trend in corporate history, changing the way companies think about and interact with their consumer audience. However, the fundamental problem with social media as a marketing platform is that the development of tools to measure its performance and effectiveness has not kept up with the fast pace of social media itself (Ulitz, 2012).

Managers who use social media for marketing are not generally aware of their financial and nonfinancial *returns on investment* (ROI). Social media is often used without a strategy in place (Ulitz, 2012). How, then, does one measure social media efforts to determine their effectiveness in marketing campaigns?

By looking at several key *metrics*, one can determine whether or not social media marketing efforts are worthwhile based on what social media offers a business compared with the necessary resources required to maintain the social media presence.

Social Media and Web 2.0

Before one understands how to measure social media efforts, one needs to closely examine two terms. These common terms are used interchangeably in the world of Internet marketing, but there is a distinct difference between the two. *Web 2.0* refers to the "next stage" of the World Wide Web, where users actively participate in the creation of information and content. *Social media* refers to the platforms and applications developed for social interaction as a result of Web 2.0. Essentially, the Internet is the whole, whereas Web 2.0 represents a segment of that whole, and social media represents only a small segment of Web 2.0 (Ulitz, 2012).

Social media, when properly integrated into a marketing strategy, helps strengthen brand awareness and build consumer relationships. Studies have shown 91% of marketers are using online advertising, but many find their budgets pressed. More than half of the study participants cut their traditional media budgets to invest more resources into online marketing (Ulitz, 2012). Social media requires a greater investment of time than of money, which makes it easier for small companies with little to no marketing budget to connect with and engage their audience.

Data and Metrics Applied to Marketing Techniques

Social media has several different metrics that can be applied to marketing techniques. The choice of metrics that marketers employ typically depend

Return on investment: *A performance measure used to evaluate the efficiency of an investment. It is usually expressed as a percentage or a ratio where return of an investment is divided by the cost of the investment.*

Metrics: *A standard of measurement used to gauge a company's performance.*

Web 2.0: *The second generation of the World Wide Web that includes features such as blogs, wikis, and social networking.*

on the social media platform being used. For example, when measuring Facebook metrics, the number of "likes" is a key piece of data.

Before exploring metrics, social media must be broken down into smaller segments to understand each aspect and how they all play into the marketing goal (Ulitz, 2012).

- **Social Networking Sites.** "Online sites, platforms or services that focus on building social networks or relations among people. Individuals, groups or companies can set up a profile and connect with others" (Ulitz, 2012). Examples of these sites include Facebook, LinkedIn, and Google+.
- **Blogs.** "A web site on which individuals, groups or business entities can publish news, opinions and commentaries [on] various topics" (Ulitz, 2012). According to Technorati and the 2011 State of the Blogosphere report, there are millions of blogs online today. Individuals maintain some, while small businesses and large corporations maintain others. ("State of the Blogosphere 2011: Introduction and Methodology," 2011) Examples of blog sites are WordPress, Blogger, and TypePad (Ulitz, 2012).
- **Microblogs.** Microblogs place a limitation on the number of characters allowed in a message. Twitter is considered a micro-blogging platform (Ulitz, 2012).
- **Social Bookmarking Sites.** "Social bookmarking helps to organize, store and manage online resources" (Ulitz, 2012). Examples of social bookmarking websites include Digg, Reddit, StumbleUpon, and Delicious.
- **Sharing Sites.** "Some platforms offer users the possibility to store and share photos (e.g., Picasa, Flickr), videos (e.g., YouTube), slides (e.g., SlideShare), and other media with other users, both for public and private use" (Ulitz, 2012).

Simply knowing and understanding the subsets of social media will not provide enough information for a successful campaign for a business. This knowledge only provides the platform for outreach and communication. Using the knowledge of various platforms, marketers can develop the social media marketing strategy best suited to their business, goals, and target audience (Ulitz, 2012).

Developing a Social Media Marketing Strategy

Strategy is an integral part of any social media marketing campaign, as it will be partially responsible for dictating ROI. Without a strategy in hand, it can be easy to interact aimlessly on social media networks, which makes it more difficult to reach the desired goal. Then, when goals are not reached, it can make it look like using social media as a marketing tool is a waste of time or an unwise investment for a business, when the truth is that it could be a very valuable tool if used properly.

There is not a clear "one size fits all" approach to social media strategy. Although there are templates and planning tools available to help businesses with this, those looking for a perfect formula will not find one. Instead, follow a process to develop a customized social media strategy for the business (Porterfield, 2012).

Step One: Assessment

A company should begin its planning by answering this question: "Why social media?" The answer will vary from business to business and niche to niche, but the answer provides the information needed to carry out the rest of the strategy creation process. Be detailed and thorough. The purpose of this assessment is to determine where the business is now versus where the business wants to go (Porterfield, 2012).

When answering the question, put the target audience at the forefront. Clarify their needs, their desires, and where they spend their time online. Do not waste time marketing on the wrong platform; if the audience is not there, it will not produce results. If assistance is required, consider surveying the customer base with any number of free or inexpensive surveying tools (Porterfield, 2012).

Knowing the audience allows the business to focus on building content that will immediately resonate with their customers, which increases engagement. The more a business listens to their audience, the better able they are to meet their audience's needs. The specific content focus also allows for a business to become an authoritative source for their consumers, enhancing trust and credibility (Porterfield, 2012).

Determine the theme of the strategy by thinking about what the desired consumer response would be. Generally speaking, there are three themes: loyalty, awareness, and sales. Although loyalty and awareness can lead to sales, it is important to choose just one of these themes and stick to it to develop the strategy to better reach the goals (Porterfield, 2012).

Get specific. Think about what the business does, what makes the customers happy, and what is truly at the core of the business. This helps find the "soul" of the business, which dictates the tone and voice of the strategy across all social media networks in which the business will be active (Porterfield, 2012).

Identify what metrics should be measured and monitoring opportunities exist. For loyalty, measure consumer engagement and influence. For awareness, measure growth, engagement, number of likes, and number of shares. For sales, measure click through rates, social sales, and conversion rates. Do not forget to monitor overall trends, including brand mentions, company name mentions, mentions of company staff, and mentions of competitors (Porterfield, 2012).

Put it all in writing. Who is responsible for what aspects of the marketing plan? What happens when? How and in what manner will information be communicated, and so on (Porterfield, 2012).

Step Two: Implementation

Create a content calendar. Turn the assessment into a feasible editorial calendar that lets the team know what needs to be written, when it should be written, and where it should be published. Think about the theme of the content, the person responsible for creating it, when and where it will shared, how often third party content will be used versus custom created content, and how the content will be delivered (Porterfield, 2012).

Create a plan for growth and promotion. There are many different ways to do this, but the main one is to start by integrating social media buttons on the company website. Consider running contests and special sales promotions to build the network of fans and followers (Porterfield, 2012).

Outline a promotional policy. What actions will be taken to promote the company? What is acceptable? What is not? Determine where to send conversions and places for potential opt-ins (Porterfield, 2012).

Step Three: Monitor and Measure

Before starting the campaign, set a meeting date for about two months after its start date. The purpose of this follow-up meeting is to gather the members of the team to evaluate the progress of the campaign and how it seems to be reaching goals so far. Make adjustments to the strategy where necessary to facilitate reaching goals by the campaign's end. If momentum is there, ramp up efforts to increase progress through Facebook advertising, for example. Move into live sessions with fans and followers through Twitter parties, live blogging, or Google+ hangouts (Porterfield, 2012).

Know what matters to the business. Some businesses may only need a small number of quality fans, or people who contribute mainly to the business' social media, to produce results, whereas others may need thousands to see a real financial impact. Do not expect to see instantaneous results because relationship building with social media marketing takes time (Porterfield, 2012).

Once the company has an understanding of social media categories and strategy, it is time to dive into metrics. However, because each of the platforms has a different goal, each of them has varying metrics to determine whether or not that goal was attained. This is part of what makes selecting a single metric and calculating its impact difficult for marketers (Ulitz, 2012).

Here are the various metrics to consider when evaluating a campaign for effectiveness:

1. **Social media leads.** Use website analytics data to determine how much traffic is coming from social media websites to the company's website. Choose a few of the social media networks to track over time. If social media traffic is bringing referrals, track this data separately to determine how many leads from social media become paying customers (Dash, 2010).

2. **Engagement duration.** Although page views are important for many companies, some companies need to be more concerned with how long they are keeping customers engaged on their sites, in contrast to how many people are seeing their content. This is particularly important for companies using Facebook applications. How much time people spend using the application is a more important metric to track. It is also important to track the visitors coming to the company's website from other social media websites (Dash, 2010).

3. **Bounce rate.** Are visitors coming to the company's website but leaving within 60 seconds? This could be a sign the landing page needs better copy or that the visitors are not finding what they are

looking for once they get to the page. Try enhancing the website copy or making the information visitors are looking for easier to find (Dash, 2010).

4. **Increase in membership versus active network size.** This refers to the portion of a company's social media presence (across all platforms used) that actively engages with the content posted on these networks. Is the social media network increasing? Is the amount of interaction with content increasing (Dash, 2010)?

5. **Activity ratio.** How active are the business' social media fans/followers? Create a ratio of active versus total members and track it for several months. Do not expect that all members will be active, but if the number is lower than expected, consider running a campaign to boost activity. Businesses can measure this activity in a number of ways, including likes, shares, comments, and application usage (Dash, 2010).

6. **Conversions.** This is important because your company wants the social media activity to convert into sales or subscriptions, either directly or indirectly. For instance, social media activity can translate to indirect sales through increasing subscriptions to a newsletter that presents sales opportunities. Social media may also translate to direct income because a customer clicks the link from Facebook and makes a purchase. Track and chart all conversions over time (Dash, 2010).

7. **Brand mentions.** Track and measure all of the company and brand mentions over time, both positive and negative (Dash, 2010).

8. **Loyalty.** Are members of one's social networks interacting just once, a few times, repeatedly, or regularly? How many of those members reshare content from one's page and how often (Dash, 2010)?

9. **Virality.** Members of a social network should be sharing updates relevant to that company. Are friends of those members also sharing those updates? How many friends of friends are resharing the posts and how quickly (Dash, 2010)?

10. **Blog interaction.** Blogs that allow comments and user interaction are part of the social media marketing tool kit, but blog interaction measures multiple metrics. Encourage readers to connect with the company via comments on the posts or via social media networks such as Facebook and Twitter. Use a widget on the blog

that makes connecting via social media easier. If the content on the blog is appropriate for social bookmarking websites, make sure to include a social sharing bar at the bottom of each post. Most of the time users will only share the content if it is easy for them to do (Dash, 2010).

The metrics applied to measuring the success of marketing via social media are quite different than the four categories used for traditional marketing, but they can all be used to track the same basic information.

1. **Traditional financial measures.** Sales revenue, profit, and cash flow.
2. **Nonfinancial measures.** Market share, quality of service, customer loyalty and satisfaction, adaptability.
3. **Input measures related to marketing**. Marketing assets and implementation.
4. **Output measures.** Effectiveness and efficiency (Ulitz, 2012).

Using social media metrics can tell a business about how much of their revenue is coming from social media marketing and lead generation. It can also provide insight into the nonfinancial measures by tracking brand mentions and monitoring customer satisfaction by using social media as a quick response branch of customer service efforts. Businesses can track input measures based on the amount of time spent on social media platforms and control implementation by developing a social media strategy. Looking at the campaign to determine if there was an increase in social media following across one or all networks, and how effective this increase or engagement push was at producing conversions, can assess output measures.

Calculating ROI/Bottom Line Impact

Social ROI is one of the important things businesses want to know. They want to know the money they are spending will produce profit, or they will not be able to justify continuing the practice. However, because of the nature of social media, calculating the ROI is not easy. Businesses are trying to put numeric values on human interaction and conversation, something that is not easily quantifiable (Ulitz, 2012).

Social media is constantly changing, and although there are a variety of tools available to help track brand mentions, number of clicks on links posted to social media, and the number of people who saw one's social media message, such as KISSmetric and Google Analytics, these tools are not always accurate.

What looks like a successful ROI for one company may look like a disaster to another company. It comes down to what the company's goals are and how they use social media to reach them.

When considering social media ROI, it is important to consider four key things:

- **What makes a social media campaign successful?** There is no right or wrong answer here, but a company needs to know what they consider success before starting out so they can choose the best path to achieve that success. For most businesses, using multiple social media channels makes their campaigns more effective because it gives consumers more ways to reach and connect with them. Putting the control of how to connect with the brand in the customers' hands is the best way to allow users to expand their connection to the brand. When the user is in control, the campaign is generally more successful.

- **How is social media monitored by advertising agencies?** How an agency monitors their social media engagement can impact the ROI. Using a variety of tools is advised, as a single tool may not be an accurate representation of what is going on in the social media spaces in which a business is active. For best results, agencies should be monitoring the progress of social media campaigns on a day-to-day basis. The fast pace of social media means it can change in just a few minutes. Keeping an eye on the progress every day will give a clearer picture of what is happening with consumer engagement.

- **How is social media measured by advertising agencies?** How an agency measures social media is a key part of whether or not it is deemed successful. Measuring from one metric may show the social media advertising campaign to be a waste of time, money, effort, whereas measuring with another metric may show it to be the most successful campaign the company has ever run. Choosing the metrics for measurement before running the campaign will more clearly define the ROI. Often, companies use built-in social analytics tools, such as the Facebook Insights (https://developers.facebook.com/docs/insights/) option, on pages to show how many new likes, how many shares, and so on take place within a certain period of time. These built-in analytics tools are beneficial, but it is important to know which metrics are important to a campaign.

- **What is the most significant social media metric measured?**
  The most significant social media metric measured will vary from company to company and goal to goal. If a company runs a campaign to increase Facebook likes to spread brand awareness, then obviously the most important metric becomes the number of Facebook likes. However, if a company runs a Twitter advertising campaign, the number of Facebook likes will not matter as much.

Instead of looking at ROI as return on investment, it will be much easier to measure if companies switch gears and look at it as return on influence or return on interaction (Ulitz, 2012).

Staying Ahead

Social media is not meant to replace other marketing campaigns completely but instead should be integrated into existing marketing campaigns as an extra set of tools. To stay ahead of the curve, make social media marketing fast and easy for the user. If users have to work for it, they are less likely to actively participate (Ulitz, 2012). Social media is ever changing, so staying ahead of the curve is not an easy task.

Create a Social Media Policy

There are many different regulations to consider, so all companies should have a social media policy (Well, 2010). Create a policy as part of one's strategy before launching a campaign.

The policy should include such topics as: What is the policy regarding negative comments? What happens when a fan/follower is disrespectful to the company or another fan or follower? What happens if an employee posts something that does not align with the campaign strategy and offends the fan base?

This policy will help employees and social media managers understand what they can and cannot do on the various corporate social media accounts, and will set forth expectations for employee usage of these networks while on the clock (Well, 2010).

A legal team should review a company's social media policy. If a legal team is not available, look at other companies' policies. Keep in mind that today's policy may not work a year from now. The policy will need to be reviewed and updated on a regular basis, such as between campaigns, and for best results, should use flexible wording (Well, 2010).

When the policy is in place, make sure all employees understand it. Consider enlisting the help of one person, or a small team of people, to handle everything related to social media in the business (Well, 2010).

Market Research

One of the best ways businesses can stay ahead of the social media curve is to actively participate in the social media niche to learn industry news. Part of staying ahead means knowing what is going on where and investing time wisely. Although it does not look like Facebook or Twitter is going anywhere soon, there are still some future social media ventures that will go bust. However, that does not mean that social media is not here to stay and will not thrive.

With the knowledge in hand before business innovations go live, businesses are able to adapt as fast as the change happens, rather than after the fact. Although this might not ensure they will survive, it will certainly increase their chances of it.

Multiplying Impact of Social Media

Social media continues to grow at a rapid rate. As more platforms develop, it will further diversify the number of options available to connect with people and to market products and services to them. With time, existing platforms will grow and adapt to better suit the needs of their target market. As the networks change, marketing strategy will need to rapidly adjust to stay current (Cray, 2012).

Social media has had a profound impact on society, changing the way people conduct business online, and generating privacy concerns. *Fortune 500 companies* are now using social media as one of their marketing tools, promoting new services and pricing tiers to their current customers with hopes of bringing in new ones. Beyond sales and marketing, these companies are also using social media as a quick response customer service option, by monitoring their brand mentions—including the negative ones (Cray, 2012).

Fortune 500 company:
A company that has been listed on Fortune magazine's annual ranking of the largest corporations in the United States.

Attempting to measure the impact of a single social media metric is almost impossible. Instead, it is best to focus on implementing the strategy and segmenting each social media platform out to how well it meets the company goals. Tracking the trends will demonstrate its impact on a business (Cray, 2012).

A difficult thing about staying ahead in the social media world is the fact that we cannot predict where it will go because it is a platform controlled by users, rather than by marketing and advertising professionals (Cray, 2012).

Conclusion

Regardless of how it is measured, social media is a huge segment of marketing. One out of every six minutes spent online is spent on social networking. Online is the one place where businesses can find nearly everyone in their consumer audience. This is the main reason why traditional media advertising is shrinking in favor of online and social media advertising and marketing (Cray, 2012).

As the world of social media continues to develop, eventually there will be a way to accurately determine its ROI. Social media will become further integrated in our lives, and brands will come along with it. As such, brands will increasingly become more transparent with consumers (Cray, 2012).

SOURCES OF ADDITIONAL INFORMATION

Fifty Shades of Social Media Measurement Tools. http://marketingland.com/fifty-shades-of-social-media-measurement-tools-14261

Five Simple Metrics to Track Your Social Media Efforts. http://www.socialmedia-examiner.com/metrics-to-track-your-social-media-efforts/

Five Social Media Metrics You Should Be Monitoring. http://socialmediatoday.com/jvocell/914271/5-social-media-metrics-you-should-be-monitoring

BIBLIOGRAPHY

Cray, E. (2012). The social ROI: Successful social media measurement from an agency standpoint. *The Elon Journal of Undergraduate Research in Communications, 3*(1), 43–52. Retrieved November 15, 2012, from https://www.elon.edu/docs/e-web/academics/communications/research/vol3no1/05CrayEJSpring12.pdf

Dash, R. (2010, February 4). The 10 social media metrics your company should monitor. *The 10 Social Media Metrics Your Company Should Monitor—SocialTimes*. Retrieved November 15, 2012, from http://socialtimes.com/social-media-metrics_b2950

Porterfield, A. (2012, March 1). 3 steps to an effective social media strategy. *Social Media Examiner RSS*. Retrieved November 15, 2012, from http://www.socialmediaexaminer.com/3-steps-to-an-effective-social-media-strategy/

StateoftheBlogosphere. (2011, November 4). State of the Blogosphere 2011: Introduction and Methodology. *Technorati Social Media*. Retrieved November 15, 2012, from http://technorati.com/social-media/article/state-of-the-blogosphere-2011-introduction/

Uitz, I. (2012). Social media—Is it worth the trouble? *Journal of Internet Social Networking & Virtual Communities, 2012*. Retrieved November 15, 2012, from http://www.ibimapublishing.com/journals/JISNVC/2012/313585/m313585.pdf

Well, D. (2010, October 18). Staying ahead of the curve. *Slide Share*. Retrieved November 15, 2012, from http://www.slideshare.net/dwell13/staying-ahead-of-the-curve-social-media-compliance-1072010-final

Convergence of Marketing, Data, and Technology

In This Essay

■ Social media is increasingly emerging as an avenue to communicate and interact with customers

■ Online customer reviews provide opportunities to analyze customer feedback and even provide customer service to those expressing negative comments, although care should be taken to verify a review is genuine

■ Social media is an important tool for companies to use for marketing purposes and requires employees skilled in communication

■ To reach customers through social media, companies should carefully establish online communities, collect relevant consumer data, and work only with established, trusted websites in collaborations

Introduction

In the modern world the means in which businesses market themselves and how they analyze their businesses have become increasingly crucial. Although it has always been important to know who is buying what products and who is the target market, today this information is more valuable than ever.

With the increase in programs that can provide website data and social media feedback, and an array of technology that allows companies to analyze the information, there is a lot for companies to look at. It is crucial that companies understand the data they are looking at, the technology they are using, and how to adjust their marketing based on the data received and the technology available.

Emerging Roles

Inevitably with the changes in technology there is an array of roles for people to play. A good example of this is in the field of social media.

Businesses are often aware of how feedback affects the image of their company. An often-quoted phrase is that "a disgruntled customer tells ten people." With the advent of social media, analysts have rephrased this saying as "the disgruntled customer has the ability to communicate with ten million people" (Gillin, 2007). Admittedly this does not literally mean that one person will create a worldwide panic. However, companies are aware that bad publicity can very quickly sink a company image. Therefore, they employ people to look at negative comments on social media sites in order to address any issues they may have (Gillin, 2007).

Bad publicity does not have to create a disastrous situation for a business. Companies can take advantage of a potentially difficult situation by quickly responding to a complaint and addressing it. As a result, the person who made the original complaint gets a quick and satisfactory resolution to the problem and then tells other people about the good customer service.

Get to the Point

To use social media successfully, a company needs to have an infrastructure that will allow for the implementation of social media. While a company may have someone who is good at looking at social media sites and checking for complaints, this is just one role in the process. Someone else then has to look at what the complaint is and how it can be resolved. Yet another individual will be responsible for communicating with people in another part of the business (Gillin, 2007).

To illustrate this, imagine that someone has ordered the most popular toy as a gift for Christmas. The customer orders it as far in advance as possible to guarantee it will arrive before December 25. However, as the date approaches and the toy has not arrived, the customer makes a complaint that the proposed delivery time has not been met (Gillin, 2007).

It is not sufficient simply to acknowledge that someone has made a complaint. Being sympathetic but not addressing the issue is likely to cause more frustration. Therefore, there needs to be someone capable of getting the right message to the right department so that a delivery can be made on time and that the issue is addressed quickly (Gillin, 2007).

Furthermore, from a data perspective this complaint needs to be *quantified*. Broadly, the following questions ought to help define what a complaint is, how it is resolved, how many complaints have occurred, and how to prevent the complaints from occurring again (Gillin, 2007; see Table 1).

However, this is just one aspect in the ever-changing world of e-commerce and social e-commerce. Although being able to respond to feedback is important, the business also needs to ensure that the company has the right tools of the trade in order to have an efficiently functioning online business (Gillin, 2007).

Even if the company is a small business and is operating at a local level, it is worth being aware of and responding to marketing data and technology. The good thing is that in recent years there are various analytical tools available that allow businesses to look at website hits, where they come from, and the terms that people are using in search engines. All of this information can be used to learn who a business' customers are, what they are looking for, what they are buying, and what their feedback is (Gillin, 2007).

In many respects the fundamental needs of customers have not changed much over time. They still want the best service at the best price. What has changed is that this need is often fulfilled by companies that can increasingly provide what customers want instantly. With this often comes a degree of obligation as customers demand products and services that satisfy their needs (Gillin, 2007).

Quantified: *To determine, express, or measure the quantity of something.*

TABLE 1 Possible Procedures in Dealing with a Complaint.

Question	Response
What was the complaint?	Complaint is noted
How was the situation resolved?	Complaint is addressed
How satisfactory was the resolution?	Note how quickly the complaint was addressed and the satisfaction of the customer
How many complaints have occurred during a set time period?	A number is quantified
How can this be prevented?	Data is analyzed and changes are implemented to improve procedures and reduce complaints

(Adapted from Gillin, 2007)

TABLE 2 A Broad Definition of Roles.

Name of role	Duties
Business owner	Establish, promote, and ensure the longevity of the business
Data analyst	Look at data and present conclusions based on it
Customer service	Engage with customers, possibly on a number of platforms, and deal with their complaints as necessary
Implementation	The people needed to make a business work. For example, if a business sells toys, this would be the people who make the toys and those who deliver them
Information professional	Check the validity of online feedback, ensuring that it is accurate
Social media consultants	Advise on the best use of social media
Content producers	Create online content, such as video production companies and bloggers

(Adapted from Gillin, 2007)

Real or Not Real

One problem with the broad example of the customer complaint detailed above is that it assumes the complaint is genuine. There have been a number of stories in recent years about counterfeit reviews or complaints that have often incorrectly damaged the reputations of businesses (Hane, 2012).

Paula J. Hane (2012) predicts in her article "Social Media News and Reviews" that 10% to 15% of social media reviews will be counterfeit in 2014. As well as incorrectly negative reviews, there is also the possibility that the positive reviews are not real. Indeed, many companies spend money to ensure that positive copy is prominent on various high-profile websites. "Many marketers have turned to paying for positive reviews with cash, coupons and promotions" (Phadnis, 2012).

The motivation for paying for reviews is fairly simple. If the number of positive reviews increases the number of sales, then it might be tempting to increase the number of positive reviews with ones created by the business itself. In some respects this is the online equivalent of "salting the tip jar," which is often done in restaurants. Members of staff will put money in the jar in order to indicate that people have given tips, and therefore customers are more inclined to further donate.

Problems

The problem with counterfeit reviews is that it makes the analysis of these reviews harder. If it is one's job to collate data about the success of a product or to talk about representative feedback, it is complicated by having to decide who is offering genuine praise or constructive criticism and who has created a "sock puppet" (a false online reviewer, usually one who gives positive reviews and often used in the context of online authors giving themselves positive praise) (Hane, 2012).

It should be pointed out that Hane has also looked at a more honorable approach that companies have taken toward counterfeit reviews. In this instance a company simply asks that a website or a reviewer remove their counterfeit reviews or they will face legal charges. This threat may work to an extent, but unless companies are capable of living up to this threat, it may prove impractical, especially if the reviews are posted anonymously (Hane, 2012).

Hane also notes that regulations have been put in place that require a reviewer to clearly state whether he has been given any rewards in exchange for a review. This has been backed up by the *Federal Trade Commission* (FTC), who has fined both high-profile and lesser-known companies for counterfeit reviews (Hane, 2012).

Federal Trade Commission: *In the United States, the agency that promotes free enterprise and competition.*

Finally, the article goes on to suggest that fines and punishment alone are not enough to change a culture and remove counterfeit reviews. What seems to work best is an additional public backlash against companies who engage in these practices so that any short-term gain is cancelled out by long-term damage to their brand (Hane, 2012). This may mean publicly claiming they are using counterfeit reviews so that potential customers can see that they are not trustworthy. This backlash could also make the company at fault lose loyal customers.

Skills Required

There are many individuals and companies that make various claims that their skills can benefit a company in the social media arena. There are those that claim they can get a company to the top of search engine results pages or others that will get it a certain amount of followers. A company has to decide who is offering genuine benefits to their business and who is making claims that are disproportionate to what they can actually deliver (King, 2012).

In some ways the best way to decide who can help get the most from a business is to go back to basics. There are certain tools to use that are necessary in order to adapt to the changing world of online business (King, 2012).

Listening

Listening is one of the first key skills. The idea is that before a business can change its online strategy, it is well worth knowing what customers are saying about the business and its products or services. As a result, the business can respond to the feedback and make the necessary changes (King, 2012).

One simple method King recommends is to include the name of one's business in a search and save that search. By periodically running the search, the business will be able to check and see if anyone has discussed the business recently and if so what they have to say (King, 2012).

To be even more specific, the business can include the local area in a saved search. This is especially useful for businesses which have long been established as part of a local community because it is an opportunity to engage with people who have been customers for a long time and also to find new customers within that local community (King, 2012).

Remember that new people arrive in local communities all the time. Therefore, it is wrong to assume that people in the local area necessarily know who the area businesses are. This is also equally true of larger and more established businesses. It is always a good idea to keep seeking out new customers and to treat all aspects of marketing as if the company is just starting out and looking to build a customer base (King, 2012).

A good example is if someone is in a local area and they are looking for car insurance. They may say in an online forum, "I am annoyed with my current insurer because they are charging me a lot and I want a better deal." This is a good chance to contact them and potentially get a new customer.

Communicating

It is the responsibility of a business to engage with customers and provide them with content to which they will want to subscribe. While promoting products and services is important, there is also the need to look at what one's subscribers are doing and to engage with their interests as well (King, 2012).

King also says that social media offers "direct access." In terms of marketing and data this offers a massive opportunity. Companies can learn more about their customers and adapt as required. Indeed, some companies (such as a recent online betting firm) have used comments people have posted and incorporated them into their advertising (King, 2012).

Answering

In order to deal with problems, it helps to know what people want to know. Although abuse of social media, such as trolling or bullying, should not be tolerated and should be reported, this should not be confused with valid constructive criticism (King, 2012).

If a question is asked about one's business, then it is strongly recommended that one answer it as soon as possible. This shows that one's company is prepared to swiftly deal with any issues that might arise (King, 2012).

Questions generally come under two different categories, direct and indirect (King, 2012).

Direct questions in this context are those that are addressed to a particular company. These are the questions that need to be responded to quickly to show that a company is able to address the concerns of its customers (King, 2012).

TABLE 3 Types of Questions.

Question	Response
Direct	Company deals with inquiry directed at them ("Why doesn't X company offer Y product?")
Indirect	Someone discusses X company or Y product with friend, saying they had a problem. Someone in the company offers a response despite not being asked the question in order to give them the information they want

(Adapted from King, 2012)

If appropriate, the business may choose to reply to those concerns. If done in the right way, this can often impress previously skeptical customers because it shows the company is looking out for potential feedback and is prepared to help them even if they are not specifically asked to do so (King, 2012).

Promoting Events via Social Media

Event promotion is another key part of promoting a business via social media (King, 2012).

Businesses may show video footage from previous successful events to give potential customers the opportunity to see what an event actually looks like. The consumer can then judge for himself whether he wants to pursue the organizers of the event (King, 2012).

One way to spread the word about an event is to ask customers to share the information via social media outlets such as Facebook or Twitter. A company may offer discounts or prizes as incentives to get customers to promote an event. It is crucial to put charismatic and creative people in the social media marketing roles in a company so that they are able to encourage customer participation and interaction (King, 2012).

Avoiding Anonymity

In the business context, social media should not be anonymous. The customer should know the people they are interacting with and feel that they can discuss issues with them directly. This becomes difficult when an employee does not have the training to interact openly with customers in a business context (King, 2012).

For some people this is easy because they may naturally have the appropriate social skills. However, it is wrong to assume that because social media is prevalent that anyone can perform this role, and adequate training needs to be provided (King, 2012).

Companies should have official social media guidelines for their corporations to establish a place where employees can go to learn how to act appropriately online when representing the business. These guidelines should cover responsibility, avoiding controversial topics, steering clear of using profanity or offensive language, and avoiding divulging confidential information. Equally, this does not mean that if they have their own private account that they are free to do as they please, because companies often monitor private accounts as well, and a quick search can often reveal indiscretions (King, 2012).

However, it is also important that a customer get a sense of the personality behind the person to whom they are talking. The posts and content should not be purely promotional because it is unlikely that someone will actively follow something that feels excessively commercial. It is often a difficult balance to get right, which is why companies need to be careful when recruiting employees and consultants dealing with online issues (King, 2012).

Buy Buy Sell Sell

It can be easy to forget that business online is not purely about dealing with customer complaints or engaging in promotion via social media. There is also the issue of how people can purchase products, the ease in which they can do this, and ensuring that transactions are secure (Boris, 2012).

This is all part of what is considered corporate entrepreneurship, defined as "the creation and pursuit of new venture opportunities and strategic renewal" by Urban Boris (2012). Boris then continues with an outline delineating how to accomplish strategic renewal using forms of corporate entrepreneurship such as sustained regeneration, organized rejuvenation, and domain redefinition (Boris, 2012).

Each of these strategic terms describes business and growth potential marketing avenues for the stagnant business concern. The different types of strategy are not necessarily right, or wrong, however, some of these strategies may be better suited to the needs of a more technologically savvy market and larger business or corporation. Others are more adaptable for the smaller, individually owned business sector and will require discernment to know what methods of promotion are appropriate for which business (Boris, 2012).

Morris (2007), as cited in Kirilka and Stokas (2012), lists the following to be the five core aspects of corporate entrepreneurship:

- Adaptability
- Flexibility
- Speed
- Aggressiveness
- Innovation

TABLE 4 Definitions of Corporate Entrepreneurship Strategies.

Strategy	Definition
Sustained regeneration	Introducing brand new places to sell goods and services. Causes mainly piece-by-piece growth (Kuratko & Audretsch, 2008)
Organized rejuvenation	Innovating is about making new, interesting, and fun organic products. Internal operations is all about growing and improving the company (Kuratko & Audretsch, 2008)
Domain redefinition	Redefining what the domain is; deciding what the new platform is for a strategy before implementing it
Strategic renewal	"Companies redefine the way to compete with competitors and/or redefine markets"

Adapted from Morris, Kuratko, & Covin, 2007

It is clear to see why these particular aspects are important in business in general. However, the nature of online business is that it is changing all the time, so being adaptable and flexible are vital. It is not just about being able to react quickly but also about being able to have everything in place to cope with sudden changes (Kirilka & Stokas, 2012).

There can be some debate as to what constitutes aggressiveness. It is not likely to be an endearing trait. Although some may argue that this is often a negative aspect inherent in those who are determined, focused, and forthright, this does not necessarily mean that everyone in an organization has to have aggressive character traits. Aggressiveness can also be equated with persistence (Kirilka & Stokas, 2012).

However, this does not mean that when things go wrong they will always right themselves. This is why the final aspect of innovation is so important. Being innovative does not solely mean invention; it can also mean being prepared to change something if it is going wrong and to adapt a strategy as necessary (Kirilka & Stokas, 2012).

Kirilka and Stokas (2012) also note aspects of e-commerce that ensure the smooth running of a business:

- Reach customers
- Learn about customers
- Establish user groups (sometimes referred to as "tribes")

- Collect/track customer reviews (and also assess their validity)
- Provide services using only trustworthy websites, such as Paypal

Each of these parts of an online business require people with certain skills and require data to be properly analyzed (Kirilka & Stokas, 2012).

Reach and Learn About Customers

To reach customers, a business needs to know who their customers are, and what they want. Thus, a business needs employees who know the right ways of communicating with customers and getting sufficient feedback (Kirilka & Stokas, 2012).

The benefit of online communication is that a company has a much wider sample to choose from than people who would be restricted to interviews or postal questionnaires. If people are allowed to respond anonymously, then this also reduces the chances of the ***halo effect***, where someone who is interviewed gives an answer based on what they think an interviewer *wants* them to say rather than their genuine opinions (Kirilka & Stokas, 2012).

Halo effect: *How the positive perception of one outstanding trait leads to an overly favorable impression of the whole.*

Establish User Groups

Building a group of dedicated followers is something many businesses aspire to, and this requires people with charisma and experience capable of amassing a dedicated following. The danger is that people can mistake a large number of members for success. It is equally important to foster discussion and engagement, ensuring that the group members have positive attitudes toward the business and promote it because they want to (Kirilka & Stokas, 2012).

Although building followers can be done via financial incentives and prizes, that is only one method of establishing a group. A local connection is often useful because people tend to identify more with companies that have been part of the local area. As with any form of networking, common ground and effective communication can mean more people want to be part of the group and encourage others to join it (Kirilka & Stokas, 2012).

Collect and Track Customer Reviews

Tracking customer reviews requires both technical skills and the right kind of personality. People assessing the reviews need to be aware of the validity of a review so that when it is used in data collection at a later point it is a valid representation of the business and its online presence (Kirilka & Stokas, 2012).

Also, the person in change of tracking customer reviews can check for false reviews and remove them as soon as possible. Although a business does not want false negative reviews, the company may also want to consider removing unsolicited positive spam messages from websites, as this could potentially harm the reputation of the business (Kirilka & Stokas, 2012).

Use Trustworthy Sites

Some businesses rely on the support of other larger brands in order to bolster their own validity. This phenomenon is not confined only to the online world. Although people may not want to admit it, there are certain brands that have an association with quality, and it is that association that people find reassuring. An example of this is the fact that if someone wants to describe something as reliable they may refer to it as "the Rolls Royce" of a certain type of product (Kirilka & Stokas, 2012).

Customers prefer to work with businesses that are well-known and trusted. Well-established businesses can reassure consumers who are nervous about online transactions that their personal information will be safe. This trusted reputation is part of a business's branding, as it can ensure they are the first stop a customer will make when looking for a product (Kirilka & Stokas, 2012).

However, this reputation will only last as long as the product or service being sold can be trusted. If the product does not work as advertised or the service is unreliable, then the business's reputation can be tarnished, along with those of its supporters (Kirilka & Stokas, 2012).

Conclusion

An online business is a convergence of marketing, data, and technology. Each of these things can be used to affect the other in various ways. A business could have the best marketing campaign, but it is useless if the company uses data that does not reflect the target demographic or if it does not have the technology or the skilled workforce in place to implement it.

Equally, a business may analyze its customers perfectly, come up with the best strategy, and use the most reliable technology. However, this is not advisable if the company does not have the right kind of marketing strategy to promote it.

The problem is that the nature of online business is always changing. Although being able to adapt is advisable, knowing how to adapt in the right way is worth remembering as well. This is why having the right data and, more crucially, knowing how to analyze it, is essential. There is never a guarantee that a company's strategy will be effective, but the right balance of experienced professionals, recognized technology, well thought out corporate strategy, and appropriate marketing can make all the difference.

SOURCES OF ADDITIONAL INFORMATION

Discovery News. http://news.discovery.com/tech/top-ten-social-networking-sites.html
Learn more about social media in general. http://www.socialmediaexaminer.com/tag/michael-stelzner/
A marketing perspective. http://www.seomoz.org/article/social-media-marketing-tactics
The Times of India Tech Section. http://timesofindia.indiatimes.com/tech

BIBLIOGRAPHY

Boris, U. (2012). The effect of pro-entrepreneurship architecture on organizational outcomes. *Journal of Business Economics and Management* 13(3).

Gillin, P. (2007). *The new influencers: a marketer's guide to new social media.* Sanger, CA: Quill Driver Books/Word Dancer Press, Inc.

Hane, P. J. (2012, November). News watch: social media news and reviews. *Information Today, Vol. 28, 1-10.*

King, D. L. (2012, November 28). Social media? *American Libraries.* Retrieved November 25, 2012, from http://americanlibrariesmagazine.org/columns/dispatches-field/social-media

Kirilka, V., & Stokas, T. (2012). Strategic renewal in retail companies by means of social e-commerce. *Jönköping University, Jönköping International Business School.* Retrieved November 29, 2012, from http://hj.diva-portal.org/smash/record.jsf?pid=diva2:528850

Kuratko, D. F., & Audretsch, D. B. (2008). Strategic entrepreneurship: exploring different perspectives of an emerging concept. *Entrepreneurship Theory and Practice, 33*(1), 1–17. Retrieved December 1, 2012, from http://onlinelibrary.wiley.com/doi/10.1111/j.1540-6520.2008.00278.x/full

Morris, M. H., Kuratko, D. F., & Covin, J. G. (2007). *Corporate entrepreneurship & innovation.* Mason, OH: Thomson Higher Education.

Phadnis, S. (2012, September 17). Marketers pay for positive reviews: Gartner. *The Times of India.* Retrieved November 28, 2012, from http://articles.timesofindia.indiatimes.com/2012-09-17/india-business/33901730_1_social-media-gartner-positive-reviews

Legal Challenges with Social Media

In This Essay

- FTC guidelines
- Sweepstakes and contests
- Hosting of content

Overview

Social media is changing the nature of how businesses relate to their customers and to Internet users in general. Interactive platforms such as Facebook, Twitter, and YouTube provide expanded opportunities for companies to collect data on consumers, enabling businesses to better decipher customers' needs and desires. However, the same technology that provides companies with a window into the world of consumer preference also presents advertisers with new legal challenges. Data collection and the voluntary provision of personal information have contributed to the blurring of lines between personal conversations and business activities (Wehner, 2011), creating legal ramifications for any advertiser unfamiliar with the statutory limits on online data delving.

In addition, deceptive advertising, copyright infringement, and defamatory postings remain a concern in the world of social media (FTC, 2010). This article addresses the types of legal issues businesses may face as they attempt to adhere to the U.S. Federal Trade Commission (FTC) guidelines dealing with social media in general, and the specific concerns raised by such activities as conducting online contests and sweepstakes and hosting user content.

FTC Guidelines

The most common legal risks for companies doing business through social media fall into a few broad categories (Tehven, 2010), including:

- Employee-generated content on behalf of the company
- User-generated content on company social media venues
- Third-party use of company social media content
- Privacy-related issues

The Federal Trade Act of 1914 (FTA) authorized the Federal Trade Commission (FTC) to, among other duties, "prevent unfair or deceptive acts or practices affecting commerce" (FTC, 2013; Legal Information Institute, 2013). To clarify what these terms mean in specific instances, the FTC has issued continuing guidelines (Guides) relating to the privacy rights of consumers, endorsements of products, and other subject matter (FTC, 2012). The Guides do not have the force of law, but, in making determinations on whether to file claims under the FTA, the FTC assesses whether marketers under investigation have attempted to comply with their provisions (Northwestern Law, 2010; Socolow, 2011).

Advertisers should be aware that the area of law dealing with social media is relatively new and is in the process of being established (Wehner, 2011). Few cases have been ruled on by the courts, so the law is not yet settled (Dubois, 2011). The criteria used by the FTC in their investigations are applied on a case-by-case basis, and the outcome of any investigation may hinge on the extent that a marketer has provided mechanisms to implement FTC recommendations (Fayle, 2008; Northwestern Law, 2010).

Privacy

Although some consumers appreciate the time-saving benefits resulting from targeted advertising, others find the collection of personal data to be intrusive or unsafe (Keller & Heckman, 2009). The FTC shares this concern. To ensure the protection of consumers' personal information, current FTC recommendations suggest that online marketers publish privacy policies, which should include the following information (FTC, 2010; Keller & Heckman, 2009; Navetta, 2011):

- Always identify who is collecting the information
- Divulge to whom information will be provided

- Identify the information being collected, including the means of collection, such as cookies

- Make the disclosure of sensitive information optional

Once a company has established a privacy policy, it has the duty to adhere to the terms of that policy (FTC, 2012; McHale, 2011). Since 2010, the FTC has settled lawsuits more than a dozen times with companies who have been accused of violating their own privacy policies (FTC, 2012; Ray, 2012).

In addition to complying with their own privacy policies, marketers are obliged to follow the policies of the platforms on which they conduct business (Merrill, Latham, Santalesa, & Navetta, 2011). However, the constant interaction between social media makes such compliance a complicated matter. Marketers may create an online presence on Facebook that incorporates content from Twitter, YouTube, a blog, or some other platform. Each of these social media outlets incorporates its own balance between users' rights to keep their personal information confidential and advertisers' need for data. A post that adheres to the privacy policy of Twitter may cause an advertiser to violate the privacy policy of Facebook when it is reposted there (Navetta, 2011).

Another form of cross-platform activity that threatens user privacy involves tracking consumer behavior across the Internet. Legal issues arise whether a marketer uses personally identifiable information or anonymous data. For businesses using this type of targeted marketing, the FTC has suggested that marketers apply self-regulatory principles for online behavioral advertising (OBA). This self-regulation encompasses seven principles, including (Keller & Heckman, 2009):

- Education of consumers about OBA

- Allowing consumers to access information about data collection and use practices

- Control by consumers of whether their data is to be collected and used for OBA

- Reasonable security for, and limited retention of, data

- New consent to be obtained upon material changes to data collection and use practices

- Parental consent requirements prior to collecting data of minors and special protection for health and financial data that can be attributed to a specific individual

- Industry-wide advancement of principles, including programs for monitoring and reporting of non-compliance

As marketers navigate the evolving legal situation, best practices dictate that they proactively analyze their methods of collection, processing, storage, distribution, and retention of the personal information they obtain through social media (Navetta, 2011). The main factors that assist marketers to avoid challenges by the FTC are concise, published policies that make sense to the reasonable consumer, and provide that consumer with control over the collection and dissemination of personal information (FTC, 2010).

COPPA

Children constitute a special category of user, and advertisers who cater to minors must follow the dictates of the Children's Online Privacy Protection Act (FTC, 2012). COPPA requires website owners and other service providers who collect information about children under the age of 13, or whose content is directed at children under the age of 13, to allow the parents of minors to have knowledge of, and the option to consent to, the collection of personal information prior to its being gathered (Sheppard Mullin, 2012). To this end, marketers should provide some means for verification of parental consent, such as e-mail confirmation, credit card number, phone call with the parent, or submission of a form signed by the parent (Shabani, 2007; Winter & Kohl, 2011).

Geolocation: *The detection of the physical location of a remote device.*

Persistent identifiers: *A long-lived, globally unique number or code allocated to an object or resource. Also known as PID.*

COPPA was recently amended to add "plug-ins and ad networks that have actual knowledge that they are collecting personal information through a child-directed website or online service" to the social media interactions that are subject to its terms (FTC, 2012). Furthermore, personal information has been expanded to include *geolocation* as well as photos, videos, and audio files that contain a child's image or voice, and *persistent identifiers* that can be used to follow minors over time and across websites and online services (FTC, 2012).

Deception

Along with protecting consumers' privacy, the FTC actively searches the Internet for deceptive acts or practices, and challenges marketers to substantiate the claims they make (FTC, 2012). To pursue a claim, the FTC does not need to show intent to deceive on the part of the advertiser, nor that any actual harm resulted from an alleged deception (Northwestern Law, 2010). Instead, Section 5 of the Federal Trade Act (FTA) defines deception as consisting of three elements (FTC, 2012; Legal Information Institute, 2013; McHale, 2012; Northwestern Law, 2010):

1. The content must represent or omit information in a way that is likely to mislead the consumer

2. The representation or omission must be evaluated from the perspective of a reasonable consumer (or an ordinary child or teenager, if targeted to that market)

3. The representation or omission must be material—likely to affect the consumer's purchasing decision

Although some advertising is blatantly deceptive, as when marketers set up websites to emulate news stories regarding the efficacy of their product (FTC, 2011), advertisers need to be aware that the FTC may challenge more subtle forms of deception as well. For example, to avoid challenges by the FTC, advertisements must clearly state whether results shown are typical, and if they are not, what the typical results are (Fair, 2012; FTC, 2009). Also, advertisers awarding "expert" badges or commendations to endorsers are required to ensure that the reviewer be properly credentialed in the presumed area of expertise (McHale, 2012).

In addition to advertising, other forms of communication can trigger an FTC investigation. In one case, Sears offered its online customers US$10 to download software that the company stated would confidentially track their online browsing. In reality, the software gathered much information about many of the customers' online activities. Although Sears did eventually disclose the extent of the data collection, that disclosure was inserted in a lengthy user license agreement, available only as part of the registration process for the software. The FTC determined that lack of a clear, easily accessible statement of intent was actionable, and eventually Sears was forced to erase all of the data that it had collected and cease further data collection (FTC, 2012).

Endorsement Guides

Endorsements can be the source of two other types of deceptive advertising. One form of deception occurs when the claims of the endorser cannot be substantiated, and the other when the relationship between the endorser and the producer of the product being endorsed is not disclosed (FTC, 2009).

The Endorsement Guides circulated by the FTC require that endorsements, like direct advertising, not contain any deceptive statements (FTC, 2009). The FTC has the authority to compel a marketer to substantiate claims made by an endorser, even if the marketer did not specifically request those claims to be made (McHale, 2012). In certain situations, advertisers may be held civilly liable for the false claims of their endorsers, even if the claims were not previously authorized, approved, or used by the advertiser (McHale, 2012; Northwestern Law, 2010). The test used by the FTC is whether the message is deemed to have been sponsored by the marketer, based on the following considerations (McHale, 2012):

- Compensation of the content generator
- Whether the product was provided for free
- The terms of any agreement between the advertiser and the poster
- The value of any previously received products by the poster, and the likelihood of such compensation in the future

The factor deemed most important by the FTC is whether the advertiser initiated the process that led to the review of the products, whether by providing samples, conducting promotions, or encouraging the posting of content (McHale, 2012; Northwestern Law, 2010). Companies that may solicit online reviews are advised to compile a procedure manual for online activities, provide guidance and training for bloggers, monitor the behavior of their online endorsers, and establish mechanisms to take immediate corrective action in the case of behavior that violates any provision of the Federal Trade Act (McHale, 2012; Socolow, 2011). To a great extent, the advertiser's policies, practices, and policing efforts will ultimately determine liability in any particular situation (Northwestern Law, 2010).

The Endorsement Guides require that any testimonials must reflect the "honest opinions, findings, beliefs, or experience of the endorser," and that any connection between the endorser and the maker of the product be disclosed. The same warning applies to research facilities whose results are posted in advertising (FTC, 2009). The duty to disclose applies to any message on any social media website that endorses a product or service when a reasonable consumer would expect that the endorsement was posted by someone not likely to have a relationship with the company whose products are being promoted (McHale, 2012; Socolow, 2011). Such messages include celebrity endorsements, whether on the celebrity's personal blogs or on others', postings on Facebook and Twitter, and bloggers who receive samples with for the purposes of review (Fair, 2012; Socolow, 2011). The Guides also apply to a company's own employees who blog about their employer's products or services (Merrill, Latham, Santalesa & Navetta, 2011; Socolow, 2011). Due to the fact that social media, by nature, encourages openness and data sharing, there is a higher threshold of disclosure for online advertising than there is for traditional media (Northwestern Law, 2010).

In determining whether the disclosure is deceptive, the FTC has adopted a "clear and conspicuous" standard, which comprises four elements (McHale, 2012):

- Prominence
- Presentation
- Placement
- Proximity

Disclosures must be large, easy to read, placed where consumers are likely to look, and close to the claims they modify. Whether disclosures meet these standards is evaluated by FTC investigation into actual consumer perception and comprehension, that is, whether what consumers understood from the totality of the ad was truthful and substantiated (McHale, 2012).

Sweepstakes/Contests

Sweepstakes and contests can be great lures to consumers and are almost irresistible tools for marketers (Dubois, 2011). Sweepstakes are prize giveaways in which the winners are chosen predominately by chance, whereas contests are promotions in which prizes are awarded primarily on the basis of skill or merit (McHale, 2012; Northwestern Law, 2010; Sacharoff & Kunick, 2010). By contrast, lotteries are random drawings for prizes, for which participants must pay to play (McHale, 2012; Northwestern Law, 2010; Sacharoff & Kunick, 2010). Lotteries are generally illegal, and marketers try to avoid having their promotions labeled as such (McHale, 2012; Northwestern Law, 2010). Sweepstakes can avoid being designated as lotteries by allowing free admission (McHale, 2012; Northwestern Law, 2010), and contests can avoid being designated as lotteries by removing the element of chance (McHale, 2012). One way to remove the element of chance from a contest is to award a prize to every contestant (Shabani, 2007).

Removing the element of consideration from sweepstakes is not as straightforward a solution, as the determination of what constitutes consideration is made on a case-by-case basis (Keller & Heckman, 2009; McHale, 2012; Sacharoff & Kunick, 2010; Shabani, 2007). Consideration may be found in the increased time it takes a contestant to enter the sweepstakes and in providing another person's e-mail address in exchange for a chance to enter (Keller & Heckman, 2009; Shabani, 2007). Other factors evaluated as potential consideration are requesting too much personal information, the necessity of downloading specific software to take part in the sweepstakes, or the requirement of subscribing to a website (Keller & Heckman, 2009).

Jurisdictional Issues

The minimum standard for sweepstakes to meet the threshold of legality in all 50 states is a requirement that the promoter prominently post the official rules, which are to include the following information (McHale, 2012; Sacharoff & Kunick, 2010):

- Clear and conspicuous alerts that "no purchase is necessary" and "a purchase will not improve one's odds of winning"

- Start and end dates, eligibility requirements, and the sponsor's name and address

- A description of each prize, with its approximate value, along with the odds of winning it

- The manner of selection of winners and method of notification, along with where and when a listing of winners may be obtained

- A "void where prohibited" statement

- The method of entry, including an alternate method of entry (AMOE), if necessary

The AMOE cannot be so burdensome as to constitute consideration itself. In addition, AMOE entrants must generally have the same chance of winning as the traditional entrants, even if the entry is online and the

AMOE is offline. Therefore, awarding prizes for the first few entrants will tend to render an online sweepstakes susceptible to a claim that it is actually a lottery (Shabani, 2007).

Some states, such as Florida and New York, have more stringent requirements, and online promoters may consider limiting eligibility in those jurisdictions (McHale, 2012; Northwestern Law, 2010; Shabani, 2007). The test of whether a contest will be deemed a lottery also differs by state, making knowledge of all applicable laws a necessity (McHale, 2012; Northwestern Law, 2010).

Online promotions may be subject, not only to the laws of each of the 50 states, but to the laws of every country in which the promoter's website is available. Any country whose citizens are targeted by such a marketing effort may assume jurisdiction and deem its laws applicable to the promotion (Northwestern Law, 2010). Therefore, a promoter unfamiliar with the myriad of laws in effect around the globe may restrict eligibility to U.S. residents (McHale, 2012; Northwestern Law, 2010). Unless a promoter is willing to take the extra precaution of verifying parental consent to entry in a promotion through the means listed in COPPA, eligibility in any contest or sweepstakes should also be restricted to persons over the age of 13 (Shabani, 2007).

Online Voting

The act of opening a contest up to online voting may transform it into a game of chance in some jurisdictions. This may be the case especially if there is a question of whether the public is qualified to apply the listed criteria pertaining to the skill being judged to the actual entries. Making public voting a percentage of the means by which a winner is chosen, while professional judges have the final say, may reduce the likelihood of a legal challenge to this type of promotion (McHale, 2012).

Online voting may also subject a promoter to allegations of fraud or unfairness, as some voters may attempt to manipulate the voting process. Promoters may consider restricting voting to one vote per person, tracked by IP address, to avoid challenges of this nature (McHale, 2012).

To address many of these issues, online promotions should always include the following statements (Shabani, 2007):

- A clause that disclaims liability for fraud, viruses, or other events that compromise the security of the contest

- A reservation of the right to terminate or modify the contest in such a situation

- Limitation of entries to a particular number per entrant

- The duration of the contest and the deadline for entries, as expressed in date and time in a specific time zone

- Clear how-to-play rules

- Special technical rules (such as the need to accept cookies)

- In the case of complex games, a clickable "I Accept" button as the only means of entry

Other Issues

Terms of use: *Rules which one must agree to follow in order to use a service. Also known as Terms of Service; TOU.*

In addition to state and federal statutes regulating promotions, each social media platform has its own rules regarding games of chance (Dubois, 2011; McHale, 2012; Northwestern Law, 2010). For example, Facebook requires that promoters collaborate with Facebook-approved ad developers, whereas LinkedIn prohibits any form of unsolicited promotional materials (McHale, 2012). Penalties for failure to comply with platforms' *Terms of Use* (TOU) include removal of the promotion from the website (Dubois, 2011). Instead of complying with a website's rules, some companies choose to move promotions to a contest-specific URL (Northwestern Law, 2010).

Contests and sweepstakes are so popular that some companies have developed apps surrounding them. Advertisers need to avoid the use of another company's patented business method, especially in the case of online instant-win games (Shabani, 2007).

Many legal issues arise when a promotion solicits content from contestants, including (McHale, 2012; Northwestern Law, 2012):

- Compliance with copyright and trademark rights

- Rights of privacy

- COPPA

- The Digital Millenium Copyright Act

- The Communications Decency Act

- The Federal Trade Act

Some of these issues, such as privacy, have previously been discussed, and others are addressed in the next section. Privacy is a special concern in promotions, where, due to the awarding of prizes, the collection of personally identifiable information is almost unavoidable. Promoters should provide a hyperlink to their privacy policy on the entry form and on any page where personally identifiable information is collected (Shabani, 2007). Best practices suggest that promoters soliciting content that includes photos or videos require releases from everyone who appears in the photo (Keller & Heckman, 2009). If minors appear in submitted photos, releases from their parents or guardians are necessary (Keller & Heckman, 2009).

Hosting of Content

Allowing or encouraging others to post on a business' website provides many advantages to that business, including increased traffic and continual updating of content. Both of those factors are vital elements in search engine optimization (SEO) (McHale, 2012). However, the decision to post user-generated content (UGC) can also expose a business to a number of legal challenges, including potential copyright infringement, defamation, and invasion of privacy issues (Fayle, 2008; McHale, 2012; Merrill, et al., 2011; Navetta, 2011; Northwestern Law, 2010; Tehven, 2010). Web hosts should also be aware that all laws, policies, and ethics regarding advertising continue to be effective online, even though users may not be aware of them (Northwestern Law, 2010).

The major *intellectual property* (IP) issue facing companies that allow UGC to be posted on their websites is copyright infringement, which is governed by the Digital Millennium Copyright Act (DCMA), among other statutes (Fayle, 2008, McHale, 2012; Merrill, et. al., 2011; Northwestern Law, 2010). The DCMA provides a safe harbor (protection and immunity from prosecution) for companies that have a mechanism in place for the owner of a copyright to ask to have material obtained without permission removed (Fayle, 2008; McHale, 2012; Northwestern Law, 2010). This safe harbor is available so long as the site also does not receive direct financial benefit from such posting (Fayle, 2008). In addition, the policy must provide for denial of access to the site for repeat offenders, with an agent appointed and on record with the Copyright Office to receive notice of any infringements (Tehven, 10/13/2010).

A second legal issue regarding IP is the posting of UGC materials that are defamatory (McHale, 2012; Merrill, et. al., 2011). The Communications Decency Act (CDA) was enacted to "promote the development of

Intellectual property:
Any idea or work that can be considered proprietary in nature and is thus protected from infringement by others.

the Internet and other interactive services and other interactive media," and provides immunity to providers arising from claims against UGC (McHale, 2012; Navetta, 2011). One method of control over content is moderation by the host, either before posting, or in response to complaints. Editing content prior to post may seem the simple solution, but undertaking the responsibility to ensure that content complies with all applicable laws can be a risky maneuver (Northwestern Law, 2010). In addition, the CDA immunity does not apply if the host materially edits the content, or in any way contributes to the "creation or development" of offensive content (McHale, 2012; Fayle, 2008). Outsourcing this particular activity to specialists, especially for companies that cater to children, may be the most advisable method of ensuring compliance with the law (Northwestern Law, 2010).

Under the Computer Fraud and Abuse Act (CFAA), hosts can protect themselves from prosecution by creating terms of service, explicitly prohibiting the uploading or posting of unlawful content (McHale, 2012). Companies that accept UGC should post the following guidelines for use of the website (Tehven, 2010):

- Prohibition of unlawful use of the site
- Specific disclaimer of responsibility for unlawful content published on the site by third party users
- Protection of proprietary information and intellectual property
- Prohibition of defamatory, libelous, harassing, offensive, profane, or indecent material
- Requirement of supervisor approval of the use of vendor, employee, or customer information

These terms of service should be required to be read and accepted through an active click before permission to post is given (McHale, 2012; Northwestern Law, 2010). Included should be a clear warning that the user is granting the host a "worldwide, royalty-free right and non-exclusive license to use, distribute, reproduce, modify, adapt, translate, publicly perform and publicly display the UGC" (Northwestern Law, 2010). A further measure of protection may be applied through prominent links that direct users to the authorized process for reported inappropriate content (Northwestern Law, 2010). Courts and regulators will take the posting of these types of policies into consideration when conducting investigations or determining company liability for violations of statutes and guidelines (Tehven, 2010).

The European Union (EU) has codified its stance on online marketing in its Directive 2000/31/EC (Northwestern, 2010). That directive applies to the nations of the EU, plus Norway, Iceland, and Lichtenstein. The Directive contains specific provisions on liability for hosting services. Providers receive protection from prosecution if they had no actual knowledge of illegal activity, or had no reasonable cause to know that a particular activity was unlawful. If a provider acts to remove unlawful content as soon as it is brought to his attention, no liability will attach (Northwestern Law, 2010).

Even if a business does not host UGC, it may incur an obligation to respond to content that is posted by users who are not connected to that company. If a company becomes aware of third parties hosting fraudulent websites that resemble the company's own, or disseminating a malware-infested application that looks to be provided by the company, that business may find itself under an obligation to take action or face legal liability (Navetta, 2012).

There are many legal challenges that companies doing business online may encounter, ranging from those raised by their own activities to those brought on by the actions of others. However such difficulties may arise, the best line of defense for marketers seems to be the creation and publication of specific, standardized policies to cover the various situations and platforms businesses tend to deal with.

SOURCES OF ADDITIONAL INFORMATION

Children's Online Privacy Protection Act. http://www.coppa.org/comply.htm
Federal Trade Commission. www.ftc.gov
Financial Industry Regulatory Authority. http://www.finra.org/

BIBLIOGRAPHY

Dubois, L. (2011, February 24). How to Avoid a Social Media Lawsuit. *Inc.* Retrieved January 25, 2013, from http://www.inc.com/guides/201102/how-to-avoid-a-social-media-lawsuit.html.

Fair, L. (2012). Shutting the Door on Deceptive Endorsements: The FTC's Revised Endorsement Guides. *Bureau of Consumer Protection, Business Center.* Retrieved January 22, 2013, from http://business.ftc.gov/documents/shutting-door-deceptive-endorsements-ftcs-revised-endorsement-guides.

Fayle, K. (2008, March 26). Understanding the Legal Issues for Social Networking Sites and Their Users. *Find Law.* [Web log post]. Retrieved January 25, 2013, from http://technology.findlaw.com/modern-law-practice/understanding-the-legal-issues-for-social-networking-sites-and.html.

Federal Trade Commission.(2009, October 9). Guides Concerning the Use of Endorsements and Testimonials in Advertising. 16 CFR Part 255. Retrieved January 28, 2013, from http://ftc.gov/os/2009/10/091005revisedendorsementguides.pdf.

Federal Trade Commission. (2010, December 10). Protecting Consumer Privacy in an Era of Rapid Change. Retrieved January 28, 2013, from http://www.ftc.gov/os/2010/12/101201privacyreport.pdf.

Federal Trade Commission. (2011, April 19). FTC Seeks to Halt 10 Operators of Fake News Sites From Making Deceptive Claims About Acai Berry Weight Loss Products. Retrieved January 28, 2013, from http://www.ftc.gov/opa/2011/04/fakenews.shtm.

Federal Trade Commission. (2012). The FTC in 2012. Retrieved January 28, 2013, from http://www.ftc.gov/os/highlights/2012/topics/deceptiveAdvertising.shtml.

Federal Trade Commission. (2012, October 10). FTC Publishes Final Guides Governing Endorsements, Testimonials. Retrieved January 22, 2013, from http://www.ftc.gov/opa/2009/10/endortest.shtm.

Federal Trade Commission. (2012, December 19). FTC Strengthens Kids' Privacy, Gives Parents Greater Control Over Their Information by Amending Childrens' Online Privacy Protection Rule. Retrieved January 22, 2013, from http://www.ftc.gov/opa/2012/12/coppa.shtm.

Keller & Heckman. (2009, August 19). Structuring Online Sweepstakes and Contests: New Challenges for Marketers. [Web log post]. Retrieved January 23, 2013, from http://www.khlaw.com/showpublication.aspx?Show=3155.

Legal Information Institute. 15 U.S.C., Chapter 2, Subchapter I – Federal Trade Commission. Retrieved January 28, 2013, from http://www.law.cornell.edu/uscode/text/15/chapter-2/subchapter-I.

McHale, R. (2012). *Navigating Social Media Legal Risks: Safeguarding Your Business.* Upper Saddle River, NJ. Pearson Education, Inc.

Merrill, T., Latham, K., Santalesa, R., Navetta, D. (2011, April). *Social Media: The Business Benefits May Be Enormous, But Can the Risks – Reputational, Legal, Operational – Be Mitigated?* [White paper]. ACE USA. Retrieved January 25, 2013, from http://www.acegroup.com/us-en/assets/ace-progress-report-social-media.pdf.

Navetta, D. (2012, January 9). The Legal Implications of Social Networking Part Three: Data Security. *Information Law Group.* [Web log post]. Retrieved January 25, 2013, from http://www.infolawgroup.com/2012/01/articles/social-networking/the-legal-implications-of-social-networking-part-three-data-security/.

Navetta, D. (2011, June 11). The Legal Implications of Social Networking: The Basics (Part One). *Information Law Group.* [Web log post]. Retrieved January 25, 2013, from http://www.infolawgroup.com/2011/06/articles/social-networking/the-legal-implications-of-social-networking-the-basics-part-one/.

Navetta, D. (2011, October 17). The Legal Implications of Social Networking Part Two: Privacy. *Information Law Group.* [Web log post]. Retrieved January 25,

2013, from http://www.infolawgroup.com/2011/10/articles/social-networking/the-legal-implications-of-social-networking-part-two-privacy/.

Northwestern Law (2010). *Network Interference—A Legal Guide to the Commercial Risks and Rewards of the Social Media Phenomenon.* Retrieved January 22, 2013, from http://www.law.northwestern.edu/cci/specialevent/Documents/SocialMedia_Hines.pdf.

Ray, N. (2012, June 29). Federal Government Targets Privacy Violations by Social Media Companies. *Social Media Law.* [Web log post]. Retrieved January 22, 2013, from http://www.socialmedialawupdate.com/2012/06/articles/social-media/federal-government-targets-privacy-violations-by-social-media-companies/.

Sacharoff, A., & Kunick, J. (2010, June 18). Don't Gamble with Internet Sweepstakes. *The National Law Review.* Retrieved January 25, 2013, from http://www.natlawreview.com/article/don-t-gamble-internet-sweepstakes.

Shabani, N. (2007, July-August). Running an Online Contest without Running Afoul of the Law. Los Angeles Lawyer. Retrieved January 23, 2013, from http://www.lacba.org/Files/LAL/Vol30No5/2395.pdf.

Sheppard Mullin (2012, October 12). FTC Proposes Updates to Children's Online Privacy Law. *Social Media Law.* [Web log post]. Retrieved January 22, 2013, from http://www.socialmedialawupdate.com/2012/10/articles/advertising/ftc-proposes-updates-to-childrens-online-privacy-law/.

Socolow, B. (2011, March). Blogs and Social Media Marketing: Complying with the FTC 's New Endorsement Guides. *Association of Corporate Counsel.* Retrieved January 22, 2013, from http://www.acc.com/legalresources/quickcounsel/Blogs-and-Social-Media-Marketing.cfm.

Tehven, L. (2010, September 23). Social Media for Business: Legal Issues Faced by Employees. *WestLaw Insider.* [Web log post]. Retrieved January 25, 2013, from http://westlawinsider.com/social-media-law/social-media-for-business-legal-issues-faced-by-employees/.

Tehven, L. (2010, October 13). Minimize Risk: Five Social Media Best Practices for Business. *WestLaw Insider.* [Web log post]. Retrieved January 25, 2013, from http://westlawinsider.com/social-media-law/minimize-risk-five-social-media-best-practices-for-business/.

Tehven, L. (2010, October 28). Website Terms and Conditions: More Important Than You Might Think. *Westlaw Insider.* [Web log post]. Retrieved January 25, 2013, from http://westlawinsider.com/social-media-law/website-terms-and-conditions-more-important-than-you-might-think/.

Wehner, J. (2011, July-August). Social Media at work: defining new legal boundaries. *Rural Telecommunications, 30.4, 40.*

Winter, S., & Kohl, J. (2011, March 7). Keep Your Online Sweepstakes and Contests on the Right Side of the Law. *Advertising Age.* Retrieved January 23, 2013, from http://adage.com/article/guest-columnists/online-sweepstakes-legal/149206/.

Marketing to a Global Segment

Overview

Domestic marketing can be a challenging endeavor. Stiff competition, constantly changing technology, and having to appeal to a wide variety of cultures within a nation's borders are key marketing concerns. When these problems are compounded in the global marketplace, it is no wonder that global marketing is so vast.

With the growing digital technology and other scientific advancements, the world is experiencing quicker modes of transporting goods and an increased number of trade and finance agreements between countries. Excelling at a global market is key for continued business growth and vitality. The integration of the global economy means that brands have to adjust their marketing angle to fit the needs and tastes of a particular location while still holding true to their product and brand image.

Challenges in the Global Marketplace

A global marketing plan is specifically tailored to address the market and consumer nuances of the region in which a company markets its brand. At first, only international companies were able to compete effectively in the international market because of the high costs associated with running a global marketing campaign. However, with the continued spread of the Internet and Internet networking systems, social media is providing small- and medium-sized businesses with the reach they need to target consumers at an international level (The Global Social Media Challenge, 2011). Even though social media has made global marketing easier, there are still a number of challenges that a business operating in the global market must face.

- Product considerations. The basic product is the same. The way the product is conveyed, however, and unintended nuances conveyed from this due to cultural and language differences, must be carefully thought about and provided for in the social media plan.

- Pricing. There are a number of factors that can affect a company's pricing schedule, including currency, where the goods are produced, the existence of any trade agreements, tariffs, cost of goods sold (COGS), government bureaucracy, corruption, the cost of the product, communication adaptations, and product level (luxury items vs. regular goods) must all be given credence when formulating a global marketing plan.

- Placement. The participants in the global economy are so intertwined that high-end purchasers in one country reflect the same tastes as high-end purchasers in other countries. When companies seek to place their goods, the positioning must ensure that it matches a particular demographic.

- Promotion. Promotion involves getting the word out about a good or service to increase sales. There are a number of avenues for global promotion of a product (The Global Social Media Challenge, 2011).

The digital marketing arena, with its overabundance of social media marketing tools and platforms, can be very exciting. It can be very daunting in terms of what is required to run an effective global marketing campaign, however. After addressing the varying factors that affect the global social media marketing arena, the next step is to identify the global social networking sites and the markets that use them.

Social Media

Companies entering the global social media arena must deal with varying languages, different time zones, cultural differences, and unfamiliar markets (The Global Social Media Challenge, 2011). Social media allows consumers around the globe to comment, promote, or destroy a company's brand. A social media faux pas can have a huge effect in a short span of time, so a company's management of its social networks in an efficient and effective manner is key.

Development of Social Media Strategy

In developing a social media strategy, a company must explore the following questions:

- Can one social media strategy manage the brand across the globe? (The answer is usually no.)

- Should social media accounts be combined or should there be a separate account for each one?

- Who is going to be in charge of managing the brand in various countries to ensure that customer interaction is always responded to in a timely manner?

- How does a business ensure that there is no overlap in your social media channels?

- Are you going to have multiple blogs—one in each language—or will they be English only?

- What are the target country's cultural trends and political status? (A key to brand building is to ensure a business knows exactly what its brand is saying no matter where its product is located) (The Global Social Media Challenge, 2011).

To reach target markets in different countries, companies must take the time to study the various social media platforms and the way different cultures interact online. In addition, paying attention to how other companies with existing social media accounts interact with their subscribers will help a company gather the information it needs to be able to operate within the social media system with zero mistakes. No matter what, an ultimate goal in regards to implementing a social media program is key (Meyer, 2006).

Basic Social Media Plan

A good method to use in the beginning is the Hub/Spoke method. In this method, everything flows from the focal point. The focal point for a business is usually a blog, forum, or some other type of online community.

From there, the second spoke is formed. This includes local market communities and special interest communities that provide specific content relevant to the communities you are targeting. Social networks and opt-in marketing form the third spoke. This can include sites such as Facebook, Twitter, and Google+ or RSS feeds and email for opt in marketing (The Global Social Media Challenge, 2011).

In addition, there are forum groups (LinkedIn/Quora), social sharing (Reddit, Stumble Upon), syndication (Blog Catalog, Demand Studios), *search engine marketing* (SEM) (Google Adwords), and *search engine optimization* (SEO) (Bing, Yahoo, Google) (The Global Social Media Challenge, 2011).

Global Target Market Data

Social media has the strongest influence on consumers in the Asia, the Pacific region, Latin America, and the Middle/East Africa markets. In fact, according to Nielsen's 2011 social media report, "30% of online consumers in the Middle/East Africa region and 29% of those in the Asia-Pacific market use social media on a daily basis to learn about brands, products, and services" (Nielsen | Social Media Report, 2012).

The five categories in which social media has the greatest influence on the global scale are as follows: "Travel/leisure (60%), appliances (58%), food/beverages (58%), clothing/fashion (58%), and restaurants (57%) (Nielsen | Social Media Report, 2012). The global average number of hours per day spent online is 5.27. This means that companies have 5.27 hours a day to interact with, market to, and assist their current and future customers (Grove, 2010). In addition, more women than men use social media ("Global Audience Spends Two Hours More a Month on Social Networks than Last Year," 2010).

Search engine marketing: *A form of Internet marketing that involves the promotion of websites by increasing their visibility in search engine results pages.*

Search engine optimization: *The process of affecting the visibility of a website or webpage in a search engine's search results through targeted keyword phrases. Also known as SEO.*

Getting information about the use of varying global markets is only the first piece of the puzzle. The next step is to see which networks are actually used and by whom. If a company sets up an account on Stumble-Upon, but their target market prefers Tumblr, then no matter how effective their message, it will not be very successful.

Facebook remains the most popular social networking site in the world, with more than 700 million users. Although Facebook is the most popular social networking site, it is not the only site that a company could leverage to build and market their brand (Social Networking Sites, 2012).

TABLE 1 Popular Global Social Media

Netlog	42 million users 27 languages Popular in Belgium, Austria, Switzerland, and Turkey
Bebo	40 million users Number 2 in the U.K. after Facebook
Xiaonei	40 million users Known as the "Chinese Facebook"
Twitter	408 million users Used by 21% of global internet population
Skyrock	10 million users French network Ranks number 2 behind Facebook in France
Friendster	105 million users 90% of traffic is from Asia
Qzone	200 million users Available only in Chinese
Google +	343 million users
LinkedIn	200 million users Located in 200 countries
Sina Weibo	400 million users

(Source: Adapted from Bloomberg BusinessWeek and Chappell, 2012)

Overcoming Language Barriers

Making the transition from a domestic brand to an international one is not easy. Companies must try to develop a cohesive brand identity in various cultures while ensuring the brand retains its strength and message. One of the biggest barriers to accomplishing this is language. As global markets expand and become more accessible via increased access to the Internet, the need for correct translation of ideas and concepts to other languages, while still retaining the original meaning, is key.

In a report commissioned by the European Union (EU) that sought to determine what language online users preferred, 80% of the population of EU member states said they used the Internet in their native language every day. In addition, 55% of the EU reported that if they used another language beyond their native one, it was usually English (User Language Preferences Online, n.d.).

TABLE 2 Top 10 Languages on the Internet (in millions)

Korean	39.4
Russian	59.7
French	59.8
Arabic	65.1
German	75.1
Portuguese	82.9
Japanese	99.2
Spanish	165
Chinese	510
English	565

Source: Adapted from World Internet Users Statistics Usage and World Population Stats, 2012

Fifty-three percent of respondents said they would use a site in English if it were not available in their language. English, however, will soon be replaced as the number one language used on the Internet by Chinese.

Content Creation Rules for Global Brand

The intended audience must be at the forefront of the social marketer's mind. Companies should make every effort to avoid content that could be considered offensive. Successfully conquering the language barrier requires a true commitment to reaching and cultivating a diverse consumer market. Success dictates that a company take steps beyond using a multilingual dictionary or content translation services (although these do have their value) (2011 The Year of International Social Media, 2011).

How can translating marketing materials assist in building a business' brand? Translation of social messages and feeds will assist a company in keeping up with ongoing trends. By translating press releases, the team gets to interact with local news resources and form professional relationships (2011 The Year of International Social Media, 2011).

Ensuring that the social media team handling interactions has someone familiar with the language and environment of that country is imperative. For example, in China and Japan, there are key cultural considerations, such as red being the color of luck and white being the color of death in China, that must be adhered to in order to avoid offense. Having a dedicated person or persons who not only have a experience with a country but who also have the ability to handle copywriting in the native language to ensure there is no dilution or skewing of information is very important (Jaster, 2008).

A perfect example of this is a campaign that Pepsi ran in China in the 1960s in which the tag line was "Come alive! You're in the Pepsi Generation." However the literal translation was, "Pepsi brings your ancestors back from the grave" (Sibley, 2012). A copywriter with experience in Chinese culture would have definitely caught this; a company translating text into Chinese might not have. This example is another reason why companies should not rely on Google Translate or other such tools.

Another reason to have someone on staff who can handle proper translations is the frequency with which business communication, be it on Facebook or a blog, is rewritten. Whenever a significant amount of a source text is modified, a company would need to submit the text for translation again—a cost that can quickly become prohibitive (Sibley, 2012).

For any business that is seeking to merge into new markets via social networking, make sure the conversation the business is having online is one that customers will find relevant. This means taking the time to research and discover what a country's hot topics are, any ongoing or upcoming trends, and any issues that need to be handled with cultural sensitivity.

Managing the Global Divide

Just as in most sectors that require infrastructure, large investment, and high levels of technology, there is a global divide between developed countries and lesser developed countries in social media marketing. The countries that are deriving the most benefit from the global market are those that have the technology and framework for a large number of citizens to have access to the Internet via home computers, tablets, or smartphones. However, there are a large number of people without the ability to participate in the digital economy on a consumer or business level (Biggs, 2012).

This gap is referred to as the digital divide. On one side of the divide, you have individuals with access to the Internet, and on the other, those who do not because of their countries' infrastructure, such as hardware deficiencies and lack of communication and knowledge. There is no reason for the digital divide to remain, however. In 2000, 4% of the world population had Internet access; by 2012, numbers declared that more than one-third of the world's population had Internet access (Biggs, 2012).

Broadband Expansion

G20 countries: *The 19 countries plus the European Union that represent two-thirds of the world's people, and 85% of the economy. The countries are: Argentina, Australia, Brazil, Canada, China, France, Germany, India, Indonesia, Italy, Japan, Mexico, Russia, Saudi Arabia, South Africa, South Korea, Turkey, United Kingdom, United States, European Union.*

The bridge to cross the global digital divide is to increase broadband and wireless to address "inequality in speed and functionality on digital devices, world wide" (Biggs, 2012). The Internet economy is a significant part of the world's economy. In *G20 countries*, it makes up 4.1% of GDP, which equals US2.3 trillion dollars. The United Nations' goal is to increase world Internet access to 60%. This would be increasing it to 50% in developing countries and to 15% in the least developed countries, whose 2011 access hovered around 6% (Biggs, 2012).

The International Telecommunication Union (ITU; http://www.itu.int), which is a specialized agency for information and communication technologies, and the United Nations Educational, Scientific, and Cultural Organization (UNESCO; http://www.unesco.org), set up the Broadband Commission for Digital Development. The purpose of this commission was to address and assist the United Nations in meeting its Millennium Development Goals (MDG). Started in May 2010, the Commission's goals are to increase broadband's importance on the international policy agenda.

The modus operandi is to expand broadband access in every country. A letter issued to the G20 countries by the Commission laid out the importance of this expansion and encouraged them to promote and develop networks, servers, and applications (Biggs, 2012). Broadband expansion is as crucial to the infrastructure of developing countries as is water, roads, railways, and electricity.

The telecommunication services industry generates around US2 trillion dollars a year. Out of the 2.4 billion people online, there are about 1 billion broadband subscriptions (Biggs, 2012). Groups that are not commonly online include people living in developing countries, people living in geographically isolated communities, people with disabilities, people who are illiterate, and women who are housebound.

Simply integrating broadband will not be enough. Countries are being called upon to include advanced online services, locally relevant content services, and support for media and information literacy development (Biggs, 2012). The increase of broadband into more countries has the potential to sustain social and economic growth. This could allow for a new range of digital careers and industries. The internet economy is also well-known for its limited barriers to entry, which allow for the proliferation and success of small- to medium-sized business to get a piece of the internet economy pie (*The Future of the Internet Economy*, 2008).

Broadband Commission for Digital Development 2015 Targets

The commission has set target dates to assist in the development of the Internet economy by assisting with the implementation of an increase in quality online service. The four targets are:

1. Developing a strategy for creating and implementing broadband policy

2. Ensuring an affordable broadband policy by 2015 by ensuring broadband services are no more than 5% of a country's average monthly income

3. Ensuring that 40% of households in developing countries will have internet access by 2015

4. Ensuring that the targeted user percentage of 60% worldwide, including 50% for developed countries and 15% for underdeveloped countries, is met (Biggs, 2012).

Additional Benefits to Broadband Expansion

There are more than just economic benefits to the expansion of broadband. The expansion of broadband could help with health initiatives such as sending out *SMS* with information regarding diseases and maternal and child health. Poverty and hunger initiatives are also benefits to increased technology. An increase of just 10% in broadband penetration can boost the GDP of a country by 1.3 percent in low- to mid-income families, depending on the country's economic structure (Biggs, 2012).

Another benefit to expanding broadband is the ability for children to access electronic educational materials. This one change has been shown to be invaluable in helping students learn. In addition, children's horizons are expanded and their literacy rate increases. Increased access to quality digital service can help women increase their literacy rates and living status, as well. Finally, the environment stands to benefit from

SMS: *A system that enables cellular phone users to send and receive text messages. Also known as Short message service; Short messaging service.*

increased broadband access as well. Smart grids reduce energy consumption via smart transportation and improved logistics.

Conclusion

Marketing to a global segment is a detailed process that requires many steps. The three most important steps include identification of target markets, choosing a strategy plan that allows a company to leverage its brand in the most efficient way, and breaking the language barriers. Each one of these steps is crucial for a successful global marketing initiative. Language is the mode by which most social media is conducted; therefore, it is understood that all the planning and strategy in the world will be for naught if your message does not connect and motivate your target market.

Finally, with the advent of the Internet economy, its low barriers to entry, and an international push for increased installation of quality Internet service, small- and medium-sized businesses are now able to compete on the global market using social media networking as a marketing and brand development tool.

SOURCES OF ADDITIONAL INFORMATION

Broadband Commission for Digital Development. www.broadbandcommission.org/
EuroMonitor International. www.euromonitor.com
Harvard Library Global Market Information Database. www.library.hbs.edu/go/gmid.html
International Telecommunication Union. www.itu.int/en/pages/default.aspx
McKinsey Global Institute. www.mckinsey.com/insights/mgi

BIBLIOGRAPHY

2011 The Year of International Social Media. (2011, January 13). *GPI| Translation Blog*. Retrieved January 29, 2013, from http://blog.globalizationpartners.com/2011-the-year-of-international-social-media.aspx

Biggs, P. (Ed.). (2012, September). *The State of Broadband 2012: Achieving Digital Inclusion For All* (Rep.). Retrieved January 29, 2013, from Broadband Commission website: http://www.broadbandcommission.org/Documents/bb-annualreport2012.pdf

Carmichael, M. (2011, May 16). The Demographics of Social Media. *Ad Age| Blogs*. Retrieved January 28, 2013, from http://adage.com/article/adagestat/demographics-facebook-linkedin-myspace-twitter/227569/

Chappell, B. (2012, July 31). 2012 Social Network Analysis Report: Demographic, Geographic and Search Data Revealed. *Ignite Social Media - The Original Social Media Agency RSS*. Retrieved January 29, 2013, from http://www.ignitesocial-media.com/social-media-stats/2012-social-network-analysis-report/

Chen, E. (2012, November 13). 20 Stats Every Global Social Media Marketer Should Know. *HubSpot's Inbound Marketing Blog*. Retrieved January 29, 2013, from http://blog.hubspot.com/blog/tabid/6307/bid/33819/20-Stats-Every-Global-Social-Media-Marketer-Should-Know.aspx

The Future of the Internet Economy (Issue brief). (2008, June). Retrieved January 29, 2013, from Organization for Economic Co-Operation and Development website: http://www.oecd.org/sti/interneteconomy/40789235.pdf

The Gallup Organization. (n.d.). User Language Preferences Online. *European Commission*. Retrieved January 29, 2013, from http://ec.europa.eu/public_opinion/flash/fl_313_en.pdf

Global Audience Spends Two Hours More a Month on Social Networks than Last Year. (2010, March 19). *Nielsen Wire*. Retrieved January 28, 2013, from http://blog.nielsen.com/nielsenwire/global/global-audience-spends-two-hours-more-a-month-on-social-networks-than-last-year/

The Global Social Media Challenge. (2011). *Lewis PR.com*. Retrieved January 29, 2013, from http://publish.lewispr.com/whitepapers/globalsocialchallenge/LEWIS_whitepaperEN.pdf

Grove, J. V. (2010, March 19). Global Social Media Usage. *Mashable.com*. Retrieved January 28, 2013, from http://mashable.com/2010/03/19/global-social-media-usage/

Jaster, M. (2008, May). Communication Breakdown. *Gear Technology*. Retrieved January 28, 2013, from https://www.evernote.com/shard/s58/res/d932cffd-e6d5-4c7f-ad0b-d51caa3d89e9/geartechnology_language.pdf

Meyer, K. E. (2006, January 25). *Market Penetration and Acquisition Strategies for Emerging Economies*. Retrieved January 29, 2013, from http://klausmeyer.co.uk/publications/2006_meyer_tran_LRP_final.pdf

Nielsen | Social Media Report 2012. (2012). *Nielsen | Social Media Report 2012*. Retrieved January 28, 2013, from http://blog.nielsen.com/nielsenwire/social/2012/

Sibley, A. (2012). Hub Spot's Inbound Marketing Blog. *8 of the Biggest Marketing Faux Pas of All Time*. Retrieved January 29, 2013, from http://blog.hubspot.com/blog/tabid/6307/bid/33396/8-of-the-Biggest-Marketing-Faux-Pas-of-All-Time.aspx

Social Networking Sites. (n.d.). *BloombergBusinessWeek.com*. Retrieved January 28, 2013, from http://images.businessweek.com/ss/09/07/0715_social_networking_sites/4.htm

World Internet Users Statistics Usage and World Population Stats. (2012, June 30). *World Internet Users Statistics Usage and World Population Stats*. Retrieved February 01, 2013, from http://www.internetworldstats.com/stats.htm

Protecting the Brand

In This Essay

- Social media policies detailing company and employee use of social media are important for businesses given the rise of social media and its ability to affect consumers' perceptions

- Employees must be given specific guidelines for social media use to ensure they represent a company or brand effectively and do not harm its reputation

- Swift, responsive interaction with consumers who leave negative feedback on social media can be an effective means of enhancing customer service

- Computer fraud is a growing concern and therefore companies should have IT teams and their employees should be trained in ways to avoid common Internet security problems

A company or business has a brand that distinguishes them from other companies and businesses. A brand is the combination of the service, the products, the marketing message, and the employees in the company. Branding is important to a company so that it can be distinguished by it within the marketplace in which it competes. Protecting that brand means the need to make sure that the messages sent via social media are going to support the integrity of the brand and not reflect in a detrimental way.

According to Par Marketing Services, "The American Marketing Association (AMA) defines a brand as a 'name, term, sign, symbol or design, or a combination of them intended to identify the goods and services of one seller or group of sellers' and to differentiate them from those of other sellers" (Par Marketing Services, 2012).

Introduction

In the social media world, protecting the brand can be more challenging than ever before. There are ways in which others can infringe on a business' trademark online that can make the brand become diluted or ultimately ineffective. One way in which this can happen is through "typosquatting" on a company's brand. In this case, it is a common misspelling used by Internet users when typing in a brand's web address. It can be an address that is similar or close to its website. The misspelling redirects searchers and potential customers to another site and in essence "hijacks" website traffic. Direct selling companies can be especially vulnerable to this problem. Being vigilant about finding and reporting these site types can be the best way to combat the problem (Kulik, 2011).

If a problem is discovered, there are actions that can be taken to halt the false websites. One is to use the Universal Domain Name Dispute Resolution Process (UDRP) to expose the third parties responsible for malicious intent with the sites. Another action step is to undertake, in a determined way, online monitoring of the company's reputation. Then, when a problem arises, a company must make sure that it is dealt with swiftly to lessen the damage that can be done. This effort can be a separate policy or one that is woven into the existing social media policy that the company has in place (Kulik, 2011).

Developing and Implementing Social Media Policy

One aspect of social media that companies appear to struggle with is how to address their employees' use of it. Many companies tend to ban social media for their employees in an effort to protect their brand. Others are beginning to discuss the use of social media with their employees to try to gain their support as "brand ambassadors." Some companies may have a policy, but it may not be implemented effectively (Harris, 2012).

Creating a social media policy can aid a company in navigating any potential problems with the use of social media and its brand. Having a policy that addresses expected employee behavior while using social media allows clear communication about the important issue of representing the company's brand (Reddick, n.d.).

A social media policy should spell out the company's expectations and should be specific so that employees understand and are able to comply with the policy. For example, a policy might dictate that employees should not engage in conversations in social media venues without first identifying they work for a particular company. Then it is clear that the employees are affiliated or could be considered a representative from that business (Reddick, n.d.). In other situations, an employee may be asked not to join in conversations or forums that might place the employee in the position of representing the company without intending to do so. An example would be an employee having a conversation about computer repair costs while employed by the Geek Squad™. People getting the information from that employee will believe that it comes from the company. The person will be viewed not as a reviewer but as a Geek Squad™ employee discussing it. In either case, the difficulty can be something that both the business and the employee have to deal with in some manner (Reddick, n.d.).

Companies should have a portion of their new employee orientation that is devoted to educating associates about pitfalls associated with social media both from a corporate and a private stance (Reddick, n.d.). This extra time can yield a return on investment many times over with employees who are careful and conscientious. "Companies must make it a priority to educate employees, including contractors and temporary staff, about the company's expectations with respect to use of social media, provide examples of what is considered acceptable vs. unacceptable/ encouraged vs. discouraged practice and make sure they understand the importance and meaning of the policies and protocols" (Reddick, n.d.).

When educating employees, it is important to remind them of online posts that one might not put up when a supervisor is close at hand. Those posts may be ones that should not be posted at all. That little bit of extra thought may be the difference between having an employee as an asset or not (Reddick, n.d.).

By bringing a concrete set of examples of how to be savvy as a social media user, the employer can set forth clear expectations and provide the reasoning behind those guidelines. Having employees agree to and sign a social media policy is a way to make certain that they are aware of what their responsibilities are when representing the company (Harris, 2012).

Some social media policies may be antiquated, given that the online climate has changed and evolved so much in recent years. Revisiting the policy, if it is a few years old, is advised to make certain that it describes the aspects of how social media is a part of the company right now and not how it was when the policy was crafted (Harris, 2012).

When developing a policy or revising it, referencing examples or templates can be helpful in wording company policy in a way that aligns with its mission and vision (Reddick, n.d.). Resources from sources such as the Social Media Governance website can be used to look at a variety of policies from a variety of companies, government organizations, and profit or non-profit organizations (http://socialmediagovernance.com/policies.php). Some companies use a policy and others have a suggested guideline for employees. The wording that is chosen may be based on several factors. Those factors can include how many employees are in the company, the type of business that is done, and possibly even how it uses social media as a marketing tool (Reddick, n.d.).

Risk assessment: *The process of identifying and evaluating possible risks and opportunities that could affect the achievement of an objective.*

Conducting a *risk assessment* before crafting the social media policy can be a good way to consider how the use of social media can be beneficial. It can also show how it can be detrimental to the reputation, the brand, and the business itself. Once the risks can be determined, then a response can be decided. A comprehensive policy can have responses to various threats and infractions. So, when something occurs, the response can be swift and well matched to the issue at hand—whether it is a crisis or a breach of protocol that requires more education about the policy (Reddick, n.d.).

Importance of Social Media Policy

Why is a policy helpful in protecting a company's brand?

Since social media is so accessible, people can easily post something online. Thus, the content might be posted before sufficient thought has been given to how the message will be received or how it will reflect back on a company or individual. Posts may be deleted in some forums, but deleting is not as easy as posting. This means businesses must be vigilant about what is online about their company (Reddick, n.d.).

With an up-to-date and well-crafted policy, employees will understand what is allowed and what is not. Enforcement of the consequences for infractions can be done promptly because the policy is understood. Without a relevant and up-to-date social media policy, policing potential problems can be a bit difficult because employees need to be aware of their parameters before they are disciplined for noncompliance (Reddick, n.d.).

According to the National Labor Relations Board, some statements that are included in some social media policies are against their regulations. When crafting a policy, Ann Purcell, the associate general counsel of the NLRB, suggests that companies keep these four pieces of advice in mind when crafting a social media policy (Harris, 2012):

- Be specific in the wording. The result is that statements made in the policies will be well defined or explained. If a policy is too broad, it could be considered unlawful.
- Do not place a disclaimer that states the policy will not be enforced in a manner that is considered unlawful by the NLRB. Such a statement will not "save" the business should there be an investigation or lawsuit. Rewording or explaining the policy is a better option than adding an escape clause.
- Prohibit harassment.
- Controlling posts that are put up without permission is important. Many companies have a statement in their policy that instructs the employee to seek permission before posting. That way, the posts do not misrepresent the employer or employee in any manner.

Managing Comments from Customers

Managing employees and their use of social media with regard to the business is only half of the equation for success. The other half of the equation is how the customers use social media to engage with the business. Making certain that the company has a plan for how to manage both positive and negative comments made through social media can mean that the company is aware of their online presence—both the positive and the negative. Once there is a sense of what is being said, then the company can begin maximizing the positive and managing the negative comments (Wilkie, 2012).

"How a company chooses to handle negative feedback says a lot about how it values its customers, and may have a profound effect on its reputation in the marketplace. Accordingly, responses to these types of posts should not be taken lightly" (Wilkie, 2012). Social media has become a way in which people/customers interact or engage with potential companies or businesses that are aligned with their interests. However, if one of those companies does not communicate in a satisfactory way for a customer, then the backlash that can occur can be very detrimental to that business. The detrimental effect can happen very quickly because of the fluidity of social media. Companies strive to be recognized in social media and to have people talking about their brand. However, having a video that goes viral on YouTube with an employee's unfortunate behavior is not the way a company needs the attention. The brand can and will suffer in the short term. How the situation is addressed may dictate how much damage is done in the longer term.

Negative comments can be costly to a business, with a loss of customer support and poor public relations deterring new customers from doing business with the company. The time that it takes for the company to react and respond to the negative comments must be short because the window of opportunity to make that customer satisfied is short. "The message is clear: You need to use social media not just as a marketing tool but as a systematic part of your customer service model" (Beesley, 2012).

The comments that are made by a disgruntled customer can possibly become more powerful depending on how the customer is ultimately treated and also on how many positive comments are online. It becomes a balancing act in some ways, yet if there is a side of the scale that is tipping in one direction, businesses want it to be on the positive side and not on the negative one (Beesley, 2012).

If there is a plethora of comments extolling the business and the service it provides and only one negative comment that describes an incident with a customer care employee in an unflattering manner, then the vast majority of the followers in the social media arena will discount that one negative comment as an isolated occurrence and not commonplace (Wilkie, 2012). However, if there is more than one comment that speaks negatively about the manner in which business is handled, then circumstances become more difficult for defending the company and its services. In this case, more work might need to be done to change how the company is being discussed in social media arenas and how the business is conducted so that more customers are satisfied than unsatisfied.

One way to combat this developing problem is to make a concerted effort to gain more loyal customers. Once more satisfied customers are onboard with a company, suggesting that their comments be shared online can support one's brand and boost the positive online reputation that the company strives to gain. Brennan Wilkie, contributor to Empathica, suggests that developing a customer management policy or strategy is one way to head off problems.

His logic is this: If dissatisfied customers take time to leave comments on social media sites about their poor experience with the company, then couldn't those same customers have been handled a bit differently immediately after the poor encounter? Customer experience management programs put into place alerts or some type of response that occurs quickly after an incident. In this way, the company can reach out when the problem is fresh and perhaps offer a solution that can create a better impression on the customer than the initial one. In this case, a problem could potentially be avoided altogether, and there is a possibility that the customer may take to social media to praise the fact that the company communicated and moved swiftly to make amends (Wilkie, 2012).

Managing Online Reputation through Social Media

Being aware of what is being said online about a company can be the important first step in the management of an online reputation. As a part of social media policies and other online regulations, many companies allude to the fact that their online presence will be monitored. This monitoring appears to be a fine idea to police employees' behavior with regard to the company online. In practice, some businesses fall short of monitoring in an efficient and diligent manner. The statement becomes just that—merely a statement—and true monitoring may not happen (Beesley, 2012).

The disconnect between policy and practice often results from a lack of understanding of the online media venue and its ramifications on a business. At other times, awareness of comments being shared online is too much to handle because there are not enough staff or no one is assigned exclusively to the task of monitoring (Reddick, n.d.).

It is important to be aware of online venues in which the company is being discussed. Some of the most popular sites include Twitter, Facebook, LinkedIn, Google+, and Pinterest, but these may not be the only places where comments can be placed about one's company. There are online forums that are "niche-based," so if the company in question sells electronics, there may be sites that are dedicated to topics related to that niche. These niche sites need to be monitored to understand customer trends or the frustrations that they are encountering (Reddick, n.d.).

Finding sites that are the most commonly used by the business' customer base can begin by doing a general search on the broader service or goods that are offered by the company. Then, search by the company name, and if there are mentions about the company, they should show up in the search. This search can yield solid information about what is being said about the product or service that a company offers and also specifically about the company itself. Once the online footprint is better understood, then it can be monitored more efficiently (Reddick, n.d.).

Social Media and Customer Service

Marketing online has blossomed as a viable method of gaining new customers. However, marketers are also realizing that to keep customers, there should be some interaction with them as well. Marketing and customer service can work together because the marketing plan should reflect the vision and philosophy of a company and how the customer is served should be consistent with that vision and philosophy (Beesley, 2012).

As customers engage with companies and businesses online instead of just looking at information and either purchasing or not, getting them involved in a positive manner can help them to become ambassadors for the brand. Online venues have given customers a voice in some ways because of the immediacy of the media and the conversational communication that has evolved. People chat about what is important to them online, so if they have a service or business that they like, they will share it with others and by contrast if a company has displeased that customer, that perspective, too, will be shared (Reddick, n.d.).

In some companies, the dedicated online watchdogs are people within the marketing department because they understand the way the brand should be represented and marketed. They should be familiar with how to market in the social media domain. In this way, information that can inform the marketing approach in a business can be gained while keeping watch on what is being said at the present time online (Reddick, n.d.).

Another important step with managing an online presence is to make sure that the process and results are communicated well to the stakeholders in the company, namely the employees, management, and even customers, if appropriate for that business. It all comes down to communication to each stakeholder of the company and keeping that communication meaningful and purposeful (Beesley, 2012).

The end result is that being aware of online discussions of a business and how they affect operations can be critical to how much success a business enjoys (Reddick, n.d.).

Defense Against Computer Fraud

Computer fraud can be a serious problem for companies. Information Technology (IT) plans guard against external threats, but internal abuses may not be considered in the same way. To understand what fraud entails, a definition is helpful. This definition may vary slightly depending on the country in which one resides, but the following are some definitions that seem relevant to this discussion.

According to an article in Infosectoday.com, there are three aspects to computer fraud. The first aspect is knowingly accessing or using a computer. The second is to use or access a computer without authorization or exceeding authorization. The third is to use a computer with the intent to commit a crime or a fraudulent act ("Insider Computer Fraud," 2004).

The Organisation of Economic Co-operation and Development (OECD) is an international organization with headquarters in Paris concerned with assisting governments with governance issues and challenges about economic, social, and governance challenges that occur as countries exist in a globalized economy. Their definition is: "any unethical or illegal behavior regarding unauthorized automatic data treatment and/or data transmission" (Georgiana, 2012).

Another international organization, Tokyo-based United Nations Asia and Far East Institute for the Prevention of Crime and the Treatment of Offenders (UNAFEI), has this as a definition: "any offense in which a computer or computer network is the subject of an offense, or computer network environment is the instrument of making an offense" (Georgiana, 2012).

According to the European Agency for Network and Information Security Agency (ENISA) in Heraklion, Greece, a computer crime is "Computer fraud, computer forgery, damage to databases and computer programs, computer sabotage, unauthorized access to computers, unauthorized interception, reproductions of fraudulent schemes, no right to alter data or computer software, computer espionage, unauthorized use of a computer or computer programs protected by law" (Georgiana, 2012).

While many strive to define computer fraud, the reality is crimes are not unique to one country and all the definitions are very similar (Georgiana, 2012). A common language used to describe crimes helps when discussing infractions or outright illegal actions.

When companies enter into online and social media venues, computer fraud becomes more of a concern (Georgiana, 2012). The global definitions of computer fraud may also become important because the Internet is not only for one country, and websites are not limited to only one, either.

What Can a Company Do to Defend Against Computer Fraud?

The first step in protecting against computer fraud is actually the same as for the individual computer user—getting good computer antivirus software can help protect the computer against worms, Trojans, spyware, viruses, and other online threats. Some malware can change its behavior over time, and it can pose unique threats to computers.

Setting up a firewall can protect the computer by restricting what is allowed into one's computer from outside computers. Users can set and monitor the parameters of their firewall to make certain that it is blocking and allowing what is critical to the company's or business' services. Some firewalls are built into routers or in a company's servers and some can be in specific software programs such as those in Windows programs (Heller, 2012). The difference with a company that has a network with several computers tied into it is stand-alone computer antivirus programs, which means that these networks must be able to combat threats on a daily basis by detecting and dealing with them quickly (Heller, 2012).

It is important for businesses to make certain that e-mail is exchanged with trusted vendors and to use spam filters to screen out threats that can come through e-mail. Also, it is important to not share any important information online while doing company business, just as it is for individuals.

Educating staff about the possibility of threats that can get into the network through e-mails can help to keep the network safer. Keeping passwords in a safe place and not online is important, as is changing passwords when a program prompts a user to do so to keep the integrity of the security measures. Sometimes completely closing out a browser after a session is advised even when working on a network. Reporting issues to the IT department is an important step, should a problem be detected. Being vigilant can make a difference in catching the smallest anomaly.

Hiring an IT person or team to make certain that the connections for the daily business are working at an optimal level is essential. They ensure safeguards are implemented and evaluated for effectiveness on a regular basis and give employees a resource to go to for assistance ("Insider Computer Fraud," 2004). An IT team is advisable so that any threats can be dealt with by being proactive, and not reactive, to those threats or computer issues.

In addition, having experts in the field can inform policy changes as needed with the decision makers of the company. Without such advisors, it is possible that new procedures or policy changes that reflect the latest online climate may not be enacted in a timely manner. Some smaller companies may outsource their IT department rather than hiring their own team, but in any case making certain that the company is protected is critical since the online environment is an ever-changing and evolving arena ("Insider Computer Fraud," 2004).

Employee Education

Another important part of the policy implementation is the education of employees around issues such as confidentiality, security, consistency, and awareness of potential threats or odd requests from any source. Leaking data of all sorts can be done by an employee who may not know that they are releasing information that can be used in a detrimental manner (Harris, 2012). Through seemingly normal interactions and connections, important online information can be given out, so helping the employees to understand how this can occur is training time well spent.

No one is immune to being targeted. Government officials, small and large businesses, the federal government, and individuals have all been targeted (Harris, 2012). Enlisting the assistance of the employees and educating them about their role in the security of the company can be a nice way to build a cohesive environment and a partnership with trusted employees who can become the eyes and ears in social media and the best advocates for one's business.

SOURCES OF ADDITIONAL INFORMATION

United States Small Business Administration. http://www.sba.gov

Rutgers Business School. http://business.rutgers.edu/events/2012/11/26/workshop-protecting-your-brand-using-social-media

Steptoe & Johnson LLP. http://www.steptoe.com

BIBLIOGRAPHY

Beesley, C. (2012, November 15). How to use social media to do a better job of customer service. Retrieved December 4, 2012, from http://www.sba.gov/community/blogs/how-use-social-media-do-better-job-customer-service.

Georgiana, R. (2012). Borderless Crime-Computer Fraud. *Database Systems Journal, 3*(1). Retrieved December 4, 2012, from http://www.dbjournal.ro/archive/7/7_6.pdf.

Harris, A. (2012, September 3). Social media policies protect contractors, brand. Retrieved December 4, 2012, from: http://www.achrnews.com/articles/120849-social-media-policies-protect-contractors—brand.

Heller, A. (2010, January/February). Defending computer networks against attack. *S&TR*. Retrieved December 4, 2012, from https://str.llnl.gov/JanFeb10/pdfs/1.10.3.pdf.

Insider Computer Fraud. (2004). Retrieved December 4, 2012, from http://www.infosectoday.com/Articles/Insider_Computer_Fraud.pdf.

Kulik, T. (2011, June 21). Protecting your brand in a social media world. Retrieved December 4, 2012, from http://www.slideshare.net/tkulik/protecting-your-brand-in-a-social-media-world#btnNext.

Par Marketing Services. (2012). Branding. Retrieved December 4, 2012, from http://www.parmarketingservices.com/Branding%20White%20Paper.pdf.

Reddick, K. (n.d.). Managing and protecting corporate brand reputation in social media. Retrieved December 4, 2012, from http://www.ccwomenofcolor.org/outside-counsel-corner/social-media-brand-reputation.html.

Wilkie, B. (2012, August 30). How to handle negative comments in social media. Retrieved December 4, 2012, from http://www.empathica.com/what-are-the-best-practices-for-setting-up-running-a-program-blog/how-to-handle-negative-comments-in-social-media/.

Winterfeldt, B. J. (2011, February/March). Protecting your brand in the social media space. Retrieved February 27, 2013, from http://www.steptoe.com/assets/htmldocuments/WTR%20Protecting%20Your%20Brand%20in%20the%20Social%20Media%20Space%20Winterfeldt%202011.pdf.

Glossary

A/B testing: An experimental approach to website testing in which two versions of a website are compared. The two versions of the website are identical except for one variation that might impact user behavior.

App: Online, downloadable programs or mobile applications for smartphones or tablets. Short for Application.

Asymmetrical transparency: In Internet discussions, when only one of the sender, receiver, and observer can see the other's identities.

Avatar: In computing, the graphical image of the user or the user's alter ego or character.

B2B: Short for business-to-business, or a commercial transaction between two businesses.

B2C: Short for business-to-consumer, or a commercial transaction between a company and a customer.

Bandwidth: The data transfer rate of a network or Internet connection.

Benchmark: A standard, or a set of standards, used as a point of reference for evaluating performance or level of quality.

Blog: A website on which an individual or group records opinions, information, etc. on a regular basis. Short for web log.

Brand: Name, term, symbol, sign, or design used by a firm to differentiate its offerings from those of its competitors.

Brand awareness: The degree to which consumers precisely associate a brand with the specific product.

Brand loyalty: A situation when a consumer is reluctant to switch from consumption of a favored good.

Brand representation: The way a company communicates about its brand to an audience.

Buzz: When discussing the Internet, excited attention relating to a new or forthcoming product or event.

Call to action: In computing, commands designed to trigger a desired action. Also known as CTA.

Click-through rate: A ratio showing how often people see an online advertisement and then click on it to learn more. Also known as Clickthrough rate; CTR.

Clickthrough rate: A ratio showing how often people see an online advertisement and then click on it to learn more. Also known as Click-through rate; CTR.

Cluster: Countries that share similar cultures.

CLV: The amount of revenue generated from one customer over the lifetime of the relationship. Also known as Customer lifetime value.

CMS: Software that manages maintenance of assets, such as articles or images, tracking modifications and recording metadata about changes including user name and date of revision. Also known as Content management system.

Content management system: Software that manages maintenance of assets, such as articles or images, tracking modifications and recording metadata about changes including username and date of revision. Also known as CMS.

Conversion: The rate at which one currency is transformed into another.

CRM: A model for managing a company's interactions with customers, clients, and sales prospects using technology. Also known as Customer relationship management.

Crowdsourcing: Obtaining services, ideas, or content by soliciting contributions from a large group of people, especially the online community.

CTA: In computing, commands designed to trigger a desired action. Also known as Call to action.

CTR: A ratio showing how often people see an online advertisement and then click on it to learn more. Also known as Clickthrough rate; Click-through rate.

Customer lifetime value: The amount of revenue generated from one customer over the lifetime of the relationship. Also known as CLV.

Customer relationship management: A model for managing a company's interactions with customers, clients, and sales prospects using technology. Also known as CRM.

Dashboard: A web page which collates information about a business.

Data mining: The analysis of large quantities of data to discover patterns within the data.

Diversification: The process of trying to increase profitability by marketing new products to new markets.

Federal Trade Commission: In the United States, the agency that promotes free enterprise and competition. Also known as FTC.

Fortune 500 company: A company that has been listed on *Fortune* magazine's annual ranking of the largest corporations in the United States.

Four (4) Ps: The balance of marketing techniques required for selling the product: 1) Price—the price of the product, particularly the price compared to competitors. 2) Product—targeting the market and making the product appropriate to that market segment. 3) Promotion—sale promotion, advertising, sponsorship or other promotions. 4) Place—how the product is distributed. Current trends are towards shortening the chain of distribution. Also known as Marketing mix.

Free-to-use system: A social media system that can be used for both individuals and companies without a fee.

FTC: In the United States, the agency that promotes free enterprise and competition. Also known as Federal Trade Commission.

Fuzzy logic: A system of logic in which statements do not have to be entirely true or entirely false.

G20 countries: The 19 countries plus the European Union that represent two-thirds of the world's people, and 85% of the its economy. The countries are: Argentina, Australia, Brazil, Canada, China, France, Germany, India, Indonesia, Italy, Japan, Mexico, Russia, Saudi Arabia, South Africa, South Korea, Turkey, United Kingdom, United States, and the European Union.

Gamification: Applying the principles of game design to non-game applications to make them more fun and engaging.

Gen Y: A person born between 1977 and 1992. Also known as Generation Y; Millennial.

Generation Y: A person born between 1977 and 1992. Also known as Gen Y; Millennial.

Geolocation: The detection of the physical location of a remote device.

Halo effect: When the positive perception of one outstanding trait leads to an overly favorable impression of the whole.

HTML: An authoring language used to create documents on the World Wide Web. Short for HyperText Markup Language.

Inbound marketing: A marketing campaign in which the staff of a company itself is the target audience.

Intellectual property: Any idea or work that can be considered proprietary in nature and is thus protected from infringement by others.

Keyword: On the Internet, a search term that a search engine uses to select websites to display in the search results.

Lurk: In Internet discussion forums, to follow conversations without contributing.

M-commerce: The buying and selling of goods and services through wireless handheld devices. Also known as mobile commerce.

Market dominance: The measure of the strength of a brand, product, service, or firm, relative to its competitors.

Marketing: The process to create, develop, and define markets that satisfy the needs and wants of individual and business customers.

Marketing channel: All sources used by marketers to get the product to the consumer.

Marketing mix: The balance of marketing techniques required for selling the product: 1) Price—the price of the product, particularly the price compared to competitors. 2) Product—targeting the market and making the product appropriate to that market segment. 3) Promotion—sale promotion, advertising, sponsorship or other promotions. 4) Place—how the product is distributed. Current trends are towards shortening the chain of distribution. Also known as the Four (4) Ps.

Metadata: Data that describes other data, or information about a certain item's content.

Metric: A standard of measurement used to gauge a company's performance.

Microsite: A separately promoted part of a larger website with a separate URL designed to meet discrete objectives.

Microtransaction: An electronic commerce transaction of very low value.

Millennial: A person born between 1977 and 1992. Also known as Gen Y; Generation Y.

Native advertising: Ad strategies that allow brands to promote their content in the actual experience of a website or app.

Network: A chain of interconnected individuals or organizations sharing information and/or services.

News feed: In social media, a constantly updating list of stories from people and pages that one follows.

Outbound marketing: A marketing campaign in which potential customers outside the business are the target audience.

Packet switching: A method of data transmission in which a message is broken into a number of parts that are sent independently and reassembled at the destination.

Paper trail: Documentary evidence of what was done, discussed, etc.

Persistent identifier: A long-lived, globally unique number or code allocated to an object or resource. Also known as PID.

PID: A long-lived, globally unique number or code allocated to an object or resource. Also known as Persistent identifier.

Podcast: A program, most often music or talk, made available in digital format for download over the Internet.

Polarity: The state in which two opinions or ideas are very different from each other.

Private messaging service: An e-mail or text message sent from one user to another on a social networking site. They are often more anonymous than e-mails, as the e-mail address and IP address of the senders are not disclosed.

Quantify: To determine, express, or measure the quantity of something.

Real time: The actual time during which a process or event happens.

Relationship orientation: A focus to establish, maintain, and enhance relationships with customers.

Reputation management: The process of building a company or brand's reputation then maintaining a positive reputation or overcome a negative one.

Return on investment: A performance measure used to evaluate the efficiency of an investment. It is usually expressed as a percentage or a ratio where return of an investment is divided by the cost of the investment. Also known as ROI.

Risk assessment: Identifying and evaluating possible risks and opportunities that could affect the achievement of an objective.

Search engine: A tool that allows Internet users to access information.

Search engine marketing: A form of Internet marketing that involves the promotion of websites by increasing their visibility in search engine results pages.

Search engine optimization: The process of affecting the visibility of a website or webpage in a search engine's search results through targeted keyword phrases. Also known as SEO.

SEO: The process of affecting the visibility of a website or webpage in a search engine's search results through targeted keyword phrases. Also known as Search engine optimization.

Short message service: A system that enables cellular phone users to send and receive text messages. Also known as Short messaging service; SMS.

Short messaging service: A system that enables cellular phone users to send and receive text messages. Also known as Short message service; SMS.

Signal-to-noise ratio: (informally) The ratio of useful information to false or irrelevant data in a conversation or exchange.

SMS: A system that enables cellular phone users to send and receive text messages. Also known as Short message service; Short messaging service.

Social commerce: The use of social network(s) to assist in e-commerce transactions.

Social media policy: A corporate code of conduct providing guidelines for employees who post content on the Internet either as part of their job or as a private person. Also known as a social networking policy.

Social metadata: Data added to content by people other than the content creator, such as tags, ratings, votes, comments, etc.

Social networking policy: A corporate code of conduct providing guidelines for employees who post content on the Internet either as part of their job or as a private person. Also known as Social media policy.

Socialeaders: Those who maximize their own digital influence in a personal or professional capacity.

Source: A number of purchasing practices, aimed at finding, evaluating and engaging suppliers of goods and services.

Symmetrical transparency: In Internet discussions, when the sender, receiver, and observer of Internet discussions can see the other's identities.

Target market: The clients or customers sought for a business's product or service.

Terms of service: Rules which one must agree to follow in order to use a service. Also known as Terms of use; TOU.

Terms of use: Rules which one must agree to follow in order to use a service. Also known as Terms of Service; TOU.

Touch point: A point of contact or interaction, especially between a business and its customers.

TOU: Rules which one must agree to follow in order to use a service. Also known as Terms of service; Terms of use.

Traffic: Visitors to a website, blog, or social media account on the Internet.

Trend: A statistical measurement used to track changes that occur over time.

Upsell: A sales strategy where the seller provides opportunities to purchase related products or services, often for the sole purpose of making a larger sale.

Viral marketing: A marketing campaign that uses social networks to increase brand awareness or sales through viral processes.

Web 2.0: The second generation of the World Wide Web that includes features such as blogs, wikis, and social networking.

Web analytics: The diagnostic information that describes how users interact with a particular website.

Index

A

A/B testing, 220
AAdvantage, 62
About.com, Small Business Guide, 256
Activity ratio, 345
Advertising, 269
Advertising Age, 102, 243
(Advertising) The Business of Advertising (Calkins), 118
Advocates, 156
Agranoff, Craig, 110
Agrawal, Roli, 290
Airtime, 173
AJAX. *See* Asynchronous JavaScript and XML (AJAX)
Alexa.com, 312
Alternate method of entry (AMOE), 374–375
Alternate reality games, 293
AMA. *See* American Marketing Association (AMA)
Amazon.com, Inc., 147, 206, 312
American Airlines, 62
American Express Company, 102
American Marketing Association (AMA), 395
AMOE. *See* Alternate method of entry (AMOE)
Amplification, 21
Analysis specialists, 112
Analytics, 90, 279, 318
Anonymity, 360–361
Antivirus software, 404
AOL, 71
Apple Inc., 135

Applications (apps), 242, 243, 289
Appraisal theory, 326
Appropriateness of culture, 197
Appropriateness of venue, 197
Apps. *See* Applications (apps)
Arlotta, CJ, 316
ARPANET (Advanced Research Projects Agency Network), 4
The Art of SEO (Enge, Spencer, Fishkin & Stricchiola), 216, 217, 222
Asia, 386
Assessment, 342–343
Associations, 88
Asymmetrical, 302
Asynchronous JavaScript and XML (AJAX), 168
Augmentation stage, 181
Augmented reality, 140–141
Australia, 35
Authority, 24
Avatars, 239, 300
Awareness stage, 272

B

B2B. *See* Business to business (B2B)
B2C. *See* Business to consumer (B2C)
Baidu.com, 312
Bandwidth, 168, 173–174
Basecamp, 154
Bax, Amy, 320
BBS. *See* Bulletin board system (BBS)

Bebo, 387
Behavioral targeting, 128
Belicove, Mikal, 222
Benchmark, 44
Benioff, Marc, 75
Berkeley Center for New Media, 133
Billboarding, 243
Bing, 386
Bitly, 187
Black & White, 211
Black, Susan, 274
Blair, Tony, 212
Blendtec, 97
Blendtech, 257
Blip.tv, 145
Block, Robbin, 3, 7
Blog Catalog, 386
Blog interaction, 345–346
Blogger, 135, 341
Blogs
  background of, 134–135
  business use, 135
  characteristics of, 341
  definition of, 36, 125
  editors, 109
  as form of social media tool, 17
  local news and, 32
  as marketing tools, 125–126
  number of, 84
  opportunities for, 277
  potential of, 274
  rank in social media networks, 86
  website referral traffic from, 46
Blogspot.com, 312
Bob Evans Farms, Inc., 113
Bookmarking, 46
Bounce rate, 344–346
Brand
  content creation rules for global, 388–389
  creating advocacy for, 209
  creation, 240–241
  cues, 209
  definition of, 30, 72, 85, 125, 184
  development, 244
  extension, 73–74

fostering recognition, 242–243
  importance of, 125
  leveraging icon, 209
  linkage, 209
  loyalty, 345
  management, 73–74
  mentions, 345
  monitoring sentiment, 279
  presence, 275
  protecting, 395–406
  reputation, 280
  storyline, 209
Brand Advertiser Solutions, 209
Brand awareness
  increasing, 46
  role of social networking in, 320
  strategies, 291
  strategy of, 7
  use as key metric, 54
  in virtual worlds, 243
Brand loyalty
  definition of, 119
  developing plan for, 286–287
  interacting with customers, 290–294
  social networking and, 272–273
  strategies for, 287–290
Brand representation
  chasing traffic, 77
  definition of, 72–73
  in long-term social media campaigns, 86–87
  in real time, 74
  role of associations in, 88
  role of social networking in, 320
  in social media, 75–76, 78
  using data from social media, 77–78
Branding
  characteristics of, 73–74
  control of, 88
  Twitter use, 245
Branson, Richard, 75
Brazil, 35, 60
Bright shiny object syndrome, 263
British Midland International, 63
Broadband Commission for Digital Development, 390
Broadband expansion, 390–392

C

D

M

M-commerce, 242

MABs. *See* Multi-author blogs (MABs)

Maier, Andrew, 219

Management

    of long-term social media campaigns, 84–86

    reputation management, 109

    responsibilities of managers, 86

Managers, 110

Market dominance, 170

Market research, 349

Market saturation, 180–181

Market segmentation

    importance of brand in, 125

    need for strategy in, 128

    niche social networks, 126–127

    targeted marketing, 118

    targeted marketing B2B, 122–123

    targeted marketing DTC, 123–124

    trends, 117–118

Marketing

    blindness, 181–182

    blogs as marketing tools, 125–126

    characteristics of, 314–315

    consumer-focused, 119

    converting followers to paying customers, 48

    cost of social media, 97

    data and metrics applied to, 340–341

    definition of, 12

    developing metrics for, 51–53

    developing strategy for, 342–346

    exterior, 157–158

    failures, 64–65

    future of, 11–12

    global marketing plan, 383–393

    goals statement, 44–51

    inbound, 155–156

    for instant gratification, 316–317

    integrating, 316–317

    integrating data with CRM and other systems, 49

    international campaigns, 65–66

    measurable lead generation from, 48

    measurable ROI from programs, 47

    outbound, 156–158

    phases of, 50

    philosophy, 43–55

    plan, 58

    recruiting interdepartmental staff to perform activities, 50

    role of, 20–21

    role of technology, 127

    targeted, 118

    transparency of, 297–310

    types of sites, 229–230

    viral, 158–159

Marketing channel, 85, 193, 200

Marketing mix, 12

Marketing strategies. *See also* Strategies

    best practices, 239–242

    budgeting to produce/license content, 248–249

    for content management, 249–251

    engagement, 244

    Facebook advantage, 60

    on FourSquare, 63–64

    fundraising approach, 59

    internal social media, 155–158

    main points in, 58

    marketing plan, 58–59

    to overcome diminishing returns, 183–185

    on Pinterest, 63

    producing content, 246–248

    step-by-step approach, 58

    trends, 242–244

    on Twitter, 62

    using crowdsourcing, 64–65

The Marketing Therapist, 7

Marketing Week, 38

MarketingSherpa, 46, 50

Mashable, 61

Massively multiplayer online roleplaying games (MMORPG), 243

Mattel, Inc., 294

McCain, John, 234

MCI, 206

MDG. *See* Millennium Development Goals (MDG)

Measure and adjust strategy, 288